The Westminster Confession into the 21st Century

Essays in Remembrance of the 350th Anniversary of the Westminster Assembly

Volume 1

The Westminster Confession into the 21st Century

Essays in Remembrance of the 350th Anniversary of the Westminster Assembly

Volume 1

General Editor
J. Ligon Duncan, III

Associate Editors
W. Duncan Rankin
Derek W. H. Thomas
Robert C. "Ric" Cannada, Jr.
Stephen R. Berry
Stephen E. Tindall

MENTOR

© J. Ligon Duncan III

ISBN 1-85792-862-8

First Published in 2003,
reprinted 2004, 2005
in the
Mentor Imprint
by
Christian Focus Publications,
Geanies House, Fearn,
Ross-shire, IV20 1TW, Scotland

www.christianfocus.com

Cover design by Alister MacInnes

Printed and bound by
W.S. Bookwell, Finland

Contents

Foreword

Almost a decade ago we marked the three hundred fiftieth anniversary of the English Parliament's ordinance calling for the historic Westminster Assembly (1643-1649/52). Reformed Theological Seminary (RTS) has a special interest in the promotion of the study of the Assembly since the *Confession* serves as our basic doctrinal position. Because we passionately believe these truths, RTS has aimed to produce pastors who believe and promote them in a way that is warmly and winsomely Reformed and biblically ecumenical, spreading the influence of these truths as broadly as possible.

This set of books is published with a view to introducing the student to some of the main issues in the history, theology and literature of the Assembly, and in hopes of spurring new interest in the work of the Westminster divines. Our aims, however, are not merely academic. They are also pastoral and devotional. We hope to provide material that will prove both interesting and helpful to the scholars, ministers, elders, candidates and congregations of the various evangelical churches influenced by the Westminster Assembly.

We catch something of the pastoral and devotional heart of the Assembly in the words of Samuel Rutherford (a Scottish commissioner to the Assembly), speaking of his Savior, Jesus Christ: "I am so in love with His love, that if His love were not in heaven, I should not be willing to go thither." This kind of passionate adoration of Christ is at the heart of Reformed theology at its best, and that is the sort of devotion we seek to promote through the work of Reformed Theological Seminary: love for God, love for his truth, love for Christ, love for people. Our message is "A mind for truth, a heart for God."

There is much indeed to feed our souls (as well as to strengthen our minds) which we can learn from these forefathers in the faith. The Westminster Assembly has provided for us both a profound, reverent, moving exposition of the doctrines of the Bible, and a worthy model of the function of truth in the pursuit of godliness.

Personally, my parents led me to memorize the *Westminster Shorter Catechism* when I was a young boy. Later I was given a copy of the complete *Westminster Standards* by my home church, First Presbyterian Church in Jackson, Mississippi, along with all others in that congregation when we completed our secondary education. My parents made sure that copy was packed in my luggage when I left home for undergraduate studies. A number of times as I discussed issues with others at Vanderbilt University, I turned to the *Westminster Confession* for guidance into the truths of Scripture. In particular the *Confession* was a great help to me in those days in my understanding and teaching on the subject of assurance of salvation and for my own personal comfort and encouragement in this vital area of the Christian life.

May our Sovereign God use these volumes to reacquaint His people with the rich spiritual heritage bequeathed to them by their Puritan forefathers and to spur them on to further study of their "affectionate, practical" theology.

Dr. Robert C. "Ric" Cannada, Jr.
    President, Reformed Theological Seminary
        Jackson, MS; Orlando, FL; Charlotte, NC; Washington, DC; Atlanta, GA, USA
    Associate Editor, Westminster Assembly Project
    March 25, 2003

Introduction

June of 1993, February of 1999 and March of 2002 respectively marked the three hundred fiftieth anniversaries of the seating, the final session and the informal dissolution of the historic Westminster Assembly. As you know, that godly gathering of divines met steadily throughout the ravages of the English Civil War, from 1643 to 1649, patiently putting together a testimony of the faith in hopes of uniting the Reformed movement in England, Wales, Scotland, and Ireland (and even continental Europe), in doctrine, worship, discipline and church government. Hence, there have been over the last decade a number of conferences and commemorations celebrating the memory of that venerable convention.

In the early 1990s, with the encouragement of the administration of Reformed Theological Seminary (Jackson, MS; Orlando, FL; Charlotte, NC; Washington, DC; Atlanta, GA), a group of eminent scholars from around the world was approached to participate in the production of literature (both popular and academic) designed to discuss and debate the most important issues in current post-Reformation studies, as well as promote interest in the Westminster Assembly and its work. This effort was designated "The Westminster Assembly Project" and received encouragement from many quarters, not the least of which came from the then-President of RTS, Dr. Luder G. Whitlock, Jr. RTS has been unwavering in its support of this long-standing project of scholarship and the whole editorial team is grateful for it. I am especially appreciative of the continuing interest and assistance of two good friends, RTS Vice President, Robert J. Bailey (a Ruling Elder of First Presbyterian Church, Yazoo City, Mississippi) and our new President of RTS, Dr. Robert C. "Ric" Cannada, Jr.

The distinguished historian of the Reformation and post-Reformation eras, Richard Muller of Calvin Theological Seminary, calls the Westminster Assembly Project "a most worthy undertaking and, to my mind, one that is quite timely not only because of the anniversary of the Assembly but also because of the clear need in Presbyterian and Reformed circles for scholarly work on the Reformed tradition and its confessions." And so, we have been busy for over a decade researching, producing literature and preparing for a multi-volume set of scholarly essays on various subjects related to the work of the Westminster Assembly. This volume is the first of four projected, with another planned for release this year. The timing of its publication, though much delayed, has turned out to be providentially propitious. Chad Van Dixhoorn's discovery of long forgotten and never before transcribed or published minutes of the Westminster Assembly has scholars keenly interested. Westminster Seminary's (Philadelphia, PA) announcement of a new center for the study of the Westminster Assembly will bring a fresh attention to this subject area.

Meanwhile, we have already produced a brief "user-friendly" bibliography of the Assembly (in conjunction with the North American Presbyterian and Reformed Council commemoration) called *The Westminster Assembly: A Guide to Basic Bibliography*, (Greenville: **Reformed Academic Press**, 1993), a revised version of William Beveridge's *Short History of the Westminster Assembly*, (Greenville: **Reformed Academic Press**, 1993) which has received some nice commendations,[1] a new

---

[1] "The rediscovery of reformed theology throughout the world has given fresh relevance to the Westminster Divines' classical exposition of biblical

edition of S.W. Carruthers', *Everyday Work of the Westminster Assembly*, (Greenville: **Reformed Academic Press**, 1994), a reprint of S.W. Carruthers', *The Westminster Confession: The Preparation and Printing of its Seven Leading Editions and A Critical Edition*, (Greenville: **Reformed Academic Press,** 1995), and a chain of articles called *"The Belgic Confession: A View from Westminster,"* in the Presbyterian Perspective Series in **Christian Observer** 1995-1996. Soon to be released is J. V. Fesko's, *Diversity within the Reformed Tradition: Supra- and Infralapsarianism in Calvin, Dort, and Westminster*, (Greenville: **Reformed Academic Press**, 2003), and three more volumes in this four-volume set on *The Westminster Confession in the 2lst Century* (Tain: Christian Focus, 2003-2004). Among the other major projects which have been initiated is a comprehensive annotated bibliography on the Assembly - *The Westminster Assembly: A Comprehensive and Selectively Annotated Bibliography*.

One of our major focuses is the Westminster theology (and the Puritan/Protestant Scholastic legacy) and its relation to the Reformed tradition as a whole. In particular, the Westminster Assembly Project aims to discuss the Westminster theology in its interrelationship to the earlier Reformed tradition–arguing for the basic continuity between Calvin and Calvinism, without ignoring developments and discontinuities. The seventeenth-century

---

teaching. To an extraordinary degree they studied in depth the same issues which trouble and challenge the church today, and their work continues to serve as an invaluable guide. In this context, Professor Ligon Duncan's fine edited version of William Beveridge's valuable study of the Assembly should be widely welcomed. Its appearance augurs well for the success and usefulness of the important work of the Westminster Assembly Project" (Sinclair B. Ferguson). Douglas F. Kelly has added: "...beautifully done; the notes and bibliography are extremely helpful for both historical and contemporary scholarship relating to the Westminster Standards. This will prove to be another incentive to the church to maintain and further our great doctrinal heritage for the rising generation."

Reformed theologians have not fared well in the hands of late nineteenth and twentieth century historical theologians. We hope to continue the current redress of that imbalance (*à la mode de* Muller, Clark, Trueman, Marsden and others) and to contribute to the rectification of a common, but bad, historiography.

The purpose of these volumes, then, is to **inform**, **evaluate**, and **commend**. We wish to inform the reader about the Assembly in its historical, theological, political and social setting. Further, we wish to challenge unhistorical assertions commonly made about Westminster in its relation to both earlier and later Reformed theology, and to provide fresh evaluation of its place in and contribution to the Calvinian tradition. Finally, we wish to commend the Westminster theology as a faithful expression of clear-headed Christian thinking to a generation in the thralls of dying modernity and nascent postmodernity.

There are many reasons why it would be beneficial for the scholars, ministers, elders, students and congregations of the various Reformed churches to study the Westminster Assembly. We will mention a few of them here. First, there is a *pastoral* reason. That learned gathering of divines was representative of a movement which bequeathed to us a tradition of pastoral theology unsurpassed in the history of Christianity in the English-speaking world. We need to hear them because a significant proportion of the church of our day has decided that its ministry should be carried out pragmatically rather than theologically, while another quadrant (more theologically sophisticated, it should be said) places a premium on contextualization and general revelation in its theology of ministry, at the expense of the divine modes and norms of church life clearly set forth in the Scriptures. The Puritans were not so tempted by such modern folly. The members of the Assembly (in their corporate work, lives and writings) offer to us a pattern of ministry that was biblically grounded, theologically informed, culturally engaged and pastorally effective.

Second, there is an *historical* reason. It hardly needs to be said that the work of Westminster has served for over three and a half centuries as the basic doctrinal formulary for Presbyterianism worldwide, but it has also been influential in several other Protestant traditions. Thus the *Westminster Confession* and *Catechisms* have made an historical contribution to the whole Reformed tradition's understanding of Christian faith and life, and have functioned either as the basis of or a major influence on the public theology not only of Presbyterianism, but also of the historic Baptist churches (e.g., via the *Second London Confession* of 1689, adopted as the *Philadelphia Confession* in 1742), the Congregational churches (e.g., via the *Savoy Declaration* of 1658) and the Anglican tradition. This alone argues for its historical importance and hence the value of its study. Nevertheless, it may be further suggested that knowledge and appreciation of the times and teachings of Westminster can serve to inoculate us against the false teachings and superficialities of our own age. "Reading old books," C.S. Lewis once said, keeps "the clean sea breeze of the centuries blowing through our minds" so that we are not so prone to modern errors and trivialities.

Third, there is a *theological* reason. All Christians are systematic theologians, the question is whether we are going to be good ones or bad ones. The mastering of the theology of Westminster will provide the minister with a wholesome and comprehensive grasp of biblical truth, which will serve our systematic theology better than prevalent alternatives in today's market. The scope and precision of the Assembly's product is an especially helpful corrective to the current, seemingly ubiquitous, anti-systematic theology sentiment, and to contemporary tendencies towards minimalism and reductionism. Indeed, many divinity halls and ecclesiastical assemblies are populated these days by self-styled "biblical theologians," (which usually means merely thematic theologians who harbor deep suspicions of the categories of historical theology, precise distinctions and larger theological systems, who have not themselves done the hard work of theological synthesis, who often unreflectively import their own philosophical presuppositions into their exegesis and redemptive historical method, while at the same time criticizing "scholastic theology" for doing this very thing, and who ironically have a more dominating, if smaller and narrower, theological grid than any post-Reformation scholastic you can name). The result of this is the total domination of the canon by "single issue" theologues – every passage turns out to be about whatever is the particular bee in their bonnet. Hence, their protest against Protestant scholastic theology turns out to be a case of the pot calling the kettle black, and that unfairly. It was Karl Barth who said "Fear of scholasticism is the mark of a false prophet." For once, he was right. The Assembly was not afraid of exactitude, distinctions, deductions, or historic categories, and yet was philosophically more self-aware (and self-critical) than most contemporary theologians.

Fourth, there is a *devotional* reason. The devotional value of the Westminster documents has never before been so underestimated as it is today. And yet there waits a deep pool of living water for the refreshing of the soul for any who will take the time to drink. The divines provide for us both a profound, reverent, affectionate exposition of the doctrines of the Bible, and a worthy model of the function of truth in the pursuit of godliness, thus making a wonderful contribution to the cultivation of "Christian piety" or "heart religion." Though it is often compared unfavorably to the *Heidelberg Catechism*, Westminster's *Shorter Catechism* is far from cold and academic, rather we find in it a warm, evangelical expression of the Christian faith. This is nowhere more evident than in the very first question and answer of the Catechism: What is the chief end of man? A. Man's chief end is to glorify God, and to enjoy him forever. (See 1 Corinthians 10:31 and Psalm 73:25-26). You can't get more basic or practical than this. What is the meaning of life? What is our purpose in life? What are we here for? If you get the answer to this question wrong, everything else will go wrong. To glorify God is to know him, trust him and serve him, according to his word. To enjoy him is to seek him as our greatest good and our greatest desire. We glorify him in enjoying him, and enjoy him in glorifying him. Nothing gloomy or pedantic about that!

For all those reasons (and more) the study of the Westminster Assembly is never a waste of time. To make the exercise even more valuable, we have assembled contributions from an impressive list of students of Westminster and its context: **William S. Barker**, former Dean of Westminster Theological Seminary (Philadelphia, PA, USA), an outstanding scholar of English Puritanism; **David B. Calhoun**, Professor of Church History at Covenant Theological Seminary (St Louis, MO, USA), an expert in the Princeton Theology; **Hugh Cartwright**, formerly of the Free Church of Scotland College (Edinburgh, UK) and now in the Free Presbyterian Church; **Mark E. Dever**, brilliant Puritan scholar, author of a major academic work on Richard Sibbes, and senior minister of the Capitol Hill Baptist Church (Washington, DC, USA); **Sinclair B. Ferguson**, formerly of Westminster Theological Seminary (Philadelphia, PA, USA), and St. George's Tron Kirk in Glasgow, Scotland, a widely known author and theologian; **Richard B. Gaffin, Jr.** of Westminster Theological Seminary (Philadelphia, PA, USA), an outstanding exegete and theologian, known for his research on the Sabbath in the Reformed tradition; **Timothy George**, Dean of the Beeson School of Divinity, Samford University, (Birmingham, AL, USA), world class Baptist historian; **Stewart D. Gill**, formerly of the Presbyterian Theological Hall (Melbourne, Australia), now Dean and Deputy Warden, Trinity College and Senior Fellow, Department of History, University of Melbourne (Victoria, Australia); **W. Robert Godfrey**, President of Westminster

Theological Seminary (Escondido, CA, USA); **David W. Hall**, formerly of the Covenant Presbyterian Church (Oak Ridge, TN, USA) and well-known scholar of and author on the Westminster Assembly; **Darryl G. Hart**, formerly of Westminster Theological Seminary (Philadelphia, PA, USA), now Dean of Westminster Theological Seminary (Escondido, CA, USA), exceptional church historian; **Paul Helm**, formerly of King's College (London, UK), noted author on issues relating to Calvin and Calvinism; **Michael S. Horton**, of Westminster Theological Seminary (Escondido, CA, USA) and President of the Alliance of Confessing Evangelicals (Philadelphia, PA, USA); **Douglas F. Kelly**, Jordan Professor of Theology, Reformed Theological Seminary (Charlotte, NC, USA); **Andrew T.B. McGowan**, Principal of the Highland Theological College (Dingwall, Scotland), known for his knowledge of Scottish Historical Theology; **Donald Macleod**, Principal of the Free Church of Scotland College (Edinburgh, Scotland), first order systematic theologian and master of Scottish theology; **James L. Macleod**, formerly of the University of Nottingham (Nottingham, UK) and now in the Department of History, University of Evansville, Indiana; **W. David J. McKay**, of the Ballylaggan Reformed Presbyterian Church (Aghadowey, Northern Ireland, UK); **Nicholas R. Needham** of the Highland Theological College (Dingwall, Scotland); **J.I. Packer**, of Regent College, (Vancouver, Canada); **Robert L. Reymond**, of Knox Theological Seminary (Ft. Lauderdale, FL, USA); **O. Palmer Robertson**, President of African Bible College (Uganda, Africa); **Morton H. Smith**, of Greenville Presbyterian Theological Seminary (Taylors, SC, USA); **Wayne R. Spear** of the Reformed Presbyterian Theological Seminary (Pittsburgh, PA, USA); **Andrew A. Woolsey** of the Crumlin Evangelical Presbyterian Church (Crumlin, Northern Ireland, UK); **David F. Wright,** of New College, University of Edinburgh (Edinburgh, Scotland); and more.

The topics we cover in this set are wide-ranging, from the history of the Westminster Assembly Commemorations; to recent objections to the Covenant Theology of Westminster Confession; the Holy Spirit in the Westminster Confession; Westminster and the relationship of Church and State (from both Scottish and American perspectives); the theology of the Westminster Larger Catechism; the Westminster doctrine of union with Christ; Westminster and Sanctification; Westminster on the Sabbath; the Westminster Doctrine of Scripture; Baptists and Westminster; Princeton and the Westminster Confession; Westminster and the Regulative Principle; Scotland and the Westminster Confession; Westminster and Australian Presbyterians; Calvin, Westminster and Assurance; Westminster and Protestant Scholasticism; revision of the Westminster Confession and the Free Church Declaratory Act of 1892; the Confession in the Fundamentalist-Modernist Debate; Westminster Confession and Missions; Westminster and the Atonement; Finney's Attacks on Westminster; Westminster and Worship: Psalms, Hymns?, & Musical Instruments?; and more.

In this volume the essays commence with David Hall's interesting "History of Westminster Assembly Commemorations" which has a fascinating subplot regarding what the commemorations themselves tell us about the denominations celebrating the Assembly. Then there is Wayne Spear's "Word and Spirit in the Westminster Confession" – which provides a nice, if partial rebuttal to the old and outmoded Rogers-McKim thesis on the Reformed doctrine of Scripture. O. Palmer Robertson provides a pastoral overview of "The Holy Spirit in the Westminster Confession" which undercuts the charge (often heard) that the role of the Holy Spirit is underplayed in the Westminster Confession. We are introduced to the "Theology of the Larger Catechism" by Morton H. Smith, a well-known scholar of Westminster, and Richard B. Gaffin critically but appreciatively engages the Confession on the currently controversial matter of "Westminster and the Sabbath." Dean Timothy George of the Beeson Divinity School, Samford University, gives us a helpful treatment of "Baptists and the Westminster Confession" thus reminding us of the importance of Westminster to and in that ecclesial tradition. David F. Wright of the University of Edinburgh brings to bear his expertise is the area of the doctrine of baptism to engage the debate about baptismal realism, regeneration and efficacy in his chapter "Baptism at the Westminster Assembly" – his findings are nuanced and provocative. Andrew McGowan, an expert in Scottish Federal Theology, demonstrates the fundamental theological continuity in pre-Westminster and post-Westminster Scottish theology (contrary to regnant historical mythology) in "Edinburgh to Westminster," while W.D.J. McKay explores the influence of the Scottish participants in the Assembly in "Scotland and the Westminster Assembly. Stewart Gill's "The Battle for the Westminster Confession in Australia" gives us insight into a sad instance of doctrinal erosion in a case study important to all who aspire to work within and maintain the integrity of confessional churches. Mark E. Dever's chapter on "Calvin, Westminster and Assurance" counters the flawed but common argument (typified in the Kendal thesis) that the Puritan tradition fundamentally undercut the Calvinian doctrine of assurance. This is an important point in the larger debate regarding Calvin and Calvinism. J. L. Macleod takes a hard look at "Revision of the Westminster Confession (Declaratory Act of 1892)" and the late nineteenth-century Free Church's departure from confessional Calvinism. Michael Horton looks at the self-conscious and even radical rejection of confessional Reformed theology by one of the most famous evangelists of the nineteenth century in "Finney's Attacks on the Westminster Confession." Finally, William S. Barker, outstanding historian and former Dean of Westminster Seminary in Philadelphia, considers the issue of church and state in "Lord of Lords and King of Commoners.

The nineteenth-century historian of Westminster William Hetherington once said that the Westminster Assembly "was the most important event in the century in which it occurred . . . and has exerted, and in all probability will yet exert, a far more wide and permanent influence upon both the civil and the religious history of mankind than has generally been even imagined." That statement, made over two centuries after the event and perhaps uncharacteristically enthusiastic and generous for a Scot talking about anything from south of the Border, may certainly be debated (I can already hear today's historian crying "Anglo-centrism"!), but is at least indicative of the magnitude of the Assembly and its work, and its significance for the English-speaking world and beyond in successive generations. After all, Richard Baxter, a contemporary of the Assembly who held some serious divergences from the Westminster theology, himself declared that "Since the days of the Apostles there has never been a Synod of more excellent divines. . . ." Whatever the hyperbole of these estimations, the Assembly marks the highpoint of Reformed confessionalism and warrants the further study and consideration that these essays of ours intend to promote.

J. Ligon Duncan, III, BA, MDiv, MA, PhD
> General Editor, The Westminster Assembly Project
> Senior Minister, First Presbyterian Church (PCA), Jackson, Mississippi, USA
> Adjunct Professor, Reformed Theological Seminary
> Convener, Twin Lakes Fellowship
> Council, Alliance of Confessing Evangelicals
> Chairman, Council on Biblical Manhood and Womanhood
> Secretary of the Board, Belhaven College
> Editorial Director, Reformed Academic Press

Acknowledgments

This first volume of the Westminster Assembly Project's essays on the Assembly has been waiting to see the light of day for more than half a decade. The General Editor wishes to express his appreciation to the authors, who have so patiently awaited its arrival, for their outstanding work. I am also appreciative of the labors of my Associate Editors, W. Duncan Rankin, Derek W.H. Thomas, Robert C. "Ric" Cannada, Jr., and Stephen Berry. Professor Rankin has been a vital part of this project from the beginning and recruited many of the contributors. Professor Thomas, who now holds the John E. Richards chair at RTS and serves with me at First Presbyterian Church, has shouldered some of the unglamorous aspects of editorial work. Dr. Cannada, now President of RTS, has continued the crucial support of the Seminary to this project and is vitally interested in its fruition. Stephen Berry, a former student and now PhD candidate at Duke did much of the initial editorial work in earlier drafts, while he was Professor Rankin's Thornwell scholar at RTS Jackson. Stephen Tindall, my intern and assistant, has painstakingly reviewed every letter and space of the final manuscript, numerous times. We are all indebted to him for his herculean labors and his liaison work with typesetters, publishers and printers in two states, three countries and two continents (not to mention his detective work in tracking down contributors world-wide). He has earned every drop of editorial attribution! Each of these men is a dear Christian friend to me and I am grateful for each of your unique contributions to this long labor.

Collectively, the whole editorial team here expresses our thanks to the Executive Committee of RTS for its ongoing encouragement and support. Many congregations and individuals have given financially toward the work of the Westminster Assembly Project, among them, James R. "Sonny" Peaster (a trustee of the Banner of Truth Trust) and A. William May (a Ruling Elder of First Presbyterian Church, Jackson) stand out. Without their gifts, we could not have brought this work to completion.

We all also wish to express our gratitude to our publisher, William Mackenzie, Managing Director of Christian Focus Publications, and our Editorial Manager, Willie Mackenzie (not to be confused with his aforementioned uncle!).

Soli Deo Gloria
L.D.

The History of Westminster Assembly Commemorations

DAVID W. HALL

Like any family which enshrines select events as anchors of that family's memory, the events which a church commemorates are clues to their self-identity. A keen observer may monitor the occasions of commemoration and infer much about the past glories and future goals of a communion. No church routinely celebrates every event of its history, nor does it ascribe equal value to them. Likewise, Presbyterian churches have a rich tradition of remembering the history surrounding the Westminster Assembly and standards.

What a family or a church celebrates signals the values they cherish. Commemoratives are spiritual versions of family reunions, which are filled with the notes of deep family love, aspects of celebration and renewal, recollections of the past, and even complete with sibling rivalries and infighting. The strength of commitment to underlying traditions is observed when a church (as with a family) carries out those celebrations, even during times of difficulty and opposition. A brief review of previous examples of commemorations may help in appreciating that legacy, as well as give guidance for the future. Such study may also reveal subtle changes of emphasis over time within the tradition of any ecclesiastical family.

When participants from various countries and denominations assembled in London in 1993 on the historic grounds where the Westminster Assembly first convened, whether they knew it or not, such a commemoration was but the latest in a tradition of Westminster commemorations.[1] Presbyterian churches already had a rich (though short) tradition of remembering the history surrounding the Westminster Assembly and it standards.

The North American Presbyterian and Reformed Council (hereafter NAPARC), an umbrella organization for six USA reformed communions, first began planning for the 350th anniversary of the Westminster Assembly in 1991. This review concentrates on the largest segment of commemorates, the American Presbyterian Churches. That however, is not to deny that other Presbyterian communions, e.g., in Scotland and Ireland, also held previous commemorations. While the primary focus is on the American efforts, it is important to realize that we are not the first—nor the only ones—to tread this ground, and we sincerely trust that we will not be the last.

The strength of commitment that Presbyterian churches have had to the Westminster history is noticeable from their earlier commemorations. The regard of the Presbyterian family for their Confession was paramount, even among various geographical or theological divisions. As the Presbyterian churches approach the dusk of the second millennium, with many other cultural and ecclesiastical issues before them, parts of the Presbyterian family would again return to their roots, and commemorate a continuing aspect of their self-identity. The abiding validity of remembering the Westminster era and properly commemorating it was a part of the best of Presbyterian churches. Had the lessons of history

---

[1] Much of this essay follows an earlier version produced in conjunction with the 350th Anniversary celebration. See *To Glorify and Enjoy God*, John L. Carson and David W. Hall eds. (Edinburgh: Banner of Truth Trust, 1994), pp. 3-24.

from the Westminster chapter of history been unimportant or fading in significance, these modern churches would have easily jettisoned such commemorations. Indeed, some Presbyterian communions did. But for those which saw themselves in continuity with history, their desire to keep this part of their self-image alive was an admirable and noble attribute. For all those who know the value of spiritual remembering, this can serve as an introduction to our own and subsequent commemorations.

The First Commemoration: The Bicentennial

Efforts to commemorate the Westminster Assembly in America began in 1842. There is no evidence of major centennial celebrations of the Assembly in colonial America. Of course, if one recalls that in 1743, one hundred years after the convening of the Westminster Assembly, America was a mere pup of a colony, not even formally a nation, the reasons for non-celebration may be self-evident. Remembering that in the 1740s, the American Presbyterian church had recently experienced controversy over the meaning of subscription to the Confession, the first wave of the Great Awakening, and a kind of youthful expansion that would hardly be looking backwards for commemorative events, it should be noted that the Westminster chapter (like most events worthy of commemoration) had not yet stood the test of time's evaluation. Hence the American (and most other) Presbyterians permitted the centennial of the Westminster Assembly (1743) to pass without comment or celebration.

The same is true for the 150th anniversary of the Westminster Assembly, for the same logic above. In addition, rarely do commemorative events begin at the half-century mark. If the event itself is worthy of commemoration, it will normally commence in a centennial year. If the Westminster Assembly had no centennial celebration in the 1740s, it could hardly be expected that a sesquicentennial commemoration would commence the tradition in the 1790s.

Earlier commemorative works such as John Flavel's half-century commemoration, released in 1692 (*An Exposition of the Assembly's Catechism*, re-issued throughout the years.) and American Old Sider, John Thomson's *An Explication of the Shorter Catechism* (1745) satisfied commemorative urges. The Church of Scotland re-issued the Assembly's *Directory for Family Worship* as a centennial token in 1745, and one hundred fifty years after the Assembly saw the publication of Isaac Watts' *Plain and Easy Catechisms for Youth* (1792), James Fisher's *The Westminster Assembly's Shorter Catechism* (1792), and John Brown's "Plain, practical" elaboration of the standards (1796).

Thus, as the Presbyterian family members approached the bicentennial (1843), the time was ripe for a due remembering of this era of family history. A bicentenary was planned for Scotland, the land perhaps with the most Presbyterian of the Presbyterians. In fact, it may be that some of the American leaders borrowed the idea of calling for the first American commemoration from their Scottish cousins.

However, the Scottish celebration reflected an earlier serious division. The Reformed Presbyterian Church of Scotland was organized in 1743, and in 1843 they combined an anniversary celebration of their first century with a zesty celebration of the bicentennial of the Westminster heritage. They gathered in Edinburgh, "the capital of Presbyterianism" (in Canon-mills Hall), the mornings and evenings of July 12-13. Among the addresses in the *Commemoration of the Bicentenary of the Westminster Assembly* (Glasgow, 1843) by this Scottish and Irish convocation were: "The Real Character and Bearing of the Westminster Assembly, and Refutations of Calumnies" by William Hetherington; "On the Leading Incidents and Characters of the Assembly" by Thomas M'Crie; "The Opposition of the Westminster Assembly to Popery, Prelacy, and Erastianism" by

William Cunningham; "The Uses and Value of Subordinate Standards" by Prof. Harper; "The Leading Features and Excellencies of the Westminster Standards" by Charles J. Brown; and "The Importance of Adhering to Sound Scriptural Standards, and Aiming at Union on that Basis" by Principal Candlish.

One of the participants and contributors, William Symington, helped capture the significance of the commemoration:

> We would not be chargeable with the enormous wickedness of forgetting that men are only what God makes them, and that to Him all the glory . . . is to be ascribed. But we are, at the same time, unable to see wherein the bestowment of a due meed of praise on the memory of such . . . contravenes any maxim of sound morality, or any dictate of inspiration. We . . . have no hesitation in attempting to awaken, in the men of the present generation, sentiments of admiration and gratitude for the memory of worthies to whom all are so deeply indebted . . . . While we claim and exercise the right of bringing these, like all other human productions, to the infallible touchstone of Revelation, ... We cannot but cherish the hope that the present commemoration, . . . may be regarded as symptomatic at once of a growing attachment to the sentiments of the Westminster divines, and of an enlightened determination to maintain them more firmly and diffuse them more extensively than ever.[2]

Meanwhile, in America, a leader of the Old School Presbyterians,[3] Dr. Robert Breckinridge of Kentucky (whose family was known for political leadership in Kentucky, as well as in the Lincoln Administration), offered an overture to the 1842 General Assembly of the Old School Presbyterians calling for a bicentennial commemoration of the Westminster Assembly. Viewing the history surrounding Westminster as "an era full of

---

[2] "Historical Sketch of the Westminster Assembly of Divines: by William Symington in *Commemoration of the Bicentenary of the Westminster Assembly of Divines* (Glasgow, 1843), pp. 69, 71.

[3] Five years earlier American Presbyterianism witnessed its first major rupture in the Old School/New School division, with the Old School unseating the New School. The disagreements were over missionary strategy, union with other bodies, the views (and discipline) of some in the denomination, and at heart, adherence to details in the Westminster Confession of Faith.

interest to the Churches under its care, and to all other Churches which adopt the Standards . . . prepared by that venerable body; and believing that the occasion can be so used, as by the Divine blessing, greatly to promote the interests of truth,"[4] Breckinridge called for the erection of a ten member Standing Committee to plan a suitable commemoration of the Assembly on July 1, 1843, which committee should also invite and seek the cooperation of other Presbyterian denominations.

The 1842 Old School Assembly agreed with this proposal, and resolved that such a commemoration should attempt to hold up "the venerable standards" which should be "more carefully studied, more perfectly understood, and more faithfully observed by all the members and office-bearers of this Church; and that the children of the Church be early and faithfully taught to understand them . . . . . That an accurate acquaintance with the history of the past trials, persecutions and faithfulness of the true Church, and especially of our own brand of it, should be diligently sought, particularly by those who are office-bearers in the Church."[5]

In answer to Breckinridge's overture, the Assembly ordered a commemoration throughout the church, to be held on July 1, 1843 "when convenient to do so, and when not convenient, on such other day during the current year, as may be deemed expedient devoted to the general instruction of our people, by the minister, in the great facts connected with this subject."[6] It is clear from this act, that a church-wide thrust was commended, but this first effort was short of a formally organized set of presentations or commemorations by the General Assembly. Nevertheless, the Old School Presbyterian church in 1843

---

[4] *Minutes General Assembly* (O.S.), 1842, p. 17.

[5] *Minutes General Assembly* (O.S.), 1843, pp. 191-192.

[6] Ibid, p. 192.

expressed the value of a historical recollection of the Westminster Assembly:

> A correct knowledge of the character of that (sic) Assembly, of the purpose for which they were convened, of the difficulties of their position, of the arduous nature of their task, and of the result of their labors, how the extent of the benefits which they have conferred on the interest of truth and freedom; and our Church in common with other Churches, which have been formed on the same model, must feel that the concurrence of the Two Hundredth Anniversary of their meeting, is a deeply interesting period in the lapse of time, and may prove profitable by its appropriate commemoration.[7]

Not only did the Old School Assembly of 1843 order a commemoration, but so did the New School Assembly—only five years after the first major rupture within American Presbyterianism. Satisfied to hitchhike on the approved celebrations of the Old School Presbyterians and other commemorations, the New School Assembly agreed to cooperate with these, stating its admiration for the standards, as well as commending to the next level of governance—Sessions and Presbyteries—that they also sponsor appropriate commemorations. The 1842 New School Assembly resolved:

> Whereas the meeting and the acts of the Westminster Assembly, now some 200 years ago, are honorably associated in the history of theology and of the protestant cause, with eternal principles of truth that are dear to every genuine Christian, to every friend of God and the progress of human society; to every love of the church and the Reformation—especially to the Puritans of illustrious memory, and to the pilgrims from whom many of us lineally, and morally are, descended, therefore Resolved, That we approve with others the measures proposed by many ecclesiastical bodies throughout the Protestant world, . . . with gratitude to God for his mercies, with a suitable review of events historically connected with it and with ardent prayers that the spirit of true religion may be diffused through all countries, and perpetuated through all ages to the end of time.[8]

This New School church also desired to commemorate the

---

[7] Ibid., p. 191.

[8] *Minutes General Assembly* (N.S.), 1843, p. 24.

Westminster history with admiration for its impact not only in America, but within all of the "protestant world," targeting the spiritual edification of its members, specifically to spur on prayer, true religion, and eternal truth. These commemorates realized the positive value of applying the truths and helpful practices of our grandparents in the faith. In that earliest commemoration, neither American church, despite their differences, acknowledged a fundamental departure from the standards or ethos of Westminster.

Also as lasting testimonies to the commemorative impulse, as would become customary, there were a number of written volumes which would add supportive testimony to particular commemorations. *A History of the Westminster Assembly of Divines* (anonymous[9]) was completed in 1841, and in 1843 William Hetherington first published his *History of the Westminster Assembly of Divines.*

The Scotsman, Hetherington, expressed his admiration for the chief product of the Assembly, the Confession of Faith:

> The existence of a Confession of Faith is ever a standing defense against the danger of any Church lapsing unawares into heresy . . . . Nothing essential is omitted; and nothing is extended to a length disproportionate to its due importance . . . . It contains the calm and settled judgment of these profound divines on all previous heresies and subjects of controversy which had in any age or country agitated the Church. This it does without expressly naming even one of these heresies,—the great Anti-Christian system alone excepted,—or entering into mere controversy. Each error is condemned, not by a direct statement and refutation of it, but by a clear, definite, and strong statement of the converse truth. There was, in this mode of exhibiting the truth, singular wisdom combined with equally singular modesty. Everything of an irritating nature is suppressed, and the pure and simple truth alone displayed; while there is not only no ostentatious

---

[9] This fine work only states that it was entered for copyright by A. W. Mitchell, who evidently was an official with the Presbyterian Committee for Publications. Suggested authors have ranged from Archibald Alexander to Samuel Miller to J. W. Alexander, but even after some investigation, the author[s] of this first American history of the Assembly remains anonymous.

parade of superior learning, but even a concealment of learning the most accurate and profound.[10]

Thomas Smyth, another eminent Presbyterian leader in Charleston, SC, also offered some succinct and valuable discourses on the influence of the Westminster Assembly in his *History, Character, and Results of the Westminster Assembly of Divines*. Smyth, who composed a short history of the Assembly prior to the release of Hetherington's 1843 history, stated the value of commemoration in this fashion:

> If the preparation of standards which have served as bulwarks to the truth as it is in Jesus, when error and heresy have come in like a flood upon the church, and which are at this moment venerated, as containing the system of doctrine taught in the word of God, by growing multitudes; and if a devotion to the cause of human rights which no bribery or persecution could extinguish; if, I say, these achievements are sufficient to demand our gratitude, then are we imperatively called upon to hail with exultation this natal day of our spiritual birthright, to consider the days of old and the years of ancient times, and to bring to remembrance the Westminster Assembly.[11]

An edition of the *Works of George Gillespie* was re-issued in 1846, and Thomas M'Crie published his *Life of Alexander Henderson* in 1840. Although not technically associated with a commemoration, the appearance of Samuel Miller's *The Utility and Importance of Creeds and Confessions* (1839) quickly became a useful tool in commemorations. Works such as the *Commemoration of the Bicentenary of the Westminster Assembly* (1843) by the Reformed Presbyterian Church in Scotland (issued in America as *Bicentenary of the Assembly of Divines at Westminster* in 1845), and individual discourses by Thomas Smyth, John Leyburn, and Robert Morris (*A Tribute to*

---

[10] William Hetherinton, *History of the Westminster Assembly of Divines* (Edmonton, AB: Still Waters Revival Books, 1991), pp. 349- 351.

[11] Thomas Smyth, "History of the Westminster Assembly" in *The Works of Thomas Smyth* (Columbia, SC: Bryan Publishing, 1908), p. 393.

Presbyterianism, A Bicentenary) were published. Commentaries on the Catechisms or Confessions during these commemorative periods by John Whitecross (1840), Alexander Patterson (1844), and Robert Shaw (*An Exposition of the Confession of Faith*, 1845), along with a re-issue of Flavel's *Exposition of the Assembly's Catechism* (1848), left the church with a legacy of materials for future celebrations.

The Semi-Bicentenary: 1893-1898

The next opportunity for commemoration saw another divided American Presbyterian church. The Old School/New School division had been repaired after the Civil War era, only to find the Presbyterian church divided along largely geographic lines by the time of its next commemoration.[12] No calls for commemoration were recorded on the 250th anniversary of the *convening* of the Westminster Assembly in 1893. Rather, it appears that in both north and south, churches chose to commemorate the Westminster contributions at the anniversary of the *completion* of that Assembly, rather than in honor of the commencement. In any event, both Northern and Southern Presbyterian churches hosted well-received and superbly planned commemoratives at the close of the nineteenth century, in 1897 and 1898 respectively.

At the 250th commemoration the participants were called on to recall, as in Hebrews 12:1-3, "that vast star-reaching amphitheater of shining immortals over looking down upon the church . . . the shadow of a vaster presence—a more imposing assemblage than mortal eyes have ever seen . . . .[to] utilize the heroism of illustrious examples, the achievements of conquering

---

[12] The separation of the Southern and Northern Presbyterians in 1861 was over the 1861 action to require southern slave holders to submit to the US government. As the Confederacy was coming into its own, this proved too much to swallow. Also at stake was the question of who should direct the church, independent boards or church-elected committees.

faith, and the ravishing glory of the victor-crowned host to animate and quicken the sacramental host on earth until the end of time."[13]

However, this commemoration occurred amidst a bitter debate over the meaning and utility of the Westminster tradition. With Archibald Hodge's 1884 "The Consensus of the Reformed Confessions,"[14] an attempt to summarize and display the creedal hallmarks of Presbyterianism, a new phase of debate was begun. In some ways Hodge's article was a delayed Old School response to Charles Briggs's earlier "Documentary History of the Westminster Assembly,"[15] which was the fruit of his research into the origins of Elizabethan puritanism. Drawing widely on original writings from many of the divines at Westminster, Briggs had contended that the role of Westminster was not to definitively settle all issues, nor best revered as normative, but rather to be seen as a consensus-building instrument reflecting many of the strong compromises necessarily arising from the Westminster Assembly.

Briggs's debates with Hodge (later succeeded by the likes of Patton, Shedd, and Warfield) led to a firestorm of calls for confessional revision. Briggs's demythologizing sentiments, e.g., "The Westminster Standards are the banners of Protestantism, but they did not claim infallibility, inerrancy, or completion. They did not propose to speak the final word in theology . . . . Theological progress is not in the direction of simplicity, but of variety and complexity,"[16] proved provocative, as Benjamin Warfield and others of the Old School tradition spewed responses. By 1890 the subject of creedal revision was so discussed that 134

---

[13] *Addresses at the Celebration of the Two Hundred and Fiftieth Anniversary of the Westminster Assembly by the General Assembly of the Presbyterian Church in the USA*, William Henry Roberts, ed. (Philadelphia: Presbyterian Board).

[14] *Presbyterian Review*, 1884, Vol. 5, pp. 266-304.

[15] *Presbyterian Review*, 1880, Vol. 1, pp. 127-163.

[16] Charles Briggs, *Whither? A Theological Question for the Times* (New York: Scribner's, 1889), p. 160.

presbyteries had called for revision, with some even proffering diminutive forms of consensus models.[17]

Warfield responded with numerous ripostes, such as "The Presbyterians and Revision," and "The Presbyterian Churches and the Westminster Confession of Faith."[18] W. G. T. Shedd's 1893 *Calvinism: Pure and Mixed* contained several essays defending the lasting usefulness of the Westminster Confession of Faith. While prior to the 250th anniversary, there were a few less partisan discussions of the Westminster Assembly, e.g., Francis Beattie's *The Presbyterian Standards: An Exposition* (1896), Francis Patton's *The Genesis of the Westminster Assembly of Divines* (1889), or Philip Schaff's *Creed Revision in the Presbyterian Churches* (1890), most published essays tended toward the strident.

Warfield, with unabashed enthusiasm for the maiden chapter of the Confession, could say (partially in response to Briggs): "There is certainly in the whole mass of confessional literature no more nobly conceived or ably wrought-out statement of doctrine than [this] chapter . . . placed at the head of their Confession and laid at the foundation of their system of doctrine."[19] Elsewhere, he would applaud of the same:

> If it be compared in its details with the teachings of Scripture, it will be found to be but the careful and well-guarded statement of what is delivered by Scripture concerning itself. If it be tested in the cold

---

[17] For an excellent summary of this whole period, which is sympathetic to Briggs, see *Charles Augustus Briggs and the Crisis of Historical Criticism* by Mark S. Massa (Minneapolis: Fortress Press, 1990), pp. 59-84.

[18] *Presbyterian Review*, Vol. 10, 1889, pp. 646-657. Also in this issue were articles by Philip Schaff on "The Revision of the Westminster Confession of Faith," John DeWitt on "Revision of the Confession of Faith," and later Shedd offered a contribution, all of which were printed under the title *Ought the Confession of Faith to be Revised* (New York, 1890).

[19] *The Westminster Assembly and Its Work* by Benjamin B. Warfield, orig. 1932, reprinted in 1972 by Mack Publishing Co., and in 1991 by Still Waters Revival Books (Edmonton, AB, Canada), p. 155.

light of scientific theology, it will commend itself as a reasoned statement, remarkable for the exactness of its definitions and the close [connection] of its parts. . . . Numerous divergences from it have been propounded of late years, even among those who profess the Westminster doctrine as their doctrine. But it has not yet been made apparent that any of these divergences can commend themselves to one who would fain hold a doctrine of Scripture which is at once Scriptural and reasonable, and a foundation upon which faith can safely build her house. In this case, the old still seems to be better.[20]

If Briggs was an exemplar of criticism of the work of Westminster, Warfield was its defender. Of the Confession of Faith as an accurate and vital compilation of Christian truth, Warfield contended, that as such, the Westminster Confession of Faith could not in its influence:

lack in spiritual quality. It is the product of intellect working only under the impulse of the heart, and must be a monument of the religious life. This is true of all the great creedal statements, and preeminently true of the Westminster Standards. Their authors were men of learning and philosophic grasp; but above all of piety. Their interest was not in speculative construction, but in the protection of their flocks from deadly error . . . . In proportion as our own religious life flows in a deep and broad stream, in that proportion will we find spiritual delight in the Westminster Standards.[21]

Benjamin Warfield challenged his contemporaries with this: ". . . the nicety of its [Westminster Confession] balance in conceiving and the precision of its language in stating truth, will seem to us scholastic only in proportion as our religious life is less developed than theirs." When Warfield saw others attempting to lessen the influence of the Confession of Faith and lower its standard, he felt "an inexpressible grief [to see the Church] spending its energies in a vain attempt to lower its testimony to suit the ever changing sentiment of the world about it."

Toward the close of the nineteenth century Francis Patton estimated that the doctrinal system of Westminster, "is the most

---

[20] *Warfield*, Ibid., pp. 256-257.

[21] Cited in Shedd, *Calvinism: Pure and Mixed* (reprinted by the Banner of Truth Trust [Edinburgh], 1986), p. 161.

luminous, logical, and consistent summary of the Calvinistic faith ever published. It is worthy of and it has ever commanded the highest admiration of those whose minds and hearts were capable of appreciating their excellence,"[22] and we "owe a debt of gratitude to a Puritan ancestry which has not been duly acknowledged."

All of this debate just prior to the 250th anniversary celebrations showed the strains over the manner of attempting to secure orthodox identity. Unfortunately at times, it also sounded as if battle lines were being drawn. The Confession of Faith, of course would be revised in due time (1903, and in scope in 1967). However, the late nineteenth century commemorations themselves contained little in way of revision, and even less in terms of polemics.

The Southern family initiated the *fin de siecle* commemorations. At the 1896 PCUS General Assembly, meeting in Memphis, TN, on May 18th, Dr. Francis Beattie of Louisville Presbyterian Seminary introduced the following overture calling for an anniversary celebration:

> The undersigned desires respectfully to call the attention of the Assembly to the fact that it is now just about two centuries and a half since the Westminster Assembly which framed our Catechisms and Confession of Faith was in session. He also brings to the attention of the Assembly the fact that several branches of the Presbyterian family are already proposing to celebrate, in various ways, the two hundred and fiftieth anniversary of that great event during the coming year. He further expresses the conviction that at the present day it is important to give prominence to the history and contents of the great doctrinal symbols which the Westminster Assembly gave to the world. We live in an age of unrest and criticism, if not of transition, in regard to many things pertaining to the Christian faith. An intelligent acquaintance with the history of the Westminster Assembly, and a clear grasp of the doctrinal system which it formulated, may be of great value in these circumstances. The undersigned, therefore, respectfully overtures the General

---

[22] Francis Patton, *The Genesis of the Westminster Assembly* (1889), p. 76.

Assembly to take steps to observe this anniversary in some suitable way, say in connection with the Assembly of 1897.[23]

In addition, another commissioner, W. D. Morton, overtured the same Assembly to, "record its sense of the inestimable blessings which have resulted from the Westminster Confession and Catechisms, not only to the churches holding these standards, but to the cause of Christianity."[24]

The Southern Presbyterian Church concurred and ordered the following: "that this General Assembly commend to the Presbyteries and Synods the propriety of observing the two hundred and fiftieth anniversary of the formulation of the Westminster symbols of doctrine, and that order be taken by this Assembly to celebrate this event in connection with the sessions of the General Assembly of 1897."[25] The 1897 Assembly of the PCUS, meeting in Charlotte, NC, was treated to a true feast, with the following honored as presenters on the following topics:

(1) Dr. Henry A. White to discuss the social and political background of the Assembly; (2) Dr. Robert Price to discuss the religious situation of Britain at the time; (3) Dr. T. D. Witherspoon to give a description of the Assembly, its personnel, proceedings, and place of meeting; (4) Dr. R. L. Dabney to discuss the doctrinal contents of the Confession; (5) Dr. G. B. Strickler to speak on the nature, value, and utility of the Catechisms; (6) Dr. Eugene Daniel (replacing B. M. Palmer) to discuss the polity and worship of the Westminster standards; (7) Dr. J. D. Tadlock to address the present relations among those churches which hold the Westminster symbols; (8) Dr. Moses D. Hoge to speak on the influence of the Westminster symbols on missionary activity; (9) Dr. Samuel M. Smith to address the relation of the Westminster standards to current theology and the needs of the future; (10) Dr. J. F. Cannon to speak on the influence of the Westminster symbols on family and society; (11) W. M. Cox to discuss the influence of Westminster on civil liberty and government.

---

[23] *Minutes of the General Assembly, Presbyterian Church, U.S.*, 1896, pp. 585-586.

[24] Ibid.

[25] Ibid.

All eleven of these addresses were given at the 1897 Assembly in Charlotte, and later collected and published by the PCUS as the *Memorial Volume of the Westminster Assembly, 1647-1897*.[26] In comparison with the *Anniversary Addresses* (1898; see below) from the northern branch of American Presbyterianism, this southern contribution was both more substantive, as well as more directly related to the Assembly rather than focusing on its North American offspring. Typical of this volume is Dabney's assessment of the Westminster contribution:

> The Westminster Assembly was convened near the middle of that age, and in the midday light of its learning and genius. Had we no histories of its members, and no record of its discussions, the contents of the Confession itself are enough to teach us that those profound and illustrious scholars were enriched with all the stores of sacred learning gathered from previous ages, and culminating in their glorious epoch. . . . Providence thus qualified them for their important task to the most eminent degree, and set them in that historic epoch most favorable to success. In speaking of their work, I propose to signalize in the remainder of this address two of its remarkable traits. One I may describe as its scripturalness, the other as its moderation. . . . Many are professing to say: Let us have a creed which shall teach the Reformed system in its substance, but let us retrench its ultraisms and excrescences. The history of doctrine shows us that the Confession has no excrescences. The Westminster Assembly has already pruned them off. The real effect of change will be an amputation of some essential member, endangering the life of the whole structure, not a cleansing away of useless accretions. Let us, then, be wise and hold fast this priceless possession of which a gracious Providence has made us heirs. Our supreme wisdom will be 'to let well enough alone,' and humbly teach our scriptural creed, instead of attempting vainly to tinker it.[27]

---

[26] Ed. by Francis Beattie, Charles Hemphill, and Henry Escott (Richmond, VA: Presbyterian Committee of Publication, 1897). See also *The Westminster Assembly: A Guide to Basic Bibliography* by David Hall and Ligon Duncan (Greenville, SC: A Press, 1993) for more detail on the contents of this volume.

[27] Cf. the whole of Dabney's "The Westminster Confession and Creeds" in *Memorial Volume of the Westminster Assembly, 1647-1897* (Richmond, VA: The Presbyterian Committee of Publication, 1897), ed. by Francis Beattie *et al.*

As a prominent part of this 1897 Assembly, the evening sessions were open to the public, whose "interest grew and the enthusiasm deepened with each succeeding address, till at the close the impression produced by eleven such addresses was profound and lasting."[28] The 1897 Assembly voted its great satisfaction to the committee with a standing ovation and also resolved to publish the entire set of addresses, as well as those of Strickler and Cannon (on the Catechisms and the relation of the standards to family and social life) in pamphlet form. The 1897 Southern commemoration concluded with the *Memorial Volume* recording the intent and value of commemorations:

> It is too soon to speak at length of the deep and widespread benefits which may flow from this celebration and others of a similar nature held in various connections throughout our bounds. With God's blessing upon these celebration, good will surely will follow. Larger knowledge of the origin and contents of our Standards will be one result. Greater devotion to the system of doctrine, polity, and worship which they contain will surely be kindled. And a renewed purpose to spread these great teachings abroad among men will no doubt be formed by many of our people. It is gratifying to notice that other branches of the Presbyterian family in America and Europe are also entering upon similar celebration during this year. A revived interest in the doctrines of the Reformed system will be the sure result, and with this will come vigorous spiritual life and quickened religious activity in the conquest of the world for the Lord Jesus Christ.[29]

From these and other words, it can be clearly seen that this celebration was designed for the primary purpose of acquainting its membership with the historic faith and of deepening the piety of those Christians. It was not a mere historical or ecclesiastical exercise, but intended to aid the spiritual interest, vitality, and activity of various churches and individuals. If such purposes will be recalled, future commemorations will benefit and the possibility of lapsing into some semblance of idolatry can be avoided.

---

[28] *Memorial Volume*, p. xiv.

[29] Ibid., pp. xvi-xvii.

Of the value of the 1897 and other commemorations, Moses D. Hoge wrote:

> In such commemorations there is a great moral element. Sometimes it is good to get free from the narrow environments of the immediate present and ascend some eminence which commands a view of ways long since trodden, and then, from what is taught in the review, learn to forecast the ever-widening way of the future. It is only by such studies that we catch the spirit of the great historic eras which have been potent in shaping the institutions of our own times. It is only when we can transport ourselves to the distant past and evoke from its obscurity the forms of its heroic men; it is only when we acquaint ourselves with the errors they combated, the difficulties they surmounted, the hardships they endured, that we can fully comprehend the character of the men who thus toiled and suffered, or appreciate the value.[30]

The Northern Church also had a well-ordered commemoration the next year. In 1898, the Northern Presbyterians sponsored a similarly structured event at Winona Lake, Indiana. The Overture first calling for the celebration to be held in 1898 asked for a committee of nine to plan the commemoration which would begin on the 250th anniversary of the adoption of the Westminster standards on the second Thursday session of the 1898 Assembly. This overture also urged that "Synods, Presbyteries and churches under its care observe at such times as may be convenient to them, during the years 1898, the anniversary of the adoption of these great Standards of faith and practice, which have been so inestimable a blessing alike to the churches and to the world."[31]

As a portion of this commemorative, a portrait of Alexander Henderson was dedicated, and a commemorative gavel consisting of marble taken from Westminster Abbey during repairs was donated by Dean C. G. Bradley of Westminster Abbey.[32] Also as part of the commemoration, a large collection of Westminster memorabilia,

---

[30] *Memorial Volume*, p. 189.

[31] *Minutes General Assembly*, PCUA, 1987, P. 86.

[32] *Anniversary Addresses*, pp. 10-11.

owned by the Rev. H. C. McCook, D. D., was housed in one of the buildings of the Winona Assembly and Summer School.

The 1898 celebration, perhaps modeled after its Southern counterpart the previous year, met with broad approval. The speakers and addresses, which were eventually published in *Anniversary Addresses* (1898), were as follows:

> (1) "Alexander Henderson" by Dr. William Henry Roberts; (2) "The Civil and Religious Conditions of the Times of the Westminster Assembly" by Dr. Samuel J. Niccolls; (3) "The Story of the Westminster Assembly" by Dr. George Norcross; (4) "The Fundamental Doctrines of the Westminster Confession and Catechisms" by Dr. James D. Moffat; (5) "The Westminster Polity and Worship" by Dr. Robert F. Coyle; (6) "The Westminster Assembly, the Men and their Work" by Dr. Wallace Radcliffe; (7) "The American Presbyterian Church and the Adopting Act" by Dr. Benjamin L. Agnew; (8) "The Presbyterian Churches and the People" by Gen. James A. Beaver; (9) "The Presbyterian Churches and Education" by Dr. John Eaton; (10) "Presbyterianism and its Influence upon Society through its Emphasis upon Childhood and Youth" by Dr. Newell D. Hillis; (11) "The Presbyterian Churches and Home Missions" by Dr. George L. Spining; (12) "The Presbyterian Churches and Foreign Missions" by Mr. Robert Speer.

A few writings became associated with this final commemoration of the nineteenth century. Of course the above noted volumes of commemorative addresses left a lasting witness to the commemorative spirit. In addition, a number of articles were contributed by Benjamin Warfield (along with his brother, Ethelbert Warfield's *The England of the Westminster Assembly*), including "The Significance of the Westminster Standards" (1898), "The Presbyterian Churches and the Westminster Confession" (1899), "On the Revision of the Confession of Faith" (1890), and later "Is the Shorter Catechism Worth While?" (1909).

Among re-issues of earlier versions at these turn of the century celebrations were the *Directory for the Public Worship of God*, and several reprintings of the Westminster Confession itself. Alexander Mitchell's *The Westminster Assembly: Its History and Standards* was reprinted in 1897 (by the PCUSA Board of

Publications) and also William Hetherington's *History of the Westminster Assembly of Divines*.

At the 250th anniversary, Dwight Witherspoon expressed the sentiment of gratitude for our forefathers:

> And so, as we contemplate the lives and characters of these illustrious men, whose lot was cast in the midst of the storms of political and ecclesiastical revolution, who heroically bared their breast to the tempest, receiving in full shock, and hurling back in defiance the waves of despotic absolutism in the state, and hierarchical oppression in the church, their majestic forms loom up before us in the thick of the conflict for the defence of the civil and religious liberties which we enjoy, and there is a majesty and a sublimity in the rugged grandeur of their natures that overawe us. We uncover our heads with reverence before them, and our souls thrill with emotions of gratitude, admiration, and love, as we remember that . . . they stood breast-deep amidst the waves, and maintained their position, inflexible and unawed, under all the fury of the tempest.[33]

Toward the end of the nineteenth century and in the vicinity of the 250th anniversary of the Assembly, an apologist for the lasting value of the Westminster standards noted:

> The significance of the Westminster Standards as a creed is to be found in the three facts that, historically speaking, they are the final crystallization of the elements of evangelical religion, after the conflicts of sixteen hundred years; scientifically speaking, they are the richest and most precise and best guarded statement ever penned of all that enters into evangelical religion and of all that must be safeguarded if evangelical religion is to persist in the world; and, religiously speaking, they are a notable monument of spiritual religion.[34]

In 1893, W. G. T. Shedd reflected: "In these struggles, however, the gem of the gospel was cut and polished, and it is on this account that the enunciation of the gospel in the Reformed Confessions attains its highest purity, and that among other Reformed Confessions the Westminster Confession, the product

---

[33] *Memorial Volume*, pp. 84-85.

[34] W.G.T. Shedd, *Calvinism: Pure and Mixed* (Edinburgh: Banner of Truth, 1986), p. 159.

of the Puritan conflict, reaches a perfection of statement never elsewhere achieved."[35]

Still, however, it must be noted that amidst all of the celebrations of this heritage, there were foundational issues which were not resolved until the twentieth century. Thus far, these commemorations were slightly nostalgic prior to confessional revision, and still treated the 1643-1648 era as a heroic episode. Many of the twentieth century descendants would differ with some of these earlier assessments.

The Tercentenary: 1943

Embroiled in the heat of warfare, English speaking churches did not turn their primary attention to commemoration of the Assembly in 1943-1947. It must be granted that a World War was certainly justification for non-commemoration. Neither North, nor South, nor Scottish Presbyterians hosted much more than scaled-down commemorations during the War. Still had the church desired to sponsor commemorations, the years of 1947 or 1948 following the war might have been suitable. Another explanation for the relative lack of commemoration at the tercentennial was that the earlier signs of declining commitment to the Westminster standards as the sole confession were growing more unmistakably apparent.

Even the young Orthodox Presbyterian Church—which only 7 years earlier (1936) had separated from the mainline American Presbyterian churches in the USA, criticizing them of doctrinal laxity— did not host a formal commemoration of the Westminster Assembly. It would remain for conservative Presbyterian churches to first formally celebrate the Assembly in 1993.

Nevertheless, in the early 1940s there were a few notable addresses and published essays in commemoration. A tradition of commemoration continued, even if waning. In 1941, the

---

[35] Shed, Ibid., p. 160.

Southern Presbyterian Assembly considered overtures from Atlanta and Concord Presbyteries calling for an observance of the 300th anniversary of the Westminster Assembly by appointing a committee of three leading historians (Henry Wade DuBose, T. H. Spence, and Ernest Trice Thompson) to plan a program for commemoration at the 1943 Assembly. The plan called for addresses to be given on the Monday night of the Assembly. Hence, on May 31, 1943, four addresses were delivered to the Assembly at Montreat, NC, and were later printed in the 1943 issue of the *Union Seminary Review*.

The *Union Seminary Review* commemorated the tercentenary by publishing 4 essays: (1) "Some Neglected Features in the Early Reformed Confessions" by Dr. James A. Cabaniss, dealing mostly with other sixteenth century confessions, (2) "The Story of the Westminster Assembly" by Dr. Walter L. Lingle, (3) "The Contribution of the Westminster Assembly to Democracy" by Dr. J. McDowell Richards, and (4) "The Contribution of the Westminster Assembly to Christian Thought" by Dr. John Newton Thomas.[36]

Flowing from these Tercentenary addresses, the Assembly was variously assessed as, "the most remarkable body of men, perhaps, which the world has ever produced,"[37] or "Whether evaluated by the work it did, or by the influence which these Presbyterian standards have had throughout the world for the past three hundred years [1943], the Westminster Assembly was the most important Protestant Assembly that ever met."[38]

In the midst of World War II, Dr. J. McDowell Richards observed, "The fact that Calvinism and Presbyterianism in general

---

[36] All four of these are contained in the *Union Seminary Review*, Vol. 54, no. 1.

[37] Ibid., p. 323.

[38] Walter L. Lingle, "The Story of the Westminster Assembly" in *Union Seminary Review*, Nov. 1943 (vol. 54, no. 1), p. 321.

have exerted a tremendous influence for human freedom has not entirely escaped the attention even of secular historians."[39] He pointed out that this Westminster doctrine impacted on western civilization not just in terms of forms of government, but also that Westminster has had an enormous indirect influence via the *character* of its adherents in civil matters. At the 300th anniversary of the Assembly, J. McDowell Richards said: "It is the glory of the Presbyterian system as set forth by the Westminster divines that it has produced citizens of intelligence, of integrity, of courage."[40] Several pamphlets and essays in 1943 were devoted to the tercentenary. Thomas H. Spence set forth summaries of the calling by Parliament, the Assembly in session, The Scottish influences, and the heritage of Westminster in a 6-page pamphlet published by the Presbyterian Historical Foundation (Montreat, NC), collating other holdings at Montreat with these topics.

In 1942, the Northern Presbyterian Church adopted recommendations proposed by the Department of History to celebrate the tercentenary during the sessions of the 1943 Assembly as planned by the Stated Clerk and the Department of History who were to prepare a "form of service for the celebration of the Westminster Assembly Anniversary for the use of our churches, and . . . a syllabus . . . sent to the pastors to enable them to make a suitable presentation of this subject."[41] In 1943 the Detroit Assembly resolved that all Synods and Presbyteries docket a "worthy recognition" of the anniversary sometime during 1943, and that "Sunday, October 31, 1943, be set apart as the day most appropriate for the churches to observe the same anniversary, and that every pastor be urged, either on that day, or whenever it will be most convenient, to make fitting plans to instruct his

---

[39] *Union Seminary Review supra*, p. 333.

[40] Ibid., p. 341.

[41] *Minutes of General Assembly, PCUSA,* 1942, p. 72.

congregation in the great principles underlying the Westminster Confession of Faith."[42]

On Sunday May 30, 1943—one day before the Southern Presbyterian celebration—the Assembly met in the Masonic Auditorium in Detroit, MI, with a commemorative celebration, including two addresses given by Dr. J. Harry Cotton ("The Sovereign God and Human Liberties") and Dr. Edward Howell Roberts ("Faith of our Fathers"), thus bringing the total number of Assembly addresses among both churches to six, as compared with 23 at the most previous 1897-1898 commemorations. In a message addressed to youth, Edward Roberts contended:

> A very penetrating thinker has observed, 'When you hear anyone say, 'Away with creeds,' you know that what he really means is 'take mine.'" Everyone has a creed. There is not a single exception. And we live according to what we really believe. How foolish then the prejudice against doctrine. Much of it is based upon ignorance.[43]

To further assist in celebration of this tercentenary, which was to be held on Reformation Sunday (Oct. 31) in 1943, every active pastor, Seminary Professor, and Chaplain received a packet containing a brochure with a historical sketch of the Assembly, a description of the documents created, and an essay on the abiding values of the Assembly's work; a suggested order of worship; an announcement of a Tercentenary Sermon Contest; a bibliography of relevant books handled by Presbyterian book stores; samples of Church Calendars for the month of October; and a folder with suggestions for celebration.[44] This occasion was also the first attempt at a commemorative radio hookup, as the PCUSA arranged with CBS for an October 17th nationwide hookup in which Henry Sloane Coffin, the Moderator, gave an address.

---

[42] *Minutes of General Assembly, PCUSA,* 1943, p. 332.

[43] *Journal of Presbyterian History,* Vol. XXI, Nos. 2 and 3, June and September, 1943, p. 102.

[44] *Journal of Presbyterian History,* op. cit., p. 80.

Furthermore, the committee also encouraged the use of new resources, e.g., *The Everyday Work of the Westminster Assembly* by Dr. Samuel W. Carruthers (1943) and *The History of the Westminster Assembly and Standards*, a small but informative pamphlet setting out the background and history of the Assembly by Dr. Gaius J. Slosser. Carruthers, in a smaller version of his 1943 work commented on the importance of the Westminster Assembly:

> Although the Westminster Assembly of Divines occupies but small space in the ordinary history books, it may reasonably be argued that it has had a wider and deeper influence than the victories of Cromwell's Ironsides, or even the great work of the Long Parliament. In England, where it met, that is perhaps not so; but in Scotland, Ireland, in America, and in other lands to which Scots and Irish emigrated, it has wielded a tremendous power, directly and indirectly.[45]

The Department of History also printed a commemorative brochure, *The Westminster Assembly: Its History, Formularies, and Abiding Values* (1943), with three addresses for use by pastors in the tercentenary. The essays contained were "The Westminster Assembly, An Historical Sketch" by Earl L. Douglass, "The Westminster Formularies, A Brief Description" by Frederick W. Loetscher, and "Some of the Abiding Values of the Work of the Westminster Assembly in the American Tradition" by Thomas C. Pears, Jr. In addition, under the direction of Dr. Norman E. Richardson and McCormick Seminary, a facsimile edition of The Shorter Catechism was issued. Earlier Eric G. Haden had written *The History of the Use of the Shorter Catechism in the Presbyterian Church in the United States of America* (Central Baptist Theological Seminary Press, Kansas City, 1941), a survey of the pedagogical value of catechetical instruction in Colonial America up to 1880.

The essays by Gaius Slosser, Edmond E. Robb, John McNaugher in the 1943 *The Westminster Assembly and Standards*,

---

[45] Ibid., p. 163.

and Samuel Wilson's (1944) *Tercentenary of the Westminster Assembly*, as well as S. Carruthers's *The Westminster Confession of Faith* were all released to be used as resources for various commemorations of this 300th anniversary. Following the completion of the celebration, in 1948 Herbert Stewart's *The Westminster Confession After Three Centuries* was printed.

A note should be added about the inchoate criticism which became visible at the tercentennial. In 1943, Samuel Carruthers was instrumental in leading the Presbyterian churches to remember their works and wrote a very up-to-date work—one of the few lasting contributions from the tercentennial. However, this work was beginning to show the trends of modernism as it began to strip away the ancient faith and challenge the motives of the divines, almost as if it were incomprehensible to the modern mind that the authors of the Confession would really mean exactly what they wrote. The dedication to "the Honored Memory of the Westminster Divines who *were also very human*" is as indubitable, as it is reflective of a questioning of their timeless validity.

Interestingly, the history of these commemorations shows both that Presbyterian churches had respect for their unifying doctrinal symbols, and that commemorative events are clues to the self-image of denominations. Such individual commemorations are like family snapshots, taken at one moment in time, while the commemorative are more closely analogous to a home movie. No one would dare suggest that these commemorations were merely to remember the surrounding history of a period devoid of its continuing significance. It was obvious that these commemorations were designed to celebrate the underlying doctrine produced by the Westminster Assembly. To the extent that the churches valued those specific doctrinal formularies, commemorations were held by those churches.

It is also apparent that development occurred between these commemorations. The earliest commemoration saw a split between the Old School and the New School, and was less a function of geography or culture. However, by the semi-bicentenary in 1897-1898, the basic line of demarcation was geographic, with north and south holding separate but remarkably similar commemorations.

In contrast, the twentieth century commemorations began to show a decidedly ideological demarcation. At present, the geographic division of North and South has been healed, although a broader theological divide is now evident. The Presbyterian Church in the United States of America had no celebration at the 350th anniversary of the convening of the Assembly. This was understandable, both in terms of their multi-confessional approach, as well as an indication that the specificity of the Westminster faith is no longer the dominant confession of the mainline, modern Presbyterians.

1993 and Beyond

By 1993 the only remaining American celebrants were the NAPARC churches, none of which had sponsored previous commemorations. These groups gathered together for the first time for a trans-denominational celebration in 1993 in London. The 350th Commemorative Conference met in Westminster itself, Westminster Chapel, and St. Margarets (Westminster) Church September 23-25, 1993. Chaired by Dr. Charles Carlisle of Erskine College in South Carolina, the conference was attended by over 225 participants from Australia, Brazil, Canada, England, Ireland, Scotland, and the USA. Program Chairman, Dr. John L. Carson, Professor of Systematic Theology at Erskine Theological Seminary, gathered an excellent consortium of speakers. Various denominational representatives alternated as liturgists for the Worship Services.

The opening Worship Service for the 350th Commemorative Conference saw Presbyterian Church in America pastor James M.

Boice—one of the few Bible-believing Presbyterians allowed in that pulpit since the Great Ejection of 1662—process at the invitation of the Anglican Canon and preach from the pulpit of Westminster Abbey. With 400 chairs set up to accommodate registrants and Londoners, the committee was pleased that additional chairs were needed for this opening service. The addresses and worship services were excellent and edifying throughout.

Several lessons were so striking as to bear noting. The participants, recalling the scant two decade interlude of Presbyterian ascendancy in England (1642-1662), were once again reminded that depth of discipleship and inculcation of truth is to be preferred over temporary enforced solutions. Modern adherents to Westminster would do well to strive for long-term sincere adoption of confessional truths, rather than coerced short-term concessions. Attenders at the conference were also treated to a rare example of reformed ecumenicity, as the various communions enjoyed common belief, excellent worship, and a spirit of true fellowship. Conferees were unavoidably challenged by modernity, as they relived a brief era of history. Within the conference the traditional lifestyle of those shaped by Westminster doctrine and practice was noticeably incongruous with the congested and frantic lifestyle of teeming London, long since removed from any impact of confessional Christianity on its culture.

Following this conference, the tapes of the addresses and the written essays were published not by denominational publishers, but by non-denominational publishers (Banner of Truth Trust: *To Glorify and Enjoy God*). The speakers and topics (with some lectures given in Westminster Chapel in London, and others on the grounds of Westminster Abbey) were:

The Context and Work of the Westminster Assembly" by Samuel T. Logan, Jr.;
The Men and the Parties" by William S. Barker;

The Preaching of the Westminster Assembly" by Robert M. Norris;
The Westminster Confession of Faith and Holy Scripture" by Wayne
  Spear;
The Westminster Shorter Catechism" by Doug Kelly;
The Westminster Larger Catechism" by W. Robert Godfrey;
The Form Of Church Government" by John Richard de Witt;
The Directory for Public Worship" by Iain Murray.

In addition to these lectures, the evening featured popular but thoughtful sermons by James M. Boice ("The Sovereignty of God"), Joel Nederhood ("The Pre-eminence of Christ"), and a final, climactic sermon by Eric Alexander ("The Application of Redemption"). After such a splendid opening, the conference concluded in the exact place where the Solemn League and Covenant had been sworn (St. Margarets) 350 years to the day. The final luncheon was enjoyed in the Dean's House, Westminster, with a stirring speech by Dr. Jay Adams on "The Influence of the Westminster Assembly." After lunch, the final Worship Service was held in St. Margarets with *a capella* singing of Psalms and preaching by Eric Alexander.

In addition, most of the speakers re-assembled in Atlanta, GA, June 4-9, 1994 to re-present their addresses in conjunction with the General Assembly of the Presbyterian Church in America ("Taking the Reformation into the 21st Century"). The 58th General Synod of the Bible Presbyterian Church (Aug. 4-9, 1994), meeting in Cape Canaveral, FL, also sponsored a commemoration, consisting of several addresses on the theme: "Building Upon Our Westminster Heritage." The mainline Presbyterian Church (PCUSA) exhibited no interest in commemorating Westminster.

Various magazines emphasized or reported on the 350th commemorative conference in London: *The Presbyterian Reformed Magazine* (April 1993), *The Associate Reformed Presbyterian Messenger* (June 1993), *TableTalk* (Sept. 1993), Reformed Theological Seminary's *Ministry* (Fall 1993), *World* (Oct. 9, 1993), *Modern Reformation* (Sept./Oct. 1993), *The Blue Banner* (March-April 1994), and *The Banner of Truth* magazine (Aug. 1994).

As had become customary a number of publishings were associated with the 350th commemoration. Work on this multi-volume set of essays was commenced in the early 1990s, along with a comprehensive bibliographical effort, as were other comments on the abiding significance of Westminster,[46] along with timely reprints of: Samuel Carruthers's *The Everyday Work of the Westminster Assembly* (Reformed Academic Press), *A Short History of the Westminster Assembly* (Reformed Academic Press) by William Beveridge, *The Westminster Confession, a Critical Edition* by Samuel Carruthers (Reformed Academic Press), and an audio version of the Westminster Confession on tape.

Several other works by Still Waters Revival Books were reprinted. *Notes of Debates and Proceedings of the Assembly of Divines at Westminster, February 1644 to January 1645* (in vol. II of *The Works of George Gillespie*) was re-issued by Still Waters Revival Books, as was Warfield's *The Westminster Assembly and Its Work*. In 1992, a once rare volume, *The Minutes of the Sessions of the Westminster Assembly of Divines*, ed. by A. F. Mitchell and John Struthers (orig. 1874) was released, as were two seminal histories of the Assembly: Alexander Mitchell's *The Westminster Assembly: Its History and Standards* and William Hetherington's *History of the Westminster Assembly of Divines* (issued as a special commemorative edition). In 1993 Still Waters Revival Books was helpful to the church in republishing a two volume commentary by Thomas Ridgely on the Westminster Larger Catechism. One of the sturdiest commentaries, Thomas Boston's *Commentary on the Shorter Catechism* (over 1300 pp. in 2 vols.), was reprinted by Still Waters Revival Books.

Soli Deo Gloria also re-issued other works by members of

---

[46] Such as: *Windows on Westminster* (Atlanta: Great Commission Publications, 1993) by David W. Hall and *The Westminster Assembly: A Guide to Basic Bibliography* (Greenville, SC: Reformed Academic Press, 1993) by J. Ligon Duncan III and David W. Hall.

the Westminster Assembly: William Greenhill's Commentary on *Ezekiel*; Obadiah Sedgwick's *The Anatomy of Secret Sins* and *The Doubting Believer*; *The Works of William Bridge*; and Jeremiah Burroughs's *Rare Jewel of Christian Contentment*; *The Evil of Evils*; *The Saint's Happiness* on the Beatitudes; *A Treatise of Earthly-Mindedness*; *Gospel Fear, Gospel Worship*—a fine statement of the regulative principle; and *The Saints' Treasury*, a collection of five sermons (e.g. "Christ is all in all," and "The Glorious Enjoyment of Heavenly Things by Faith"). Also released were Edward Reynolds's *The Sinfulness of Sin*, *The Select Works of Thomas Case* (an Assembly member), and a collection of *Farewell Sermons* preached by many of the divines at the 1662 Great Ejection.[47]

Another unique feature of the 350th commemoration was the distribution of a NAPARC-wide resource packet. Nearly 2,000 resource packets were sent, one to each local congregation of the ARP, KAPC, OPC, PCA, and RPCNA. Contained in these packets were: suggested Orders of Worship from the period, information about the September 1993 conference, a copy of the April 1993 *Presbyterian Reformed Magazine*, a copy of *The Westminster Assembly: A Guide to Basic Bibliography*, a copy of the *Westminster Directory for Family Worship*, a copy of Hetherington's *History of the Westminster Assembly of Divines* (specially printed for these packets), and other information to assist each church in having its own commemorative celebration. Certainly the amount of publication and ecumenical participation reached a zenith for these commemorations.

Looking forward to the 400th anniversary in 2043, one final observation may be in order relative to the evolution of commemorations. The earliest commemorations were only

---

[47] For a fuller listing of recent and older works, see *The Westminster Assembly: A Guide to Basic Bibliography* by J. Ligon Duncan III and David W. Hall (Greenville, SC: Reformed Academic Press, 1993).

concerned with local churches (1843). Then by the 1897-1898 commemoration, Synods, Presbyteries and Assemblies were targeted. The same was true in 1943, with the slight commemorations held. Yet, the scope of the commemorations grew by 1993, reaching still another stage perhaps unpredicted by earlier declines of interest. The 1993 celebration was not merely interdenominational, but international. This commemoration marked an upsurge in expansion, a new stage of celebration. The remaining question was: Will this be the climactic, final peak, or the beginning of a new resurgence of the Westminster communions? Certainly, it was at the peak of geographical expanse, the largest geographical segment ever involved in a single commemoration. The only geographical expansion which could be greater would be if the Westminster faith spread missiologically and dramatically to the third world and to countries where it had heretofore not held sway.

Could the ideological conquest over rival theologies resume? That was a real question on the minds of many participants in the 1993 commemoration. By the next half century, will the Westminster faith grow among its own adherents, or shrink as it had among the mainline participants? Will the family of Presbyterians have a 400th anniversary of the Assembly? If they do not, it is also likely that the family would not exist, so basic is the Westminster Confession to the heart of Presbyterianism.

Following the 1993 commemoration, as many participants pondered, "Whither?", a helpful distinction between nostalgia and memory was beneficial. Culture critic Christopher Lasch has posited that an awareness of the difference between nostalgia and memory can help ward off falling prey to various progressivist idolatries. Lasch suggests, that if any type of recollection of the past does not employ an intelligent eye toward the future as well, then the "ideological twin" of proper memory, nostalgia," undermines the ability to make intelligent use of the past. Memory, in contrast, does not idealize the past to condemn the present, but draws hope from the past in order to enrich the present and guide the future."[48] In any commemoration, it is prudent to mark this distinction. As others have stated in previous histories, a proper memorial is worthwhile, if it stirs us toward the future; while a bare recollection with no purpose save nostalgia is worth very little, or perhaps even idolatrous.

An appropriate assessment of the motive and utility of commemoration was summarized well 150 years ago by William Symington:

> The disposition to commemorate events, whether of public or private interest, springs from a law of our nature. It is true, the law has been abused,—grossly abused, for purposes of a superstitious character, advantage having been taken of it to impose on men's consciences a whole host of cumbrous, and useless, nay, pernicious, observances. Nevertheless, the law is good, if men use it lawfully . . . . Matters of great and permanent utility, the due consideration of which is fitted to exert a continued beneficial influence on society, are thus held forth to the view of the community, and prevented from passing into oblivion. The very act of reminiscence itself is calculated to call into operation, and consequently to improve by exercising, some of the higher moral principles of the heart, such as gratitude for benefits received, veneration for departed worth, and imitation of praiseworthy excellence.[49]

Commemorants are in good biblical company. As David, "the man after God's own heart," meditates, he remembers the past, the "days of long ago" (Ps. 143:5). The pledge of the exiled Israelites is "may my right hand forget its skill," if I do not *remember* you . . . May my tongue cling to the roof of my mouth if I do not remember you, if I do not consider Jerusalem my highest joy" (Ps. 137:5-6). Clearly, remembering God's past providence is a benefit for the covenant people. It is an aid for spiritual growth and perseverance. Remembering how the Lord worked previously

---

[48] Fredrick Jones, *Stewardship Journal*, Fall 1992, vol. 2, no. 3, p. 62.

[49] William Symington, *supra*, pp. 31-32.

is a fine weapon in the arsenal of the faithful, which is ignored to their own peril.

Perhaps as we face ebbing and flowing tides of human thought, we can share the sentiments expressed by Samuel Smith almost one hundred years ago:

> No other system has the inherent force to resist this rising tide as the Westminster has; it stands, therefore, today invested with an importance perhaps transcending all present possible appreciation, for should this new theology win the day there is danger that the world may be ultimately orphaned of its God as it is fast being robbed of its Bible. The part, then, that Calvinistic theology must play in the needs of the future is that of a granite ledge against the insidious encroachments of a troubled sea casting up mire and dirt; its office is to say, with the voice of that God, whose humble mouth-piece it has been privileged to prove in many a stormy period of the past, 'Hitherto shalt thou come, But no further: And here shall thy proud waves be stayed.'[50]

Alexander Solzhenitsyn remarked about the necessity of remembering: "To destroy a people you must first sever their roots."[51] Another insightful commentator said, "The first step in liquidating a people is to erase its memory. Destroy its books, its culture, and its history; before long the community will forget what it is, and what it was."[52] This amnesia can fall on the church, too, if she does not actively remember how God has worked in history.

As Hebrews 10:23 says, "Let us hold unwavering to the confession of our hope." It is not only appropriate, but also imperative for us to renew our commitment to these old truths from time to time. To the extent that the things taught by these Westminster divines are scriptural, then we must return to these ancient landmarks, repair them from time to time, and hold fast.

---

[50] *Memorial Volume*, p. 254.

[51] Cited in Rush Limbaugh's *The Way Things Ought to Be* (New York: Simon and Schuster, 1992).

[52] Milan Hubl, cited in George Grant's *The Third Time Around* (Franklin, TN: Woglemuth & Hyatt, 1991), p. 136.

G. K. Chesterton analyzed that, "all conservatism is based upon the idea that if you leave things alone you leave them as they are. But you do not. If you leave a thing alone you leave it to a torrent of change. If you leave a white post alone it will soon be a black post. If you particularly want it to be white you must be always painting it again; that is, you must be always having a revolution. Briefly, if you want the old white post you must have a new white post. . . . An almost unnatural vigilance is really required . . . because of the horrible rapidity with which human institutions grow old."[53] It may be time to clasp a paintbrush to repaint the ancient fenceposts. Thomas Smyth assessed the value of proper commemorations in 1843: "Like the members of a large family we have been scattered, and lived apart, and gathered around us new and separate interests. But we are on this occasion brought together. We revisit our old ancestral homestead. We read over the original deeds by which we became heirs to the same rich inheritance. The ties of blood draw our hearts together, and we embrace one another in the arms of spiritual affection."[54]

This prayer comes from a commemorative a century ago:

God of our fathers, preserve us, 'lest we forget, lest we forget' thy hand in our deliverance, thy mighty hand in our prosperity! . . . Forget not that the Puritan, the Huguenot, and the Covenanter were thy master builders, that their principles and religious faith were inwrought in thy structure, and that their sacred dust has consecrated thy soil to civil and religious liberty for ever! . . . Forget not the type of religion which dominated these men; because nations are the product of religious faith; religion shapes and molds their political character and destiny.[55]

Moreover, the challenge was also posed:

The supreme inquiry for us is, whether we are serving our generation by that same will, and are laying such foundations for the future as shall make the men of 2148 look back on this Assembly as we have been looking back today to the men and the Assembly of 1648? What sort of men we are and what sort of men our children will be is of

---

[53] G.K. Chesterton, *Orthodoxy* (New York: Doubleday, 1990), p. 114.

[54] Thomas Smyth, op. cit., p. 428.

[55] *Anniversary Addresses*, 1898, p. 276.

vastly more consequence to this world than the kind of men our ancestors were. There is a story of an Austrian nobleman, who, risen from the ranks of the common people, was taunted once by a group of degenerate princes because of his want of ancestry. 'Gentlemen,' he replied, 'you are descendants; I am an ancestor.' If I must make my choice, I would rather be the ancestor of a new Westminster Assembly than the descendant of an old one. I would rather be the architect of two hundred and fifty glorious years of future history than the product of two hundred and fifty years of great history past.[56]

Conclusion

Remembering God and his dealings with people in history must be important, as it certainly is prominent. At least it was for the saints in biblical ages, who surpass many moderns in spirituality. To the staggering church at Ephesus, which was in danger of forsaking her first love, the Apostle of Love does not tell her to forget about the past and set her sights only on current or futuristic perspectives. On the contrary the Apostle of Love urges the people to remember: "Remember the height from which you have fallen! Repent and do the things you did at first" (Rev. 2:5). Remembering is positive and necessary. Also to the church at Sardis, the church which was in the terminal ward, the one which was nearly dead, he called for her to strengthen any remaining spiritual vital signs. Specifically he said, "Remember, therefore, what you have received and heard; obey it, and repent" (Rev. 3:3).

The Prophet Isaiah—in a time of national and spiritual decline— seemed to highly value remembrance. It may even be, that in those times of spiritual declension, spiritual commemorations are most needed. In Is. 63:11, as a means of revival, God's "people remembered the days of old, the days of Moses and his people. . . ." Could it be that revival might be hastened by the covenant people of God re-acquainting themselves with God's history? Many peers might imagine that to be far from true, but the biblical pages reveal

---

[56] Ibid., pp. 320-321.

an uncanny association between revival and remembering. G. K. Chesterton issued a biting reminder about the timelessness of truth:

> An imbecile habit has arisen in modern controversy of saying that such and such a creed can be held in one age but cannot be held in another. Some dogma, we are told, was credible in the twelfth century, but is not credible in the twentieth. You might as well say that a certain philosophy can be believed on Mondays, but cannot be believed on Tuesdays. You might as well say of a view of the cosmos that it was suitable to half-past three, but not suitable to half-past four. What a man can believe depends upon his philosophy, not upon the clock or the century. If a man believes in unalterable natural law, he cannot believe in any miracle in any age. If a man believes in a will behind law, he can believe in any miracle in any age.[57]

An earlier historian of the Assembly supported the plea for a reintroduction of these Westminster standards in our homes. Invariably, as others have sought an improvement of the old faith, "it has been found, that while under this pretext, one step of deviation from the old orthodoxy has been taken, no convenient stopping place has been found; . . . No doubt, there are many 'hard sayings' in the Bible; many difficulties which no human ingenuity can entirely remove or solve. Sometimes by rejecting that part of the truth which appears most objectionable, it is hoped, that the difficulty will be removed, and the truth recommended to reasonable men. But in such departures from orthodoxy, the relief is only apparent; for although we may escape a more obvious and prominent difficulty, we are sure to find one more untractable, arising out of our new hypothesis."[58]

As if warning against a spirit which elevates openness to the level of ultimate value, much as in our own day, the 1841 history continued (fully aware of the full-blown humanity of the divines): ". . . and if to avoid this [objection], we reject something more of the orthodox doctrine, we only plunge deeper into the mire, until at

---

[57] G.K. Chesterton, *Orthodoxy* (New York: Doubleday, 1990), pp. 74-75.

[58] *A History of Westminster Assembly of Divines*, anon. (Philadelphia, 1841), p. 86.

last, we are obliged, for consistency sake, to give up the whole system, or retrace our steps, and return to the point of our first deviation from the straight line of truth."[59] Thus does the work of the Westminster Assembly have much lasting validity for us today.

As observed at the commemoration of the Westminster Assembly a century ago, we would do well to affirm: "Ah, the past is never dead! All history is God's mighty electric battery charged to the full with slumbering forces which have subdued kingdoms, overturned thrones, and shaken the world to its center."[60]

Let me conclude with two perceptive comments from previous commemorations. George L. Spining (1898) noted: "The end of this anniversary is not self-glorification and an ostentatious parade of denominationalism. Nay, God's hand is in it, and it means remembrance, stimulus, inspiration, life from the dead, and a glorious flood of light on some of the dark problems of history."[61] John Murray (1943) extolled: "Language fails to assess the blessing that God in His sovereign providence and grace bestowed upon His church through these. . . . The influence exerted by them is beyond all human calculation. We should indeed be remiss if we did not make this [commemoration] the occasion for grateful remembrance of God's inestimable favor. Other men labored and we have entered into their labors. Truly the lines are fallen unto us in pleasant places and we have a goodly heritage."[62]

---

[59] Ibid., p. 86.

[60] *Anniversary Addresses*, p. 273.

[61] *Addresses at the Celebration of the Two Hundred and Fiftieth Anniversary of the Westminster Assembly by the General Assembly of the Presbyterian Church in the USA* (Hereafter, *Anniversary Addresses*), edited by William Henry Roberts (Philadelphia: Presbyterian Board of Publication and Sabbath-School Work, 1898), p. 274.

[62] "A Notable Tercentenary" in *The Presbyterian Guardian*, June 10, 1943; reprinted in *The Collected Works of John Murray* (Edinburgh: Banner of Truth, 1976), Vol. I, p. 312.

Word and Spirit in the Westminster Confession

WAYNE R. SPEAR

The conjunction of Word and Spirit has been an important feature of Reformed theology since the time of Calvin. In an important study, Jackson Forstman found that Calvin's principle of authority is "the correlation of word and Spirit."[1] "Word and Spirit" is also an important theme in the Westminster Standards. In the Westminster Confession of Faith, the working of the Holy Spirit in conjunction with the Word is mentioned in the discussion of the application of redemption by Christ, effectual calling, sanctification, saving faith, good works, assurance, and the efficacy of the sacraments.[2] Word and Spirit are joined seven times in the Larger Catechism, and once in the Shorter Catechism.[3] The relation between Word and Spirit is crucial also for understanding the Confession's doctrine of revelation in Chapter One, and this study will focus on that doctrine.

Several contemporary Presbyterian scholars who wish to be known as "evangelical" have made the conjunction of Word and Spirit central in their efforts to reconstruct Reformed theology

---

[1] H. Jackson Forstman, *Word and Spirit; Calvin's Doctrine of Biblical Authority* (Stanford, CA: Stanford University Press, 1962), p. 49. See his survey of the literature, pp. 2-5.

[2] Westminster Confession, 8.8; 10.1; 10.4; 13.1; 14.1; 16.1,3; 18.2,3; 27.3.

[3] Larger Catechism, Q. 2, 4, 43, 67, 72, 155; Shorter Catechism, Q. 24.

by using the theological method of Karl Barth. Donald Bloesch proposes "a theology of Word and Spirit" which would avoid the subjectivism inherent in the mysticism and existentialism which shapes much modern theology, and the objectivism of what he calls "evangelical rationalism." He would follow the lead of Luther and Calvin and early Protestant orthodoxy, and reject the later orthodoxy in which "the paradoxical unity of Word and Spirit was sundered, being replaced by an objectivism of the Word." Bloesch does not say whether he places the Westminster Confession in the realm of later orthodoxy. However, in his one reference to the Confession, he faults the advocates of biblical inerrancy for their failure to examine such confessions critically "in the light of new truth that the Spirit brings to his church through God's holy Word."[4]

Jack B. Rogers and Donald McKim have also tried to present a "middle way between rationalism and subjectivism . . . a way that holds in balance the objective and the subjective, the Word and the Spirit."[5] They advocate the unusual thesis that the Westminster Confession, like Calvin and in contrast to later Protestant Scholasticism and the Princeton theology, holds a view of inspiration that does not entail inerrancy, and understands "the Word" to refer primarily to "the saving message of the Bible," not to the Bible itself.

The purpose of this article is to investigate the meaning of "Word and Spirit" as it relates to the doctrine of revelation in the Westminster Confession. The investigation will make use of an important but neglected source for understanding the Westminster doctrine of Scripture: William Whitaker's *Disputation on Holy*

---

[4] Donald G. Bloesch, *A Theology of Word & Spirit*, Downers Grove, IL. InterVarsity Press [1992], PP. 14,225.

[5] Jack B. Rogers and Donald K. McKim, *The Authority and Interpretation of the Bible; An Historical Approach* (San Francisco: Harper & Row, [1979], p. 461. See also Jack B. Rogers, *Scripture in the Westminster Confession* (Grand Rapids, MI: Wm. B. Eerdmans, 1967.

Scripture.[6] Whitaker was Professor of Divinity at Cambridge from 1579 or 1580 until his death in 1595. His book (in Latin) was published in 1588. Whitaker's influence upon the Assembly is indicated by the frequency with which he was quoted in the debates, as recorded in the unpublished Minutes. In the *Disputation*, he treats the doctrine of Scripture under questions or topics which later became the standard topics in Reformed theology: canon, authentic versions (and vernacular translations), authority, perspicuity, proper interpretation (and the supreme judge in controversies), and sufficiency.[7] These topics are covered in the first chapter of the Westminster Confession, with strong parallels to the views published by Whitaker seventy-five years earlier. In Chapter I, Section viii, the Confession comes close to quoting Whitaker *verbatim*.[8]

The Word and the Holy Spirit, according to Scripture and Reformed theology, are connected in three ways: the Holy Spirit is the ultimate author of Scripture (inspiration); the Spirit persuades the believer to accept the Scripture as the Word of God (inward

---

[6] William Whitaker, *A Disputation on Holy Scripture*, trans. and ed. by William Fitzgerald for The Parker Society (Cambridge, 1849). I have discussed Whitaker's contribution to the Westminster Confession in two previous articles: "William Whitaker and the Westminster Doctrine of Scripture," *Reformed Theological Journal* (Reformed Theological College, Belfast) Vol. 7, Nov., 1991, pp. 38-48; "The Westminster Confession of Faith and Holy Scripture," *To Glorify and Enjoy God*, ed. by John L. Carson and David W. Hall (Edinburgh: Banner of Truth Trust, 1994, pp. 85-100.

[7] See Heinrich Heppe *Reformed Dogmatics* (Grand Rapids, Mich.:Baker Book House, 1978); Francis Turretin, *The Doctrine of Scripture*, ed. and trans. by John W. Beardslee III (Grand Rapids, Mich.: Baker Book House, [1981]). To my knowledge, no writer before Whitaker covered this complete list of topics.

[8] *Disputation*, pp. 235, 236, 240. Warfield notes that John Arrowsmith, a member of the committee which put the Confession in its final form, cited Whitaker as well as Calvin in support of his views on the inward witness of the Spirit. B.B. Warfield, "The Westminster Doctrine of Holy Scripture," in *The Westminster Assembly and its Work* (Grand Rapids, Mich.: Baker Book House, 1981), p. 218.

witness); and the Spirit guides the believer and the Church to a proper understanding of the Word (interpretation). On these three aspects of the conjunction of Word and Spirit, Calvin, Whitaker, and the Westminster Confession are in fundamental agreement.

This article will investigate the topics of inspiration and the Spirit's inward witness. The topic of interpretation awaits further study.

The Holy Spirit and the Inspiration of the Word

One of the features in common among Calvin, Whitaker, and the Westminster Confession is that none of them treats the doctrine of the inspiration of Scripture as a distinct topic in theology. One reason for this is that inspiration was not a controversial subject at the time of the Reformation, nor in the first part of the seventeenth century.[9]

It is not difficult to ascertain Calvin's belief about inspiration, though a variety of theological concerns and prejudices may lead to disagreement among scholars.[10] Both in the *Institutes* and in the commentaries, Calvin frequently refers to the Scriptures as having been written by the Holy Spirit. His comment on II Timothy 3:16 is unequivocal:

> This is the principle that distinguishes our religion from all others, that we know that God has spoken to us and are fully convinced that the prophets did not speak of themselves, but as organs of the Holy Spirit uttered only that which they had been commissioned from heaven to declare. All those who wish to profit from the Scriptures must first accept this as a settled principle, that the Law and the prophets are not teachings handed on at the pleasure of men or produced by men's minds as their source, but are dictated by the Holy Spirit.[11]

Calvin's use of the term "dictated" is characteristic of the way in which he speaks of the Spirit's activity in the production

---

[9] Forstman, *Word and Spirit*, p. 50; Rogers, *Scripture*, p. 301.

[10] Forstman, *Word and Spirit*, pp. 49ff.

[11] John Calvin, *The Second Epistle of Paul the Apostle to the Corinthians and*

of the Scripture. He regards the writers of the inspired books as the "scribes" or "amanuenses" of the Holy Spirit.[12] The criticism of the concept of dictation has often missed the mark, when the "dictation theory" of inspiration has been treated as if it made the human authors of Scripture to be merely passive instruments, "an almost negligible element in the production of Scripture."[13] Thus understood, dictation is rejected as the mode of inspiration because of the obvious differences of style and content found in various books of the Bible. Warfield is persuasive, however, when he contends that Calvin's use of the term had to do, not so much with the exact process by which Scripture was written, but with the final product: " . . . the result of inspiration is as if it were by dictation, viz., the production of a pure word of God free from all human admixtures [of error]."[14]

Like Calvin, William Whitaker regards the Holy Spirit as the ultimate author of the Scriptures.[15] Though there were many human authors with differing styles and vocabularies, they were all taught by the Holy Spirit. "We should not regard the various men who wrote,

---

the Epistles to Timothy, Titus and Philemon, trans. by T. A. Smail, ed. by David W. Torrance and Thomas F. Torrance (Grand Rapids: Wm. B. Eerdmans, [1964], p.330. See also the numerous citations in B. B. Warfield, *Calvin and Calvinism* (Grand Rapids: Baker Book House, 1931; rpt.1981), pp. 60-62.

[12] John Calvin, *Institutes of the Christian Religion*, ed. by John T. McNeill, trans. by Ford Lewis Battles, in *The Library of Christian Classics*, vols. XX and XXI (Philadelphia: Westminster Press, [1960]), IV.viii.9, Vol. XXI, p. 1157.

[13] Forstman, *Word and Spirit*, p. 50. Calvin's idea of dictation was not drawn, of course, from the business office, but from the university, where students with limited access to books wrote down their teachers' lectures in their notebooks.

[14] *Calvin and Calvinism*, pp. 63,64. Forstman suggests that Calvin's view of dictation differs from that of "arch-conservatives" such as Henry, Carnell, and Van Til, but gives no evidence to support the remark. *Word and Spirit*, p. 52.

[15] *Disputation*, pp. 26,410.

but the one Spirit under whose direction and dictation they wrote. Thus there is one continuous body of doctrine in these books, various as they are."[16] As one of the evidences that the Scripture is the very Word of God, he repeats and expands one of Calvin's arguments:

> *Eighthly*, the authors themselves guarantee, in a great measure, the credit of these books. What sort of men were they before they were raised up to discharge this office by the Holy Ghost? Altogether unfitted for such a function then, though afterwards endowed with the noblest gifts of the Holy Spirit. Who was Moses, before he was called by God? First, a courtier in Egypt, then a shepherd, and finally, endued with the richest outpouring of the Spirit, he became a prophet. . . . Who was Peter? A fisherman, an ignorant and illiterate person. . . . Who was Paul? An enemy and persecutor of that doctrine which he afterwards professed. . . . How could such men have written so divinely without the divine inspiration of the Holy Ghost? They were, almost all, illiterate men, learned in no accomplishments, taught in no schools, imbued with no instruction; but afterwards summoned by a divine call, marked out for this office, admitted to the counsels of God: and so they committed all to writing with the exactest fidelity; which writings are now in our hands.[17]

Jack B. Rogers is formally correct when he asserts that "The Westminster Confession gives no definition of inspiration but simply points to its result: a Word of God written. . . ."[18] What Rogers draws from this is that Westminster, unlike the Princeton theology, had no "theory" of inspiration.[19]

What the Assembly meant by "inspiration," however, can be accurately determined from numerous statements in the Westminster Confession itself, as well as by considering the

---

[16] *Disputation*, p. 661; see also pp. 391, 644.

[17] *Disputation*, p. 294. The germ of the argument is in *Institutes*, I.viii.11.

[18] *Scripture*, p. 298.

[19] It is ironic that Rogers would claim to be following Calvin, who repeatedly spoke of dictation as the mode of inspiration, and then be so sharply critical of the Princeton theology on this point. Hodge and Warfield held that in Scripture "The human agency...is everywhere apparent, and gives substance and form to the entire collection of writings....This is true *except in that comparatively small element of the whole body of sacred writing* in which

influence of earlier writers such as Calvin and Whitaker.

In I.i, the Confession states that "... it pleased the Lord to reveal himself, and to declare that his will [necessary to salvation] unto his Church, and afterwards ... to commit the same wholly to writing." Here "the Lord" is the subject of the action "to commit the same wholly unto writing." In I:ii the 66 canonical books are said to constitute "the Word of God written" and to have been given by inspiration. By contrast, the books of the Apocrypha, "not being of divine inspiration," are to be used like "other human writings." (I.iii) I.v gives a number of evidences that the Scripture is the Word of God, and speaks of its "infallible truth and divine authority." The Old Testament in Hebrew and the New Testament in Greek are finally to be appealed to in controversies, because they were "immediately inspired by God." (I.viii) In the chapter on Saving Faith, the Confession declares that "By this faith, a Christian believeth to be true whatsoever is revealed in the word, for the authority of God himself speaking therein." (XIV.ii) This is a *general* response of faith to the Scripture, as possessing divine authority because it is God's own Word; the section then goes on to speak of specific aspects of faith: "accepting, receiving, and resting upon Christ" is not the whole of faith, but the "principal acts" thereof. In discussing the Law of God, the Confession asserts that the moral law was "delivered by God upon mount Sinai," and is permanently binding upon all "in respect of the authority of God, the Creator, who gave it." (XIX.2,5) The ceremonial and judicial laws are also declared to be given by God. (XIX.3,4) With regard to the Fourth Commandment, the Confession says that "[God] in his word, ... hath particularly appointed one day in seven for a sabbath." (XXI.7) The power of synods, which the Assembly derived by "good and necessary consequence" from Scripture texts, is to be respected as "an ordinance of God, appointed thereunto in his word." (XXXI.3.)

These declarations of the Confession reveal a fundamental conviction that God the Holy Spirit is the ultimate author of Scripture, in this the Confession is fully in accord with Calvin and Whitaker.

Rogers and McKim have challenged the common view that the Westminster doctrine of Scripture implied inerrancy. Their argument is that concern about the infallibility of the details of Scripture is a product of dependence on Aristotelian philosophy and reaction to the rise of Enlightenment science. They maintain that such influences did not seriously impact the Puritan movement in Britain until after the time of the Westminster Assembly, so that the Confession represents the earlier, "Augustinian" view of Scripture.

The argument is built on circumstantial evidence. In his earlier work, Rogers cited statements from divines which acknowledged differences of style in various biblical writers, and the fact that their writings draw on their own experiences, as evidence that they did not hold to a theory of verbal inspiration.[20] Both Calvin and Whitaker, however, who speak of "dictation" in connection with inspiration, are fully aware of individual differences of style in the various human authors. Rogers gives no examples of the members of the Assembly stating that the Scripture contains errors, or giving examples of such.

The discovery of Whitaker's influence on the Assembly provides decisive evidence against the historical scenario drawn by Rogers and McKim. As a teacher in one of great universities of England, a scholar revered by members of the Assembly, Whitaker held explicitly to the inerrancy of Scripture. Rejecting the view of Erasmus that Matthew might have suffered a lapse of memory in writing a detail of his Gospel, Whitaker responds:

> But it does not become us to be so indulgent as to concede that such a lapse could be incident to the sacred writers. They wrote as

---

the human authors simply report the word of God objectively communicated, or, as in some of the prophecies, they wrote by dictation." Archibald A. Hodge and Benjamin B. Warfield, *Inspiration* (Grand Rapids, MI: Baker Book House, 1979; orig. pub. 1881), p. 12. [emphasis added]

[20] *Scripture*, pp. 298-302. Rogers does quote Rutherford, who spoke of "dictation," but contends that his views are not representative of the Assembly as a whole (though Rutherford is cited positively for other sections of Chapter One.)

they were moved by the Holy Ghost, as Peter tells us, 2 Pet. 1.21. And all scripture is inspired of God, as Paul expressly writes, 2 Tim. iii.16. Whereas, therefore, no one may say that any infirmity could befall the Holy Spirit, it follows that the sacred writers could not be deceived, or err, in any respect. . . . For, whatever Erasmus may think, it is a solid answer which Augustine gives to Jerome: "If any, even the smallest, lie be admitted in the scriptures, the whole authority of scripture is presently invalidated and destroyed."[21]

The Inward Witness of the Spirit and the Authority of the Bible

According to classic Reformed theology, the work of the Holy Spirit in conjunction with the Word was not finished when the Canon was completed. The Scripture, produced by the "immediate inspiration" of the Spirit, is the trustworthy Word of God. But how does it comes to be known to be such by Christian believers?

To this question, Calvin, Whitaker, and the Westminster Confession give a two-fold answer: first, there are several evidences that the Scripture is God's Word; secondly, our full persuasion of this fact comes from the internal testimony of the Holy Spirit.

Calvin, Whitaker, and Westminster are in agreement that there are various arguments or evidences which indicate that the Bible is God's own Word.

There are significant similarities in the listing of evidences, but there are also differences. The Westminster Confession has some omissions which may be significant. The arguments are briefly presented in the table below. Because a brief summary of evidences by George Gillespie seems to have significantly influenced the Westminster statement, it is included in the table.[22]

---

[21] *Disputation*, p. 37.

[22] George Gillespie, *A Treatise of Miscellany Questions*, in *The Works of Mr. George Gillespie*, Vol. II (Edinburgh: Robert Ogle and Oliver and Boyd, 1846), pp. 105-106. For the other arguments, see *Institutes*, I.viii; *Disputation*, pp. 293-294; *Westminster Confession*, I.v.

Calvin	Whitaker	Gillespie	Westminster
heavenly character of doctrine	majesty of doctrine	heavenliness of matter	heavenliness of matter
agreement of all the parts		marvellous consent of all parts	consent of all parts
uncultivated and rude simplicity	simplicity, purity, and divinity of style	majesty of style	majesty of style
power to affect the reader		irresistible power over the conscience	efficacy of the doctrine
antiquity	antiquity		
unselfish honesty of Moses		holiness and honesty of the penmen	
confirmation by miracles	confirmation by miracles	confirmation by miracles	
predictive prophecy	predictive prophecy	fulfilling of prophecies	
providential preservation	providential preservation	conservation vs. enemies	
consent of the church	unbroken judgment of the church		[testimony of the church]
testimony of martyrs	testimony of martyrs		
	weakness of human authors		
		scope: to abase man & exalt God aims at God's glory and man's salvation	scope: all glory to God revelation of only way of salvation
			entire perfection

48

The three sources agree that full confidence in the truth of Scripture requires the inward witness of the Spirit. Rejecting disputation as the method by which firm faith may be achieved, Calvin writes, " . . . the testimony of the Spirit is more excellent than all reason. For as God alone is a fit witness of himself in his Word, so also the Word will not find acceptance in man's hearts before it is sealed by the inward testimony of the Spirit."[23]

Calvin, unlike Whitaker and the Confession, places the discussion of the Spirit's testimony *before* the treatment of the evidences.

B. B. Warfield gives an extensive discussion of the testimony of the Spirit in his treatment of Calvin's doctrine of the knowledge of God.[24] He raises the important question of the relation between the Spirit's testimony, and the arguments or *indicia* for the authority of Scripture. His conclusion is this: that while Calvin does not state it explicitly, " . . . on Calvin's ground, . . . when the soul is renewed by the Holy Spirit, it is through the *indicia* of that divinity that it is brought into its proper confidence in the divinity of Scripture."[25] As Warfield acknowledges, it is not entirely clear that this is Calvin's view, because the latter seems to place the usefulness of the arguments later in Christian experience: " . . . once we have embraced it devoutly as its dignity deserves . . . , those arguments—not strong enough before to engraft and fix the certainty of Scripture in our minds—become very useful aids."[26]

There is no ambiguity in Whitaker's treatment of this question.

---

[23] *Institutes*, I.vii.4.

[24] B.B. Warfield, *Calvin and Augustine* (Philadelphia; Presbyterian and Reformed Publishing Company, 1956; rept. From *Princeton Theological Review*, vii, 1909),pp. 29-130

[25] *Calvin and Augustine*, p. 87.

[26] *Institutes*, I.viii.]. Calvin is confident, however, that he can silence the objections of scholarly opponents through the use of arguments, I.vii.4

After citing his arguments for the divine inspiration of the Bible (which he takes from Calvin), Whitaker adds, "These topics may prove that these books are divine, yet will never be sufficient to bring conviction to our souls so as to make us assent, unless the testimony of the Holy Spirit be added. When this is added, it fills our minds with a wonderful plenitude of assurance. . . ." The witness of the Spirit " . . . causes us most gladly to embrace the scriptures, giving force to the preceding arguments." The testimony of the Spirit is not " . . . external, nor separate, or alien from the books, because it is perceived in the doctrine delivered in those books; for we do not speak of any enthusiastic influence of the Spirit."[27]

The Westminster Confession echoes Calvin and Whitaker regarding the inward testimony of the Spirit: " . . . our full persuasion and assurance of the infallible truth, and divine authority [of the Scripture], is from the inward work of the Holy Spirit, bearing witness by and with the word in our hearts."[28] The Assembly appears to share Whitaker's view of the connection between the evidences and the testimony of the Spirit, as is indicated by the assertion that the Holy Spirit bears witness "by and with the word." The Spirit's testimony does not give new revelation, or a purely mystical experience, but opens a person's spiritual vision to appreciate the marks of truth which were objectively present in Scripture all along. Whitaker describes what is ordinarily the unfolding experience of the believer:

> We do not immediately understand everything ourselves; we must therefore listen to the church which bids us read these books. Afterwards, however, when we either read them ourselves, or hear others read them, and duly weigh what they teach, we believe their canonicity, not only on account of the testimony or authority of the church, but upon the inducement of other and more certain arguments,

---

[27] *Disputation*, p. 295.

[28] I.v.

as the witness of the Holy Spirit, and the majesty of that heavenly doctrine, which shines forth in the books themselves and the whole manner of their teaching.[29]

The presentation of arguments or evidences for the divine origin and character of the Bible raises the important question of apologetic method. Modern Reformed theologians who adhere to the theology of the Westminster Confession are divided on this question. Some adherents of "classical" apologetics maintain that there are valid rational arguments which, without any special enlightenment by the Holy Spirit, will prove the inspiration of the Bible to any person of normal intelligence.[30] Presuppositionalists, on the other hand, believe that without divine illumination the sinful human consciousness will not be persuaded of the divine origin and trustworthiness of the Scripture.[31] Calvinists in both camps agree that evidence is useful to faith, and that *saving* confidence in the Scripture is the result of the inward witness of the Spirit. The difference appears to lie in differing views of the nature of the evidence, and of the effects of sin upon human thought processes.

In assessing the significance for apologetics of the Westminster Confession's statement about evidence in I.v., it may be helpful to notice that the Confession gives a shorter list of arguments than any of its predecessors, and appears to have selected only those which would clearly appeal to the consciousness of one who has saving faith, or is in the process of being drawn to Christ by the Spirit. Is there anything in the Confession's enumeration which would have any compelling force of persuasion to an unbeliever? "Majesty of style" might seem to be a quality perceivable by a neutral observer, but only if

---

[29] *Disputation*, p. 369.

[30] R.C. Sproul, John Gerstner, and Arthur Lindsley, *Classical Apologetics* (Grand Rapids, Mich., Zondervan Publishing House, [1984]).

[31] Cornelius Van Til, *The Defense of the Faith* (Philadelphia: Presbyterian and Reformed Publishing Company, 1963), p. 212.

there can be found a generally agreed-upon standard of excellence. (Curiously, the Confession, following Whitaker and Gillespie, differs here from Calvin on the matter of style, for he does not use elegance of style as a positive argument, but says that the "sublime mysteries" and the "force of truth" in Scripture bear witness to its inspiration *in spite of* its "mean and lowly words," and the "uncultivated and almost rude simplicity" of its style.)[32] As for the rest of the evidences: one must believe in heaven to be impressed by "the heavenliness of the matter"; must have felt the Word to be living and powerful to note "the efficacy of the doctrine"; must have begun to see Christ and truth in all the Scriptures (Luke 24:27) to be able to speak of "the consent of all the parts." Only a regenerate person, having come to realize his true position as creature and sinner could be impressed with the Scripture's scope or objective, "which is to give all glory to God," and could rejoice in "the full discovery [Scripture] makes of the only way of man's salvation." These are not, then, arguments which could appeal to neutral human reason. They hardly belong in the category of discursive argument, but are expressions of the religious experience of those renewed by the Spirit. In Calvin's metaphor, as one does not need elaborate instruction to distinguish light from darkness, white from black, or sweet from bitter, so "Scripture exhibits fully as clear evidence of its own truth as white and black things do of the color, or sweet or bitter things of their taste."[33] Ability to perceive these qualities, however, rests upon the work of the Spirit to renew the sinner's capacity: "Our mind has such an inclination to vanity that it can never cleave fast to the truth of God; and it has such a dullness that it is always blind to the light of God's truth. Accordingly, without the illumination of the Holy Spirit, the Word can do nothing."[34]

---

[32] *Institutes*, I.viii.1.

[33] *Institutes*, I.vii.2.

[34] *Institutes*, III.ii.33.

The Confession's use of arguments for the divine authority of the Bible, then, does not indicate that rational argument is the necessary foundation for faith. Here, Warfield's apologetic method appears to depart from the position taken by the Confession. In principle, Warfield holds that the evidences which will prove that the Scripture is divinely inspired are valid according to the principles of universal human reason, prior to and apart from the regenerating work of the Spirit.[35] At the point, the criticism of the Princeton Theology as "evangelical rationalism" has some validity.

Abraham Kuyper, Warfield's contemporary and friend, gives a description of how a person comes to have confidence in Scripture which seems more fully in accord with the view of Calvin and Whitaker, and with the language of the Confession:

> In a later period it has been made to appear that the "heavenly majesty of the doctrines, the marvellous completeness of the prophecies, the wonderful miracles, the consent of all its parts, the divineness of the discourse," and so much more, formed a system of outward proofs able to convince the reason without *enlightenment*; but our first theologians, at least, did not attach such a meaning to them. They taught that these inner relations of the Scripture were understood . . . only when, by enlightening, the spiritual understanding had been clarified and purified. He only, who in palingenesis had experienced *a miracle* in his own person, ceased to react against miracles, but rather invoked them himself. . . . He who heard the music of the Divine melody of redemption in his own soul was rapt in wonder . . . in listening to the Oratorio of Salvation proceeding from the heavenly majesty of doctrine in the Holy Scripture.[36]

Some recent discussions of the conjunction of Word and Spirit have claimed that the "Word" to which the Spirit bears witness is not the Scripture as a whole, but rather its saving message or central content. Rogers and McKim understand the Reformers to teach that "The Spirit witnessed to the divine, Christological

---

[35] B.B. Warfield, "Apologetics." in *Selected Shorter Writings*, Vol II, ed. By John E. Meeter (Nutley, NJ: Presbyterian and Reformed Publishing Co., 1973).

[36] Abraham Kuyper, *Principles of Sacred Theology*, trans. J. Hendrik De Vries (Grand Rapids, Mich.: Wm. B. Eerdmans Publishing Co., 1965). p. 558.

content of Scripture, not its human, linguistic form." "We should look for no other knowledge in the Bible than of Christ and his benefits towards us, according to them."[37]

This view drastically changes the meaning of "Word and Spirit" as it was understood by Calvin, Whitaker, and Westminster. While acknowledging that the Scripture's central purpose is to make known Christ and salvation through him, they held that the Scripture as a whole is God's Word to us, and made no distinction between the merely human (and therefore fallible) aspects of the Bible and that which was truly divine.

In Calvin's discussion of faith, he emphasizes that at the heart of saving faith, which comes by illumination of the Spirit, is confidence in God's promise of salvation. But faith also has a more general object, namely the Scripture as a whole.

> Faith is certain that God is true in all things whether he command or forbid, whether he promise or threaten; and it also obediently receives his commandments, observes his prohibitions, heeds his threats. Nevertheless faith properly begins with the promise, rests in it, and ends in it . . . when we say that faith must rest upon a freely given promise, we do not deny that believers embrace and grasp the Word of God in every respect: but we point out the promise of mercy as the proper goal of faith . . . our slanderers unjustly charge us with denying, as it were, that faith has regard to all parts of the Word of God.[38]

According to William Whitaker, the Holy Spirit not only bears witness to the Gospel, but also to the Scripture as a whole, that is, to the books that comprise the Scripture. "For we say that there is a more certain and illustrious testimony [than that of the church], whereby we are persuaded of the sacred character of these books, that is to say, the internal testimony of the Holy Spirit. . . ."[39] His conviction that the Spirit persuades believers of the divine authority of the Scripture as a whole as well as of "saving truth"

---

[37] *Authority and Interpretation*, p. 126

[38] *Institutes*, III.ii.29,30.

[39] *Disputation*, p. 279.

is clearly stated: As the Holy Spirit " . . . he seals all the doctrines of faith and the whole teaching of salvation in our hearts, and confirms them in our consciences, *so also* does he give us a certain persuasion of these books, from which are drawn all the doctrines of faith and salvation, are sacred and canonical."[40]

The authors of the Westminster Confession appear to have had Calvin's discussion of faith in mind when they formed the description of saving faith in Chapter XIV.2. In that significant statement, faith is said to involve assent to the whole content of Scripture as God's authoritative voice; experiential response to particular aspects of that content (commandments, threatenings, promises), and, as the central part that response, "accepting, receiving, and resting upon Christ alone for justification, sanctification, and eternal life. . . ." Spirit-given faith does not grasp the saving message of Scripture apart from the trustworthy Scripture as a whole, sees that message as the center of the whole revelation regarding God, creation, providence, human nature, human sinfulness, the destiny of man and all things, God's law, the church, and much else of which the Bible speaks. Separated from the whole content of revelation, the "saving message" evaporates into thin air, or becomes something else than the Bible says it is.[41]

According to the Westminster Confession, what the inward work of the Spirit bears witness to is the fact that *Scripture* is the Word of God, not just its saving message. This is reinforced by the fact that in the Confession "the Word" always means "Scripture."

---

[40] *Disputation*, p. 295. [emphasis added]

[41] Showing the influence of Barth on his theology, Donald Bloesch says, "To walk by faith means to walk in . . . the uncreated light of Jesus Christ himself, which is reflected in the church, in Scripture, and in consciencer. Paradoxically, to walk by faith also means to walk in darkness, for the light and truth of Jesus Christ are hidden from all sight and understanding." *A Theology of Word & Spirit*, p. 207.

Conclusion

In its doctrine of Scripture, the Westminster Confession does not differ significantly from the views which Calvin held in the first period of the Reformation. In a historical situation in which Roman Catholicism was still a significant political and theological adversary, the Assembly continued to maintain with Calvin that the Scripture was immediately inspired by God, and thus was to be listened to "as if there the living words of God were heard."[42] The organization of the material in Chapter I, the topics covered, and even the wording show the influence of William Whitaker, who is the bridge for the Assembly to Calvin's thought. The Confession captures the essence of Calvin's thought about the absolute necessity of the inward testimony of the Spirit for assured faith in the Scripture, and follows Whitaker in making it clear that the Spirit opens the eyes of the regenerate sinner to see the marks of divine origin which are in the Scripture and its teaching.

Authors such as Donald Bloesch, and Rogers and McKim have rightly called attention to the crucial importance of the conjunction of Word and Spirit for understanding the theology of the Reformation. However, their understanding of the "Word" in that conjunction, differing as it does from the view of Calvin, Whitaker, and the Westminster Confession, leads to a changed view of what saving faith involves. In the Reformation doctrine, faithfully repeated in the Westminster Confession, the Spirit persuades the mind and heart that all the books of the Old and New Testaments differ from all human writings in that they have the Spirit of God as their author, and therefore make known to us in a trustworthy manner all that we need to know for our salvation, faith and life.

---

[42] *Institutes*, I.vii.1. (The "as if", of course, did not indicate that Calvin was uncertain about it.)

The Holy Spirit in the
Westminster Confession of Faith

O. Palmer Robertson

Introduction

More than once the Westminster Confession of Faith has been charged with a deficiency in its doctrine of the Holy Spirit.[1] In the first half of the twentieth century, American presbyterianism made an effort to correct this perceived deficiency by adding a separate chapter entitled *Of the Holy Spirit*.[2] In the second half of

---

[1] Among others, cf Thomas F. Torrance, *The School of Faith. The Catechisms of the Reformed Church*. James Clarke & Co. Limited, 1959, p. XVI, who remarks concerning the Westminster *Shorter Catechism*: "Like *The Larger Catechism*, it has little to say about the Holy Spirit."

[2] In a special introduction to Abraham Kuyper's book on the work of the Holy Spirit, B. B. Warfield offers an analysis of the role of the doctrine of the Holy Spirit in reformed thinking. Warfield notes that although John Calvin has been identified especially with the doctrine of predestination, he was in this regard only echoing the teachings of Augustine. But one of the major creative contributions from Calvin according to Warfield was his extensive development of the doctrine of the Holy Spirit (p. xxxiv). In Warfield's estimation, "the developed doctrine of the work of the Holy Spirit is an exclusively Reformation doctrine, and more particularly a Reformed doctrine, and more particularly still a Puritan doctrine" (p. xxxiii). In evaluating the absence of a chapter specifically on the Holy Spirit in the Westminster Confession of Faith, Warfield points to the extensive

the twentieth century, great restlessness has been manifested regarding the limitations in the treatment of the "gifts" of the Spirit found in the Westminster Confession of Faith.

What is the reason for this restlessness regarding the doctrine of the Holy Spirit in the Westminster Confession of Faith? A similar kind of unease about the doctrine of the person of Christ does not appear to be a factor in people's thinking. Obviously a man-made document like the Confession penned at Westminster could not be perfect. Quite possibly the reformed church, ever reforming, has come to a new and richer comprehension of the person and work of the Holy Spirit. In any case, the subject deserves exploration. It may be that the church today may improve on the formulations of the doctrine of the Holy Spirit as they are found in this old document. At the same time, it may be that buried in this statement of antiquity is to be found something instructive for the church today.

A twentieth-century effort at correcting a perceived deficiency in the Confession's doctrine of the Holy Spirit has an interesting history. In the Presbyterian Church in the United States, more popularly known through its hundred-year history as the Southern Presbyterian Church, strong adherence to all the doctrines of the Westminster Confession prevailed through the 1920s. This "predominantly conservative" denomination adhered to the doctrinal system of the Standards, "strictly construed."[3] Even as

---

development of the subject throughout the rest of the Confession: "The sole reason why it does not give a chapter to this subject . . . is because it prefers to give *nine* chapters to it; and when an attempt was made to supply the fancied omission, it was found that pretty much all that could be done was to present in the proposed new chapter a meager summary of the contents of these nine chapters" (p. xxvi). Cf Benjamin B Warfield, "Introductory Note" in Abraham Kuyper, *The Work of the Holy Spirit.* (Grand Rapids: Eerdmans, 1900 [reprint of August, 1969]), pp. xxv-xxxix.

[3] Ernest Trice Thompson, *Presbyterians in the South*, Richmond: John Knox Press, vol. 3, 1973, p. 486.

late as the 1940's, vigorous support for full subscription to all the doctrines of the Westminster Confession was manifested in an editorial appearing in the first year of publication of *The Presbyterian Journal*. "The *Southern Presbyterian Journal* accepts without any reservation the standards of the Southern Presbyterian Church contained in the Confession of Faith and Catechisms" stated an editorial in the newly formed magazine.[4] While the "Northern" Presbyterian Church already had largely succumbed to the rationalistic doctrines of liberalism by the 1930's, the Southern Church kept to its ancient heritage. This observation is vividly illustrated by the fact that J. Gresham Machen, minority champion of historic Christianity at Princeton Theological Seminary, was invited by the president of Union Theological Seminary in Virginia to become its professor of New Testament even as the modernist/fundamentalist controversy raged in the North[5]. Though regretfully declining the invitation to come as Professor of New Testament, Machen accepted the invitation to deliver the prestigious James Sprunt lectures at Union, which he did in the spring of 1921.[6] One of the great "what ifs" of church history emerges with speculations about the

---

[4] Henry B. Dendy, "Offering You Shares in the *Ministry* of the Southern Presbyterian Journal", in *The Southern Presbyterian Journal*, Feb.1943, vol.1, no.10, p.2. While this testimony itself displays that it was responding to current challenges to the Confession, its vigor indicates the strong commitment of a significant body within the Southern Presbyterian Church at the time.

[5] Ned B. Stonehouse, *J. Gresham Machen. A Biographical Memoir*. (Edinburgh: The Banner of Truth Trust, 1978), pp.233-235. The President of Union Seminary in Virginia sought an indicator from Machen of a willingness to accept the invitation before he formally presented a nomination to the Board. But he indicated that the matter was fully known to our large and widely scattered Board." He expressed his confidence in the outcome if a nomination had been made: "There is no doubt that he would have been unanimously elected if he could have seen his way to let the Board proceed" (p.234).

[6] Stonehouse, *Machen* p.235; 324-326. Machen indicates that he enjoyed his time with the faculty and students at Union immensely.

hypothetical effect of Machen's going to Union Theological Seminary in Virginia.

But the seeds of liberalism had been planted in the South as well, and came into full bloom with a movement to rewrite portions of the Westminster Confession of Faith. The formal effort began with a 1935 report from churches in Virginia that called attention to what were regarded as some of the "extreme statements" in the Westminster Confession of Faith. This report presented to East Hanover Presbytery also noted that the Confession contained no chapter on the Holy Spirit or on missions. A number of overtures came to the 1935 General Assembly of the church responding to these observations, and the whole matter was referred to a committee consisting of the Moderator and the professor of theology from each of the four denominational seminaries. Three years later, in 1938, the committee recommended changes to eighteen paragraphs of the Confession and the addition of two new chapters, one on the Holy Spirit and one on the Gospel.[7] Some of the proposed changes simply involved the use of more modern language. But others sought to modify the reformed distinctives regarding election and predestination as they are developed in the theology of the Confession. All the changes were approved by the Assembly, and during the next year almost all were passed by a sufficient number of the various presbyteries with a vote of more than two to one.[8]

The General Assembly of 1939 was a tense one, since it had the responsibility of finally ratifying the proposed changes to the Confession. These alterations were vigorously opposed by Professor William Childs Robinson of Columbia Theological

---

[7] Thompson, *Presbyterians*. p.491.

[8] Thompson, *Presbyterians*, p.491. Cf. *Minutes of the Seventy-ninth General Assembly of the Presbyterian Church in the United States*. Austin: von Boechmann-Jones Co., 1939, pp. 68-71

Seminary, even though Professor J. B. Green of the school had served on the committee that formulated the changes. Professor Green had written an article during the previous year attempting to clarify the modifications to the doctrinal standards of the church that were being proposed to the presbyteries. An Atlanta paper had interpreted the action of the Assembly with the headline: *"Presbyterians Modify Canons, Omit Predestination Doctrine."*[9] In his response, Professor Green had argued that the changes involved no omission of the doctrine of predestination. In his view, the statements that were to be deleted with their references to foreordination to everlasting death and to a numbering of the elect that could not be changed, "contribute nothing useable to the materials of preaching." He argued that the church should not confess what it does not pray, and 'We never ask God . . . to visit any with dishonor and wrath for their sins, to the praise of his glorious justice." Professor Green concluded his article by noting he would be pleased if the changes passed, but would "not be greatly disappointed" if they failed.[10]

Under the influence of Professor Robinson, the Assembly voted to retain the doctrinal standards of the church in their original form, even though certain minor modifications were enacted. As one historian has noted:

> There was no one of equal weight to uphold the affirmative, and the matter was decided practically without debate.[11]

But three years later, in 1942, the two additional chapters on

---

[9] J.B. Green, "Regarding the Revision of the Confession of Faith and the Catechism," *Presbyterian of the South*, June 15, 1938, p.13.

[10] Green, "Revision," p.13. The observation that a doctrine may or may not currently be preached or prayed by a particular segment of the Christian community hardly seems to be the best way to argue the validity of a theological truth. It also may be wondered if a matter of such significance should be properly viewed with a willingness to be content whether or not it is included in a church's creedal statements.

[11] Thompson, *Presbyterians*, p. 492.

the Holy Spirit and the gospel were added "over the strenuous opposition of Dr. Robinson[12]." These chapters were identical to the alterations made to the Westminster Confession by the "Northern" Presbyterian Church almost 40 years earlier. It had taken two generations longer, but the seeds of modernist thought now had infiltrated the Southern Church.

What was the effect of the addition of these two chapters? The assessment of some contemporaries is summarized by a plea offered by a person advocating the changes:

> Let us take down the picture of God which Calvinism has hung in [the Standards], presenting to our view a God who has unchangeably elected some men to eternal life and unchangeably ordained the rest of mankind to eternal death.[13]

After the changes were made, the author of this statement attached an addendum to his book. In these further comments he argued that the latest laws passed by a governing body must be viewed as superseding all previous laws that might be in conflict with the new law. So he concluded that the "objectionable" chapter on predestination now must be viewed as subordinate to the new chapter. In his enthusiasm over his perception of the effect of these changes, the author concluded his addendum by exclaiming: "Glory be to God! Amen! And Amen!"[14] Obviously the author felt that the addition of the two new chapters had accomplished what he felt needed to be done. No longer was the theology of the reformed faith as developed in the confessions of the church viewed as binding on its ordained officers. As has been explained:

> In the generation that followed ministers (and officers) have continued to accept the system of doctrine set forth in the Confession of Faith,

---

[12] Thompson, *Presbyterians*, p.492. Cf. *Minutes of the Eighty-second General Assembly of the Presbyterian Church in the United States*, Austin: von Boechmann-Jones Co., 1942, pp.67-69.

[13] Robert Ware Jopling, *Studies in the Confession of Faith or the Five Points of Calvinism Examined*, Clinton, S.C.: Jacobs Press, 1942, p. 53.

[14] Jopling. *Studies*, p.90.

but the General Assembly has interpreted this to mean only the essentials of the system, and it has become quite clear that the essentials of the system are understood quite differently from what they were one or two generations earlier. Which indeed must be the case if there is not to be stagnation and death.[15]

Restlessness over the binding character of the Confession has emerged surprisingly in the relatively young Presbyterian Church in America. The need to change the confession itself has been made unnecessary in the minds of some by a broad interpretation of the significance of the vow taken by ministers and other officers to uphold the doctrines of the document. But a sense of the inadequacy of the Confession's treatment of the doctrine of the Holy Spirit, particularly as it relates to the validity of the gifts of "prophecy" and "tongues" today, continues to create an atmosphere in which the church searches for some formulation beyond what the Confession states.

It is in this context that a fresh look at the teaching of the Westminster Confession on the doctrine of the Holy Spirit needs to be reexamined. The present study will develop that doctrine as it is presented in the Confession, setting it in the context of the scriptural evidence that lies behind this teaching. After this material has been presented, an evaluation of the current significance of the doctrine of the Holy Spirit in the Westminster Confession of Faith will be offered. A basic outline of the subjects to be covered is as follows:

I.   Who is the Holy Spirit?
   A. He is God
   B. He is a Person
II. What does the Holy Spirit Do?
   A. Outside of Us
   B. Within Us

---

[15] Thompson, *Presbyterians*, p.493.

In a unique sense the present era since the ascension of Christ may be designated as the age of the Holy Spirit. Three great epochs in the history of God's working among men may be distinguished, and the three persons of the Trinity have a relative prominence corresponding to these three epochs. Beyond dispute all three persons of the Trinity have been active in working salvation for men in all ages. Yet some distinction may be made respecting the prominence of the various persons of the Trinity in these different epochs. During the times of the old covenant, God the Father was most evident; during the period of the incarnation, God the Son was more fully manifested; and since the time of Christ's ascension, God the Holy Spirit has stood out more prominently. This perspective is summarized in a succinct statement by Herman Bavinck:

> As in the ontological trinity the Father is first in the order of subsistence, the Son second, and the Holy Spirit third; so also in the *history of revelation* the Father preceded the Son, and the Son preceded the Holy Spirit. The economy of the Father pertains in a special sense to the Old Testament, Hebrews 1:1; the economy of the Son began with the incarnation; and the economy of the Holy Spirit commenced at Pentecost, John 7:39; 14:15.[16]

This order of the divine working in the world stresses the importance of properly understanding the person and work of the Holy Spirit for those on whom the end of the ages has come. Consider then the witness of Scripture and the Church's confession first concerning the person of the Holy Spirit and then concerning his work.

I. Who Is the Holy Spirit?

A. *The Holy Spirit is God*

First and foremost it must be affirmed that the Holy Spirit is God. Generally people readily recognize the Father to be God in

---

[16] Herman Bavinck, *The Doctrine of God*, (Grand Rapids: Eerdmans), 1951, p. 320.

all his distinctive attributes. Though some people may have hesitations, the Son also is normally acknowledged to be God. But many people think of the Holy Spirit in a very different way. To them he is an emanation, a "force" that goes out from God.

The wording of Christ's Great Commission underscores the fact that the Holy Spirit is God on an equality with the Father and the Son. People are to be baptized in the name of the Father and the Son and the Holy Spirit (Matt. 28:18-20). In this formula, each of the three persons of the Trinity is treated equally. In the original language, a definite article is used for each of the three persons, and yet the "name" of God which indicates his essence appears in the singular. The one God exists in three persons. To leave out the name of any one of the three is to deny the essence of God himself. The Spirit stands alongside the Father and the Son as God in all his glory.

Scripture clearly indicates that respect for the Holy Spirit as a person must not be any less than the honor paid to the Father and the Son. Jesus said sin and blasphemy against the Father may be forgiven (Matt. 12:31). The person who speaks against the Son also may be forgiven (Matt. 12:32). But, blasphemy against the Spirit will not be forgiven (Matt. 12:31). Though words spoken against the Father and the Son may receive God's forgiveness, words spoken against the Holy Spirit will not be forgiven.

In the light of this teaching of Jesus, it hardly could be suggested that the Holy Spirit is merely an *it* and not a person. He could not be less than the Father and the Son if sin against him can never be forgiven.

The designation of the third person of the Trinity as "Spirit" should not detract from his full deity. The "spiritual" character of the Holy Spirit must not lead to the misconception that he is only an extension of the godhead in a manner similar to the way in which wind is a "force" created by a fan. In a unique sense, the "spiritual" nature of the Holy Spirit captures the essence of deity. Nowhere does Scripture say in so many words, "God is a Father" or "God is a Son." But Scripture does say "God is a Spirit" (John

4:24). The Father and the Son are "spiritual" beings just as much as the Holy Spirit, so that any aspects of spirit-ness that belong to the Holy Spirit also characterize the Father and the Son.

This reality of the essence of the godhead is recognized immediately in the classic definition of God in the Westminster Shorter Catechism: "God is a *spirit*, infinite, eternal and unchangeable. . . ." (SC Q. 4). But the significance of this fact is brought out more fully in the Confession's opening statement about God:

> There is but one only, living, and true God who is infinite in being and perfection, a most pure spirit, invisible, without body, parts or passions . . .. (WCF II, 1).

In light of this spiritual essence of God in all his persons, it may be concluded that the common misconception of the Holy Spirit as something less than God because of his "spiritual" nature is symptomatic of a larger problem. An improper conception of God in each of his persons troubles the church. Man's existence is so intertwined with his corporeality that he finds it almost impossible to think of personhood without body. In this circumstance, the essential nature of the Holy Spirit as God in all his glory should prove to be significantly edifying for the church.

Recognizing the divine nature of the Holy Spirit may deliver the Church from a number of errors. Consider these consequences that flow from the full deity of the Holy Spirit:

(1) Because the Holy Spirit is God, he never will contradict himself. The Spirit that inspired the Bible cannot say one thing while the Spirit that indwells the believer says another. A young person may hear his parents clearly say, "You cannot go to the Bible study tonight. You must complete your schoolwork." This young person knows that the Scripture instructs children to obey their parents (Eph. 6:1). But because of the pious pull he feels toward going to the Bible study, he may conclude that the Holy Spirit is telling him to disobey his parents.

But the Holy Spirit possesses all the integrity that belongs to God. He will not contradict himself. His work of enforcing the truths of God in the hearts of men never will contradict his previous work of inspiring the Scriptures.

(2) Because the Holy Spirit is God, he never will confront an insoluble problem. What should be done when a woman in a polygamous relationship is converted to Christ? The situation can be very perplexing, having an impact on her children as well as other family members. This type situation may baffle the wisest of God's servants. But the problem never should be viewed as insoluble. For the wisdom of the Holy Spirit that indwells the believer has no limit. Because the Holy Spirit is God, he can determine the proper response to any situation in life however perplexing it may appear.

(3) Because the Holy Spirit is God, he never will find a sinner too hardened to be converted. The powers of the Holy Spirit to create a new life within the soul of a person are limitless. His infinite might can cause the most hardened sinner to be born again. It is no more difficult for the Holy Spirit to convert a sinner than it was for Christ to cleanse a leper. As Christ transformed the crusted, putrefied skin of the leper into the likeness of a baby's soft skin, so the Holy Spirit renews the most defiled sinner's heart by the new birth.

(4) Because the Holy Spirit is God, he cannot be manipulated as human beings. Men are inherently changeable, but God does not change. An effort may be made to modify the testimony of the Spirit. But the witness of the Spirit does not change. He will not deviate from the perfections of holiness that are an essential characteristic of his own nature.

The Holy Spirit is not a part of God, a will-weakened form of the Deity. The "spiritual" nature of the Holy Spirit in no way diminishes his power, his wisdom, his volition. He is the unchanging God. He is God in all his glory. It is with this understanding that the Westminster Confession of Faith affirms: "Religious worship is to be given to God, the Father, Son, and Holy Spirit; and to him alone"(WCF XXI, 2). No being other than God himself is worthy of receiving the adoration and worship of men; and the Holy Spirit is all that God is.

B. The Holy Spirit is a Person

1. As a person, he has a will.

Because people often think of the Holy Spirit as a "thing" or a "force," they consider the Spirit of God as something that can be programmed or managed. Even if the Spirit is affirmed to be a "person," it is supposed that he like other persons can be manipulated into doing what people want him to do. So for some years a course on "signs and wonders" was taught in an evangelical seminary. In this course, people supposedly were trained in what they must do to get the Holy Spirit to perform certain wonders for them.

Still with great embarrassment, I remember as a young person "demanding" in a prayer meeting that the Holy Spirit send a revival to the church. The old elder with the hearing aid kneeling next to me didn't catch all that I dictated to the Almighty, but he heard enough. "We don't demand anything of you," he intoned in his off-key way, "we only humbly plead."

God the Holy Spirit has his will, and can be deeply grieved when men attempt to tamper with his purpose and plan for the perfection of the saints (Eph. 4:30). Even "true believers" may have their assurance of salvation "shaken, diminished, and intermitted" by their grieving the Holy Spirit (WCF XVIII, 4; cf XVII, 3).

Figuratively speaking, the wind has a "will" and "blows where it will." Man can do little about the direction and the force with which the wind wills to blow. In a similar way, the Holy Spirit wills to regenerate whoever he will, whenever he will. "So [like results of the willful wind] is everyone that is born of the Spirit," says Jesus to an educated but unwise Nicodemus (John 3:8). The Holy Spirit is personhood personified, as displayed by his exercise of personal will in the regeneration of deadened sinners.

The personal will of the Spirit is seen also by his determining the way the gospel shall spread. Asserting himself into the worship of the church at Antioch, the Holy Spirit said, "Set apart *for me* Barnabas and Saul *for the work to which I have called them*" (Acts 13:2). So the two were *"sent on their way by the Holy Spirit"* (Acts 13:4). Clearly the Holy Spirit has a will that goes beyond the conversion of individual sinners. His determinations embrace the whole direction of an expanding church. By his force of will he says "Yes" to some missionary endeavors and "No" to others. In the mysteries of his providential ordering Paul was "kept by the Holy Spirit from preaching the word in the province of Asia" and was sent to Europe instead (Acts 16:6-8). The Spirit is not an "it" or a "force"; he is a person with a will.

2. As a person, he has moral standards.

Impersonal "forces" have no moral standards. But why would the Spirit of God be mainly characterized as "Holy" if he had no standard of purity? He embodies in his very essence the moral perfections of the personhood of God, who is the ultimate and only source of a true moral standard for humanity.

It is against the Spirit of God that the flesh lusts (Gal. 5:17), and it is by living in the Spirit that the believer is freed from gratifying the sinful desires of the flesh (Gal. 5:16). So the Westminster Confession of Faith emphasizes the work of the Holy Spirit in its chapters on Sanctification and the Law of God:

> (Those who have been regenerated) "are further sanctified really and personally . . . by his word and Spirit dwelling in them" (WCF XIII, 1).

> " . . . through the continual supply of strength from the sanctifying Spirit of Christ" the saints "grow in grace, perfecting holiness in the fear of God" (WCF XIII, 3).

"The law of God supports the gospel in the life of the believer because)
"the Spirit of Christ" is constantly "subduing and enabling the will
of man to do that freely and cheerfully which the will of God revealed
in the law requireth to be done" (WCF XIX, 7).

How could the Spirit of God sanctify personally, perfect
holiness, and enable the will of man to do the will of God
cheerfully without possessing the moral characteristics of a
person? That moral perfection to which the Spirit leads believers
the Spirit himself already possesses.

3.   As a person, he communes with people.

On the eve of his departure from this earth, Jesus pointed his
disciples to the person of the Holy Spirit as that one who would
stand in his place. He would not leave them as orphans. God's
Spirit, the "Comforter," would provide counsel, consolation and
encouragement (John 14:16). This coming Counselor would teach
the disciples all things, and would offer irrefutable testimony about
the person of Jesus Christ (John 14:26; 15:26). These offices and
functions as described by Christ could be fulfilled only by a person.

So the Westminster Confession affirms the personhood of the
Spirit by noting that he speaks to men in the Scriptures (WCF I, 1),
he persuades sinners to believe and obey (WCF VIII, 8), he governs
the human heart (WCF VIII, 8), he provides personal assurance of
salvation by testifying to the human spirit (WCF XVIII, 2), and he
makes possible personal communion with God through prayer
(WCF XXI, 3). All these functions of the Spirit undergird the reality
of his personhood. If personhood is defined in part as an ability to
commune with other human spirits, then the Spirit of God clearly
must be viewed as the source of all human personhood.

God the Holy Spirit is a person. His manifestation of will, his
moral essence, and his capacity for intimate communion
establishes his personhood. He must not be insulted by being
considered as nothing more than a form of God's manifestation.
If God is person, the Holy Spirit is a person.

II. What does the Holy Spirit Do?

Commonly the working of the Spirit in the hearts of men is recognized in the church. But the objective as over against the subjective role of God's Spirit is a matter sadly neglected today. One of the healthy dimensions of the doctrine of the Holy Spirit found in the Westminster Confession of Faith is its thorough treatment of the objective work of the Spirit. It would do today's church some good to concentrate on the important works of the Spirit outside the soul of man. Perhaps it would help in correcting the imbalanced focus on people's subjective experiences. Consider then the seven different categories of the Spirit's objective work as treated in the Westminster Confession of Faith:

A. The Activities of the Spirit Outside Us

1. The Spirit proceeds from the Father and the Son.

In speaking of this profound subject, a person cannot help but be painfully aware of the limitation of human conceptions concerning the essence of God. Any effort to comprehend the inter-trinitarian relationship can only speak in limited human terminology. Yet Scripture provides some insight into this aspect of the divine essence.

In one sense the essence of a spirit is that it emanates. As the aroma of a perfume naturally moves outward, so the human spirit communicates happiness, worry, joy, excitement. This concept may provide in a limited sense a weak illustration of the fact that the Spirit is "proceeding" from the Father and the Son. The Spirit is not enslaved to the other persons of the trinity. But he processes from the Father and the Son, always himself being in himself all that God is. In this way the Holy Spirit profoundly communicates the essence of God.

Jesus taught his disciples that the Holy Spirit would come from him and from the Father:

"When the Comforter is come, whom *I will send (pempso)* to you *from the Father*, even the Spirit of truth, which *proceeds from the Father (ho para tou patros ekporeuetai)*, he shall bear witness of me" (John 5:26).

In this passage, Jesus is not directly referring to an "eternal procession" of the Spirit. Jesus speaks of the Spirit as being sent by him after he has accomplished redemption. But just as something of the essence of the second person of the Trinity is reflected in his designation as "Son" of God who is "begotten" of the Father, so also something of the essence of the third person of the Trinity is communicated by his designation as the "Spirit" who is "sent" by the Father and the Son. The name Spirit hints at the idea of emanation. His procession from the Son as well as from the Father is suggested by the statement that Jesus will "send" the Holy Spirit (John 16:7). Subsequently, Jesus breathes symbolically on his disciples after his resurrection, declaring "Receive the Holy Spirit" (John 20:22). In other scriptures, the Holy Spirit is related immediately to the Son by several designations. He is called:

'The Spirit of Jesus" (Acts 16:7)
'The Spirit of his Son" (Gal. 4:6)
'The Spirit of Christ" (Rom. 8:9)
'The Spirit of Jesus Christ" (Phil. 1:19)

The Spirit's proceeding from the Father and the Son binds the person and the work of the triune God into an indivisible unity. Where the Father is, there also is the Spirit and the Son; where the Son is at work, there also the Spirit sent by the Father always shall be found. In the context of this unity of the three persons of the godhead the Westminster Confession of Faith speaks of the procession of the Spirit:

In the unity of the Godhead there be three persons, of one substance, power, and eternity; . . . the Holy Ghost eternally proceeding from the Father and the Son. (WCF II, 3).

The Christian church has not been united in its assertion regarding the procession of the Spirit from the Son as well as from the Father. In 1054, the Eastern orthodox church split from the Western church over what has become known as the *filoque* controversy. The Eastern church insisted that the Spirit proceeded from the Father alone, while the Western church held that the Spirit proceeded from the Father "and from the Son" (*filoque*), agreeing with the Council of Toledo (589).

This controversy may appear to be nothing more than a typical example of middle-ages hair splitting over matters inconsequential. But as has been pointed out, " . . . a denial of the *filoque* leads to an unhealthy mysticism."[17] For denying that the Spirit proceeds eternally from the Son as well as from the Father risks undermining the equality of the Son to the Father. Furthermore, denying the eternal procession of the Spirit from the Son may well lead to a minimizing of the significance of the temporal procession of the Spirit from the Son. In any case, failing to recognize the procession of the Son from the Spirit " . . . tends to isolate the work of the Holy Spirit in our lives from the work of Jesus."[18] This view opens the door to the possibility of viewing the work of the Holy Spirit apart from the redemption accomplished by Christ. Gradually communion with the Spirit becomes more significant than the atonement accomplished by Christ. Sanctification then can take on a role disproportionate to justification, personalized communion with the Spirit becomes larger than objective church life, and the inner illumination of the Spirit is treated as though it could occur apart from the Word.

---

[17] Edwin H. Palmer, *The Holy Spirit* (The Presbyterian and Reformed Publishing Company, 1964), p.18. Palmer refers to the fuller treatment of this subject by Abraham Kuyper in his work on the Holy Spirit (see reference below).

[18] Palmer, *Holy Spirit*, p. 18.

If these trends may be traced in the Eastern Orthodox Church over past centuries, they also may be seen in open display throughout the evangelical church today. Modern choruses that play prominent roles in contemporary worship services take little notice of the atoning sacrifice of Christ for condemned sinners, or of Jesus' blood that is our beauty and our righteousness. Exclusive concentration on the working of the Spirit in the soul has virtually excluded an awareness of the fact that the Spirit proceeds in his work only from the sacrificed Son of God.

2.   The Spirit Created and Sustains Life

The opening verses of Scripture attest to the direct involvement of the Spirit of God in the creation of the world. The "hovering" of the Spirit over the nondescript mass of creation gave promise of meaningful life that eventually would emerge (Gen. 1:2). The term used to describe this early activity of the Spirit in relation to creation occurs only one other time in the Old Testament, where it describes an eagle "brooding" over its young in the nest, infusing life by its warmth (Deut. 32:11). The poet John Milton has captured the impact of this imagery in the lines of his *Paradise Lost*:

> His brooding wings the Spirit of God outspread,
> And vital virtue infuse, and vital warmth
> Thruout the fluid mass.[19]

The Spirit joins with the whole of the trinity as the ultimate source of life for every living thing. As the Westminster Confession indicates, God the Father, Son and Holy Spirit in the beginning created all things out of nothing, whether visible or invisible (WCF IV, 1). This creative activity includes the formation of man and the breathing into him the breath of life. As Elihu

---

[19] Cited in Leon Morris, *Spirit of the Living God*, (London: Inter-Varsity Press, 1967), p.19.

testifies to Job:

> The Spirit of God
>   has made me;
> The breath of the Almighty
>   gives me life (Job 33:4).

As the parallelism of this verse indicates, the activity of the Spirit in providing animation extends to the constant sustaining of life as well as to its original creation. The psalmist confirms this same fact when he notes that all creation looks to God for the sustaining of its life, and that apart from the work of the Spirit no living thing can continue:

> When you hide your face,
>   they are terrified;
> when you take away their breath,
>   they die and return to the dust.
> When you send your Spirit,
>   they are created,
>   and you renew the face of the earth (Psa. 104:29, 30).

It would be a healthy thing for Christians to look out onto the vast array of divergent life and see the work of God the Holy Spirit in creating and sustaining all things. Each moment the life-breath of every human being rests on the sustaining work of the Spirit of God. Not merely in the refreshment of the soul, but in the sustaining of life itself, every single person depends on the working of God's Spirit.

3.   The Holy Spirit Inspired the Men who Wrote the Scriptures

The work of the Holy Spirit in the inspiration of the Scriptures is today a truism among evangelical Christians that arouses little debate. The magisterial work of B. B. Warfield on the inspiration of the Bible has stood the test of time in establishing that Scripture was "breathed out" by the Holy Spirit, so that every word is God's word.[20] It is furthermore generally understood that the mode of

---

[20] B.B. Warfield, *The Inspiration and Authority of the Bible*, (Philadelphia: Presbyterian and Reformed Publishing Company).

the Spirit's inspiration was organic in nature, so that the personalities of the writers was a factor in the Spirit's direction. These concepts find classic Scriptural expression in the passages that affirm that "all Scripture is God-breathed" (II Tim. 3:16) and that "holy men of God spoke as they were borne along by the Holy Spirit" (II Pet. 1:21). The Westminster Confession of Faith refers to this vital work of the Spirit by affirming that all the canonical books of the Old and New Testaments were given "by inspiration of God," even though it does not specifically state that this inspiration was the work of the Spirit (WCF I, 2, 4). The evangelical church currently seems to have little difficulty in affirming this aspect of the Spirit's work.

More pointed with respect to current issues is the Confession's negation in this area. To get the full impact, each element of the statement should be emphasized:

> *Nothing*
>> at any time
>>> is to be added
>>>> whether by new revelations of the Spirit,
>>>>> *or traditions of men . . .*

. . . to the completed Scriptures for man's salvation, faith and life (WCF I, 6). The statement could not be made more all-inclusive in its negation. Not a single bit of information ever at any time, can be added to the perfected words inspired by God's Spirit as found in the Scriptures. Not even supposedly new revelations that have come from the Holy Spirit can be allowed to supplement Scripture. This affirmation of the Confession unequivocally supports the *sola Scriptura* principle of the reformation, but often does not find ready acceptance in the modern evangelical church. Yet it is a vital aspect in the understanding of the working of the Spirit across the ages. In most ancient times, God revealed himself to individual patriarchs on varied occasions. Then in the time of Moses God established the office of prophet to serve as the instrument for delivering his word (Deut. 18:15,18). This office continued into the days of Christ and his Apostles. But now the finality of revelation through the Son has brought to perfection the previous process of the Spirit's work. To assert a continuation of the Spirit's activities in revelation would change the character of the present age from one in which all things necessary for life and godliness had been provided to one in which some things still are lacking in the divine leadership of men's lives. That possibility the Confession intends to close off by affirming that there is no longer any valid work of the Spirit in this area.

4. The Holy Spirit Caused the Conception of Jesus

The virgin birth of Christ has been an essential tenet of the Christian faith since the time of its prophecy by Isaiah. But the specific role of the Holy Spirit in his conception may not have been given due attention. Apart from the Spirit's work in forming Jesus in the womb of the virgin Mary there would be no savior. Only by the imposition of the Spirit's working in holiness could the infant Christ be kept from possessing a sinful nature. It was not enough simply that God be his Father to preserve him from all taints of original sin, since a sinful human being was his mother. It took the preserving work of the Holy Spirit to keep Jesus from all defilement.

Without this preservation from sin there could have been no savior. This essential work of the Spirit is brought out in Scripture with the response of the angel to Mary's inquiry:

> The Holy Spirit
>   will come upon you,
> and the power of the Most High
>   will overshadow you.
> So the holy one to be born will be called the Son of God. (Luke 1:35).

The identification of the Holy Spirit with all the power that resides in God is made plain by the parallelism of the passage. The "Holy Spirit" is nothing less than "the power of the Most

High." This personified Power of the Almighty will have the effect of "overshadowing" Mary so that the infant child of the virgin will be "holy," sinless, "the Son of God." Nothing but the Holy Spirit of God could have accomplished this result of a holy child being born of a sinful woman. The erroneous idea of an "immaculate conception" in which Mary herself was kept free of original sin must be rejected as a myth without revelational base; but it does at least give recognition to the problem that had to be overcome by the work of God's Spirit. This reality is worthy of deepest contemplation. Apart from the preserving work of the Holy Spirit in keeping Christ from all sin, he could not have been the Holy One who died substitutionally for others.

The essential role of the Spirit in the accomplishment of the great mystery of the incarnation is developed quite fully by the Westminster Confession of Faith. According to its formulation, the second person of the Trinity, who was of one substance and equal with the Father, took on himself human nature with all its essential properties and common infirmities, yet without sin, "being conceived by the power of the Holy Spirit in the womb of the virgin Mary." As a consequence, "the Godhead and the manhood were inseparably joined together in one person, without conversion, composition, or confusion" (WCF VIII, 2). Apart from the working of the Holy Spirit, this union of God and man is incomprehensible.

5. The Holy Spirit Anointed Jesus for the Fulfillment of His Offices.

Throughout the days of the old covenant, prophets, priests, judges and kings were anointed by the Holy Spirit to enable them to fulfill their commission to serve the Lord. But in all these instances, the anointment of the Spirit had limitations. The Spirit came and went on Samson and Saul (Jdg.13:25; 14:6,19; 16:20; I Sam. 10:10; 11:6; 16:14). The sons of Aaron, the anointed high priest, were consumed in the Lord's anger because they presumed to offer "strange fires" (Lev. 10:1,2). Though David's experience of the Spirit's anointment is contrasted with Saul's, he nonetheless falls into grievous sin against the holiness of the Lord (I Sam. 16:13,13; II Sam. 11:1-4).

But the saving hero of the new covenant was anointed by the Spirit "without measurement" (John 3:34). At his baptism, the Holy Spirit flew downward as a dove from heaven and rested on Jesus, symbolizing the direct descent of the power of God on his chosen servant (Matt. 3:16). This anointing occurred as a fulfillment of the prophesied coming of God's Spirit on the One who was to be king in Israel while at the same time filling the role of the servant of the Lord (Isa. 11:1, 2; 42:1). As the Confession says, he "was sanctified and anointed with the Holy Spirit above measure," and so being holy, harmless and undefiled, he was "thoroughly furnished to execute the office of a Mediator" (WCF VIII 3). By this testimony, it becomes evident that the work of redemption is accomplished only in the unity of the Godhead. The Spirit of God must not be perceived as playing a part in man's salvation only after Christ had completed his work. Instead, he embodied the enabling power by which the Son fulfilled his commission.

It was in the power of this anointing Holy Spirit that Jesus presented his body as a sacrifice unblemished by sin which therefore could remove sin (Heb. 9:14). The presence of the Spirit in the offering of Christ assures the believer that this sacrifice was acceptable to God, and so the conscience of the sinner can be freed to live a life of worshipful service. From the beginning of his ministry at the time of his baptism to the climactic offering of his life-blood in substitution for sinners, the power of the Holy Spirit was at work in him. According to the testimony of the Confession, Christ offered his perfect obedience and sacrifice of himself "through the eternal Spirit" (WCF VIII, 5), and without the Spirit's work his obedience and sacrifice would have been impossible.

6. The Holy Spirit Raised Jesus from the Dead.

As the Spirit of God hovered over the formless abyss at creation, so he brooded over the body of Jesus in the tomb. That tomb was like a nest, and the graveclothes of Jesus like the thin shell of an egg. By the powerful working of the life-creating Spirit, a most radical transformation took place. For "if there is a natural body, there is also a pneumatic body" (I Con 15:44), a body permeated by the Spirit of God. For "through the Spirit of holiness" Jesus "was declared to be the Son of God with power by his resurrection from the dead" (Rom. 1:4). God the Holy Spirit judged Jesus to be innocent of all charges that had been directed against him. The Spirit of holiness therefore vindicated Christ in his innocence by raising him from the dead. The resurrection accomplished by the Spirit involved the creation of a new form of existence never before known, in which the Spirit of God thoroughly permeated the human body, making it possible among other things for Jesus to pass through doors without opening them (John 20:19, 26).

The resurrection of Christ by the power of the Spirit provides the believer with a basis for sure hope of his resurrection. As Paul says, "if the Spirit of him who raised Jesus from the dead is living in you, he who raised Christ from the dead will also give life to your mortal bodies through his Spirit who lives in you" (Rom. 8:11). This Spirit of the resurrection that now lives in the Christian provides a certain hope that he shall experience the same resurrection as Christ.

But we in our resurrection will represent only the beginning of the Spirit's renewing activity. For "the whole creation has been groaning as in the pains of childbirth," waiting for the redemption of our bodies (Rom. 8:22, 23). For with our resurrection will come also the Spirit's work in the restoration of the whole of the earth.

So the Christian of today must not fall into the modern trap of a purely subjective Christianity. The "great men" of the world are not considered first for the impact they have had subjectively within other men. Instead, they are measured by their objective accomplishments as historical figures.

In a similar way, the person of the Holy Spirit must be considered first in terms of the great things he has accomplished across the ages. He is the Creator and Sustainer of all life in the universe. He is the author of Christ's incarnation, the way by which he offered himself as a sinless sacrifice to God. In him is the embodiment of the power that raised Christ from the dead, and by that same power the final transformation of every believer is assured.

It would do the modern evangelical church some good to take time and contemplate the objective work of the Holy Spirit. Then it might be ready to perceive more properly his subjective work.

B. *The Activities of the Holy Spirit Within Us*

The church generally is much more aware of the teaching of Scripture concerning the work of the Holy Spirit within people's lives. But no more thorough and balanced a presentation may be found than that which is developed in the Westminster Confession of Faith. In this respect, a most mature doctrine of the work of the Holy Spirit is unfolded in the Confession. Not only in terms of the Spirit's work in the life of the believer, but in terms of the Spirit's work in the life of the unbeliever as well the teaching of the Confession offers good guidance for the faith of the church.

1. The Holy Spirit works even among hardened unbelievers.

Already it has been indicated that the Holy Spirit works constantly to sustain the life of every living creature. Because he works to maintain all the organs of every human life, men see the testimony of God in the creation around them. Their sense of smell that detects the faint odor coming from the bare earth after a rain, their capacity to hear with the depths of their soul the rhythmic vibrations of a violin string, their sensitivity to the touch of a human hand or a balmy breeze — all these pleasures of human existence derive from the life-sustaining Spirit of God. These activities are included among some of the "common activities of the Spirit" experienced by those who have been passed over and left in their sin as well as by those who have been predestined to eternal life (WCF X, 4).

In addition, those who remain hardened in their sinful condition may nonetheless be "called by the ministry of the Word" through the working of the Holy Spirit (WCF X, 4). Just how far the working of the Spirit goes into the soul of those who reject the gospel must remain a mystery beyond the knowledge of men. But the Scriptures indicate that they may "become partakers of the Holy Spirit" (Heb. 6:4). They may taste the heavenly gift, they may taste the goodness of the word of God, and in some undescribed way they may participate in the reality of the Holy Spirit (Heb. 6:4, 5). This description must serve forever as a warning to the presumptuous who would dare to treat lightly the things of God, though it should not be allowed to terrify those who have experienced more than merely a taste of these realities.

As he comforted his disciples on the night before his departure from this earth, Jesus spoke of this significant work of the Holy Spirit even among the most hardened of sinners. The Spirit of God that he and the Father were about to send would "convict the world of sin, of righteousness and of judgment" (John 16:8). Wherever the disciples would have the boldness to testify of Jesus, the Spirit would do his convicting work. The world at large would be convinced of the reality of sin even as they refused to believe on Jesus. They would accept the presence of righteousness in the world when they heard that Jesus' innocence had been vindicated by God's raising him from the dead. And they would be persuaded that judgment was coming when they learned by the work of the Spirit as the gospel was preached that even the Prince of this world had been brought under judgment in the cross of Jesus

Christ (John 16:8-10). The small band of original disciples must be encouraged by this powerful working of God's Spirit throughout the whole world. Although all men and authorities before whom they testified would not be converted, they would be convicted. The presence of the Holy Spirit in all places and at all times that the gospel is preached guarantees that the power of the truth will not be suppressed no matter how hard men try.

Christians today need this confidence to aid them in their witnessing to a resistant world. Tell people about the unjust sufferings of the innocent Jesus. Repeatedly declared innocent during his trial, he nonetheless suffered the abusive death of a criminal. These facts will convict the world of human sin like nothing else. Tell them about the vindicating resurrection of Christ from the dead, and his glorious ascension to the right hand of God. It will convince them that God is righteous after all. Explain to them that Satan the Prince of this world has been condemned even in his seeming victory over Christ at the cross. The Holy Spirit will convince them that they too will be judged.

This working of the Spirit even among the people of this world without a loyalty to Christ has great importance. To the degree that the present evil age manifests some sanity in its order, it is dependent on the consistent working of God's Holy Spirit.

2. The Holy Spirit works from beginning to end in the life of those who have been chosen by God to be sharers in Christ's redemption.

At least ten different operations of the Holy Spirit may be identified in the life of those who have been claimed by the electing grace of Christ. Each of these works of the Spirit provides comfort and encouragement, confirming a person's eternal election by the grace of the Lord:

(1) The Holy Spirit sovereignly calls and regenerates a person while he still is dead in his trespasses and sins.

The priority of the Holy Spirit in effectively calling and regenerating a person still dead in his trespasses and sins underscores the sovereignty of God in the salvation of sinners. If the new birth occurred as a consequence of faith, or if the only call to sinners came through the general invitation of gospel preaching and the common stirrings in the lives of all sinners by the Holy Spirit, then men rather than God would be making the final determination concerning their salvation. But the Scriptures plainly teach, as the Confession affirms, that the Spirit works uniquely in the souls of some people to draw them to God, persuade them to believe, and recreate a new life within. In a number of ways corresponding to the varied testimony of Scripture on this subject, the Confession upholds the sovereignty of God's Spirit as he effectively brings chosen sinners to eternal salvation, while not working with the same power in the lives of others. These undeserving but favored sinners:

"are effectually called unto faith in Christ by his Spirit working in due season" (WCF III, 6).

[are promised] "his Holy Spirit, to make them willing and able to believe" (WCF VII, 3).

[are effectively persuaded] "by his Spirit to believe and obey" (WCF VIII, 8).

[God is pleased] "effectually to call by his word and Spirit, out of that state of sin and death in which they are by nature, to grace and salvation by Jesus Christ; enlightening their minds spiritually and savingly to understand the things of God; taking away their heart of stone, and giving unto them an heart of flesh; renewing their wills, and by his almighty power determining them to that which is good; and effectually drawing them to Jesus Christ; yet so as they come most freely, being made willing by his grace" (WCF X, 1).

[are] "altogether passive" [in the receiving of God's sovereign call to salvation] "until, being quickened and renewed by the Holy Spirit," [they are] "thereby enabled to answer this call, and to embrace the grace offered and conveyed in it" (WCF X, 2).

In one sense it may be said that this doctrine of the Confession provides the single key for understanding the saving work of God's sovereign Spirit among sinners. How is it to be explained that some men humble themselves before Christ and others do not? On what basis may it be asserted that the initial experience of salvation in regeneration can never be reversed? What can encourage a gospel preacher to carry on with his proclamations despite the stubborn resistance of sinners? The sovereign priority of the divine Holy Spirit in calling and converting the most hardened of sinners provides the answer to all these legitimate questions.

But is the consistent affirmation of the Confession scripturally based? Is it not true that the Scriptures constantly present a picture in which the gospel is offered to all who will receive it? Does not the "whosoever will" of the Scriptures imply a call of God to all men everywhere to come and receive eternal life from the hand of a gracious Christ?

Yes, there is a call that goes out to all men, often accompanied with the working of the Holy Spirit, and the Confession fully affirms that call. Those sinners who have not been chosen of God to experience the grace of eternal life nevertheless "may be called by the ministry of the word, and may have some common operations of the Spirit," even though they will not come to the point of actually calling on the Lord for their salvation (WCF X, 4).

The Scriptural teaching on this subject is extensive, as the biblical references in these sections of the Confession indicate. But the simple words of Jesus in the gospel of John make the point plain enough. Never does Jesus even hint that a person must "born himself again." His teaching indicates that the sinner is just as passive in being born of the Spirit of God as he was when he was born the first time. There is no exception. No one. Not even the most religious can ever see the kingdom of God unless he first has been born again by the sovereign Spirit of God, who works as freely as the wind blows (John 3:3-8). As Jesus said, "No one can come to me unless the Father who sent me draws him" (John 6:44) But this "drawing" of sinners by the Father is not merely a general summoning that effects all people who hear the gospel preached. For as Jesus indicates, those who come to him for salvation are those and only those that the Father has sovereignly "given" to Him (John 6:37).

This perspective on the initial working of the Holy Spirit in the soul of chosen sinners has great usefulness to the church. Let no man despair of his salvation, for the other side of the Holy Spirit's "drawing" men to Jesus is the fact that any person who comes to him must have been drawn by the Spirit and so shall be received by Christ (John 6:37). Let no evangelist become discouraged because of the apparent sparseness of response to his proclamation of the gospel.

For in his appointed time the sovereign Spirit will effectively call and regenerate whoever he wishes.

  (2) The Holy Spirit confirms the authority of Scripture as the word of God in the heart of the believer.

From the point of his entry into the kingdom of God through rebirth by the Spirit, the believer needs guidance from God concerning what he is to believe and how he is to live. In the midst of the many voices contending for his attention, one calm word keeps speaking to his soul. It is the Holy Spirit "bearing witness by and with the word in our hearts" (WCF I, 5). The Holy Spirit never speaks without the word, and the word never speaks without the Holy Spirit. Although the Bible is a most impressive book in and of itself, "our full persuasion and assurance" of its "infallible truth, and divine authority" rests on the confirming testimony of the Holy Spirit, its divine author (WCF 1, 5).

Jesus anticipated the Spirit's work when he explained to his disciples that the Holy Spirit would guide them into all truth (John 16:13). He was not concerned about the many things he still needed to teach them, because he had the confidence that "the Spirit will take from what is mine and make it known to you" (John 16:15). While this description of the Spirit's activity refers in the first place to his work of inspiration, it also anticipates his work in confirming the Lord's truth in the hearts of his disciples throughout the ages.

(3) The Holy Spirit illumines the Scriptures for the individual believer and for the church as a whole.

The will of God has been recorded plainly in the Scriptures for all men to see and examine. But even the regenerated soul has difficulty grasping the most basic truths in the word of God because of the remnants of sin that constantly cloud his mind and heart. It is not without good reason that the Confession balances its denial of any further revelations through the Spirit by affirming:

> "Nevertheless, we acknowledge the inward illumination of the Spirit of God to be necessary for the saving and understanding of such things as are revealed in the word" (WCF I, 6).

As Paul indicates, no one can know the mind of a man except as the spirit of the man wills to reveal himself. In the same way, "no one knows the thoughts of God except the Spirit of God." But we have the assurance that we have received the Spirit who is from God "that we may understand what God has freely given us" (I Cor. 2:11,12). What a privilege it is for the believer to have the Holy Spirit as his companion, who continually reveals to him wondrous things new and old out of the treasury of God's word.

(4) The Holy Spirit works in the life of the believer to grant him the assurance of his salvation.

The testimony of Paul is quite clear about the role of the Holy Spirit in assuring the believer of his salvation, and the Confession only echoes the teaching of the Apostle. The Spirit has a distinctive role among the persons of the Trinity by serving as the divine seal in the soul of the saved, for He is the "deposit guaranteeing our inheritance" (Eph. 1:13, 14). The Spirit of God himself "testifies with our spirit that we are the sons of God," since he is the "Spirit of adoption" that enables us to cry "Abba, Father" (Rom. 8:15,16). According to the Confession, the believer's assurance of his salvation is not based on a "bare conjecture," but among other things on "the testimony of the Spirit of adoption witnessing with our spirits that we are the children of God" (WCF XVIII, 2). In this connection, the Spirit is identified as the "earnest of our inheritance" by which the believer is "sealed to the day of redemption" (WCF XVIII, 2).

The Westminster Confession of Faith has developed this doctrine of assurance and the process by which it may be gained, lost and regained in its own distinctive way. The Confession clearly affirms that salvation may not be lost. But it is equally clear in stating that the "infallible assurance" of salvation may be gained, diminished, lost and regained. "Enabled by the Spirit," the believer may know for certain the things given to him by God. His heart "may be enlarged in peace and joy in the Holy Ghost." Some circumstances such as a "special sin" may grieve the Holy Spirit resulting in a shaking of the believer's assurance. Yet "by the operation of the Spirit, this assurance may in due time be revived." In the meantime, the Spirit continues to work so that the believer is "supported from utter despair" (WCF XVIII, 3, 4).

It would be difficult to discover a more balanced treatment of the question of the believer's assurance of salvation. While giving all encouragement and hope, it guards against the abuses of presumption that so regularly plague the modern church scene.

(5) The Holy Spirit guarantees the perseverance of the saints until the end.

No comfort could be gained from a doctrine of perseverance to the end that depended on the determination of a person's own free will. For the fickleness of the human will is known too well.

Instead, perseverance hinges on the saving work of the sovereign God. Among other workings, "the abiding of the Spirit" serves to guarantee that the believer will continue trusting until the end (WCF XVII, 2). Indeed, the believer may grieve the Holy Spirit by different acts of disobedience (Eph. 4:30; cf. WCF XVII, 3). But the effective work of the Spirit in calling and sanctifying the believer guarantees that he "shall certainly persevere" until the end, and be "eternally saved" (Phil.1:6; cf. WCF XVII, 1).

Even at this point in the present discussion, it should have become apparent that the work of the Holy Spirit in the life of the believer stretches from the beginning to the end. Starting with effectual calling and regeneration, the Spirit works steadily until the believer has come to the point of his perfection in glory.

(6) The Holy Spirit applies and seals to the believer all the various benefits of his redemption.

From eternity past God determined to justify all those who were chosen in Christ and at his crucifixion Jesus suffered the penalty these sinners deserved for their violation of God's law. But none among sinners actually are declared righteous "until the Holy Spirit doth in due time actually apply Christ unto them" (WCF XI, 4). In a similar way, the full benefits of union with Christ come to the believer only as he is "united to Jesus Christ . . . by his Spirit" (WCF XXVI, 1). True fellowship in the body of believers hinges on the mutual work of the Spirit in binding all members of Christ's body to one another as they are united to Him. Still further, the saving grace that is available to the believer in the sacraments of baptism and the Lord's supper does not come through any power inherent in the sacraments themselves. Instead, grace is conferred through the sacraments only by "the work of the Spirit and the word of institution" (WCF XXVII, 3). Though the effectiveness of baptism is not inseparably tied to the moment of its administration, yet the grace symbolized by the sacrament is "not only offered" but "really exhibited and conferred by the Holy Ghost" to those to whom that grace properly belongs (WCF XXVIII, 6).

So life in the body of the church depends always on the constant working of God's Holy Spirit. This aspect of the blessing of God must not be forgotten. Since the Spirit of God is holy, God's people constantly must remain in unbroken union with Him if they are to experience the benefits of the body. This consideration leads to the next vital work of the Spirit of God.

(7) The Holy Spirit sanctifies the church of Christ.

It would appear obvious that the work of sanctification distinctly belongs to the Holy Spirit of God. Since man even in his regenerated state still has within himself strong remnants of sin, a powerful force originating from without but working within must accomplish sanctification. The Holy Spirit supplies that power in two ways: by permeating and by purifying.

"Be being filled with the Spirit" is the admonition of Paul to the church at Ephesus (Eph. 5:18). "One baptism, many fillings" appropriately summarizes the Scriptural perspective on the believer's experience of the sanctifying work of the Holy Spirit. This "being filled with the Spirit" in contrast with being "drunk with wine" suggests the idea of permeation. Even as alcohol enters the bloodstream and affects every part of the person's being, so the Spirit of God must permeate the believer's life. Rather than simply creating an emotional "high," this permeation by the Spirit powerfully influences the life of the believer in practical ways, as the immediately succeeding verses of this Scripture indicate. A string of dependent participles elaborates on the effect of being filled with the Spirit. The Spirit will affect the person's speech so that he will praise God among the brothers (Eph. 5:19a). The Spirit will lead a person to sing hymns of praise in his heart to the Lord (v. 19b). The Spirit will enable him to give thanks to God in everything (v. 20). The Spirit will lead a person to submit his will to others in maintaining an order that will glorify the Lord (v. 21).

This last-mentioned effect of sanctification receives extensive elaboration by the Apostle, showing just how practical is the effect of a person's being "filled" with the Spirit. Wives will submit to their husbands as to the Lord, and husbands will love their wives as Christ loved the church (Eph. 5:22-33); children will submit to their parents (Eph. 6:1-4); and servants will submit to their masters (Eph. 6:59).[21] Far from promoting a concept of heightened emotionalism as the effect of the Spirit's filling a person's life, this Scripture underscores the down-to-earth practicality of the Spirit's work.

This same perspective is found in the affirmations of the Confession on this subject. The sanctifying Spirit applies the benefits of redemption to elect sinners by "effectually persuading them by his Spirit to believe and obey," and by "governing their hearts by his word and Spirit" (WCF VIII, 8). The "Spirit of Christ" so permeates the will of the regenerated saint that he "freely and cheerfully" does all that "the will of God revealed in the law requires to be done" (WCF IX, 7). The new covenant saint now has the blessing of "fuller communications of the free Spirit of God" as a consequence of his greater liberty in Christ (WCF XX, 1). His worship is directed to none other than the triune God, Father, Son and Holy Spirit, and to him alone (WCF XXI, 2); and it is "by the help of his Spirit" that prayer is made (WCF XXI, 3). In perceiving the extent of the Spirit's work of sanctification, the believer should be greatly encouraged despite the many failures in piety of which he is so painfully conscious.

This permeation of the Spirit must result in an ever-increased holiness in the life of the believer. Though the struggle with sin may be fierce, growth in a more righteous walk must be the result.

---

[21] The idea of mutual submission between husband and wife runs totally counter to the further development of the concept of submission in this passage. It hardly could be supposed that parents are to "submit" to the authority of their children and masters to the authority of their servants.

As the Confession states, those who have been regenerated "are further sanctified really and personally . . . by his word and Spirit dwelling in them" (WCF XIII, 1). Because of the remnants of corruption in every part of a man, there is "a continual and irreconcilable war; the flesh lusting against the Spirit and the Spirit against the flesh" (WCF XIII, 2). Yet "through the continual supply of strength from the sanctifying Spirit of Christ," the saints will grow in grace perfecting holiness in the fear of God (XIII, 3).

Where else can the saint that is constantly bantered by the world, the flesh and the devil look other than to the Holy Spirit of God for true progress in his sanctification? His own "arm of flesh" will fail him. The church and its ministries, though clearly appointed by Christ, display their weaknesses on every hand. But the indwelling Spirit of God, the same all-powerful Spirit that raised Jesus from the dead, can defeat the strongest temptations and accomplish the greatest victories in the struggle with indwelling sin. In the ministry of the Spirit the saint of God can be confident. Since he is "being led by the Spirit of God" into an ever greater holiness, he can be confident that he is a "son of God" (Rom. 8:14).[22]

(8) The Holy Spirit enables the believer to bear the fruit of saving graces and good works

Although Paul in Galatians 5 enumerates nine different products of the Spirit in the soul of the believer, he designates them

---

[22] The sermon of B. B. Warfield on this passage is well worth noting. Contrary to popular impressions, this text does not speak of being "led" of the Spirit into a revelational knowledge of God's hidden will for the life of the individual. Instead, the passage clearly speaks of being "led" into a life of holiness. As the immediately preceding verse indicates, "If by the Spirit you put to death the misdeeds of the body, you will live." Cf. B.B. Warfield, "The Leading of the Spirit" in *Biblical and Theological Studies*, (Philadelphia: Presbyterian and Reformed Publishing Company, 1968), pp.543-559.

singularly as the "fruit" of the Spirit (Gal. 5:22-23). The "acts" of the sinful nature are multiple, and include disorders such as sexual immorality, fits of rage, selfish ambition and envy (Gal. 5:19-21). A particular sinner may be guilty of any number of these transgressions of God's law. But the person in whom the Spirit of God is at work will bear the entirety of the "fruit of the Spirit," since this fruit is singular in number. The believer may be encouraged that the fruit of love, joy and peace, to name only three aspects of the Spirit's by-product in a person's life all shall be his.

The Westminster Confession of Faith makes it plain that even the initial faith by which "the elect are enabled to believe to the saving of their souls," is "the work of the Spirit of Christ in their hearts" (WCF XIV, 1). In addition, any ability that believers possess to perform good works "is not at all of themselves, but wholly from the Spirit of Christ." As a matter of fact, the performance of any particular good work is wholly dependent on "an actual influence of the same Holy Spirit to work in them to will and to do of his good pleasure" (WCF XVI, 3). To the extent that any works of man are good, "they proceed from his Spirit; and as they are wrought by us, they are defiled and mixed with so much weakness and imperfection, that they cannot endure the severity of God's judgment" (WCF XVI, 5). Yet the believer is warned against waiting for some "special motion of the Spirit" before he attempts to perform his various duties (WCF XVI, 3).

This absolute dependence on the constant working of the Holy Spirit should have a salutary effect on the outlook of each person who trusts in Christ for his salvation. On the one hand, he should be encouraged to suppress any hints of pride within himself, since every good work that he performs comes immediately from the influence of God's Holy Spirit. On the other hand, he should be encouraged in his efforts to do good service in the kingdom of Christ. For no matter how weak or limited he may feel in terms of his own abilities, he may be confident of the powerful work of the Spirit within him.

> (9) The Holy Spirit provides gifts by which the whole body of Christ is strengthened and edified.

If there is any area of the person and work of the Holy Spirit where the Westminster Confession of Faith may be regarded as deficient, it would be at this particular point. Yet interestingly the chapter on the Holy Spirit added to the Westminster Confession of Faith by American Presbyterianism in the first half of the twentieth century says very little about the gifts of the Spirit. It simply states that the Holy Spirit "calls and anoints ministers for their holy office, qualifies all other officers in the Church for their special work, and imparts various gifts and graces to its members."[23] This statement hardly says anything that would resolve questions being raised in the church today relating to the special gifts of the Spirit. It would appear that the formulation of this statement preceded the invasion into mainline American presbyterianism of issues regarding the charismatic gifts of tongues and prophecy.

How is the absence of an extensive treatment of the subject of the gifts of the Spirit in the original Westminster Confession of Faith to be understood? It could be suggested that the issue of the Spirit's gifts was not a live one at the time of the Assembly. But another consideration may be the fact that the Assembly felt it had dealt sufficiently with this issue in its Directory for the Public Worship of God and the Form of Presbyterial Church-Government, as well as in the statement of the opening chapter of the Westminster Confession concerning the cessation of revelational gifts.

In its Directory for Public Worship, which was completed

---

[23] *Minutes of the Eighty-second General Assembly of the Presbyterian Church in the United States*, (Austin: von Boechmann-Jones, 1942), p.68.

two years before the Confession of Faith, the Assembly began by noting the negative effect of the Church of England's Book of Common Prayer on the exercise of the "gift of prayer, with which our Lord Jesus Christ pleaseth to furnish all his servants whom he calls" to the office of the ministry.[24] The document proceeds to develop the significance of the reading of the Scriptures in public worship, recommending that at least one chapter of each testament be read at every meeting. This reading was to be done by a person ordained to the gospel ministry, preceded by appropriate prayer. The Directory offers suggestions spilling over five pages for this prayer that is to anticipate the solemn reading of the Word of God.[25]

In its treatment of the subject of preaching, the Directory for Worship notes that the minister of Christ must be "in some good measure gifted for so weighty a service," including skill in the original languages, knowledge of the whole body of theology, and "the illumination of God's Spirit" as well as "other gifts of edification."[26] A recognition is made of "different gifts" which may exist among ministers within the same church, and these gifts are categorized in terms of "doctrine or exhortation."[27]

In the Form of Presbyterial Church-Government, which was the first order of business to be addressed in the Westminster Assembly, opening statements make plain the distinction between the "ordinary and perpetual" offices in the church and the

---

[24] *The Directory for the Publick Worship of God Agreed upon by the Assembly of Divines at Westminster with the Assistance of Commissioners from the Church of Scotland (February 1645) as published in The Subordinate Standards and Other Authoritative Documents of the Free Church of Scotland*, (Edinburgh: William Blackwood & Sons Ltd, 1973), p.136.

[25] *Directory*, 1973, pp.139-144.

[26] *Directory*, 1973, p.144.

[27] *Directory*, 1973, p. 148. The context discussing these gifts makes it evident that the special charismatic "gifts" are not in view in these passages.

"extraordinary . . . which are ceased". The "extraordinary" offices "which are ceased" are identified as apostles, evangelists, and prophets. The "ordinary and perpetual" offices are "pastors, teachers, and other church-governors, and deacons."[28] It would seem clear from this distinction that the Westminster Assembly had determined at its earliest stage to register its opinion that the foundational offices by which revelation was brought to the church no longer were functional in the church's life. This understanding is supported by the first chapter of the Westminster Confession of Faith, where it is stated that Scripture provides to men "the whole counsel of God . . . unto which nothing at any time is to be added, whether by new revelations of the Spirit, or traditions of men."[29]

It might be wished that the Westminster divines had been more specific in dealing with issues related to the validity of gifts of "prophecy" and "tongues" as the issue confronts the church today. But in order to do so, they would have had to exercise the gift of "prophecy" themselves in foreseeing the current state of the church, which, according to their own theology, they could not be expected to do.

But the lines of continuity with their thinking that would address the current scene are easily drawn. The "extraordinary" gift of prophecy continues in the church no longer, since all new revelations of the Spirit have ceased. if, as Peter indicated on the day of Pentecost, "tongues" is an exercise of the prophetic gift, then this gift also must be classified among the "extraordinary" operations of the Spirit associated with the founding of the church that no longer function today (cf Acts 2:16, 17).

It is understandable that the fathers of Westminster centered their attention on the centrality of the gift of prayer and on the

---

[28] *Form of Government* p.172. This document was adopted in 1645, four years before the completion of the Westminster Confession of Faith.

[29] Westminster Confession of Faith, I, 6.

significance of the reading of the Scriptures in a language understandable by the people. In addition, the preaching of the Word had to be established as the primary gift of the Spirit that would infuse new life into their churches. On these matters the rebirth and the continuation of the church hinged.

It may well be that the situation is not much different today. In the present church scene, prayer often sinks to the level of a mundane repetition of trite phrases. Hardly ever is a complete chapter of Scripture read, and nowhere can a plan be found for the reading of the whole of the Word of God publicly in worship before the people. In place of consistent exposition of the Scriptures too often drama, dance, a movie or other inventions of the human imagination are substituted. It may be that a revitalization of the church at worship is needed. But new life hardly can be expected to come when devices not designed by the Spirit are employed. The church today would do well to be instructed once more in the doctrine of the Spirit's gifts as found in the Westminster Confession of Faith, despite the abbreviated character of its expressions.

> (10)　　The Holy Spirit resurrects the body of believers, just as he brought Christ from the dead.

The statement of this truth by the Westminster Confession of Faith is simple but profound. The bodies of the just shall be raised "by his Spirit, unto honour, and be made conformable to his own glorious body" (WCF XXXII, 3). This affirmation rests on the hope presented by the Apostle Paul:

> And if the Spirit of him who raised Jesus from the dead is living in you, he who raised Christ from the dead will also give life to your mortal bodies through his Spirit, who lives in you (Rom 8:11).

It is indeed a glorious hope, and one that should live constantly within the heart of every believer. Since this powerful Spirit of the resurrection already has taken up residence in our hearts, we should live every day with the reality of this eternal expectation. The Holy Spirit's transformation of our vile bodies will mark the inevitable climax of his work throughout the ages in perfecting the saints of God in body and in soul.

Conclusion

So it may be concluded that the Westminster Confession of Faith contains a very full doctrine of the person and work of the Holy Spirit. This fuller teaching on the Spirit is a doctrine much needed in the church today. As B.B. Warfield has said:

> Wherever men are busying themselves with holy and happy meditations on the Holy Ghost and His work, it is safe to say the foundations of a true spiritual life are laid, and the structure of a rich spiritual life is rising.[30]

A rich deposit of holy and happy meditations on the Holy Spirit may be found in the Westminster Confession of Faith. Rather than being found deficient, development of the doctrine of the Holy Spirit reflects the nature of the scripture's teaching on the subject by integrating the person and work of the Spirit to the whole of God's eternal purposes as they have been expressed in creation and throughout redemption.

But what about the lingering charge that the Confession deals inadequately with the matter of the "gifts" of the Spirit?

In response, it should be noted that if this issue were to be treated further, it could be considered exactly along the guidelines already provided by the Westminster divines in their distinction between the "extraordinary" offices and gifts that have ceased operating in the life of the church today, and the "ordinary and perpetual" gifts and offices that continue to function.

In one sense it might be said that no greater need may be found in the church today than a clear exclusion of pretensions of continuing gifts of prophetic utterances that contradict the teaching of the Confession. Just one demonstration of the ill effects brought about by a wrong perception of this issue may be illustrated by a

---

[30] Warfield, "Introductory Note," p. xxxix.

missionary's letter describing the tragic disruption of the fruit of many years of hard ministerial labor in a difficult field. In this case, a vital church had been built in a country dominated by the Roman Catholic church. A native-speaking pastor had been installed, who went away for further study. He returned with the conviction that the Lord had revealed to him that the church would grow to over a thousand members, but only if the officers and people submitted to the instructions he had received in his vision. In the following weeks, the church was splintered, the native-speaking pastor estranged from his governing ecclesiastical body, and the sheep of Christ scattered. Years of work invested by the missionary came to a tragic conclusion — and all in the name of new prophetic revelations of the Spirit.

It would be a great blessing to the church if it could come to appreciate afresh the full and balanced perspective of the Westminster Confession of Faith in its teaching on the person and work of the Holy Spirit. God would receive the glory he deserves, and men would be encouraged to a humbler walk with the only source of their creative and redemptive life.

Theology of the Larger Catechism

Morton H. Smith

Introduction:

The Westminster Assembly was called by the English Parliament to consult and advise it regarding such a Church government "as may be most agreeable to God's holy word and most apt to procure and preserve the peace of the Church at home, and nearer agreement with the Church of Scotland, and other Reformed Churches abroad."[1] A secondary purpose was "to vindicate and clear the doctrine of the Church of England from all false calumnies and aspersions." Though doctrine was not the intended purpose of the Assembly as it was first gathered, all would agree that it was in this area that it made its most significant contribution through the production of the Westminster Confession and *Catechism*. These documents have been adopted by Presbyterian Churches throughout the world as the confession of their faith.

After some three years of labor the Assembly completed the Confession with scriptural proofs which was presented to the House of Commons on April 29, 1647. Though it had worked on

---

[1] As cited by B.B. Warfield, *The Westminster Assembly and Its Work*, (New York: Oxford University Press, 1931), p. 3.

a catechism earlier, this work was abandoned, but a fresh start was made, under the mandate of Parliament, toward producing a single catechism. This attempt also failed, for it appeared to them to be an impossible task. The Scottish commissioners wrote to their General Assembly saying that the divines were attempting "to dress up milk and meat both in one dish."[2] The Assembly then called a halt and "recommitted the work that two formes of Catechisme may be prepared, one more exact and comprehensive, another more easie and short for new beginners."[3] The result was that the Assembly produced both the Larger and the *Shorter Catechism*s. They worked on the *Larger Catechism* from April 15, 1647 through October 15, 1947. The scripture proofs for both catechisms were presented to Parliament April 14, 1648. Though the *Shorter Catechism* was approved by Parliament, the *Larger Catechism* received only the approval of the House of Commons. It was never approved by the House of Lords. In Scotland both catechisms were approved by the General Assembly of 1648, and ratified by the Estates of Parliament, February 7, 1649. Warfield comments, "In the later history of the Westminster formularies, the '*Larger Catechism*' has taken a somewhat secondary place; but no product of the Divines has been more widely diffused or has exercised a deeper influence than their '*Shorter Catechism*.'"[4] He goes on to treat the primary source of the catechisms. He summarized the background of the *Larger Catechism* as follows: "The doctrinal portion of the '*Larger Catechism*' is very much a catechetical recension of the Assembly's *Confession of Faith*; while in its ethical portion (its exposition of the Ten Commandments) it seems to derive most from Ussher's 'Body of Divinity' and Nicholl's and Ball's 'Catechisms'; and in its

---

[2] As recorded by B.B. Warfield, *The Westminster Assembly and Its Work*, p. 63.

[3] *Ibid.*

[4] *Ibid.*, p. 64.

exposition of the Lord's Prayer to go back ultimately through intermediary manuals to William Perkins' treatise on the Lord's Prayer.[5]

I. The Structure of the Larger Catechism

If one examines a harmony of the Westminster Standards in which the corresponding sections of the *Confession* and *Shorter Catechism* are compared with the *Larger Catechism*, some of the differences between these three documents become obvious.[6] There are some places where the *Confession* alone speaks at some length, and both of the catechisms are very brief. Examples of this are found in connection with the doctrine of Scripture and the decrees of God. There are some doctrines that are treated only in the *Confession*, such as Good Works, Christian Liberty, Lawful Oaths and Vows, the Civil Magistrate, Marriage and Divorce, Church Censures, Synods and Councils. On the other hand, the catechisms treat some subjects that the *Confession* does not. For example, both catechisms expound the Ten Commandments and the Lord's Prayer, neither of which are found in the *Confession*. Some of the most significant differences are to be found in the passages where the catechisms, particularly the *Larger Catechism*, expand on the doctrines found in the *Confession*. Among the most significant of these are found in the sections on Christology, Sanctification and the Sacraments, particularly, the Lord's supper. The effort shall be made in this essay to note the overall doctrinal teaching of the *Larger Catechism*, and, specifically to consider the most significant distinctives of this document.

---

[5] *Ibid.*, p. 65.

[6] See the author's *Harmony of the Westminster Confession and Catechism*, (Greenville: Greenville Seminary Press, 1991).

II. General Doctrinal Teaching of the Catechism

A. The Doctrine of Scripture

The *Larger Catechism* opens its presentation of the doctrine of Scripture with a simple statement to the effect that the light of nature both in man and in the works of God declare that there is a God, but that only the Scripture and the Spirit sufficiently and effectually reveal God to men for their salvation.[7] It then defines the Word of God as the Scriptures of the Old and New Testaments. This word is the only rule of faith and life.[8] Here we find a brief affirmation regarding the doctrine of general revelation to the effect that it simply declares that there is a God. The *Catechism* does not enter further into this subject. General revelation is sufficient for the purpose of pointing to the existence of God, but it does not tell us how sinners may approach God for forgiveness. This information is found only in special revelation—the Scriptures of the Old and New Testaments. The Scripture is declared to be the word of God, and thus to be the only infallible rule of faith and practice.

B. The Doctrine of God

In its treatment of the nature of the Godhead, the *Larger Catechism* stands between the two comprehensive paragraphs of the *Confession* and the concise answer of the *Shorter Catechism*. In its definition of God, it summarizes the *Confession*, bringing out that God exists in and of himself, and that he is all-sufficient in all his attributes. Under the section on the Trinity the *Larger Catechism* expands on the personal properties of each of the Persons of the Godhead. It also lists evidences of the fact that the Bible teaches the equality of the Son and the Holy Ghost with the

---

[7] Q&A 2.

[8] Q&A 3.

Father. In these amplifications there is no addition to the doctrine of the *Confession* and *Shorter Catechism*, but simply a further clarification.

C. The Decrees of God

The *Larger Catechism* goes beyond the *Shorter* in speaking explicitly on the doctrines of election and reprobation of both men and angels. It is fully in accord with the *Confession*, though much briefer on this subject.

D. Of Creation

The *Larger Catechism* adds a specific question on the creation of angels that is not covered in either the *Confession* or the *Shorter Catechism*. Otherwise it is in full harmony with them.

E. Of Providence

The *Larger Catechism* continues its interest in angels in teaching on providence. In particular, it deals with the fall of the angels, which is limited and ordered to the glory of God. The elect angels are also treated briefly as established in holiness and happiness and employed by God in the administrations of his power, mercy and justice.

F. Of the Fall of Man and Sin

The *Larger Catechism* introduces the term "publick person" to describe the relation of Adam to his posterity. Theologians designate this as federal headship. The *Confession* lays the stress on the natural relation that Adam and Eve had as "the root of all mankind." The *Larger Catechism* also stresses the natural relationship with the phrase, "all mankind descending from him by ordinary generation, " which, of course, excludes Christ. The

Larger and the *Shorter Catechism* expand on what is included under the term "original sin." It is first, the guilt of Adam's first sin, second, the "want of original righteousness, " and third, the corruption of his whole nature.

The *Larger Catechism* has a particular question on how original sin is conveyed from our first parents unto their posterity. The answer is that it is passed through natural generation.

Under its treatment of the misery of the estate of sin, the *Larger Catechism* speaks particularly of the punishment of sins in this world and in the world to come.

G. Of God's Covenant with Man

Both of the Catechisms use the term "covenant of life" to describe the Adamic covenant, in contrast to the Confession, which calls it the "covenant of works." The *Larger Catechism* contrasts the Covenant of Works and the Covenant of Grace, thus it uses both terms. It also lists the creation ordinances: namely, Adam's task to tend the garden, putting the creatures under his dominion, ordaining marriage, instituting the Sabbath, as well as the probation of the Covenant of Works.

The *Larger Catechism* specifies that the covenant of grace is made with Christ as the second Adam, and in him with all the elect as his seed. It then describes how grace is manifested in the covenant of grace. Next in the catechism the different adminstrations of the covenant of grace are considered under the Old and New Testaments, which parallels the *Confession of Faith*.

H. Of Christ the Mediator

The three Standards treat Christ as the Mediator of the covenant of grace, both in his person and his work. The *Larger Catechism* expands on the reason why the Messiah must be divine, human, and both in one person.

The *Larger Catechism* closely parallels the *Shorter* in its treatment of the three offices of the Redeemer. It enlarges on the various stages of the humiliation and exaltation of Christ. Of particular interest is question 50 which defines the humiliation after his death. "Christ's humiliation after his death, consisted in his being buried, and continuing in the state of the dead, and under the power of death till the third day; which hath been otherwise expressed in these words, He descended into hell." This understanding of the phrase "He descended into hell" is in accord with the history of the phrase in the Creed. It differs, however, from the position of the *Heidelberg Catechism*, which says, "That in my greatest temptations, I may be assured, and wholly comfort myself in this, that my Lord Jesus Christ, by his inexpressible anguish, pains, terrors and hellish agonies, in which he was plunged during all his sufferings, but especially on the cross, hath delivered me from the anguish and torment of hell."

In answer to the question of how Christ was exalted in his resurrection, the *Larger Catechism* not only lists the event of the resurrection, it describes something of its nature. It then lists the effect of the resurrection in that it declared him to be the Son of God, to have satisfied divine justice, to have vanquished death and him that had the power of it, and to be Lord of the quick and the dead. It is added that he did all of this as a public person, namely as head of the church, for their justification, quickening in grace, support against enemies, and to assure them of their resurrection from the dead at the last day.

The *Catechism* then asks a series of four questions speaking of the exaltation of Christ in his ascension, his session at the right hand of God, his intercession, and in his coming again to judge the world. The *Larger Catechism* thus adds material on each of these subjects that is not found in either the *Confession* or the *Shorter Catechism*.

I. Of Effectual Calling

As the *Larger Catechism* treats the application of salvation to mankind, it adds a particular question defining the union which the elect have with Christ. "The union which the elect have with Christ is the work of God's grace, whereby they are spiritually and mystically, yet really and inseparably, joined to Christ as their head and husband; which is done in their effectual calling." The *Larger Catechism* in this section stresses the fact that the redemption is applied only to those for whom Christ died, which it elsewhere calls "the elect." "All elect, and they only, are effectually called. . . ." (Q. 68).

J. Of Justification

The *Larger Catechism*, in addition to defining justification in parallel with the *Confession* and *Shorter Catechism* gives a definition of justifying faith in question 72. It speaks of the three aspects of faith, namely, knowledge, assent and trust. "Justifying faith is a saving grace, wrought in the heart of a sinner by the Spirit and Word of God; whereby he, being convinced of his sin and misery, and of the disability in himself and all other creatures to recover him out of his lost condition, not only assenteth to the truth of the promise of the gospel, but receiveth and resteth upon Christ and his righteousness, therein held forth, for pardon of sin, and for the accepting and accounting of his person righteous in the sight of God for salvation." In the next question the *Catechism* elaborates on how faith justifies the sinner. It concludes that faith is only "an instrument by which he receiveth and applieth Christ and his righteousness."

K. Of Adoption

The *Larger Catechism* does not add anything to the teaching of the *Confession* and *Shorter Catechism* on Adoption.

L. Of Sanctification

On the subject of sanctification, the *Larger Catechism* in parallel with the *Confession* and *Shorter Catechism* defines sanctification as based upon the decree of God and the result of the powerful operation of the Spirit. It speaks of the whole man as being renewed after the image of God, which is not found in the other Standards. It also speaks of the seeds of repentance unto life, and all other graces as being put into the hearts of the elect, and these graces are strengthened so that they are enabled more and more to die to sin and to rise unto newness of life.

The *Catechism* explains on why there is imperfection of sanctification in believers as being the result of remnants of sin remaining in every part of them. The Christian life is portrayed as one of conflict between sin and the spirit.

Particularly helpful is question 77 which spells out how justification and sanctification differ. A proper understanding of these differences would save much theological confusion. Rome confused these two doctrines, and all too often Protestants also fail to understand the differences. The two doctrines are inseparably joined, but they are not to be confused.

Justification	Sanctification
by imputed righteousness of Christ,	the Spirit infuseth grace and enableth to the exercise thereof,
sin is pardoned,	sin is subdued,
equally frees all believers from wrath of God, and that perfectly in this life,	not equal in all, or in this life perfect in any,
never to fall into condemnation	but growing to perfection.

M. Of Saving Faith

As already noted, the *Larger Catechism* gives a more expanded definition of justifying faith than is found in either the *Confession* or *Shorter Catechism*. It distinguishes between the intellectual and the volitional aspects of faith. Emphasis is laid upon that though other graces accompany saving faith, and good works are the fruits of it, these are not the ground of justification. Nor is the grace of faith itself imputed to the believer for justification. Faith is but the instrument by which justification is received.

N. Of Repentance unto Life

The *Larger Catechism* in its treatment of repentance unto life closely parallels the first two paragraphs of the *Confession* on this subject.

O. Of the Perserverance of the Saints

The *Larger Catechism* states the doctrine of the perseverance of the saints in parallel with that of the *Confession*.

P. Of Assurance of Grace and Salvation

Again the *Larger Catechism* closely parallels the *Confession* in its statement of the Assurance of Grace and Salvation.

Q. Of the Law of God

The Larger *Catechism* has a number of distinctive statements under the section on the Law of God. The first is to identify the moral law as the rule of obedience given to Adam and to all mankind in him in the estate of innocence. This moral law 'is the declaration of the will of God to mankind, directing and binding everyone to personal, perfect and perpetual conformity and obedience thereunto, in the frame and disposition of the whole man, soul and body.

The *Catechism* has four questions that go beyond both the *Confession* or *Shorter Catechism* in treating the use of the moral law to man since the fall, to all men, unregenerate, and regenerate. The law informs all men of the holy nature and will of God. It also convinces them of their inability to keep it, and of their inherent sinful nature. It is suited to humble man and to help him see his need of Christ and the perfection of his obedience to the Law. For the unregenerate the law awakens their conscience to flee from the wrath to come, and thus to draw them to Christ. If they remain in the way of sin, then the Law serves to leave them inexcusable and under its curse.

For the regenerate, the Law reminds them of their obligation to Christ for having fulfilled it for them, and enduring the curse of the broken Law for them. It also directs them in the way of greater obedience to Him as their rule of obedience.

One of the most useful questions of the *Larger Catechism* is question 99, which gives eight rules for the right understanding of the ten commandments. These eight rules are based upon the way in which the Bible itself interprets the Law. They are most helpful to the proper understanding of how the two Catechisms interpret the law in the detail that they do.

The *Larger Catechism* expands on each of the commandments beyond that of the *Shorter Catechism*, but this does not represent any divergence in its teaching. It concludes the commentary on the law with an expansion on the subject of what aggravations make some sins more heinous than others. It lists these aggravations in four categories; namely, from the parties offending, from the parties offended, from the nature and quality of the offense, and from the circumstances of time and place.

Both of the Catechisms speak to a number of the ethical issues of our own day, and it may be useful to note some of the positions taken. First, both Catechisms affirm the "regulative principle of worship" in connection with the Second Commandment. The

Shorter Catechism question 50 says, "The second commandment requireth the receiving, observing, and keeping pure and entire, all such religious worship and ordinances as God hath appointed in his word." The *Larger Catechism* in question 108 adds a number of the elements of worship that are clearly specified in the Word of God. The same is true of the sins forbidden by this commandment. Both Catechisms assert that the commandment forbiddeth the worshiping of God in any way not prescribed in his word. The *Larger Catechism* amplifies this by listing a number of the kinds of sins and acts that are forbidden by the commandment.

Under the third commandment both Catechisms speak of the "holy and reverent use of God's names, titles, attributes, ordinances, word, and works." (SC 54) This broad application of the commandment speaks to our use of creation. All of it is revelatory of God, and is all thus to be used with reverence and to the glory of God. Biblical Christianity thus has its implications for the use of the environment. It is not a deifying of the environment, but it is a recognition of it as a part of God's creation, and thus to be used to the glory of God.

Of course, both Catechisms hold to a high view of the Sabbath, to the effect that the whole day is to be devoted to the Lord. It is of interest to observe that while the *Larger Catechism* elaborates on sins forbidden under some of the other commandments, it simply states the basic principle, without an expanded lists of do's and don't's for the Sabbath.

Under the sixth commandment, both Catechisms speak of lawful endeavors to preserve the life of ourselves and others. The *Larger Catechism* elaborates on the kinds of things to do in order to promote the preservation of life. The *Larger Catechism* specifically states that cases of "publick justice, lawful war, or necessary defence" are not forbidden by this commandment.

These examples are sufficient to show that the *Larger* and the *Shorter Catechism*s of the Westminster divines were very practical and very relevant documents speaking to issues that are still very much a part of our modern sinful condition.

R. Of Christian Liberty, and Liberty of Conscience

The Catechisms do not speak to the question of Christian Liberty.

S. Of Religious Worship and the Sabbath Day

The Catechisms both consider the Lord's Prayer. The *Larger Catechism* is more expansive, but does not add any significant doctrinal content.

T. Of Lawful Oaths and Vows; Of the Civil Magistrate; Of Marriage and Divorce

Neither *Catechism* has any questions on these three chapters.

U. Of the Church

The *Larger Catechism* in parallel with the *Confession* gives definitions of the church invisible and visible. It then speaks of the special privileges of the visible church. It then indicates that not all who are in the visible church are saved, but only those who are true members of the church invisible.

V. Of the Communion of Saints

The *Larger Catechism* indicates that members of the invisible church enjoy union and communion with Christ in grace and in glory. It defines union with Christ as being joined to Christ as head and husband spiritually, mystically and really.

The *Catechism* speaks of the communion in glory that members of the invisible church enjoy in this life. They enjoy "the sense of God's love, peace of conscience, joy in the Holy

Ghost, and hope of glory." This is contrasted to the "sense of God's revenging wrath, horror of conscience, and a fearful expectation of judgment" experienced by the wicked in this life.

For the members of the invisible church, immediately after death their souls are made perfect in holiness and received into the highest heavens, where they behold the face of God in light and glory. Their bodies remain united to Christ, and rest in their graves as in beds. The wicked in contrast have their souls cast into hell, "where they remain in torments and utter darkness." Their bodies are kept in the graves as in prisons awaiting the resurrection and day of judgment.

Moving from the intermediate state to the day of judgment, the *Catechism* lists the blessings that shall come to the righteous. They are:

1. being caught up to Christ in the clouds,
2. to be set on his right hand,
3. to be openly acknowledged and acquitted,
4. to join with Christ in judging the reprobate angels and men,
5. to be received into heaven, fully and forever freed from all sin and misery,
6. to be filled with inconceivable joys,
7. to be made perfectly happy both in body and soul in company of innumerable saints and holy angels,
8. to be in the immediate vision of God the Father, of our Lord Jesus Christ, and of the Holy Spirit to all eternity.

W. Of the Word and Sacraments

The Catechisms both treat the outward means of grace. These means are defined as all of his ordinances, but especially the word, sacraments and prayer. In specifying prayer as a means of grace, the Westminster Standards differ from the Heidelberg *Catechism* which limits the means to the word and sacraments. The *Larger*

Catechism limits those who are to read the word publicly saying, "Although all are not to be permitted to read the word publickly to the congregation. . . ." It does not, however, specify who are to be permitted to read it publicly. In a separate question it sets forth the requirement for those who are to preach the word, "The word of God is to be preached only by such as are sufficiently gifted, and also duly approved and called to that office." In other words, only those licensed to do so, or ordained to the office of the ministry of the word and sacraments may preach the word.

Having specified that only the duly approved may preach, the *Larger Catechism* considers how the word is to be preached. It teaches that ministers of the word are to:

preach sound doctrine:

diligently, in season and out of season;

plainly, in demonstration of the Spirit and power;

faithfully, making known the whole counsel of God

wisely, applying themselves to the necessities and capacities of the hearers;

zealously, with fervent love to God, and the souls of his people;

sincerely, aiming at his glory, their conversion, edification and salvation.

Not only does the *Larger Catechism* speak of how the word is to be preached, but it gives direction to those who hear the word preached. They are to attend upon it with diligence, preparation and prayer. They are to examine to be sure that the preaching is true to the word. They are to receive the truth with faith, love, meekness, and readiness of mind, as the word of God. They are to meditate upon it, confer on it, hide it in their hearts, and to bring forth fruit of it in their lives.

In defining a sacrament, the *Larger Catechism* spells out more explicitly than either the *Confession* or the *Shorter Catechism*, that it signifies, seals and exhibits "unto those within the covenant of grace the benefits of his mediation." It also elaborates on the fact that the sacrament is designed to strengthen the faith and all other graces, and "to oblige them to obedience." This is not due to any magical power in the sacraments, but is due to the working of the Spirit upon the recipients. Another result of the right use of a sacrament is the encouragement that recipients have to cherish their love and communion one for another. Finally, the *Catechism* speaks of the sacraments as distinguishing us from non-believers.

X. Of Baptism

In defining baptism, the *Larger Catechism* speaks in unison with the other two Standards in defining it as the sign and seal of our ingrafting into Christ. It is more explicit in adding that it is the sign and seal of the remission of sins by his blood, and of regeneration by the Holy Spirit. It then adds that baptism is also the sign and seal of adoption, and resurrection unto everlasting life. As a visible sign and seal baptism is the means by which "the parties baptized are solemnly admitted into the visible church." The implication of this is that those who may be believers or their seed, while members of the covenant, are not formally recognized as members of the church visible until they are initiated into it by baptism. A proper implication then is that one who is not a member of the church visible should not be admitted to the table of the Lord.

The *Larger Catechism* joins with the other two Standards in affirming that baptism is to be administered both to believers and to children of believers, because they are thus in the covenant of grace. It then goes on to elaborate on how baptism is to be "improved" by us, that is, how we are to grow in grace thereby. It teaches that this is a "needful, but much neglected duty," that is to be performed all of our lives. This is especially true when we are present at the baptism of others. We are to be thankful for the nature of baptism as designed by Christ as the sign and seal of the covenant of grace. We should be reminded of our own vow made in baptism, and be humbled for our failures to keep our vow. Positively, we are to draw strength from the death and resurrection of Christ, into whom we are baptized for the mortification of sin, and to draw quickening grace from Christ. In addition to this, we are to strive to walk in holiness and righteousness into which we have been baptized. In these ways we are to strive to grow in the grace of which baptism is the sign and seal.

Y. Of the Lord's Supper

The *Larger Catechism* in the question defining the Lord's supper is most explicit on the real presence of the body and blood of Christ with the physical elements of the Lord's supper. It speaks of the worthy communicant as "feed[ing] upon his body and blood, to their spiritual nourishment and growth in grace." This presence is not a form of consubstantiation. The elements remain bread and wine in the mouth, while the communicant feeds upon Christ's body and blood spiritually in the heart. This concept is spelled out explicitly in question 170,

> As the body and blood of Christ are not corporally or carnally present in, with, or under the bread and wine in the Lord's supper, and yet are spiritually present to the faith of the receiver, no less truly and really than the elements themselves are to their outward senses; so they that worthily communicate in the sacrament of the Lord's supper, do therein feed upon the body and blood of Christ, not after a corporal and carnal, but in a spiritual manner; yet truly and really, while by faith they receive and apply unto themselves Christ crucified, and all the benefits of his death.

Having thus stated the classic Reformed position regarding the spiritual feeding upon Christ, the *Larger Catechism* then treats the question of how the sacrament is to be received and who may receive it. First, in order properly to partake, the communicant is to prepare himself by self-examination: first that he is in Christ, second of his sins and failures, third of the truth and measure of his knowledge, faith and repentance, fourth of his love to God and the brethren, and charity to all men, fifth of his desire after Christ, and his new obedience, and renewing his exercise to this. All of this examining is by serious meditation and fervent prayer. It should be observed that the communicant is to be able to thus meditate and pray, which indicates that the Westminster divines did not consider paedo-communion to be proper.

The next two questions (172, 173) treat the question of who may properly partake of the Lord's supper. The first group considered are true believers, who do not have assurance of salvation. Though he has professed to believe in Christ, because of sin, he has doubts about being in Christ, or has doubts about his proper preparation for the sacrament. The *Larger Catechism* gives several grounds of encouragement for such to come to the table. First, his doubts may not be well founded. Some who once had assurance may lose that assurance because of waywardness. Our salvation does not depend upon our assurance of it, but upon Christ and his finished work appropriated by simple trusting faith. The very fact that a person is exercised over whether or not he belongs to Christ, or over assurance, may itself be evidence of his having the heart of the matter, namely, saving faith. The sacrament is appointed by Christ for our nourishment in the faith, and should not be neglected by such persons, who desire assurance and holiness of life. He is not to be content with this state, but to "bewail his unbelief," and labor to remove his doubts, "and in so doing, he may, and ought to come to the Lord's supper that he may be farther strengthened."

Having dealt with the weak believer, the *Catechism* turns to consider the case of the presumptuous believers, who believe they are properly prepared to come, despite sin that should bar them from the table. Here the *Catechism* refers to the power that Christ has vested in his church to keep the ignorant or scandalous from the table. This power, of course, has reference to the duty of the church to exercise discipline. The Standards do not treat this subject at length, but simply assert its validity.

The *Larger Catechism* next speaks of duties we have while observing the Lord's supper, and after receiving it. First, we are to observe the sacramental elements and actions, recognizing that they represent to us the body and blood of Jesus and his death in behalf of sinners. Such consideration should stir up the vigorous exercise of the graces of God in us. We should judge ourselves and be sorrowful for our sin. We should be earnest in our hungering and thirsting for Christ, and by feeding upon him, we should renew our covenant with God, and show increased love for all the saints.

We not only have responsibilities in the way we observe the sacrament, but also are to continue applying the benefits after having received it. We should review how we have observed the sacrament, and to seek to carry out those vows that were made at the sacrament. If we find we have not benefitted from our observance of it, then we are to look to the Lord yet to bless us by it. If we do not receive such blessing, then we should be humbled by our failure in properly observing the sacrament, and to take care on future occasions of celebrating the sacrament.

Two final questions consider the ways in which baptism and the Lord's supper are alike and how they differ. We shall list each category:

Alike:
God is the author of both,
Christ is the spiritual part of both,
Both are seals of the same covenant,
Both are administered by ministers of the gospel, and by none other, Both are to be continued in the church until the second coming.

Differ:

Baptism	**Lord's supper**
administered just once with water to be sign and seal of regeneration and of ingrafting into Christ, and that even to infants.	administered often with bread and wine, to represent and exhibit Christ as spiritual nourishment to the soul, and to confirm our continuance of growth in him, and that only to such as are of years and ability to examine themselves.

Z. Of the State of Men after Death, and of the Resurrection of the Dead

The *Larger Catechism* deals with the question of death and why the righteous are not delivered from it. Death was the threat for sin. Since all have sinned, it is now appointed unto all men once to die. In answer to the second question, the *Catechism* affirms that the righteous shall be delivered from death at the last day. For them the sting and curse of death is removed. Death is the means by which God frees them from sin and misery, so that they become capable of further communion with Christ, which they enter into immediately after death.

The *Catechism* then treats the "intermediate state." The souls of believers are made perfect in holiness and received into the highest heaven, where they behold the face of God, waiting for the day of redemption of their bodies, which rest in Christ in the graves. The souls of the wicked, on the other hand, are cast into hell, where they are tormented, awaiting the day of judgment. Their bodies are kept in their graves as in prison.

In question 87 the *Larger Catechism* affirms that there shall be a general resurrection of all the dead. All those alive on the last day, shall be changed. The souls and bodies shall be reunited and raised up by the power of Christ. The righteous shall be raised in power, spiritual, incorruptible, and made like his glorious body. The bodies of the wicked shall be raised to dishonor.

AA.   Of the Last Judgment

Having affirmed that there is to be a general resurrection of all, the *Larger Catechism* asserts that immediately following there is to be a general and final judgment of angels and men, contrary to the view that there is a series of judgments. The *Catechism* specifically treats the judgment of the wicked, in which it emphasizes that their condemnation is "upon clear evidence, and full conviction of their own consciences." The punishment involves being cast from the "favourable presence of God, and the glorious fellowship with Christ, his saints, and all his holy angels into hell, to be punished with unspeakable torments, both of body and soul, with the devil and his angels for ever." It is clear that the Westminster divines understood the punishment of the wicked to be eternal. Note that the consideration of angels, which had begun in the chapter on creation, carries through to eternity.

The state of the righteous on the day of judgment is also considered. First, they are to be caught up into the clouds with Christ. There they are openly acknowledged and acquitted. They shall then join with Christ in the judging of the reprobate angels and men. Finally, they will be received into heaven, where they shall be freed from all sin and misery, and enter into a state of being most holy and happy, both in body and in soul. They will have the privilege of the immediate vision of the Triune God. This is to be their eternal state.

III. Conclusion

Though often neglected, even by Presbyterians who profess it to be a part of their confession of the faith, the *Larger Catechism* is worthy of careful study. It presents the most complete commentary on the Law and on the Lord's Prayer, as well as its theological insights into the person and work of Christ and the sacraments. As such, it deserves much greater consideration by the Church than it has had. It can be of special value to the minister of the Word to guide him in the sound understanding of the Biblical faith and ethic. Were the Church to take seriously the Westminster Standards, including the *Larger Catechism*, we could expect a genuine spiritual awakening.

Westminster and the Sabbath

Richard B. Gaffin, Jr.

1.

In the middle of the last century, the Dutch theologian A. van Selms speculated that in Holland at that time there was a serious quarrel weekly in 10,000 homes, on average, about what kind of activities are permissible on Sunday. That amounted to some half-million quarrels a year, he observed, and left it to the statisticians to calculate how many nervous breakdowns had resulted![1]

Van Selms likely had in view, at least primarily, the Dutch Calvinist community of his day. But his colorful surmise no doubt aptly describes countless English-speaking Presbyterian households in generations past. This state of affairs prompts a couple of further observations preliminary to an examination of the Sabbath in the Westminster Standards. For one thing, the difference between the Puritan Sabbath and Continental Sunday should not be exaggerated, especially so far as the actual practices of churches in the Reformed tradition are in view. To be sure, at the confessional level, there are differences, although these, too, are not as substantial as sometimes

---

[1] J. Douma, *The Ten Commandments* (trans. N. D. Kloosterman; Phillipsburg, NJ: P&R, 1996), p. 146 (cited from van Selms' *De zondag* published in 1937, in the Dutch original, *De tien geboden* [Kampen: Van den Berg, 1992], part 2, p. 56).

maintained. The Three Forms of Unity, the confessional standards of Continental Calvinism, do treat the Sabbath much less extensively and with a somewhat different accent than the Westminster Standards.[2] But in the main, especially beginning in the seventeenth century following the Synod of Dort, British-American Presbyterianism and Continental Calvinism became of one mind on what Sunday observance should look like: in view of the continuing validity of the fourth commandment, Sunday is to be a day of rest from our daily work, devoted primarily to the worship of God.[3] We may speak here of a Reformed consensus or, as it may also be put, a consensus of generic Calvinism.[4]

---

[2] The sole reference is in Lord's Day 38 (Q&A 103) of the Heidelberg Catechism:

Q. What does God require in the fourth commandment?

A. First, that the ministry of the gospel and the schools be maintained; and that I, especially on the Sabbath, that is, the day of rest, diligently attend the church of God, to learn God's Word, to use the sacraments, to call publicly upon the Lord, and to give Christian alms. Second, that all the days of my life I rest from my evil works, let the Lord work in me by His Holy Spirit, and thus begin in this life the eternal Sabbath.

(The words "the Sabbath, that is," were not part of the German original of 1563 ["am Feiertag"], but were added in the Dutch translation of 1566 and have been retained in most official English translations.)

[3] Cf. Douma, *The Ten Commandments*, pp. 142-46 ("Not Overestimating Confessional Differences"). Anecdotal evidence would suggest that until roughly a generation ago this was the case, for instance, in the Christian Reformed Church in North America.

[4] See, for instance, the *Message to the Churches*, issued by the Reformed Ecumenical Synod in 1976 after an extensive study of the Sabbath/Sunday issue (*Acts of the Reformed Ecumenical Synod, Cape Town 1976*, pp. 59-60).

The interesting (and disputed) question of the relation between the earlier Reformers, particularly Calvin, and the Westminster Standards (the Puritan Sabbath) will have to be left to the side here. On Calvin, my own view, briefly, is that there is an ambiguity in his statements as a whole because he does not do justice to the Sabbath as a creation ordinance. In his commentary on Gen 2:2-3 (1554), he does recognize that the fourth commandment is perpetually binding because the Sabbath institution antedates the fall. But in his discussion of the fourth commandment in the final (1559) edition of

Secondly, one cannot help but note van Selms' quip with a certain nostalgia or at least a sense of looking back on a time largely past. Where are the 10,000 arguments per week today? Serious debates about appropriate activities on the Lord's Day can only take place where the day itself is taken seriously. In that respect, leaving to the side broader cultural trends as well as developments in non-Reformed churches, I doubt if anyone will question the dramatic decline in Sabbath observance even among Presbyterians during the past generation or so. Is not concern for their distinctive confessional commitment to the sanctity of the Lord's Day as the Christian Sabbath rapidly eroding today, at a time when that commitment is being challenged as never before? The question is rhetorical. It is probably not overstating to speak of the Sabbath in crisis.[5]

How should we further assess the causes of this crisis and respond to it? Before taking up that challenging question, it will

---

the *Institutes* (2:8:28-34), consistent with earlier editions and virtually all statements elsewhere, the weekly Sabbath is viewed entirely as necessitated by the fall and conditions resulting from human sinfulness; in Israel it regulated worship and typified the spiritual rest brought by Christ, so that, since his coming, it is no longer binding. What obligates the New Testament church for Calvin, as it could be put, is the "general equity" of the fourth commandment: believers are to cease sinning and worship God (as often as possible – one day in seven is not mandatory but useful as a minimal guideline). See my, *Calvin and the Sabbath* (Fearn, Ross-shire: Christian Focus – Mentor, 1998); cf., for a somewhat different assessment, J. H. Primus, "Calvin and the Puritan Sabbath: A Comparative Study," in ed. D. E. Holwerda, *Exploring the Heritage of John Calvin* (Grand Rapids: Baker, 1976), pp. 40-75. In the line of Calvin, see Z. Ursinus, *Commentary on the Heidelberg Catechism* (Phillipsburg, NJ: Presbyterian and Reformed, 1985 [1591]), pp. 557-74.

5   The above comments have in view primarily the situation in churches, whose office bearers are still committed, by subscription, to the Westminster Standards. For a revealing survey of the larger Presbyterian scene, see Benton Johnson, "On Dropping the Subject: Presbyterians and Sabbath Observance in the Twentieth Century," in ed. M. J. Coalter, *et al*, *The Presbyterian Predicament: Six Perspectives* (Louisville: Westminster/John Knox, 1990), pp. 90-108, 167-72.

be well to remind ourselves briefly of what the Westminster Standards affirm concerning the Sabbath.[6]

2.

The weekly Sabbath is dealt with in three places in the Standards: in the Confession, chapter 21 ("Of Religious Worship and the Sabbath Day"), sections 7-8, and, under the section on the Decalogue, in the Larger (Q&A 115-21) and Shorter (Q&A 57-62) Catechisms. Immediately noteworthy in the Catechisms is the fact that, with the exception of the fifth commandment in the Larger Catechism, no commandment is treated anywhere nearly as extensively as the fourth. The link between the teaching of the Confession and the Catechisms is the chapter in the former on the Law of God (19), especially the universally and perpetually binding nature of the moral law (section 5).

Key elements of this teaching may be summarized under the following four points:

1. As a part of the moral law, "summarily comprehended" in the Decalogue, the fourth commandment is a "positive, moral, and perpetual commandment binding on all men in all ages" (CF 21:7). Its distinguishing concern is *worship*. Specifically, it mandates *time* for worship, more particularly that one day of the week be a day of rest, a Sabbath. This weekly Sabbath-rest is

---

[6] My exposition here is necessarily brief. Among more extensive treatments, see Ashbel Green, *Lectures on the Shorter Catechism* (Philadelphia: Presbyterian Board of Publication, 1841), vol. 2, pp. 99-144; A. A. Hodge, *A Commentary on the Confession of Faith* (Philadelphia: Presbyterian Board of Publication, 1869), pp. 379-84; Thomas Ridgeley, *Commentary on the Larger Catechism* (Edmonton: Still Waters Revival, 1995 [1731], vol. 2, pp. 34-63.; Thomas Watson, *The Ten Commandments* (London: The Banner of Truth, 1965 [1692]), pp. 92-122; more recently, R. S. Ward, *The Westminster Confession for the Church Today* (Melbourne: Presbyterian Church of Eastern Australia, 1992), pp. 149-56; cf. Ward's brief but excellent monograph, *The Goal of Creation* (Melbourne: Presbyterian Church of Eastern Australia, 1994), 24 pp.

called "holy" in the sense of being set apart for worship, especially the public worship of God.

This Sabbath commandment has as its background the more general "law of nature" (CF 21:7) that a proportionate amount of time ought to be set aside for worship. The association with the correlative, if not identical, notion of "the light of nature," with which the Confession opens (1:1) and chapter 21 begins, seems clear.[7]

Concerning the weekly Sabbath specifically, however, there is "less light of nature for it" (LC 121). This qualification is likely prompted by the "positive" stipulations contained in the fourth commandment, namely that one day each week and the seventh day particularly are to be set apart for worship. Still, the weekly Sabbath is a "moral" obligation, that is, rooted in the nature of God and the makeup of creation; in language that has since become commonplace, at least in Reformed theology, it is a "creation ordinance."

2. Originally, from the time of creation, the weekly Sabbath was the seventh day. With Christ's resurrection it has become the first day and in the New Testament is called the Lord's Day. As such, it is "the Christian sabbath" (CF 21:7; LC 116; SC 59). This notion, under the aegis of the fourth commandment, that the Lord's Day is the Christian Sabbath encapsulates the Standards' teaching, apparently for the first time in a major confessional document.

3. Given the design of the weekly Sabbath, "the whole time" is to be spent "in the public and private exercises of worship" (CF 21:8; cf. LC 117; SC 60). "Private" here covers "in private families daily, and in secret, each one by himself" (section 6). The "exercises," both public and private, in view are principally those "ordinary" parts of worship stipulated in section 5 (prayer, reading and preaching the Word, singing psalms, administering and receiving the sacraments).

The nature of this "holy resting" is highlighted, negatively,

---

[7] I will have to leave to the side here the interesting question whether and, if so, to what extent the Standards are influenced at this point by contemporary natural law theories.

by what it excludes. Forbidden are not only "all profaning the day by idleness" but also "all needless works, words, and thoughts" about those "worldly employments and recreations as are on other days lawful" (LC 119, 117; cf. CF 21:8; SC 60, 61). The only exception to this exclusive stress on worship is allowance made for "the duties of necessity and mercy" (CF 21:8; cf. LC 117; SC 60). These duties are not specified further.

4. Presbyterians have continued to debate how the Sabbath is related to the "system of doctrine," taught in Scripture and summarized in the Westminster Standards. A remarkable indication of just how integral to that system the Standards themselves view the Lord's Day is found in Larger Catechism 121: Keeping the fourth commandment helps us "better to keep all the rest of the commandments, and to continue a thankful remembrance of the two great benefits of creation and redemption, which contain a short abridgement of religion." Conversely, "Satan with his instruments much labor to blot out the glory, and even the memory of [the Sabbath], to bring in all irreligion and impiety" – a sobering thought, especially in a time of declining Sabbath-keeping.[8]

3.

With this brief sketch, we may now consider some objections to this view of the Sabbath. I begin with several specific problems often raised and then mention a couple of more general and, in my judgment, more substantial lines of opposition.

Among frequently raised particular difficulties,[9] there is, for instance, the fact that the first mention of Sabbath-keeping in the Old Testament is not until the time of the Exodus. Why don't we read anything about Sabbath practice during the long patriarchal

---

[8] "*No Sabbath, no religion*, is a maxim which you may safely apply, both to individuals and to communities" (Green, *Lectures on the Shorter Catechism*, p. 143).

[9] I follow here the listing and, to a certain extent, the detailing of difficulties by Douma, *The Ten Commandments*, pp. 109-12.

history from Eden to Sinai? In view of that silence is there any compelling warrant for holding that the Sabbath was (to be) observed before the Exodus, or for viewing the Sabbath as a "creation ordinance"?

That relates to a second problem. Genesis 2:2-3 states that God rested on the seventh day and so blessed it and made it holy. But what warrant is there for concluding from this fact that Sabbath-keeping was *prescribed* for humanity already in paradise? Perhaps at Sinai the appeal to this divine resting (Exod 20), like the appeal to God's deliverance of Israel from Egypt (Deut 5), provides the basis for God, as he had done for himself previously, at creation, *now*, for the first time, setting apart and hallowing the seventh day for his covenant people.

A third problem emerges when we turn to the New Testament. Nowhere is the church commanded to keep the weekly Sabbath; nor, unlike the other nine, is the fourth commandment cited as normative for the church. There is clear evidence that the first day of the week has become the Lord's Day, apparently as the day of Christ's resurrection, and that the church assembled on it. But where is the evidence that the Lord's Day is the Christian Sabbath? Where is there even a hint that the weekly Sabbath day has been changed from the seventh to the first?

These arguments from silence are reinforced by several statements of Paul (Rom 14:5; Gal 4:10; Col 2:16-17) that warn or at least express indifference about regarding one day of the week as more important religiously than the others. Especially the Colossians passage, it would seem, states that Israel's weekly Sabbath was a "shadow" whose function has ceased now that the "substance," Christ, has arrived.

A fourth problem is the ambiguity at best of the first few centuries of church history. There is certainly no evidence that in this period Sunday was viewed as the Sabbath. It seems, rather, that at first believers gathered for worship on Sunday early in the morning and perhaps again in the evening, but that the remainder of the day was spent like any other in work. Only gradually does

Sunday become a day of rest from labor, and not until well into the Middle Ages is a link made theologically, by appeal to the fourth commandment, between Sunday and the Sabbath.

Implicit in and also reinforcing these four areas of objection are two arguments of a more sweeping character. One is the view, traditional and widespread outside the Reformed tradition, that the Decalogue as such is not normative for the New Testament church. Again, Paul is seen as the key witness for this view. The law-gospel antithesis he expresses in passages like Romans 6:14, 7:4-6, and 2 Corinthians 3:6ff. means, it is argued, that the legislation given at Sinai, in its entirety, is now obsolete and as such does not obligate believers in any respect.

Further, it is alleged, the threefold distinction between moral, ceremonial, and judicial law with which the Standards operate (CF 19:3-4) is artificial, and their view that the latter two have been abrogated (except for the "general equity" of the judicial laws) while the former, summarized in the Ten Commandments, continues in force (CF 19:3-4), cannot be maintained exegetically. This line of criticism has become further entrenched by the consensus emerging over the past two decades on the place of the law in Pauline theology.[10]

Obviously, then, where the Decalogue as a whole is held to be abrogated, so is the fourth commandment, and with that the notion of a Christian Sabbath is rejected out of hand.

Secondly, my strong surmise is that nothing more explains the accelerating disregard for the Sabbath in recent decades, even among Presbyterian and other Reformed churches, than what may be viewed as the rediscovery of eschatology. Briefly, that recovery, one of the most important developments in biblical studies in this century, has taken place across a broad front. It began, toward the close of the last century, in scholarly reaction against the anti-

---

[10] This development is largely bound up with the "new perspective" on Paul, triggered principally by E. P. Sanders' *Paul and Palestinian Judaism: A Comparison of Patterns of Religion* (Philadelphia: Fortress, 1977).

eschatology stance of the so-called Older Liberalism (its ethical idealism). This de-eschatologizing animus was especially glaring in its distortion of Jesus' proclamation of the kingdom of God/ heaven. Subsequently, it has become widely recognized that eschatology is not only essential to Jesus and the biblical writers but that their teaching is pervasively eschatological.

This development, it should not be missed, also provides a not unimportant corrective, or at least enrichment, of historic Christian doctrine and preaching. Eschatology involves much more than is taken up, conventionally, in the last chapter in systematic theology – those things having to do with Christ's still future return (often including a treatment of the intermediate state following death) – usually with little or virtually no connection to preceding chapters, like those on Christology, soteriology and ecclesiology. In contrast, according to Scripture, particularly the New Testament, it has become more and more clear, "eschatology" is to be defined in terms of the first as well as the second coming of Christ, by both what has already arrived in Christ and what awaits his return. In this sense biblical eschatology is elliptical; that is, determined by not one but two points. The New Testament teaches what is often termed an "inaugurated," already "realized" eschatology, to be consummated at Christ's return.

It seems difficult to deny that this resurgent awareness of realized eschatology has had a decisive impact on the Sabbath debate. The argument runs something like this: The fourth commandment/the Sabbath is woven into the eschatological fabric of Scripture. Specifically, the Sabbath in Israel was a large-scale system of signs (day, week, year, Jubilee year), all pointing to eschatological rest. That rest has already arrived in Christ (with an appeal, for instance, to his statement in Matt 11:28: "... I will give you rest," in the context of his central proclamation that the eschatological kingdom is now, at last, present in his person and work). Therefore, the argument continues, because the eschatological rest (Christ) has already arrived, the sign pointing to that reality has discharged its function, now lacks a rationale for continuing, and so is no longer in force. To put it bluntly, on this view the notion of a New Testament or Christian Sabbath is a contradiction in terms.[11]

These, I take it, are the principal arguments against the view of the weekly Sabbath found in the Westminster Standards. I hope to have represented them fairly, if not fully. In responding to them briefly, I do so, for the most part, in reverse order.

4.

The eschatological argument against the New Testament Sabbath fails not because it (quite correctly) connects the Sabbath with eschatology but because it does so in a *one-sided* fashion. It is wrong not in what it affirms: Sabbath-fulfillment in Christ, but because of what it denies: a continuing place for the Sabbath-sign under the new covenant. Its eye for the link between the Sabbath and the eschatological "already" is so exclusive that it is blind to the link as well with the "not yet," and so it misses the rationale for the New Testament continuation of the weekly sign.

But does the New Testament in fact provide such a rationale? Does it tie the weekly Sabbath to still future eschatological fulfillment (at Christ's return) so that the former continues to point to the latter? The writer of Hebrews utilizes just that connection, within the overall framework of his teaching, principally in the passage, 3:7-4:13, where he refers explicitly to the Sabbath theme in 4:4 and 9. Here I can do little more than sketch the outlines of his argument and note the conclusions it points to.[12]

1. This passage (3:7-4:13) primarily serves the writer's pervasive hortatory concern (he himself calls the entire document a "word of

---

[11] This, for example, as much as any is the central thesis of ed. D. A. Carson, *From Sabbath to Lord's Day: A Biblical, Historical, and Theological Investigation* (Grand Rapids: Zondervan, 1982).

[12] For a more extensive treatment, see my "A Sabbath Rest Still Awaits the People of God," in eds. C. G. Dennison & R. C. Gamble, *Pressing Toward the Mark. Essays Commemorating Fifty Years of the Orthodox Presbyterian Church* (Philadelphia: Orthodox Presbyterian Church, 1986), pp. 33-51.

132

exhortation," 13:22). In it he draws an analogy from covenant history based on an interpretive handling of Psalm 95:7-11. He compares the present situation of the church (between the ascension and return of Christ, the high priest in heaven) with Israel in the wilderness, between Egypt/slavery (3:16) and Canaan/rest (4:8); the church is the new and final wilderness community. This covenant-historical parallel serves to picture both the already/not yet indicative of the eschatological salvation brought by Christ, the high priest in heaven, and the need for the imperatives that accompany that indicative.

Two key expressions, picked up from the Psalm 95 citation, become focal in the writer's own comments: "today" and "my [God's] rest." "Today," on the one hand, is the *present* situation of the church, the *wilderness*-day, the day of tested and persevering faith (3:12-13, 15; 4:6-7). "My rest," in contrast, refers to what is *still future* "as long as it is called today" (3:13). Believers are not at rest but are to seek it, persistently (4:11). "My rest" is the antithesis of present exposure to hardship and temptation; it is a matter of "promise" (4:1), in the sense that it stands before the church as Canaan before Israel in the desert (4:8), as the land about to be inherited (cf. 1:14).

2. No doubt we must be careful not to over-interrogate this passage. I am not suggesting, for instance, that Sabbath-keeping under the new covenant is the writer's explicit concern. Nor should 4:9 be read: "it remains for God's people to keep the fourth commandment." It would be equally remiss, however, to overlook or minimize what careful exegesis is able to show: "rest" for the church in Hebrews 3-4 is (1) eschatological (as the overall context shows), (2) entirely future (as I will presently argue), (3) called "Sabbath-resting" (4:9) and (4) grounded in God's rest at creation (4:4).

In the Sabbath debate, (2) especially is at issue.[13] The most substantial objections are the tenses of the main verbs in 4:3a and 10a. Of itself the present tense form in verse 3a gives no more than a presumption of a present sense. Here contextual

---

[13] Cf., e.g., A. T. Lincoln in *From Sabbath to Lord's Day*, pp. 205-14.

considerations, decisive as usual on a grammatical issue like this, exclude a true present, because, as already noted, it would violate a key aspect of the writer's wilderness-model: Israel in the wilderness, even on the brink of entering the land, is not yet Israel entered into the promised land/rest.[14]

In view of the various forces the present indicative can have, either of two translations fits: "we will enter," the use of the present tense giving a note of certainty, or perhaps a progressive sense ("we are entering"), actually underway but not yet there.[15] The closest New Testament parallel to 4:3, apparently, is Acts 14:22: "through many tribulations we must enter the kingdom of God." In Luke-Acts the kingdom is obviously a comprehensive eschatological reality and elsewhere is emphatically present (e.g., Luke 7:28; 11:20; 17:21), yet, to my knowledge, none of the commentators find a present meaning here; an entirely future sense is obvious.

---

[14] In the interests of clarifying this point, note that in terms of his own eschatological structure the writer *could* quite properly have spoken of the rest as present (as Jesus, for instance, does in Matt 11:28), just as he does say that (in solidarity with Christ, cf. 3:14, their high priest/forerunner in heaven) believers have already come to "the heavenly Jerusalem," the eschatological "city of the living God" (12:22). That (along with the fact that the writer has a realized eschatology) is not the issue. What is at issue is whether *in this passage* (3:7ff.) (Sabbath-)rest is entirely future or in some sense present.

[15] For the future sense of the present, see, e.g., N. Turner, *A Grammar of New Testament Greek*, vol. III, *Syntax* (Edinburgh, T. & T. Clark, 1963) p. 63 (These presents differ from the future "mainly in the tone of assurance which is imported," quoting Moulton); A. T. Robertson, *A Grammar of the Greek New Testament in the Light of Historical Research* (Nashville: Broadman Press, 1934), pp. 869-870 ("It affirms and not merely predicts. It gives a sense of certainty."); cf. E. D. Burton, *Syntax of the Moods and Tenses in New Testament Greek* (Edinburgh: T. & T. Clark, 1898), pp. 9f. For the progressive sense, see R. Funk, *A Greek Grammar of the New Testament* (The University of Chicago Press, 1961), p. 168 ("Verbs of going [coming] however also have the meaning of 'to be in the process of coming [going]' for which reaching the destination still lies in the future."

Verse 10, in fact, brings to light a basic (but often missed) flaw in the present rest view, one that in my judgment renders it inherently implausible, perhaps impossible. The verse expresses a direct, *positive* comparison between believers and God: their resting is to their works as God's resting is to his.[16] The present rest view holds (and apparently must hold in some form), that the writer's point is spiritual rest/justification by faith already experienced (cf. Matt 11:28). But on that understanding we are left with a jarring incongruity to say the least: a direct, positive parallel between our sinful, self-justifying works and God's works! Where else does the New Testament even remotely approach the notion that "repentance from dead works" (6:1) is analogous to God's resting from his labors at creation?[17]

The believer's works in view are, in a word, *desert*-works, "love and good works" (10:24; cf. 6:10) in the present *non*-rest situation. The aorist tense of the main verb in verse 10a ("has rested") has a generalizing or gnomic force.[18] The clause as a whole describes a *future* state of rest, toward which, as the writer immediately goes on to exhort, believers, for now in the wilderness, are to *exert* themselves to enter (vs. 11). The contrast with rest here (and elsewhere in the passage) is not unbelief/sin (the present rest view) but faith on trial, faith under wilderness conditions.[19]

---

[16] The view of John Owen (*An Exposition of Hebrews* [Evansville, Ind.: Sovereign Grace Publishers, 1960 (1674)]), vol. 2, pp. 331-336) that in vs. 10a "the one who enters" refers to Christ (not the believer) hardly fits the context.

[17] Note that in this passage, in terms of the controlling wilderness model, justification by faith is Exodus from Egypt/redemption (cf. 3:16), not entrance into Canaan/rest.

[18] Cf. Burton, *Moods and Tenses*, p. 21; a proleptic use of the aorist also fits well here, see M. Zerwick, *Biblical Greek* (Rome: Pontifical Biblical Institute, 1963), p. 84.

[19] The closest New Testament parallel to verse 10a appears to be Rev 14:13: "Blessed are the dead who die in the Lord ... they will rest from their labor, for their deeds will follow them."

3. With these objections to rest as entirely future in Hebrews 3-4 removed, that and the three other exegetical givens noted above[20] prompt the following conclusions:

1) The (weekly) Sabbath, whatever else its significance, is an eschatological sign or type, a pointer to eschatological rest. To deny that would necessarily involve accepting something like the following scenario: The writer himself not only (a) apparently coined the term "Sabbath-resting" for eschatological rest (4:9) but also (b) connected that rest with Genesis 2:2-3 (4:4), which only functions elsewhere in Scripture for instituting the weekly Sabbath (Exod 20:11; 31:17), yet (c) did so without any thought of the weekly ordinance – a rather unlikely supposition.

2) Because the rest in view is future the weekly Sabbath continues in force under the new covenant. To deny that is to suppose that for the writer the weekly sign has ceased, even though the reality to which it points is still future – again, an unlikely supposition. What rationale could explain such a severing, by cessation, of sign and unfulfilled reality?

3) The weekly Sabbath is a "creation ordinance." To deny that is to disagree with the writer's own interpretive treatment of Genesis 2:2. He finds there, in an interesting and instructive example of New Testament use of the Old, not only a report of God's rest at creation but the (eschatological) design and mandate that humanity enter and share it (4:3b-4). Genesis 2:2 is in fact *prescriptive* as well as descriptive; in the flow of his argument it supports the first premise in 4:6 ("it remains for some to enter it"), which otherwise would be without foundation. As the writer sees it, the fulfillment of the church's hope (its eschatological rest) represents nothing less than the fulfillment of the original purpose of God in creation. Or, more accurately, the realization of his purposes of redemption (through Christ, the rest-bringing high priest) is the means to the end of realizing his purposes for creation.[21]

---

[20] See the last sentence of the first paragraph in point 2 of this section.

[21] Cf. P. Fairbairn, *The Typology of Scripture* (Grand Rapids: Zondervan, n.d.), vol. I, p. 420. A similar pattern of thought, apparently, is present in 1 Cor

All this suggests that the sign pointing to the reality mandated at creation is itself grounded in that mandate; stated formally: as eschatology is the goal of protology, so the eschatological sign has a protological basis. Nothing in the immediate context offsets this inference.[22]

4) *Sum*: For the writer the weekly Sabbath is an eschatological sign, grounded in creation and continuing under the new covenant until the consummation. He does not support the view that because of the spiritual rest already brought by Christ, weekly Sabbath-keeping is no longer necessary or even appropriate. The notion of a New Testament or Christian Sabbath is entirely in harmony, its denial at variance, with the teaching of Hebrews 3-4.

4. It may be noted at this point that the Hebrews passage provides a response to three of the four particular arguments against the Christian Sabbath noted earlier: (1) The New Testament is in fact not silent about but supports an ongoing weekly Sabbath. It shows, among other things, that (2) Genesis 2:2-3 teaches that the weekly Sabbath is a creation ordinance, so that (3) the question of a patriarchal, pre-Mosaic Sabbath (that is, explicit evidence for a weekly Sabbath prior to the Exodus) is

---

15:42-49, where, as the *argument* of vs. 44b and the supporting quotation of Gen 2:7 in vs. 45 especially show, Paul finds an eschatological design and goal in the original, pre-fall creation order; cf. G. Vos, *The Pauline Eschatology* (Grand Rapids: Baker, 1979 [1930]), pp. 169-70 (n. 19). "The eschatological is an older strand in revelation than the soteric" (G. Vos, *Biblical Theology - Old and New Testaments* [Grand Rapids: Eerdmans, 1948], p. 157). Eminently valuable for a theology of rest and the Sabbath is his entire discussion of the fourth commandment (pp. 155-159).

[22] Lincoln writes, "The writer's quotation of Genesis 2:2 in Hebrews 4:3-4 is not in order to ground the Sabbath in creation but rather to ground the eschatological salvation rest, which God has for His people, in the divine rest at creation"; in Scripture "the notion of God's rest in Genesis 2 was treated eschatologically" but "was not held...to be a `creation ordinance'" (*From Sabbath to Lord's Day*, p. 351). Why the disjunction? Why not both?, especially since the writer himself draws a connection between the Sabbath institution (4:9) and the rest of Gen 2:2-3 (4:4).

not critical to the Sabbath debate.[23]

Further, Paul's negative statements (Rom 14:5; Gal 4:10; Col 2:16-17) are best understood from this perspective; they must not be unduly absolutized.[24] They do not address the weekly Sabbath mandated at creation but the Sabbath system instituted at Sinai and its typological function in Israel (week, year, and Jubilee year, as well as day). That system as a whole has ceased with the finished work of Christ, but without prejudice to the continuation of the *weekly* Sabbath in view of its prior and deeper creation origin. From this perspective, too, Jesus' declaration in Mark 2:27-28, in relation to his eschatological lordship as the Son of Man (who is the last Adam), may have more to say than is sometime recognized in support of the Sabbath as a creation ordinance.

5. The eschatological orientation of the Sabbath is helpful in resolving another objection to the Christian Sabbath, namely the nettlesome difficulty, for many, of the change of day. Briefly, the shift from the seventh to the first day reflects the present eschatological situation of the church under the new covenant; the change of day is an index of eschatology already realized, of the new creation rest inaugurated by Christ, especially at his resurrection. Correlatively, the continuation of a weekly rest day is a sign of eschatology still future, a pointer to the eschatological rest to come at Christ's return.

---

[23] The fourth of the above objections, from early church history (the Lord's Day was not a rest day), is not as compelling as the other three, at least for those committed to the final authority of Scripture, and will have to be assessed in that light. A rough parallel from New Testament canon history may help here: the fact that in the ancient church Hebrews, for instance, was widely rejected at first and then eventually accepted largely for the wrong reason (alleged Pauline authorship) is not decisive against its canonicity.

[24] In this regard Herman Ridderbos is not helpful, especially as a Reformed theologian, when he simply asserts, in just one sentence and in the small print section of his comments on Col 2:16: "That Paul writes in this way about the Sabbath shows that for him the fourth commandment of the Decalogue did not have continuing significance" (*Aan de Kolossenzen* [Kampen: Kok, 1960], p. 190).

6. Finally, from a broader perspective, the Sabbath-theology of Hebrews helps to facilitate a proper understanding of the church's present place in redemptive history and in that regard to preserve the balance of biblical eschatology. That theology is an important corrective against the tendency to express the already/not yet pattern of the New Testament as a dialectic of paradoxical, virtually undifferentiated eschatological statements.

In fact, the weekly Sabbath is an important safeguard against the overreaching "enthusiasm" that constantly threatens Christian faith; it protects the church against tendencies to blur or even lose sight of the differences between the eschatological "already" and "not yet." The Sabbath is a sure sign to the church that it is a pilgrim congregation that it is still "on the way." The weekly Sabbath is a recurring reminder to believers that while most assuredly they already belong to the new creation (2 Cor 5:17), are already resurrected with Christ (e.g., Eph 2:5-6; Col 3:1), and daily are being renewed inwardly (2 Cor 4:16); nevertheless, in the body, in their psycho-physical existence, they are short of the final resurrection-rest that "awaits the people of God."

5.

My response to the first of the general arguments noted above, that the Decalogue (and so the fourth commandment) is not binding on the New Testament church, will have to be much briefer. Anything like an adequate assessment is beyond the scope of this chapter and would involve, among other things, considering in depth the larger issue of the place of the law in the Westminster Standards.

1. We should agree, as recent exegesis for the most part concludes, that "law" in the New Testament refers, with few exceptions, to the law given at Sinai and so to an entity that as a whole has passed away along with the redemptive-historical epoch distinguished by it (e.g., Luke 16:16; John 1:17; Rom 6:14; Heb 10:1). Also, it is no doubt true that Israel under the Mosaic law did not think of it as having distinct subsets or experience it as anything other than a seamless whole. Well and good.

At the same time, however, something close, if not identical, to a moral-ceremonial distinction is plainly implicit in both Testaments. That appears, for instance, in the contrast between animal sacrifice and doing justice for the oppressed (Isa 1:11-17) or in Jesus' distinguishing between tithing herbs and spices and "the more important matters of the law," like justice, mercy, and fidelity (Matt 23:23).

Among such "weightier" matters – few, if any, will deny – the Decalogue has special prominence. Here, it was evident in Israel and to Jesus and the New Testament writers, are the *central* commandments, "the Torah in the Torah," as it has been put.[25] That eminence is reflected in several ways: in the distinctive origin of the Decalogue – it was separately engraved on two stone tablets "by the finger of God" (Exod 31:18); it was placed in the ark (Deut 10:1-2); it was read together with the Shema daily in the temple and later in the synagogue (cf. Deut 6:4-9; 11:13-21; Num 15:37-41). Again and again and in different settings, various of the Ten Commandments are listed to get at the heart of God's holy will and encapsulate rebellion against it (e.g., Jer 7:9; Hos. 4:2; Matt 19:18-19; Rom 13:9; 1 Tim 1:9-10; Jam 2:11).[26]

Further, the ceremonial aspect of the law is provisional, the moral continues. That is intimated in the New Testament passages cited in the preceding two paragraphs and reinforced by the likes of Romans 8:4, 13:8-10, and 1 Corinthians 7:19.[27] The New Testament stipulates a positive role for the law in the life of the

---

[25] Ed. J. van den Berg, *De thora in de thora* (Aalten: de Graafschap, n.d.), 1:5.

[26] For the substance of this paragraph see J. Douma, *Christian Morals and Ethics* (Winnipeg: Premier, 1983), pp. 38-39. The entire chapter on the Ten Commandments (pp. 38-49), as well as the book as a whole, is most helpful.

[27] Having to argue that "keeping God's commandments" in 1 Cor 7:19 is limited to Pauline and perhaps dominical commands, with no direct reference to the Mosaic law, seems to me a rather uncomfortable position to be in exegetically, particularly in view of Paul's positive use elsewhere, in parenetic contexts, of elements of the Decalogue, more or less clearly identified as such (Rom 13:9; Eph 6:2-3).

believer, its "third use," summarized in the Decalogue and focused in the love command.

2. The complaint that this view of the law ignores the redemptive-historical context and function of the Decalogue is puzzling. Certainly, the Decalogue in its form and as given at Sinai is part of the Mosaic legislation whose covenant-historical role, as a whole, is finished. But where in each of the ten words do we find redemptive-historical limitations? There is the reference to the seventh day in the fourth, to the land in the fifth, and perhaps the reference to the generations in the second (as well as the social circumstances relative to that time mentioned in the fourth and tenth). But for the rest they are terse, unqualified expressions, mostly in negative form, of perennial demands inherent in the unchanging person of God and his holiness. Further, the New Testament makes the necessary redemptive-historical adjustments – for the fifth in Ephesians 6:2-3 and, as already noted, points to the change of day for the fourth. To generalize: God's law, given with man's creation in his image and subsequently "summarily comprehended" in the Decalogue, is, since the fall, a dynamic, redemptive-historical entity with shifting elements around an unchanging core, such that, in essential continuity with the Mosaic law, there is law before Moses[28] and after Christ.

3. The fact, then, that the fourth commandment is not explicitly quoted in the New Testament is far from being a presumption for its cessation. To the contrary, its inclusion as a part of the Decalogue carries the presumption that it continues in force, unless its abrogation be made explicit.

6.

Scripture vindicates the view of the Sabbath in the Westminster Standards. That view is capable of withstanding more

---

[28] Note esp. Gen 26:5, where the Lord says of Abraham that he "obeyed me and kept my requirements, my commands, my decrees and my laws."

extensive scrutiny and of a more adequate defense than it has been given here.

I conclude, briefly, with a couple of observations for further reflection. First and most importantly, it may be asked whether the eschatological aspect of the Sabbath, which has figured so prominently above in defense of the Standards, receives adequate recognition in them. We should not overlook that "... is to be continued to the end of the world..." (CF, 21:7; LC, 116; SC, 59) and perhaps "... a thankful remembrance of the two great benefits of creation and redemption..." (LC, 121) may provide an oblique intimation of an eschatological outlook. But that outlook is surely not prominent. The primary reason, it seems, is because the Sabbath is considered almost exclusively in terms of worship – at the close of the chapter on worship in the Confession (21) and also treated in that vein in the Catechisms.

My point here is not to depreciate the importance of worship or what the Standards say about it, but that the Sabbath involves something more. The Sabbath is not merely a more or less pragmatic arrangement to ensure adequate time each week for "the public and private exercises of God's worship"; it is preeminently an eschatological sign.

Secondly, and related to the preceding comment, a perennial problem is that many fully convinced that the Lord's Day is the Sabbath have difficulty with what the Standards teach about its observance, or at least with putting that teaching into practice consistently. Hence, the 10,000 arguments per week about what is permissible on Sunday, noted at the outset. In this regard the Standards seem problematic in the way they juxtapose the "holy rest" of Sabbath worship to "works, words, and thoughts about ... worldly employments and recreations" (CF, 21:8); "six days ... for our own affairs, ... but one for himself," "a day for his service" (LC, 120).

Is not this polarity ("his service"/ "our own affairs") in tension, at least without some qualifying, with the characteristic Reformed outlook on all of life as religion, resting as it does on the apostolic injunction, for instance, that the we are to "offer" ourselves as "living sacrifices" in "worship" (Rom 12:1; cf. Heb 13:15; 1 Pet 2:5)?[29]

My point here is hardly to blur the distinctiveness of the Lord's Day or to deny that on it we are to rest from our callings belonging to the other six. Nor is it to question that worship – public and private, as defined by its "parts" or "elements" in the preceding sections (3-5) of chapter 21 of the Confession – is central to the proper observance of the Lord's Day. But should our lives on the Lord's Day and on the other six – the "holy" and the "worldly" – be isolated from each other (as much as "duties of necessity and mercy" permit)? Can our lives in fact be compartmentalized in this way? The Lord's Day ought rather to be a time of restful reflection on our "worldly" concerns *coram Deo*. Does not a good sermon, like many preached by framers of the Standards themselves, promote such reflection?

The resolution here lies in appreciating the eschatological significance of the weekly Sabbath. That rest, cessation from callings legitimate on the other six days, has a positive meaning of its own. It is not just a means to an end (worship – although it does provide for that) but an end in its own right. Sabbath-cessation is an eloquent sign, a testimony to the church itself and to a watching world that believers are not dependent on their own efforts, that our lives are not trapped in an endless, ultimately meaningless cycle of days, but are going somewhere: toward the eschatological goal of Sabbath-rest that awaits the people of God (Heb 4:9). For those who presently live out of the resurrection-Sabbath already brought by Christ and so are "steadfast,

---

[29] To suppose that this language is metaphorical and that "real" worship is not in view, undervalues what the apostle says. The word used here (*latreia*) is from the NT word group for worship with the narrowest semantic range, referring almost always to the temple cultus and priestly duties (e.g., Rom. 9:4; Heb. 9:1, 6); Paul's thought is that, for believers, life in its entirety is to be "your appropriate priestly activity"; cf. 1 Pet 2:5: the church is "a holy priesthood" and so the Christian life in its entirety consists in "offering spiritual sacrifices."

immoveable, always abounding in the work of the Lord," the weekly rest day shows that their "labor is not in vain in the Lord" (1 Cor 15:58). To keep the Sabbath is itself an act of confession, a confession that God is the Lord over our time, that "our" time is not really ours but his. That as much as anything is the significance of the weekly Sabbath.

Geerhardus Vos, writing around the middle of the last century, is still worth hearing at length on this point today:

> The Sabbath is not in the first place a means of advancing religion. It has its main significance apart from that, in pointing forward to the eternal issues of life and history. Even the most advanced religious spirit cannot absolve itself from taking part in that. It is a serious question whether the modern church has not too much lost sight of this by making the day well-nigh exclusively an instrument of religious propaganda, at the expense of its eternity-typifying value. Of course it goes without saying that a day devoted to the remembrance of man's eternal destiny cannot be properly observed without the positive cultivation of those religious concerns which are so intimately joined to the final issue of his lot. But, even where this is conceded, the fact remains that it is possible to crowd too much into the day that is merely subservient to religious propaganda, and to void it too much of the static, God-ward and heavenly-ward directed occupation of piety.[30]

What do these observations entail for Sabbath-keeping, concretely and in detail? That pastoral question needs to be thought through more than has so far happened. Nor can I address it here except to suggest that a deepened appreciation of its eschatological dimension will do much in our time to bring about a renewed "delight" (Isa 58:13) in the Sabbath. And perhaps along with that delight, instead of all those inconclusive, counterproductive quarrels each week, we may witness an abundance of fruitful and edifying discussions about its proper use that result in the Lord's Day, the Christian Sabbath confessed together with the Westminster Standards, actually being spent by God's people to their increased profit and his greater glory as their Creator-Redeemer-Consummator.

---

[30] *Biblical Theology*, p. 157.

Baptists and the Westminster Confession

Timothy George

It is not too much to say that traditional Baptist historiography has been obsessed with the issue of denominational origins. Christopher Hill has bluntly evaluated the method which has characterized this approach to church history: "There seems to me sometimes to be as much fiction and unwarranted assumption—and sheer waste of time—in tracing the genealogy of sects as of individuals."[1] For all this, the role of the Westminster Confession in the development of the Baptist tradition is a topic which raises important historical and theological questions about the origin and identity of the Baptist movement.

The debate over Baptist beginnings has been shaped by three distinct theories of historical origins. First, Baptist successionism has argued for an unbroken chain of true Baptist churches stretching back across the centuries to the New Testament itself— to Jerusalem, Jesus, and John the Baptist (not John the Presbyterian!). Second, others have traced the beginnings of the Baptist movement to sixteenth-century continental Anabaptism. Clearly, there are many strong affinities between Anabaptists and later Baptists in England and America including believers'

---

[1] Christopher Hill, *Economic Problems of the Church* (London: Oxford University Press, 1956), p. xii.

baptism, voluntary church membership, and the requirements of moral discipline. But the differences between these two streams of congregationalism are even more distinct and the case for genetic influence remains: "not proved."[2] Both the successionist and Anabaptist theories, though widely held in some circles, have tended to isolate Baptists from the Reformation matrix which gave birth to their early theological and confessional writings.

Still other historians have identified two separable beginnings of the English Baptist movement in early seventeenth-century Puritanism: the General Baptists, who evolved out of the church planted by Thomas Helwys at Spitalfields near London in 1612, which was an offshoot of the rebaptized exiled congregation of John Smyth; and the Particular Baptists, who arose among the underground London congregations of the 1630s.[3] The General Baptists stressed the universal scope of the atonement, holding with the Dutch theologian Jacobus Arminius that Christ died for all persons. The Particular Baptists, on the other hand, were strict Calvinists who were in basic agreement with the five heads of doctrine propounded by the Synod of Dort (1618-19). Older historians tended to blur the distinct origins of these two Baptist streams. Thus John Marsham wrote, "They early fell into contention upon points of doctrine and split in 1611, into two great parties, called the particular and general Baptists."[4]

The Particulars, however, tended to be better educated, better organized and more successful than the Generals who were more

---

[2] Timothy George, "The Reformation Roots of the Baptist Tradition," *Review and Expositor* 86 (1989), 9-22.

[3] Michael R. Watts, *The Dissenters* (Oxford: Clarendon Press, 1978), 41-50, 99-168.

[4] *An Epitome of General Ecclesiastical History* (New York: J. Tilden and Co., 1847), 408. A more accurate reconstruction is given in B. R. White, *The Enghsh Baptists of the Seventeenth Century* (London: Baptist Historical Society, 1983).

and more drawn into the orbit of that "swarm of sectaries and schismatics,"[5] as John Taylor put it, which included Levellers, Ranters, Seekers, Quakers, and, at the end of the Puritan movement, the mysterious Family of Love." Needless to say, the Particulars also shared a closer theological kinship with the Westminster divines than with their Arminian Baptist cousins. For all that, one of the most substantial Baptist confessions of the seventeenth century was produced by the Generals. This was the Orthodox Creed of 1678. This document reflected a robust orthodoxy and sought to mediate some of the sharper differences between the Calvinist and Arminian soteriological schemes. It also included the Apostles', Nicene, and Athanasian creeds of the early church, all three of which, it was declared, "ought to be thoroughly received and believed. For we believe they may be proved, by most undoubted authority of Holy Scripture and are necessary to be understood by all Christians."[6]

In the following century, the General Baptists declined rapidly as the strong doctrinal commitments of their forebears gave way to the laxity and latitudinarianism of the times. Many English Baptists, along with many English Presbyterians, were in fact swept into the rising Unitarian movement. In the wake of the revivals led by John Wesley and George Whitefield, the Generals experienced an evangelical awakening which doubtless saved them from extinction. Led by Dan Taylor, they established the New Connection which eventually merged with the Particulars to form the Baptist Union of Great Britain and Ireland in 1891.[7]

Exactly one year after the Westminster divines had assembled

---

[5] Quoted, Watts, *Dissenters*, 79.

[6] Timothy George, ed., *Baptist Confessions, Covenants, and Catechisms* (Nashville: Broadman & Holman, 1996).

[7] Robert G. Torbet, *A History of the Baptists* (Valley Forge: Judson Press, 1978), 116.

in London to begin their work, the Particular Baptists of that city set forth their first major confession of faith. The London Confession of 1644, also known as the First London Confession, was published in the name of seven local congregations, "the poor despised churches of God in London." These early Baptists had felt the sting of criticism brought against them by established religious leaders of the day.

"They finding us out of that common roadway themselves walk, have smote us and taken away our veil, so that we may by them be recommended odious in the eyes of all that behold us, and in the hearts of all that think upon us, which they have done both in pulpit and print, charging us with holding free-will, falling away from grace, denying original sin, disclaiming of Magistracy, denying to assist them even in person or purse in any of their lawful commands, doing acts unseemly in the dispensing of the ordinance of baptism, not to be named amongst Christians."[8]

They deny such charges as "notoriously untrue" and set forth their own positive theological commitments which reflect the kind of consensual Calvinism set forth at the Synod of Dort.

One of the innovations introduced by the Particular Baptists was their insistence on baptism for believers only by full immersion under the water. Their opponents ridiculed this "scandalous" practice. They accused the Baptists of practicing baptism in the nude thus polluting all the streams, rivers, and lakes of England. The article on baptism (Article 40) in the 1644 Confession responds to this calumny: "The word *Baptizo*, signifying to dip under the water, yet so as with convenient garments both upon the administrator and subject with all modesty." The 1644 Confession was used widely by Baptists outside of London. Its chief value lies in the precedent established for later confessional developments among Baptists: a strong commitment to historic Christian orthodoxy and the doctrines of grace embodied in Reformation theology alongside a careful

---

[8] W. L. Lumpkin, ed., *Baptist Confessions of Faith* (Valley Forge: Judson Press, 1959), 154-55.

declaration of Baptist distinctives including congregational governance, believers' baptism by immersion and religious liberty.

In the three decades following the publication of the 1644 London Confession, Baptists in England were buffeted by the cataclysmic events of the times including civil war, regicide, the Protectorate of Oliver Cromwell, the restoration of the Stuart monarchy, and renewed persecution against religious dissenters. The Clarendon Code imposed severe penalties on those who would not conform to the religious requirements of the Book of Common Prayer and the newly reestablished church. In 1662 some two thousand Protestant dissenters were expelled from their ministry for nonconformity, among whom was the grandfather of John Wesley, the Reverend Samuel Annesley.

Baptists too were implicated in these events; many of them suffered fines, imprisonment, and torture for their faith. During these turbulent times of revolution, Particular Baptists in England came to identify themselves even more closely with the mainstream Protestant tradition. This effort culminated in the promulgation of a new confession of faith in 1677. In that year an impressive company of Baptist leaders throughout England gathered in London to reaffirm their faith in what came to be known generally as the Second London Confession. Twelve years later, following the Glorious Revolution and the Act of Toleration, which granted statutory freedom of worship to religious dissenters, another Baptist assembly representing more than one hundred congregations throughout the land, met in London July 3-11, 1689 and approved the Confession of 1677, a second addition of which had been published in 1688.

The Second London Confession was soon transplanted to America where it was adopted by the Philadelphia Baptist Association which secured the services of Benjamin Franklin to publish it in 1742. The Philadelphia Confession, as the American recension came to be called, contained two new articles: "Of Singing Psalms" and "Of Laying On Of Hands." In England, many

Baptists, along with other Reformed believers, had insisted that only the Psalms were proper material for singing in church. The Philadelphia Confession takes the contrary position declaring that Christians should "sing God's praises according to the best light they have received" including the use of hymns. This statement also recognized the laying on of hands as an ordinance of Christ intended "to confirm, strengthen, and comfort" newly baptized believers. The Philadelphia Confession became the most widely used and most influential Baptist statement of faith in America.

The Second London/Philadelphia Confession was, with some significant changes, almost a word for word duplication of the Westminster Confession. Before considering the differences between the two confessions, however, we should first ask a prior question: What prompted the Particular Baptists of England to adopt in such a wholesale manner the standard of Westminster? Fortunately, the framers of the 1677 Confession drafted a preface declaring quite clearly their reasons for this procedure. It appears that four considerations were uppermost in their mind. First, the Congregationalists had already used the Westminster Confession in a similar way in their Savoy Declaration of 1658. The Savoy Declaration was only a slight modification of the Westminster Confession, the principal changes touching on matters of church government and discipline. Significantly, several members of the Westminster Assembly including Goodwin, Nye, Bridge, Caryl, and Greenhill, were also framers of the Savoy Declaration. The Baptists of 1677 were well aware of the extensive debates on the nature of church government introduced by these Independent divines at the Westminster Assembly. They acknowledged their affinity for the Congregationalist position even as they moved forward with their own distinctively Baptist statement.

Second, the Baptists of 1677 wanted to show their solidarity with other believers who espoused the kind of Reformed theology set forth in the Westminster Confession. Thus, they declared their explicit agreement with the Westminster divines in all the fundamental articles of the Christian religion, as also with many others whose orthodox confessions have been published to the world, on the behalf of the Protestants in diverse nations and cities; and also to convince all that we have no itch to clog religion with new words, but to readily acquiesce in that form of sound words which hath been, in consent with the Holy Scriptures, used by others before us; hereby declaring before God, angels, and men, our hardy agreement with them, in that wholesome Protestant doctrine, which, with so clear evidence of Scripture they have asserted.

Third, they joined other Protestants in appealing to Holy Scripture as the final arbiter in all matters of faith and doctrine. For this reason, they eschewed harsh and unnecessary polemics in favor of a straightforward confessional declaration. They intended to exercise love and meekness toward each other, they said, and not "spend our breath in fruitless complaints of the evils of others, but may everyone begin at home, to reform in the first place our own hearts and ways."

Fourth, the framers of the Second London Confession were deeply concerned to pass on the faith intact to the rising generation. They regarded the neglect of family worship and careful religious instruction as the "one spring and cause of the decay of religion in our day." The Baptists were, of course, well aware of the Westminster Shorter Catechism and set about creating various Baptist versions of the same. Henry Jessey, an early Baptist pioneer, had published a *Catechism for Babes* as early as 1646. The most influential document of this kind was the *Baptist Catechism*, commonly called *Keach's Catechism*, published in 1693 and widely used by Baptists on both sides of the Atlantic.[9] In the nineteenth century Charles Haddon Spurgeon would publish

---

[9] Benjamin Keach, and his son Elias Keach, were strong leaders in the Particular Baptist movement. See the study on Benjamin Keach by J. Barry Vaughn in *Baptist Theologians*, eds. Timothy George and David S. Dockery (Nashville: Broadman & Holman, 1990), 49-76. Both the Jessey and Keach catechisms are reprinted in George, *Baptist Confessions, Covenants, and Catechisms.*

his own *Baptist Catechism* which was in essence another Baptist recension of the Westminster Shorter Catechism.

We have seen thus far that the most substantial and most influential Baptist confession of the seventeenth and eighteenth centuries belongs to the confessional family inspired by the Westminster standards. However, despite the strong doctrinal affinity and striking verbal parallels between the two confessions, significant differences can be detected as well. Not surprisingly, the most obvious differences are ecclesiological. Baptism and the Lord's Supper are declared to be ordinances rather than sacraments. The proper subjects of baptism are declared to be "those who do actually profess repentance unto God, faith in, and obedience to our Lord Jesus," rather than infants. Immersion is the only proper mode of baptism. Each local church shall be governed congregationally, with full authority to call and dismiss pastors and to maintain proper discipline over all its members. In the chapter, "Of Christian Liberty," the Baptists follow Westminster in declaring that "God alone is Lord of the conscience," but they omit the section in which those who oppose any duly constituted power, civil or ecclesiastical, are said to be resisting the ordinance of God. The advocacy of unrestricted religious liberty was deeply rooted in the Baptist experience, and this commitment is reflected in the refusal of Baptist confessions to concede coercive power to religious establishments.[10]

---

[10] Some Baptists, however, were willing to draw the line at the toleration of Roman Catholics. John Tombs, a noted Baptist theologian, declared in 1659: "Nor do we desire . . . that popery should be tolerated... nor any persons tolerated that worship a false God; nor any that speak contentiously and reproachfully of our Lord Jesus Christ; nor any that deny the Holy Scriptures...to be the Word of God. And yet we are not against tolerating of Episcopacy, Presbyters, or any stinted form, provided they do not compel others to a compliance therewith." *A declaration of several of the people called Anabaptists in and about the city of London* (1659), quoted by H. C. Vedder, *A Short History of the Baptists* (Philadelphia: American Baptist Publication Society, 1907), 61.

In the articles dealing with theology proper, the Second London Confession largely echoed the language of Westminster, although here too there were different nuances and contrasting emphases. The first chapter in both confessions is a strong Reformed statement on Holy Scripture. In section six of this chapter, the Westminster Confession declares that the whole counsel of God related to human life "is either expressly set down in Scripture, or by good and necessary consequence" deduced there from. The wording about necessary consequence is omitted from the Baptist Confession which declares that God's counsel is "expressly set down or necessarily contained in the Holy Scripture." The Baptists insisted on a strict application of the regulative principle finding in the Bible a blueprint for Christian living and a clearly-defined, universally binding model of church life including the details of polity and discipline.

Another important difference surfaces in chapter three, "Of God's Eternal Decree." The Westminster divines declared that by the decree of God, some men and angels are "predestinated unto everlasting life; and others foreordained to everlasting death." The Baptists were quite willing to embrace foreordination of the elect to eternal life, but the "others" are merely "left to act in their sin to their just condemnation, to the praise of [God's] glorious justice." On this controverted point of predestinarian theology, the Particular Baptists echoed more closely the canons of the Synod of Dort which declare that God "leaves the non-elect in His just judgment to their own wickedness and obduracy."[11] The debates over infra- and supralapsarianism would surface again among the Particular Baptists in the eighteenth century as hyper-Calvinism was embraced by some of their leading theologians. The mainstream Particular Baptist tradition,

---

[11] Philip Schaff, *Creeds of Christendom* (Grand Rapids: Baker Book House, 1977), vol.3, 582.

however, represented by Andrew Fuller and Charles Haddon Spurgeon, would continue to affirm the traditional doctrines of grace while resisting hyper-Calvinistic notions such as eternal justification, antinomianism, and the restriction of the offer of grace to the lost.[12]

Another important debate in Reformed theology is echoed in chapter eleven, "Of Justification." Westminster declares that "the obedience and satisfaction of Christ" is imputed to those whom God effectually calls. On this point the Baptists are more explicit in distinguishing the active and passive obedience of Christ: God imputes to those who are called "Christ's active obedience unto the whole Law and the passive obedience in His death, for their whole and soul Righteousness." Calvin himself had emphasized the active obedience of Christ as an essential dimension of His atoning work. This holistic view of Christ's work was also reflected in the extra emphasis given in the Second London Confession to the threefold office of Christ;

> "This number and order of offices is necessary; for in respect of our ignorance, we stand in need of his Prophetical Office; and in respect of our alienation from God, and imperfection of the best of our services, we need his Priestly Office, to reconcile us, and present us acceptably unto God: and in respect of our averseness, and utter inability to return to God, and for our rescue, and security from our spiritual adversaries, we need his Kingly Office, to convince, subdue, draw, uphold, deliver, and preserve us to his Heavenly Kingdom."

The Westminster standards, then, stand at the headwaters of the Reformed Baptist tradition. Although the First London Confession (1644) antedated Westminster by two years, the latter had a decisive shaping influence on both the form and content of all subsequent Particular Baptist confessions. At the same time, Baptists put their own stamp on the theology of Westminster by significantly modifying its ecclesiology especially with reference

---

[12] Peter Toone, *The Emergence of Hyper-Calvinism in English Nonconformity, 1689-1765* (London: The Oliver Tree, 1967), 70-89.

to the sacraments, church polity, and the civil magistracy.

Among Baptists in America the theology of Westminster was transmitted through the enormously influential Philadelphia Confession of Faith. Despite a persistent Arminian strain within Baptist life, until the twentieth century most Baptists adhered faithfully to the doctrines of grace as set forth in the Pauline-Augustinian-Reformed theology. David Benedict, following an extensive tour of Baptist churches throughout America in the early nineteenth century, gave the following summary of the Baptist theology he encountered: "Take this denomination at large, I believe the following will be found a pretty correct statement of their views of doctrine. They hold that man in his natural condition is entirely depraved and sinful; but unless he is born again— changed by grace—or made alive unto God— he cannot be fitted for the communion of saints on earth, nor the enjoyment of God in heaven; that where God hath begun a good work, He will carry it on to the end; that there is an election of grace— an effectual calling, etc., and that the happiness of the righteous and the misery of the wicked will both be eternal."[13] On the eve of the Civil War Francis Wayland, noted Baptist statesman and educator, echoed the same sentiment:

> "I do not believe that any denomination of Christians exists, which, for so long a period as the Baptists, have maintained so invariably the truth of their early confessions...the theological tenets of the Baptists, both in England and America, may be briefly stated as follows: they are emphatically the doctrines of the Reformation, and they have been held with singular unanimity and consistency."[14]

This same theological trajectory is also reflected in the major writings of Baptist theologians of this period including John L.

---

[13] David Benedict, *A General History of the Baptist Denomination in America* (Boston: Lincoln and Edmands, 1813) 2:456.

[14] Francis Wayland, *The Principles and Practices of Baptist Churches* (London: J. Heaton and Son, 1861), 15-16.

Dagg, James Petigru Boyce, B. H. Carroll, and Augustus H. Strong.

It cannot be denied, however, that Baptist confessionalism in general, and Reformed theology in particular, has lost much of its appeal among Baptists in America during the past century. Many factors have contributed to the blurring of this part of the Reformation heritage which shaped Baptist identity: the routinization of revivalism, the growth of pragmatism as a denominational strategy, an attenuated doctrine of the Holy Spirit, and a general theological laxity which has resulted in doctrinal apathy.

Among Baptists in the North, the Fundamentalist-Modernist Controversy left deep scars and a fragmented denomination less concerned with confessional integrity than individual autonomy and prudential diversity. In 1922 the Northern Baptists refused to adopt the moderately Calvinistic New Hampshire Confession of 1833 declaring instead that "the Northern Baptist Convention affirms that the New Testament is the all-sufficient ground of our faith and practice and we need no other statement."[15] In the 1940s a similar proposal for a denomination-wide confession of faith was again defeated. In recent decades, several blue-ribbon committees and task forces have studied the continuing fragmentation and loss of theological vision within the American Baptist denomination. As a former president of the ABC put it recently in a blunt statement: Mere pluralism and diversity "is a lousy identity. "[16]

The reception of Reformed theology among Baptists in the South has been affected by three major controversial movements in the nineteenth century: Campbellism, Landmarkism, and hyper-

---

[15] *Annual*, Northern Baptist Convention, 1922, 133.

[16] Quoted, William H. Brackney," 'Commonly, (Though Falsely) Called . . .': Reflections on the Search for Baptist Identity," in *Perspectives and Churchmenship: Essays in Honor of Robert G. Torbet*, ed. David M. Scholer (Macon, GA: Mercer University Press, 1986), 81.

Calvinism. In different ways, each of these movements led to a loosening of historic Reformed theology and confessional commitment among Southern Baptists. The restorationist movement led by Alexander Campbell was both Arminian and anti-confessional. Campbell introduced slogans such as "No creed but the Bible" and "Where the Bible speaks, we speak; where the Bible is silent, we are silent" into the parlance of Baptist polemics.

In two important senses, of course, Baptists have never been advocates of creedalism. They have always held to the Reformation principle of *sola Scriptura,* believing that the Bible, and the Bible alone, is the only normative rule of faith and practice for all Christians. Furthermore, Baptists have never regarded their confessions as divinely inspired artifacts of revelation. On the contrary, they hold that confessional statements are true only to the extent that they faithfully represent the teaching of Holy Scripture. For this reason, confessions of faith are always revisable in the light of God's infallible Word in Holy Scripture. Historically, however, Baptists have not regarded conscientious adherence to an explicit doctrinal standard as compatible with biblical authority. The struggle with Campbellism brought this issue to the fore and bequeathed to many progressive Southern Baptists in the twentieth century a bias against confessions of any sort. The Southern Baptist Convention, however, unlike American Baptists in the North, have adopted a denomination-wide confession of faith, The Baptist Faith and Message. This statement, published in 1925 and revised in 1963, more nearly parallels the New Hampshire Confession of 1833 than the Philadelphia Confession with its roots in the Westminster tradition.

Landmarkism was a powerful populist movement which strongly emphasized the independence of each local congregation and Baptist distinctives over against the practices of other denominations. Thus the landmarkers opposed alien immersion (the recognition of believers' baptism in other denominations), open communion (the practice of sharing the Lord's Supper with those of other denominations), and pulpit affiliation (inviting non-Baptist preachers to speak from Baptist pulpits). Although some landmarkers were, and still are, strict Calvinists in their theology, the narrow ecclesiology of the movement as a whole tended to isolate Baptists from other evangelical Christians. By so strictly defining the church as "a local assembly of baptized believers," landmark ecclesiology also denied the catholicity of the church as set forth in the historic Baptist confessions based on the Westminster standards. Significantly, when the Baptist Faith and Message was revised in 1963, the article on the church was amended to include the statement: "The New Testament speaks also of the church as the Body of Christ which includes all of the redeemed of all the ages." Not surprisingly, many landmarkers shied away from acknowledging any linkage between the Baptist tradition and the classic heritage of the Reformation. Instead, they taught a form of Baptist successionism attempting to trace the lineage of true Baptist churches through various dissenting groups throughout the history of the church including the Cathari, the Petrobrusiani, the Donatists, the Montanists, and others with equally questionable theological pedigrees!

Among Southern Baptists hyper-Calvinism took the form of a virulent anti-missionary, anti-evangelistic emphasis. Primitive or "Hard Shell" Baptists were opposed to theological seminaries, Sunday Schools, mission boards, and other cooperative efforts to share the Gospel promiscuously. They saw little need for such strenuous evangelistic efforts, since, from their perspective, it was obviously useless to exhort unconverted sinners to do what they neither could do, nor indeed had any obligation to do! Charles Haddon Spurgeon encountered a similar hyper-Calvinistic movement in nineteenth-century England. He claimed that it had "chilled many churches to the very soul," leading them "to omit the free invitations of the Gospel, and to deny that it is the duty of sinners to believe in Jesus."[17] Spurgeon's own evangelical Calvinism was more typical of Southern Baptist leaders as well. In the tradition of Andrew Fuller, William Carey, Adoniram Judson, Luther Rice, and Richard Furman, they continued to affirm both the sovereignty of God in salvation and the obligation of the church to proclaim the Gospel to all peoples everywhere. Nonetheless, the skirmish with hyper-Calvinism left an indelible mark on subsequent Southern Baptist history. Today many Baptists find it difficult to distinguish hyper-Calvinism from the kind of evangelical Calvinism modeled by Spurgeon and embodied in the historic Reformed Baptist confessions.

In recent years there has been a growing awareness of Reformed theology among Southern Baptists. While certain skeptics regard this renewed emphasis as a resurgence of hyper-Calvinism, the Westminster confessional tradition does not assert divine sovereignty to the exclusion of human responsibility. Seen in proper perspective, a renewed commitment to the sovereignty of God in salvation, as set forth in the Westminster Confession of Faith and the Baptist documents which derive from it, will issue in worship that centers on the glory of God rather than the entertainment of the audience. It will also bring a perspective on history and culture which sees Jesus Christ as Lord of time and eternity. And it will also guard faithful believers against lethargy and laziness, against defection and darkness on every hand. All of this can only result in the building up of the Body of Christ and the setting forth of the glory of God in ever increasing measure. *Soli deo gloria!*

---

[17] Raymond Brown, *The English Baptists of the Eighteenth Century* (London: The Baptist Historical Society, 1986), 76.

Baptism at the Westminster Assembly

David F. Wright

Introduction: Baptism's Neglect

The choice of subject may surprise readers. Baptism did not provoke any of the Westminster Assembly's momentous debates—although, as will be seen, it did give rise to some lengthy and divisive discussions. Nor can the Westminster divines be said to have made any remarkable contribution to the church's understanding or practice of baptism.

Yet a reaction of surprise that baptism should enjoy a paper of its own in a volume commemorating the Westminster Assembly may have more to do with a wider neglect or devaluation of baptism, at least when compared with the Lord's Supper. Modern ecumenical conversations have paid it little attention—and the section on baptism in the landmark Faith and Order statement *Baptism, Eucharist and Ministry* (World Council of Churches, Geneva, 1982) has been judged the least accomplished of the three. We have no history of Christian baptism nor a comprehensive account of baptism in the Reformation. The magisterial Reformers' differences from the Old Church on baptism were relatively slight, and both joined in scornful dismissal of the Radical Anabaptists' protest. Compared with the mass and the inner-Protestant 'Supper-strife', baptism was very trivial. One has only to reflect on the massively contrasting weight of preoccupation displayed over the proper minister of baptism on the one hand and of the Lord's supper on the other.

Whether this relative depreciation of baptism faithfully reflects the witness of the New Testament is a large question for another occasion. Let me simply affirm my judgment that it would be far truer to the apostolic testimony to portray the church as a baptismal community than as a eucharistic community, as it is commonly called today. The conviction grows on me that the devaluing of baptism, in much of British evangelical church life, for example, cannot be understood in detachment from the predominance of infant baptism and its large-scale failure—its failure, that is, in such a high proportion of cases measured on any realistic assessment, actually to initiate people into the church. Inevitably, if paedobaptism is so often ineffective, it cannot sustain grandiose theological pretensions. Inevitably, the focus shifts to some later occasion of confirmation or admission to communion or to full membership. Inevitably, reductionist treatment is meted out to the New Testament presentations of baptism, to make them fit our experience of the administration of infant baptism on the ground.

Such contemporary concerns may help to sharpen our investigation of baptismal deliberations at the Westminster Assembly. After all, the Westminster documents have to a major degree shaped baptismal understanding and practice in the Reformed churches in the West. And the very fact that our instinctive initial reaction at the pairing of baptism and Westminster suggests that its approach to the sacrament has been assimilated among our churches without much controversy may point up the special value of bringing to it the harder questions of the present—the kind of questions, for example, that the dissolution of Christendom in the western world poses to the practice of baptizing infants. For, as Karl Barth well recognised, Christendom and paedobaptism go together.[1]

---

[1] Cf. *The Teaching of the Church Regarding Baptism*, translated by E. A. Payne (SCM Press, London, 1948), 52-4; 'the really operative extraneous

The Westminster Documents and Minutes

Four of the Westminster documents deal with baptism: the Confession of Faith, the Directory for Public Worship, and the Larger and Shorter Catechisms. The minutes of the Assembly record next to nothing of the discussions on the contents of the Catechisms, and, as far as baptism is concerned, very little of those on the Confession. The only extended minutes of baptismal debate relate to the Directory for Public Worship.

Not that the extant minutes are a high-quality record. This is the verdict of the late Robert Paul:

> [T]hese manuscript 'Minutes' are something of a misnomer, since they appear to be little more than the hasty notes of a scribe, probably written in preparation for a fuller account to appear at some later date. The speeches are often cryptic to the point of being almost meaningless, there are frustrating gaps in the text where the scribe had possibly intended to insert summaries of the speeches to be obtained from the notes of the speakers themselves, and the whole is written in an execrable seventeenth century hand of extraordinary abstruseness and complexity.[2]

Fortunately, not least for the purposes of this paper, the Library of New College, Edinburgh holds an invaluable manuscript transcript in highly legible copper-plate script of the original manuscript minutes (which are in Dr. Williams' Library, London). The transcript was made in the late 1860s and early 1870s under

---

ground for infant-baptism, even with the Reformers, and ever and again quite plainly since, has been this: one did not want then in any case or at any price to deny the existence of the evangelical Church in the Constantinian *corpus christianum*—and today one does not want to renounce the present form of the national church (Volkskirche)?' (52).

2 Robert S. Paul, *The Assembly of the Lord. Politics and Religion in the Westminster Assembly and the 'Grand Debate'* (T&T Clark, Edinburgh, 1985), 72-3; cited henceforth as 'Paul'. See also his Appendix IV, 'Interpreting the Minutes'", 562-4. Among the oddities of the manuscript is the misspelling of names. George Gillespie, one of the Scottish commissioners, commonly appears as 'Gelaspi'.

the auspices of a Church of Scotland committee.[3] The published copy of part of the minutes, edited by Alexander F. Mitchell and

---

[3] On these matters see Paul, 73, with notes. In June 1867 the Church of Scotland's General Assembly appointed a committee to obtain a transcript of the manuscript minutes held in Dr. Williams' Library, London (*Principal Acts of the General Assembly of the Church of Scotland . . .* 1867, 60). This committee, convened until his death by Professor Alexander F. Mitchell and then from 1899 by Thomas Leishman, until it was discontinued by the 1904 Assembly, arranged for the completion of the transcript (on the difficulties of this task see *Principal Acts . . . 1868*, 63-5, and subsequent annual reports to the Assembly), which it presented to the 1875 Assembly which deposited it in the General Assembly Library (*Principal Acts . . .* 1875, 85). The committee also secured the publication of most of volume III of the minutes, in 1874 (see next note), and in 1892 also of *The Records of the Commissions of the General Assemblies of the Church of Scotland holden in Edinburgh in the Years 1646 and 1647*, ed. Mitchell and James Christie (Scottish History Society, II; Edinburgh, 1892; see *Principal Acts . . . 1890*, 82; *1892*, 78), but failed despite years of effort to find adequate funds for the publication of the rest of the Westminster Assembly's minutes (*Principal Acts . . . 1881*, 64; *1904*, 68). The completion of this task of publication I hope to achieve soon. Further investigation is called for to clarify some of the General Assembly reports on the progress of the project (e.g., *Principal Acts . . . 1870*, 75; *1871*, 69; *1872*, 76; *1887*, 68).

The transcript secured by Mitchell's committee was largely, if not wholly (see next note), the work of Edward Maunde Thompson, of the Manuscripts Department of the British Museum. On Thompson (1840-1929), later Principal Librarian of the British Museum 1888-1902 (with title of Director from 1898), see *Dictionary of National Biography 1922-1930* (1937), 834-6, although this tribute by F. G. Kenyon does not mention Thompson's transcript of the Westminster Assembly's minutes. On the Church of Scotland's General Assembly Library see briefly John Howard. 'New College Library', in Wright and Badcock (eds), *Disruption to Diversity* (*op. cit.*, n. 58 below), 187-202, at 192-3. The transcript appears in the printed *Catalogue of Books, Pamphlets and Manuscripts in the Library of the General Assembly of the Church of Scotland* (Blackwood, Edinburgh, 1907), 441: 'Minutes of the sessions of the Assembly of Divines at Westminster, August 4, 1643 - March 25, 1652. 3 vols. in 5. folio.' In the preparation of this paper I have been wholly dependent on the New College transcript, which, following Paul, I cite as 'TMs.' and not on the original manuscript. In manuscript the minutes extend from April 4, 1643 to April 24, 1652.

John Struthers in 1874, presents this transcript.[4] This volume covers the Assembly's proceedings from November 1644 to March 1649 and hence does not include the debates on the Directory for Public Worship and contains little about baptism.

The minutes can be supplemented, and sometimes corrected, from the accounts of participants, especially the *Journals* of the noted Hebraist, John Lightfoot, covering July 1643 to December 1644, and the *Notes* of George Gillespie of debate February 1644

---

[4] *Minutes of the Sessions of the Westminster Assembly of Divines, While Engaged in Preparing the Directory for Church Government, Confession of Faith and Catechisms*(November 1644 to March 1649). *From Transcripts of the Originals Procured by a Committee of the General Assembly of the Church of Scotland*, Edited for the Committee by Alex. F. Mitchell and John Struthers (William Blackwood & Sons, Edinburgh, 1874, reprinted, Still Waters Revival Books, Edmonton, Alberta, 1991), cited hereafter as 'Mitchell and Struthers'. On Mitchell, see briefly Nigel M. de S. Cameron *et al.* (eds), *Dictionary of Scottish Church History and Theology* (T&T Clark, Edinburgh, 1993), 594, and on Struthers, *Fasti Ecclesiae Scoticanae*, 2nd. edit., I (1915), 391. Only further research will clear up some uncertainty over Struthers' contribution to the transcripts published by Mitchell and Struthers. According to the General Assembly record, E.M. Thompson (see previous note transcribed volume II, and Struthers an important part of volume Ill (*Principal Acts* . . . 1868, 64: the Assembly Acts give no more detail). Mitchell and Struthers, ix, state that the transcripts of volume III were made by Thompson and Struthers, but also that 'the Minutes throughout stand in [their published] text as, after repeated and careful revision, it was fixed by Mr. Thompson. Furthermore, the five folio volumes of the transcript in New College Library appear to be all in single hand. Paul, 73, with n. 5, if anything compounds the confusion. It may well be that the transcript we now have is wholly Thompson's production.

It should be noted that where Mitchell and Struthers insert an ellipsis (. . .) in their text, it does not indicate omission of material in the minutes but merely gaps in the transcript itself, nearly always immediately evident from parts of lines or several lines at a time left blank. Here the transcript faithfully reproduced the original: see Paul, 73, cited above. Mitchell and Struthers might have obviated any misunderstanding of their practice had they been fully consistent. but cf. 180, 'Her   '; 182, 'Debate of   '. The present essay uses ellipsis (. . .) to indicate only my omission of material from the source. I have modernised the spelling of the manuscript minutes only in giving 'that' for 'yt' and 'and' for the copula.

to January 1645, together with the briefer general comments in Robert Baillie's *Letters and Journals*.[5] Both Lightfoot and Gillespie are of value in supplying some of the deficiencies of the minutes in relation to the sessions on baptism.

The Confession of Faith and the Grace of Baptism

The Second Committee appointed to work on the Confession of Faith, whose assigned subjects included the sacraments, brought its report on baptism to the full Assembly on December 29, 1645.[6] Debate is recorded as having taken place on nine days in January, possibly ten, and again on September 11, 1646, with the chapters on the sacraments (27) and on baptism (28) winning final approval on November 10, 1646.[7] But apart from some tantalizingly brief indications (for example, a small group was instructed on September 11 to consider 'what children are to be baptized'),[8] the minutes record nothing of the debates except on January 5, one of several days on which the 'grace of God in baptism' (so January 9) was on the table.

The Assembly on January 5 began with a phrase which was

---

[5] *Lightfoot. The Journal of the Proceedings of the Assembly of Divines, from January 1, 1643, to December 31, 1644 . . .* , ed. John Rogers Pitman (*The Whole Works . . .* , XIII; J. F. Dove, London, 1824), cited as 'Lightfoot'; Gillespie, *Notes of Debates and Proceedings of the Assembly of Divines and Other Commissions at Westminster, February 1644 to January 1645,* ed. David Meek (Robert Ogle and Oliver and Boyd, Edinburgh, 1846), cited as 'Gillespie'; *The Letters of Robert Baillie, A.M., Principal of the University of Glasgow, M.DC. XXXVII - M.DC.LXII*, ed. David Laing. 3 vols. (Robert Ogle, Edinburgh, 1841-2), cited as 'Baillie'.

[6] Mitchell and Struthers, 164, 173. For the composition of the Second Committee see Paul, 555-6.

[7] Mitchell and Struthers, 173-82, 280, 299. The uncertainty concerns January 19, 1646 '*Ordered*—Report of that Committee concerning Baptism (be taken) be made on Wednesday morning' (*ibid..*, 180).

[8] Mitchell and Struthers, 280; cf. 175, 'Debate of Baptism. Debate about dedication to God' (January 2), 'Debate upon Baptism; "the grace of God bestowed sometimes before"' (January 5).

presumably in the Second Committee's draft but did not survive into the Confession itself, 'the grace God bestowed sometimes before'. Let us recall the statement in the Confession as approved:

> The efficacy of baptism is not tied to that moment of time when it is administered; yet notwithstanding, by the right use of this ordinance, the grace promised is not only offered, but really exhibited and conferred by the Holy Ghost, to such (whether of age or infants) as that grace belongeth unto, according to the counsel of God's own will, in his appointed time (28:6).

We can only presume (for we have no way of knowing) that it was a draft something like this which elicited some disagreement on January 5, 1646, between Jeremiah Whitaker and a more prominent member of the company, Herbert Palmer, who was the first divine to be nominated by parliament to the Assembly and later on one of its assessors (roughly, deputy chair) and the Master of Queen's College, Cambridge. Whitaker declared

> That it doth confer grace I do not find, but our divines do hold it. When they oppose the Papists, they say it is more than a sign and a seal. Chamier saith the grace that is signified is exhibited, so it is in the French Confession; it doth *efficaciter donare*.[9]

Whitaker takes his stand on Scripture:

> That which the Scripture ascribes to baptism we are to ascribe. Baptism is an ordinance to effect these ends. . . . Baptism saves, 1. Accompanied with the sign and thing signified, it is a saving ordinance. For without grace none of these things can be.[10]

Palmer's response is not easy to follow with entire clarity. He asserts that 'What the Scripture speaks of efficacy of baptism, it speaks of those that are grown up. We must suppose the person to be baptized a believer.'[11] He certainly denies that the sacrament is a naked sign—'there is no nakedness in a seal'—but he apparently envisages baptism as conferring its gifts on those who already enjoy

---

[9] Mitchell and Struthers, 175.

[10] *Ibid.*

[11] *Ibid.*, 176.

grace. He seems to reject the notion that baptism imparts the grace of conversion; 'he that is without the first grace hath nothing to make him in a capacity of receiving; he is dead'.[12] Whitaker is not satisfied: Palmer has not answered the Scriptures he quoted. 'The Scripture speaks more about conferring than it doth either of signing and sealing.'[13]

Such is our intriguingly brief glimpse of a debate that must have engaged weighty theological considerations. On my reading of the minutes, the draft before the Assembly at this point did not contain the language now present—'not only offered, but really exhibited and conferred'—but the text is not lucid enough to allow certainty on this question. Whitaker not only advances the word 'exhibited' but also evinces awareness of its Latin original—'*in conjuncta exhibitione*, Ursin[us]'. The verb was widely used in Reformation disputes on the Lord's supper, especially by Martin Bucer, but its currency in this context goes back at least to Aquinas.[14] Its pairing with 'conferred' reveals its meaning, which is stronger than 'exhibit' in modern English. The word 'convey' comes near to the double reference of *exhibere*, as does 'present' itself.

Baptismal Regeneration

What then about the efficacy of baptism according to the Westminster Confession? Its central affirmation seems clear: 'the grace promised is not only offered, but really exhibited and conferred by the Holy Ghost' (28:6). It is true that a variety of

---

[12] *Ibid.*, with n. 1.

[13] *Ibid.*

[14] *Ibid.* On *exhibere.* cf. D. F. Wright, 'Infant Baptism and the Christian Community', in Wright (ed.), *Martin Bucer: Reforming Church and Community* (Cambridge University Press, Cambridge, 1994), 95-106 at 99-100; W.I.P. Hazlett, 'Les entretiens entre Melancthon et Bucer en 1534; réalités politiques et clariflication théologique', in M. de Kroon and M. Lienhard (eds), *Horizons Européens de la Réforme en Alsace . . . Mélanges offerts à Jean Rott . . .* (Librairie Istra, Strasbourg, 1980), 207-25, at 223 n. 40.

qualifications to this assertion are entered in the chapter on baptism: efficacy is not tied to the moment of administration (*ibid.*), grace and salvation are not so inseparably annexed to baptism that no person can be regenerated or saved without it (28:5) or that all the baptized are undoubtedly regenerated (*ibid.*). But these qualifications serve in fact only to highlight the clarity of the core declaration, which is set forth as follows in the preceding chapter on sacraments in general:

> neither doth the efficacy of a sacrament depend upon the piety or intention of him that doth administer it, but upon the work of the Spirit, and the word of institution; which contains . . . a promise of benefit to worthy receivers (27:3).

The Westminster divines viewed baptism as the instrument and occasion of regeneration by the Spirit, of the remission of sins, of ingrafting into Christ (cf. 28:1). The Confession teaches baptismal regeneration. We should note also that while the Catechisms use the language only of 'sign and seal',[15] the Directory for Public Worship has the following passage in the model prayer before the act of baptizing:

> That the Lord . . . would join the inward baptism of his Spirit with the outward baptism of water; make this baptism to the infant a seal of adoption . . . and all other promises of the covenant of grace: That the child may be planted into the likeness of the death and resurrection of Christ.[16]

---

[15] Larger Catechism A. 165: 'Baptism is a sacrament of the New Testament, wherein Christ hath ordained the washing with water . . . to be a sign and seal of ingrafting into himself, of remission of sins . . . '; Shorter Catechism A. 95: ' . . . a sacrament, wherein the washing . . . doth signify and seal. . . .'

[16] The words 'join the inward baptism . . . with the outward' did not win immediate acceptance from the Assembly on July 19, 1644, according to TMs. II, 261-3. Whitaker declared the child to be as capable of the working of the Spirit in baptism as afterwards, Stephen Marshall was sure that, as a sign, baptism fulfilled all three functions of a sign, viz., to signify, to seal (*obsignare*) and to exhibit, and Palmer affirmed that, since God baptizes through ministerial instruments, 'If he does it he doth it inwardly as well as outwardly' (263).

But if the Assembly unambiguously ascribes this instrumental efficacy to baptism, it is not automatically enjoyed by all recipients: it contains 'a promise of benefit to worthy receivers' (27:3), who from one point of view are 'those that do actually profess faith in and obedience unto Christ, but also the infants of one or both believing parents' (28:4), and from another, 'such (whether of age or infants) as that grace belongeth unto, according to the counsel of God's own will, in his appointed time' (28:6). But it would surely be a perverse interpretation of the Confession's chapter on baptism if we allowed this last allusion to the hidden counsel of God to emasculate its vigorous primary affirmation.

Profession of Faith

I have been struck, in re-reading the Confession and Directory for Public Worship and scrutinizing records of the debates, at the Assembly's relatively muted concern with faith as a prerequisite for baptism to have effect. The key stipulation is, of course, present: baptism is for 'those that do actually profess faith in and obedience unto Christ, but also the infants of one or both believing parents' (28:4). Westminster provides no support for a tendency observable in recent years for the requirement of sincere and credible Christian faith on the part of at least one parent to be transposed into an emphasis on the faith of the receiving congregation. While heightened congregational involvement is to be welcomed, this shift is motivated to some measure by a desire to accommodate the baptism of children whose parent or parents cannot with any honesty be acknowledged as believers or church members. Increasingly, indeed, granny is the one pressing for the baptism. From other angles also infant baptism is becoming a more tangled pastoral issue as the norms of marriage and family disintegrate.

In the light of these present-day concerns, it is instructive to note the absence from the Directory for Public Worship of any provision for the parent(s) to be called upon to profess their faith afresh at the baptism, or to undertake any vows or commitments in relation to the child. The question was one which occupied the assembled divines on two occasions, in July 1644 (July 12 and 15) and again on October 9-11 later that year. For the second debate we have invaluable reports by Lightfoot and Gillespie. The latter records that the Assembly voted by 28 to 16 to include a parental profession of faith, in the form of affirmative answers to credal questions.[17] The deletion of such a section from the Directory was the work of the English Parliament in early 1645.[18] What the Commons and Lords dropped was the following paragraph:

> It is recommended to the parent, to make a profession of his faith, by answering these and the like questions:
>
> Dost thou believe in God the Father, Son and Holy Ghost?
>
> Dost thou hold thyself bound to observe all that Christ hath commanded thee, and wilt thou endeavour so to do?
>
> Dost thou desire to have this child baptised into the faith and profession of Jesus Christ?

All that Parliament added by way of compensation was the phrase 'requiring his [the parent's] solemn promise for the performance

---

[17] Gillespie. 91.

[18] *Journals of the House of Commons* IV, 70; *Journals of the House of Lords* VII, 264.

[19] For the text, *Journals of the House of Lords* VII, 264 (March 5, 1645) and Gillespie, 91; and TMs. II. 493, in part only. See A.F. Mitchell, *The Westminister Assembly. Its History and Standards* (Nisbet & Co., London, 1883; reprinted. Still Waters Revival Books. Edmonton, Alberta, 1992), 218 -19. The omitted paragraph would have appeared immediately after "if he be negligent', i.e., where the inserted phrase is now placed. Lightfoot, 314- 15, includes an earlier form of the questions proposed to the Assembly by its committee:

1. Do you believe all the articles of faith contained in Scripture?

2. That all men and this child are born in sin?

3. That the blood and Spirit washeth away sin?

4. Will you have, therefore, this child baptized?

of his duty.'[19]

The minutes together with the reports of Lightfoot and Gillespie enable one to follow with reasonable confidence a quite surprising range of arguments batted to and fro on the desirability of recommending such a profession.[20] The Scots, with Alexander Henderson to the fore, 'did urge it mightily, because of the use of it in all reformed churches,'[21] Citing Calvin's exegesis of 1 Peter 3:21, Henderson reckoned a profession in the form of questions and answers as 'ancient as the baptizing of infants and taken from that practise used in baptizing of adults'. It added to the solemnity of the occasion.[22] For others like Thomas Wilson and Philip Nye, the usage of the Reformed churches and Scotland was inadequate ground, if it did not satisfy the criteria of Scripture or prudence. 'We may pray reformed churches may be reformed more than are they.[23] The Scots were clearly not of one mind, for Samuel Rutherford opposed it as lacking warrant in Scripture, and he wanted nothing in the Directory that could not command full uniformity.[24] George Walker reminded his colleagues that they were constructing a directory, not 'an obligatory'.[25]

Taking a stand on the Bible proved no easy matter. No parental profession had been required in circumcision, Stephen Marshall pointed out, and Thomas Valentine concurred.[26] For Samuel Gibson

---

This came forward for discussion on October 9, 1644, according to Lightfoot. The manuscript minutes contain neither this set of questions nor the form that later failed to secure Parliament's approval.

[20] TMs. II, 251-3 (July 12 and 15), 479-93 (October 9-11, 1644); Lightfoot, 314-16 (October 9-11); Gillespie, 88-91 (October 9-11).

[21] Lightfoot, 315.

[22] TMs. II, 489, 481; Gillespie, 91.

[23] TMs. II, 483-4.

[24] Gillespie, 90; TMs. II, 481, 486.

[25] TMs. II, 487.

[26] TMs. II, 481; Gillespie, 91.

the conversion of the Philippian jailor was decisive; neither he nor his family were baptized until he made a profession of his faith.[27] William Bridge was unmoved by this precedent, for it would place members of the church on a par with non-members.[28] Strong support was raised by Edmund Calamy for whom 'the parents' profession is the ground of the admission of the child',[29] which unnerved William Bridge, lest this argued that the federal holiness of the parent was not the ground of baptizing his offspring.[30] More than one divine was worried that the requirement of a profession would look like a concession to the Anabaptists. As Bridge put it,

> This confession must be either in regard of the child, and that holds out the necessity of actual confession in baptism, as the Anabaptists hold; if in regard of the parent , then it is a wrong to the parent.[31]

The questions and answers at baptism were indeed very ancient, conceded Charles Herle, who followed William Twisse as prolocutor in the chair of the Assembly, 'but in those times the Anabaptists were not risen in the world'.[32]

Fear of seeming to appease 'the Anabaptists' surfaced on other occasions in the baptismal debates, as we shall see, for 'Anabaptism' was no merely historical threat. Robert Baillie's letters from the Assembly years sound the alarm at 'the great increase and insolencie, in diverse places, of the Antinomian and Anabaptisticall conventicles'.[33] Such apprehension in relation to a parental profession of faith added a further complication to the difficult task of reaching a consensus when the criteria—scriptural warrant, antiquity, uniformity as a feasible goal, etc.—were inadequate.

---

[27] TMs. II, 483; Gillespie, 90.

[28] TMs. II, 485.

[29] TMs. II, 485.

[30] TMs. II, 480.

[31] Gillespie, 90.

[32] TMs. II, 480; Gillespie, 89.

[33] Baillie II, 215; cf. 218, 224.

Jeremiah Burroughes of Stepney thought it ironic that 'this explicate profession' should be urged by those who regarded the church covenant as a human intervention, for it was equally so.[34]

The silence of the Directory on the need for a profession of faith—after, that is, Parliament had dispensed with it—contrasts starkly with the first attested adaptation of the early church's baptismal liturgy to accommodate children who could not answer for themselves. When a child was brought forward, parents were asked by the minister 'Does he/she believe?', in this direct third-person form.[35] The procedure could not have attested more unambiguously that infants were being included in a rite devised for faith-professing candidates. The outcome of the Westminster Assembly's tortuous deliberations reflected many centuries of practice, undisturbed by the mainstream Reformation, in which infant baptism, not faith-baptism, had been *de facto* the norm.

In Public or in Private?

Two other issues likewise kept the assembled divines busy for days during consideration of the Directory's draft section on baptism. One was whether dipping, i.e. immersion, should be mentioned, and if so in what terms, and the other was what emerged eventually in the Directory as the stipulation that baptism was not to be

> administered in private places, or privately, but in the place of publick worship and in the face of the congregation, where the people may most conveniently see and hear, and not in the places where fonts, in the time of Popery, were unfitly and superstitiously placed.

'Here', records John Lightfoot, 'began we to enter into the ocean of many vast disputes'.[36] They spent all of July 11, 1644, on it,

---

[34] TMs. II. 480.

[35] Cf. J. C. Didier, 'Une adaptation de la liturgie baptismale au baptême des enfants dans l'Eglise ancienne' *Mélanges de science religieuse* 22 (1965), 79-90.

[36] Lightfoot, 297.

and returned to it on October 9 when the location of the font was on the table. The Scots, as Gillespie tells us, claimed that there was 'no place so fit for seeing and hearing of the people as the pulpit . . . the pulpit is chosen for the fittest place'.[37] Not surprisingly they did not prevail, but Scottish practice reflected their plea, with basins affixed to the outside of the pulpit and bairns held up aloft by parents to ministers to sprinkle with baptismal dew from above.[38] The height of the pulpit determined how hazardous the elevation was.[39]

The prior question—in private, or only in public?—implicated weighty considerations of theological import. Robert Baillie's letter expresses his relief.

> We have carried, with much greater ease than we expected, the publickness of baptisme. The abuse was great over all this land. In the greatest parosch in London, scarce one child in a-year was brought to the church for baptisme. Also we have carried the parents presenting of his child, and not their midwives, as was their universall custome.[40]

Edmund Calamy made the same point more sharply: 'great abuse in the city [of London: he was vicar of St Mary's, Aldermanbury],

---

[37] Gillespie, 89; Lightfoot, 315.

[38] See the present writer's article in Cameron (ed.), *Dictionary* (*op. cit.* n. 4 above), 57.

[39] Paedobaptism in other forms has occasionally afforded an unwitting recollection of the etymological and symbolic links between baptism and death by immersion in water. According to the *Financial Times* of March 2, 1996, President Boris Yeltsin was nearly drowned by a tipsy priest when being baptized in a Siberian village as a child. I recall a story that used to go the rounds of the Anglican theological colleges. What should a vicar do if he accidentally dropped a baby into a deep stone font? Replace the lid on the font and turn in the Prayer Book to the service for Burial at Sea! Karl Barth commented scornfully on the loss in dramatic vividness as complete immersion yielded to affusion which itself was reduced from a real wetting to a sprinkling and eventually to the 'mere moistening with as little water as possible' of 'the innocuous form of present-day baptism'; *The Teaching of the Church Regarding Baptism*, 9-11.

[40] Baillie II, 204-5.

[41] TMs. II, 244.

in 2 or 3 yeares none baptized in the church'.[41] For centuries in the medieval West the majority of babies may well have been baptized by midwives or other lay persons. The custom rested, of course, on the Augustinian premise of the necessity of baptism for eternal salvation. The Westminster Confession and the Directory for Public Worship trod delicately in eschewing this notion with its abusive consequences but without relaxing the reins irresponsibly. Thus the Directory:

> [O]utward baptism is not so necessary, that, through the want thereof, the infant is in danger of damnation, or the parents guilty, if they do contemn or neglect the ordinance of Christ, when and where it may be had.

And so 'to propound the case of sickness' as justification for private baptism 'is to go too near the tenet of the absolute necessity', as Thomas Wilson put it.[42]

The argument between public and private baptism again reveals the company of divines searching in vain for decisive scriptural guidance. Was not circumcision done in private houses? Gillespie was not convinced, and in any case 'circumcision and baptism differ, because of the wound and plastering it'. No blood on the synagogue floor![43] 'All the nation was baptized when they were to come out of Egypt; but this could not be done in a congregation', retorted John Lightfoot.[44] Stephen Marshall could cite 'reasons a man may give many why in the publique congregation, but noe instance of it in the new testament'.[45] Lazarus Seaman added that it provided 'noe instance . . . in a private place by any ordinary minister either'.[46] The quest for precise scriptural precedent threatened at such junctures to issue

---

[42] Lightfoot, 297; TMs. II, 244-5.

[43] Lightfoot, 297; TMs. II, 245.

[44] Lightfoot, 298.

[45] TMs. II, 245.

[46] TMs. II, 249.

in absurd minimalism.

A more substantive aspect of this question was the child's relationship to the church. Calamy is credited with asserting that 'Baptisme properly is noe church ordinance/Baptized and then added to the church', but Samuel Rutherford retorted: 'It is admission to the church; *ergo*, it must be in the face of the church.'[47] It was left to Seaman to supply another word of sanity: 'If the church go to the child, when the child go to church, this is not to be thought private baptism.'[48] Amid the ebb and flow of conflicting opinions, in which one reluctantly admires the ingenuity of the assembled minds more than their sweet reasonableness, it is astonishing to find on this issue no forthright appeal to the principle of holding Word and sacrament together. One might have expected it to clinch the argument, so that baptism could only properly take place when and where the Word was ministered. The divines too easily lost sight of the theological wood amid varied individual trees of New Testament baptisms.

Debate over Dipping

At times when one eavesdrops on the Assembly's deliberations, one can only marvel at the providence that produced such a majestic outcome from such an astonishing pot-pourri of discussion. This is nowhere more keenly felt than in the protracted altercations over whether the Directory should mention dipping. Herein, says Lightfoot, 'fell we upon a large and long discourse',[49] on which they spent at least three days, July 21 and August 7-8, 1644, according to the minutes. Lightfoot was absent on August 7. In the end, the Directory kept silent. To baptize the child,

which, for the manner of doing of it, is not only lawful but sufficient,

---

[47] Lightfoot, 297; TMs. II, 244.

[48] Lightfoot, 297; TMs. II. 245.

[49] Lightfoot, 299.

and most expedient to be, by pouring or sprinkling of the water on the face of the child, without adding any other ceremony.

As Lightfoot commented, 'it was thought fit and most safe to let it alone'.[50] Later the Confession would be explicit, 'Dipping of the person into the water is not necessary' (28:3), but the course of reasoning that led to this change of mind is hidden from us.

On August 7 the company voted and split down the middle: 24 were for keeping a mention of dipping, 25 were against. And this was after a re-count: 'it was voted so indifferently that we were glad to count names twice', wrote Lightfoot. 'And there grew a great heat upon it: and when we had done all, we concluded upon nothing in it.[51] The arguments were truly wondrous in their variety and virtuosity:

> if dipping is needed to depict burial, 'what must answer dying?' (Francis Woodcock);[52]
>
> if we say dipping is necessary, 'we shall further anabaptisme' (John Ley, and John Lightfoot);[53]
>
> what was the 'proper native signification' of the Greek verb *baptizo*? (Gillespie);[54]
>
> how could 5000 be dipped in a day? (George Walker);[55]
>
> what happened in Jewish proselyte baptism, which was followed by John the Baptist and the disciples of Jesus? (Thomas Coleman and Lightfoot gave different answers);[56]

Lightfoot was in his element citing the rabbinic commentators;

> others reported what was the practice in Muacovy and Spain, or

---

[50] *Ibid.*, 301.

[51] *Ibid.* 300.

[52] TMs. II, 265.

[53] TMs. II, 265, 275.

[54] TMs. II, 267.

[55] TMs. II, 266.

[56] TMs. II, 271 (Coleman: proselytes went in up to their necks and dipped themselves all over), 272 (Lightfoot: sprinkling attested by Rabbi Solomon).

[57] TMs. II, 270, 276.

registered that 'those that incline most to popery are all for sprinkling';[57]

the Hebrew host 'baptized into Moses' were not immersed (John Arrowsmith);[58]

the meaning of Hebrew words was ventilated and Latin terms flew to and fro.

And early on Lazarus Seaman posed one of the Assembly's dilemmas: we must follow the mind and institution of Christ, but if that turns out to be dipping, we will be hard put to it to persuade parents to have their children baptized.[59]

I Corinthians 7:14: Holiness, Federal or Real?

With some relief, we turn to some contested exegesis. In one of his letters from Westminster Robert Baillie wrote home as follows:

> We have ended our Directorie for baptisme. Thomas Goodwin one day was exceedinglie confounded: He has undertaken a publicke lecture against the Anabaptists: it was said, under pretence of refuting them. he betrayed our cause to them, that of the Corinthians, our chief ground for the baptisme of infants, 'Your children are holy', he exponed of a reall holiness, and preached down our ordinare and necessare distinction of reall and federall holiness. Being posed hereupon, he could no wayes cleare himselfe, and no man took his part.[60]

---

[58] TMs. II, 266. John Macleod in his *Scottish Theology in Relation to Church History since the Reformation* (Publications Comm. of Free Church of Scotland, Edinburgh, 1946), 253,5, relates Macmichael's exposition of I Corinthians 10:1-5:

1. The Israelites were baptised, both adults and infants; for the Apostle declares it. 2. They were not immersed, a fact which Moses and other inspired writers testify. 3. The Egyptians who pursued them were immersed. 4. The Israelites had baptism without immersion, and the Egyptians immersion without baptism. 5. The baptism of Israelites was salvation, and the immersion of the Egyptians drowning.

I owe this reference to Donald Macleod, 'The Free Church College 1900-1970'. in D. F. Wright and Gary D. Badcock (eds), *Disruption to Diversity: Edinburgh Divinity 1864-1996* (T&T Clark, Edinburgh, 1996), 221-37, at 231-2.

[59] TMs. II, 265.

[60] Baillie II, 218.

The Directorie ended up with the statement that the children of believers 'are Christians, and federally holy before baptism, and therefore are they baptized'. John Lightfoot was unfortunately absent from the Assembly on July 16, 1644, when the meaning and implications of I Corinthians 7:14 were rehearsed at length and in depth. We may judge it one of the company's better days. The minutes are ample but not clear at every point.

Goodwin kept up his end from first to last.

> It is such a holynesse as if they dy they should be saved/whether a holynesse of election or regeneration I know not; but I thinke it is they have the holy ghost.[61]

Lazarus Seaman spelt out the alarm that others showed: all agree that this holynesse is the ground of baptisme . . . except he can make out this, the baptizing of infants is gone as touching his judgment.'[62] Goodwin in effect denied any distinction between real and federal holiness: the holiness predicated of the children of a single Christian parent by Paul is the same as that of 'I will be your God and you shall be my people. Therefore be holy.' If 1 Corinthians 7:14 speaks of any other holiness, then baptism is the seal of some other holiness than the holiness of salvation.[63]

But saving holiness is what infallibly saves, commented Stephen Marshall anxiously.[64] As Rutherford put it, 'wher ther is reall and inherent holynesse ther must be a seeing of god, and being in the state of salvation'. But 'the Lord hath election and reprobation amongst Infants noe lesse than those of age'.[65] This emerged as the main objection to Goodwin's interpretation, which

---

[61] TMs. II, 256.

[62] TMs. II, 256; cf. 256: Goodwin's interpretation removes the 'common and ordinary' ground of infant baptism and lays new ground.

[63] TMs. II, 275: 'that which you call federall holynesse and that which I call real doe both coincidere in this'.

[64] TMs. II, 257.

[65] TMs. II, 256.

was alleged to imply that all such infants would indubitably be saved (Marshall) and that the decrees of election and reprobation could not stand (Rutherford).[66]

So argument ensued on the difference between an indefinite proposition and a universal proposition. Goodwin's case rested on the former: 'an indefinite faith founded upon an indefinite promise'.[67] Herbert Palmer could not concur: Paul's answer to the 'inconvenience' to a child from one parent's infidelity must be 'a universal proposition and *de fide* we are bound to believe it *de omnibus et singulis*'.[68] To be sure, Goodwin did not entertain every notion that some divines read into his position. He denied that he was speaking of a holiness received by the child by traduction from the parent, as Richard Vines had supposed ('and so they shall be borne regenerate and really holy'),[69] but only of a holiness by way of designation.[70] Calamy came back at Goodwin: 'he judges of the reall holynesse of the infant by the reall holynesse of the parent'. But this is how we all proceed, rejoined Goodwin; it is the children of believers that we baptize.[71]

The combined learning and piety of the Westminster theologians did not resolve the exegesis of 1 Corinthians 7:14. The verse had inevitably engaged the attention of previous generations of expositors, and had found the early Fathers and

---

[66] TMs. II, 256, 257.

[67] TMs. II, 258: the 'terminus' of human judgment is to be the infant's salvation, but the minister is not to have an infallible judgment of it, but 'such a judgment as answers the promise'. But at 260, if the minute is reliable, Goodwin apparently accepted that the verse in some sense embodied 'a universal proposition': 'if the children are by a warrant from the apostle accounted holy soe as to be brought into the bosome of the church/then the unbeliever must needs be sanctified to the believers bed'.

[68] TMs. II, 260.

[69] TMs. II, 258.

[70] TMs. II, 259.

[71] TMs. II, 261.

the Reformers of the sixteenth century espousing a variety of theories that, if not universally comprehensive, was at least indefinite.[72] But whereas earlier exegetes had been especially preoccupied with avoiding the attribution to the children of a holiness which they could not comfortably credit also of the unbelieving partner, the dominant concerns of the divines at Westminster led in other directions. The irony lay in their very captivity to this verse in the first instance, for at least one thing can be incontrovertibly deduced from it—that the children in question who are declared 'holy' had not been baptized, nor, if the parallel with the unbelieving spouse extends this far, is their imminent baptism implied. This is, I think, the only place in the New Testament where children are in view of whom we know for certain whether they have or have not been baptized. They have not—but are said to be already 'holy'.

The sentence that eventually appeared in the Directory for Public Worship—'they are Christians, and federally holy before baptism'—appears to owe the inclusion 'federally' to Goodwin's opposition. If the minutes can be trusted, the wording before the Assembly at the outset of this discussion was 'they are Christians and holy. . . .'[73] This is not the only statement in the Westminster documents' deliverances on baptism that ventures explicitly into the special language of covenant theology. This latter species of theology is in no way my territory, but I raise a question for others to ponder and adjudicate upon. It was a comment by Sinclair Ferguson on the renewed interest displayed in the sixteenth and seventeenth centuries in the Bible's teaching on the covenant that set me thinking.

---

[72] My paper 'I Corinthians 7:14 in Fathers and Reformers' is forthcoming in a volume edited by David Steinmetz based on an Arbeitsgespräch held at the Herzog August Bibliothek at Wolfenbüttel in March 1994 on the Fathers in sixteenth-century biblical exegesis.

[73] TMs. II, 255, at the beginning of session 254 the morning of July 16, 1644.

[I]t was given fresh impetus by the Anabaptist accusation that the mainstream Reformers had thoughtlessly acquiesced in the 'unbiblical' practice of infant baptism. In response the Reformers argued that God had made one covenant with men with Jesus Christ at its heart, administered in two dispensations, the 'old' and the 'new'. Since the children of believers received the initiatory sacrament of this covenant in the restricted administration of the 'old covenant', they must also receive the initiatory sacrament of baptism in the 'new covenant.'[74]

Was it the case, as this statement suggests, not only that covenant theology afforded strong defence of baptizing infants, but also that the imperative to defend the baptizing of infants enhanced the attractiveness of doing theology covenantally? I find the implication—or is it my inference?—intriguing. There is no doubt in my mind that infant baptism was the single most substantive constitutive element of the church that the Reformers perpetuated from the Old Church without explicit biblical authorisation. In vindicating it they displayed immense versatility, but it was no easy task. Does the pressing necessity of doing so help to explain the shift towards the federalization of theology? Can it be shown that the apologia for paedobaptism was a significant organizing centre in the structural elaboration of covenant theology?

Concluding Assessment

It is not part of the purpose of this paper to enter into critical engagement with Westminster's presentation of Christian baptism in the light of more recent theological viewpoints. It should probably be faulted, for example, for not relating church baptism to Christ's own baptism, or perhaps to his whole work of identification with us understood as his baptism for us.[75] More

---

[74] Sinclair B. Ferguson, 'The Teaching of the Confession', in Alasdair I. C. Heron (ed.), *The Westminster Confession in the Church Today* (St Andrew Press, Edinburgh, 1982), 28-39 at 37.

[75] Cf. George S. Hendry, *The Westminister Confession for Today. A Contemporary Interpretation* (SCM Press, London, 1960), 225: 'The

serious would be a demonstration of internal inconsistency, such as that hinted at by George S. Hendry in reporting hypothetically a contention that 'even the definition of the sacrament given in the Confession implies conditions which cannot be literally fulfilled in the case of infants.'[76] He gives no more detail than this, but we might well ask whether baptism can be 'unto [the party baptized] a sign and seal of the covenant of grace . . . and of his giving up unto God through Jesus Christ, to walk in newness of life' (28:1) if the party is incapable of discerning the signification or walking in newness of life. But that may be too harsh a judgment. If it is guilty of deep-seated inconsistency, the Westminster Confession would be in good company, according to Karl Barth, who finds serious incoherence between John Calvin's treatment of baptism in general and defence of infant baptism in particular.

> One may read the 15th and 16th chapters in Book IV of the *Institutio* after the other and convince oneself whether the great Calvin was sure of his subject and where he obviously was not sure, but visibly nervous, in a hopelessly confused train of thought, abusing where he ought to inform and when he wants to convince, seeking a way in the fog, which can lead him to no goal, because he has none.[77]

Barth here points up the continuing dilemma of church and theology in seeking to defend infant baptism from a Bible—or at least a New Testament—which knows only the baptism of converts.

Yet there can be no respectable future for paedobaptism which does not treat it fully as Christian baptism. In these terms, its hopes lie in being made more central and fundamental to Christian

---

sacrament of baptism rests ultimately on Christ's own baptism, in which he became "ingrafted" into us, to bring us the benefits of the covenant of grace (Matt. 3:13-15), and which he consummated by his death (Mark 10:38; Luke 12:50).

[76] *Ibid.*, 226.

[77] Barth. *The Teaching of the Church Regarding Baptism*, 49; cf. 48, where he accuses Calvin in 4:16 of forgetting what he wrote in 4:15.

education and nurture. One of the gravest scandals attending the practice of infant baptism is that too often baptized children growing up are unaware of their baptismal identity. From time to time young adults coming forward for full membership turn out to be unsure whether they were baptized as babies. One major answer to this ignorance is the 'improvement' of baptism inculcated explicitly by the Larger Catechism (Q/A 167), and indirectly by the Directory for Public Worship, both in the home and in Sunday school and Bible class. According to the New Testament, baptism, not conversion, is the locus of our acquiring Christian identity. As the Directory puts it, in baptism children are 'received into the bosom of the visible church, distinguished from the world, and them that are without, and united with believers'.[78]

'Distinguished from the world': in the early church there was no doubt about this. But it has been one of the sad features of the story of infant baptism, not least to the present day in the declining churches of post-Christendom, that it has so often served to obscure that distinction. Perhaps a revisiting of Westminster may help us to recover it.

---

[78] Cf. Confession 27:1, on sacraments in general: 'instituted . . . to put a visible difference between those that belong unto the church and the rest of the world.'

Edinburgh to Westminster

Andrew McGowan

There is a prevailing mythology abroad in Scotland, fostered for two generations by a number of neo-orthodox theologians and historians, to the effect that the pure pristine Calvinism of the *Scots Confession* was polluted and destroyed by the evil virus of federal theology resulting in a perverted and scholastic theology which ultimately found expression in the *Westminster Confession of Faith*.

This is, of course, only one strand in a more general argument which asserts that Calvin himself was entirely misunderstood (or deliberately misrepresented) by Beza, his closest friend and colleague, such that what has come to be known as Calvinism is entirely at odds with what Calvin himself believed. The argument usually ends with the affirmation that Karl Barth has gloriously recovered what was lost and is therefore the true standard bearer of Calvinistic orthodoxy. This "Calvin versus Calvinism" debate has spawned an enormous body of literature and the arguments on both sides are, by now, well known.[1]

The concern of this paper is not with the debate in general, but with the Confessional strand of the debate in particular. Specifically,

---

[1] Some sections of the following essay are drawn from my doctoral thesis in which I interact more generally with this debate: *The Federal Theology of Thomas Boston* (Paternoster, due 1996).

the purpose is to examine the claim that the *Scots Confession* is Christological in its structure and character whereas the *Westminster Confession of Faith* is deterministic, and that the reason for this difference is their respective presentations of the doctrine of election.

The Two Confessions

The *Scots Confession* marks the consummation of the Reformation in Scotland.[2] It was written in 1560, being drawn up in four days by John Knox, John Winram, John Spottiswoode, John Hillock, John Douglas and John Rowe (the six Johns). It was written by instruction of the estates of parliament and, after private revision by Lord James Stewart and Lethington, "who tempered its language and secured the omission of an article on the 'dysobediens that subjects owe unto their magistrates', it was approved by parliament as 'hailsome and sound doctrine'."[3] The majority of scholars agree that it was primarily the work of John Knox,[4] it sometimes being called 'Knox's Confession',[5] although some would argue that the work was done more equally by the six.[6]

---

[2] A.F. Mitchell *The Scottish Reformation* (R. Blackwood & Sons, Edinburgh, 1900) pp.99-122. D.H. Fleming *The Scottish Reformation* (Scottish Reformation Society, Edinburgh, 1904) pp. 100-112. J.D. Mackie *A History of the Scottish Reformation* (Church of Scotland Youth Committee, Edinburgh, 1960) pp. 131-152 (esp. pp.137-140).

[3] W.A. Curtis *History of Creeds and Confessions of Faith* (T & T Clark, Edinburgh, 1911) p. 257.

[4] J.A. Duke *History of the Church of Scotland to the Reformation* (Oliver & Boyd, Edinburgh, 1937) p. 247. W.A. Curtis op cit., p.257. J. MacPherson *History of the Church in Scotland* (Paisley, 1901) p. 247. H. Cowan *John Knox* (New York, 1905) p.224.

[5] J.S. McEwen *The Faith of John Knox* (Lutterworth, London, 1961) p. 110.

[6] J. Macleod *Scottish Theology* (Free Church Publications, Edinburgh, 1943) p. 15. A.R. Macewen *A History of the Church in Scotland* (Hodder & Stoughton, London, 1918) vol. 2, p. 151.

The *Westminster Confession of Faith* took a little longer! It was written by the Westminster Assembly of Divines,[7] one hundred and fifty in all, who met from the first of July 1643 until the twenty fifth of March 1652. The *Westminster Confession of Faith* itself however, was finished and presented to Parliament on December 4-7, 1646.

Scots versus Westminster

The *Scots Confession* deals with the doctrine of election in chapter viii. The section begins, "That same eternal God and Father, who by grace alone chose us in his Son Christ Jesus before the foundation of the world was laid, appointed him to be our head, our brother, our pastor, and the great bishop of our souls." It then goes on to speak of Christ and the fact that to be Mediator he must be both God and man in one person.

The *Westminster Confession of Faith* presents its doctrine of election in chapter 3, having first of all dealt with the nature and authority of Scripture and with the doctrine of God and the Holy Trinity. In section 3 of that chapter we have the following words which sum up the Confession's position: "By the decree of God, for the manifestation of his glory, some men and angels are predestined unto everlasting life, and others foreordained to everlasting death."[8]

Thus there is posited a double decree whereby God chose certain individuals who would eventually go to heaven and passed

---

7 For the details of the Assembly see: A.F. Mitchell & J. Struthers (eds) *Minutes of the Sessions of the Westminster Assembly of Divines* (W. Blackwood and Sons, Edinburgh, 1874). G. Gillespie *Notes of the Assembly of Divines at Westminster* (Ogle, Oliver & Boyd, Edinburgh, 1846). C.G. McCrie *The Confessions of the Church of Scotland* (Macniven and Wallace, Edinburgh, 1907). J.H. Leith *Assembly at Westminster* (John Knox Press, Richmond, 1973). For a Calvinistic commentary on the Confession see: A.A. Hodge *Classbook on the Confession of Faith* (T. Nelson & Sons, London, 1870). R. Shaw *The Reformed Faith* (Christian Focus Publications, Inverness, 1974).

8 (FP Publications, Inverness, 1981) p. 29.

over others who would eventually go to hell (every human and angel being in one of these two groups). God completed this act of 'selection' before the foundation of the world and it is attributable only to the "most wise and holy council of his own will"[9] and not to foreknowledge nor any other contingent factor.

The difference between the Confessions at this point is expressed by J. G. Riddell,

> "In the Scots Confession Articles i and ii - of God and of the Creation of man - are followed by the articles which deal with original sin and the revelation of the promise. In the Westminster Confession there is inserted between chapter ii—on God and of the Holy Trinity—and chapter iv—on Creation—the section entitled God's Eternal Decrees, which has no direct counterpart in the earlier document."[10]

Was the *Westminster Confession* simply enlarging upon and clarifying the *Scots Confession* in a way which is entirely compatible with the theology of the earlier writers, or did there take place a change in the doctrine of election such that we have incompatibility between the two Confessions?

Riddell himself was in no doubt. He believed that there had taken place a fundamental change. Not only so, but he regarded this change as having "deplorable" consequences.[11]

James McEwan agreed with Riddell. He argued that the *Scots Confession*, in dealing with the doctrine of election, was Christological in emphasis: ". . . Predestination is not discussed at all, and under the heading of election we are told that it was Christ who was predestined from all eternity to be our Saviour, and that we are elected in him."[12]

For McEwan and those who share his position there is an irreconcilable disharmony between the Scots and Westminster

---

[9] *Westminster Confession of Faith* chapter 3, section i.

[10] "God's Eternal Decrees" *SJT* vol.2 (1949) p. 352.

[11] Idem

[12] J.S. McEwen op cit., p.78.

Confessions on the subject of election. In particular they say that we cannot argue from silence. In other words, we cannot guess at what the *Scots Confession* would have said had it been spelled out more clearly. There is no trace, they argue, of the double decree of individuals and hence to argue that such is the underlying position is utterly indefensible.

This argument is developed by noting that in the *Scots Confession* the doctrine of election is expounded after the doctrine of the Mediator (as it is in Calvin's *Institutes*) whereas in the *Westminster Confession of Faith* election is expounded as part of the eternal decrees of God.

We shall come back to this matter of the place assigned to the doctrine of election in the *ordo salutis* but for the moment it is important to understand the theological issues which most concern those who reject the Westminster doctrine of election.

In the first place, those who take this view do not regard election as the predetermination of certain individuals to heaven and others to hell but as grace being worked out in human history or, as J. K. S. Reid would have it, as ". . . grace traced".[13] This is also the view of Karl Barth,[14] who argued that the proponents of Double Predestination had failed to see that election, like all other doctrines, must be dealt with Christologically. Hence when he spoke about election he spoke about Christ.[15]

In the second place there is a concern for the doctrine of God. Barth himself spoke of the danger which the Westminster doctrine could do to our doctrine of God.[16] J. K. S. Reid enlarges upon

---

[13] "The Office of Christ in Predestination" *SJT* vol.1 (1948) p.175.

[14] K. Barth *Church Dogmatics* (henceforth CD) 2/2 (T & T Clark, Edinburgh, 1957).

[15] ibid., pp. 3-76.

[16] cf. C. Gunton "Karl Barth's Doctrine of Election as part of his Doctrine of God" *Journal of Theological Studies* N.S. 25 (1974).

this: "The classic doctrine of Predestination, as Barth points out[17] transmitted an unfortunate impression that God is equally well disposed to election and reprobation, and that he, in perfect equilibrium between the two, indifferently consigns some certain individuals to the right hand and salvation, and others to the left hand and damnation."[18] The point at issue is this: How can we continue to teach that God in his innermost being is essentially love when, in his dealings with the vast majority of men, he appears to be something else? Barth insisted that God in and of himself is the same as he is towards us.

In the third place, there is the affirmation that we are *all* chosen for salvation 'in Christ' and thus we are all *elect* in Christ. In other words, Christ didn't die to put into effect an election which was prior to grace[19] (since nothing can be prior to grace) and hence essentially non-Christological. We are elect in the Person of Christ and not because of a 'work' done on our behalf. Central to this whole line of thought is the fact that Christ is both the electing God and the elect man.[20] That is to say, Christ as God was a word of grace saying to us "I forgive you", and Christ as man by his active and passive obedience said "yes" to both the love and the judgement implicit in this statement. For Barth, every doctrine must face the Christological test. Thus, for example, our worship is real only when it is participation in Christ's worship. In the same way, our election is only real when it is understood as participation in his election. Barth insists that we retain this bi-polarity in order to give the doctrine of election the Christological character without which it is clearly suspect.

---

[17] *CD* 2/2 p. 187.

[18] J.K.S. Reid op cit., p. 177.

[19] Discussed in J.B. Torrance "Covenant or Contract?" *SJT* vol.23 (1970) pp. 51-76.

[20] K. Barth op cit., pp. 94-145

But how does this relate to our actual Christian experience and our understanding of other doctrines? Barth's definition of Christian faith helps to clarify the matter, ". . . the gift of the meeting in which men become free to hear the word of grace which God has spoken in Jesus Christ in such a way that, in spite of all that contradicts it, they may once for all, exclusively and entirely, hold to his promise and guidance."[21] When, by the grace of God, we come face to face with Christ, there takes place a moment of 'crisis' and in that moment we are set free to realise that we are (in Christ) elect. In this 'crisis experience' we are enabled to lay hold on the promises of God in a way that is both unique and permanent.

This being the case we are told that we must resist the temptation to make election into a decree or decrees prior to grace. J. K. S. Reid writes, "To crystallise the gracious will of God into a 'decree' is to take the dangerous step of 'minuting' what is supremely activity: crystallisation under certain conditions becomes petrifaction."[22] Thus election must always be seen, to use a linguistic example, as being in the present continuous tense, since election is another way of saying 'sola gratia'.[23] There are then, on this thesis, no certain individuals predestined to heaven with others consigned to hell; on the contrary we are all in ourselves rejected but in Christ we are all elect. Or, to put it more accurately, in Christ we are both elect and reprobate there being only "existential possibilities".[24]

Some have argued that Barth's position must needs end in Universalism[25] but both he and those of like mind have rejected

---

[21] *Dogmatics in Outline* (SCM, London, 1966) p. 15.

[22] op cit., p. 175.

[23] ibid., pp. 174,5.

[24] ibid., p. 183.

[25] For example, G.C. Berkower *The Triumph of Grace in the Theology of Karl Barth* (Eerdmans, Grand Rapids, 1956) pp.287- 96. E. Brunner Dogmatics (Westminster, Philadelphia, 1950) vol.1 pp. 346-53.

this, arguing that there always remains the possibility of our saying "no" to the word of grace which God speaks to us (this being their understanding of the 'sin against the Holy Spirit').[26] For the Barthian, then, reprobation is accidental to the Gospel and is only caused by God in the same way as it could be said that a shadow is 'caused' by the sun. T. F. Torrance summarises the position thus: ". . . to be reprobate can only be the choice of a Godless man. The Gospel tells us that in the death of Jesus Christ God has enacted a justification of the ungodly. Still to be reprobate is an un-understandable mystery—the mystery of iniquity. To choose our own way in spite of God's absolute choice of us, to listen to the voice of his infinite love and to know that we are already apprehended by that love in the death of Jesus, and by that very apprehension of love to be given the opportunity and capacity to respond in faith and love, and still to draw back in proud independence and selfish denial of God's love, is an act of bottomless horror. If the light that is in us be darkness, how great is that darkness."[27]

Response

However, to say, as James McEwan does, that the *Scots Confession* says nothing about predestination of anyone except Christ and that election is only referred to as being "in Christ" is less than fair, particularly if the suggestion is being made that the authors of the Confession were really crypto-Barthians!

Throughout the *Scots Confession* there are words and phrases which would later be taken up and expanded in the *Westminster Confession of Faith*. For example, in chapter iii we are told that

---

[26] *CD* 2/2 pp.417-429, 476, 480. J.D. Bettes "Is Karl Barth a Universalist?" *SJT* vol.20 (1967).

[27] op cit., pp. 316, 7.

the grace of rebirth is wrought by the Holy Spirit "creating in the hearts of God's elect an assured faith in the promise of God revealed to us in his Word". Whatever else these words mean, they certainly affirm that regeneration is limited to God's elect.

Then there are the references in chapters iii and xxv to the "reprobate" who are contrasted with the regenerate. As will be readily apparent by looking at the work of John Knox, the word "reprobate" is an essential element in his vocabulary of predestination. It certainly did not mean, for Knox, "to choose our own way in spite of God's absolute choice of us" as T. F. Torrance defined it in the quotation used earlier

W. A. Curtis, in his introduction to the Calvinistic Confessions, notes a number of features which are peculiar to them as opposed to the Lutheran Confessions. One of these is, "The eternal and absolute decree of God, whereby, . . . he has foreordained some portion of the human race . . . to eternal salvation and others . . . to eternal damnation."[28] When Curtis comes to speak of the *Scots Confession* he writes, "The articles on election (vii and viii) are characteristic . . ."[29] By this he seems to mean that they are in harmony with the 'special features' of Calvinism, including the one on election mentioned above. Curtis then, is one of those who sees no difference in the doctrine of election between the two Confessions.

It is also important to remember that the Scots Confession was put together very quickly in a time of turbulent political activity and in an era of the Church's life when the important thing was to define itself as a Reformed Church leaving the intricacies of theology to be worked out at a later period. Some writers go so far as to say that its lack of theological finesse is one of the *Scots Confession's* greatest strengths.[30] G. D. Henderson

---

[28] op cit., pp. 215, 216.

[29] ibid., p. 258.

[30] W.A. Curtis op cit., p. 260.

writes, "The Scots Confession is neither so carefully complete nor so rigidly systematic as the Westminster Confession. It was produced by men who were worried, not so much by the niceties of theological controversy, as by practical problems of the Christian life, worship, government and discipline."[31] He is, nonetheless, convinced that the two Confessions are in theological agreement. He writes, ". . . nothing new or strange in the sphere of doctrine was brought from Westminster . . ."[32]

The Teaching Of John Knox

In defence of the view that there was no difference between the Scottish Reformers and the Westminster Divines on the doctrine of election, some appeal must be made to the work of John Knox on Predestination.[33] Since he was the primary author of the Confession his own published writings on the subject deserve special attention.

David Laing, in his Introduction to John Knox' treatise on election,[34] describes it as "the most elaborate production of the Scottish Reformer".[35] Indeed, it is a most lengthy and significant work. For this paper it is neither possible nor necessary to give the space which would be required for a full appreciation of the work, rather it will be sufficient to demonstrate that Knox' understanding of the doctrine of election did not differ from that of Calvin or of

---

[31] op cit., p. 18.

[32] idem.

[33] *The Works of John Knox* (Wodrow Society, Edinburgh, 1856).

[34] An Answer to a great number of blasphemous cavillations written by an Anabaptist, and adversarie to God's eternal predestination. And confuted. in The Works of John Knox edited by D. Laing, Vol.5 (Johnstone and Hunter, 1856) pp.7-468.

[35] ibid, p.9 cf. Calderwood's remark, "How profound he was in Divinitie, that work of his upon Predestination may give evidence." (p. 17).

the Westminster Confession. To prove this fact, several of his most telling arguments and statements shall be drawn out.

This volume on predestination was originally published in 1591 and no other Scottish theologian, before or since, has produced such a massive contribution to the study of the doctrine. It was directed against Anabaptists who denied the doctrine of predestination, and responds in detail to one in particular. Knox saw this as an attack on God, whose "free grace is openly impugned and disdainfully refused".[36] The strength of his feeling on this matter is apparent when he writes,

> "But yet I say, that the doctrine of God's eternal Predestination is so necessarie to the Church of God, that, without the same, can Faith neither be truely taught, neither surely established; man can never be broght to true humilitie and knowledge of himself; neither yet can he be ravished in admiration of God's eternal goodnes, and so moved to praise him as apperteineth. And therefor we feare not to affirme, that so necessarie as it is that true faith be established in our hartes, that we be broght to unfeined humilitie, and that we be moved to praise him for his free graces receaved; so necessary also is the doctrin of God's eternall Predestination."[37]

The book is divided up into sections, each section constituting a reply on a specific point to his Anabaptist opponent. The first section is a reply to the charge of "Stoicall Necessitie".[38] Knox says that he fully supports the view of Calvin (whom his opponent had been rash enough to describe as the 'God' of those of a Reformed persuasion!) and then writes,

> "As touching the opinion, we are falsly and maliciously burdened therewith; for we imagin not a Necessitie which is conteined within Nature by a perpetual conjunction of natural causes, as did the Stoikes; but we affirme and menteine that God is Lord, Moderator, and Governor of all things; whom we affirm to have determined from the beginning, according to his wisdom, what he wold do; and now we

---

[36] ibid, p. 25.

[37] ibid, pp. 25, 26.

[38] ibid., p. 31

say, that he doth execute according to his power whatsoever he hath determined."[39]

In the course of the book the most striking feature is the total dependence of Knox on Augustine, Calvin and Beza, all of whom he quotes, but none more so than Calvin. This dependence is obvious from the summary he gives of his own position,

"God, in his eternall and immutable counsels, hath once appointed and decreed whom he wold take to salvation, and whom also he wold leave in ruyne and perdition. Those whom he elected to salvation, he receaveth of free mercie, without all respect had to their own merites or dignitie, but of undeserved love gave them to his onelie Son to be his inheritance; and them in tyme he calleth of purpose, who, as his shepe, obey his voice, and so do they attein to the joy of that kingdom which was prepared for them before the foundations of the world wer laide. But to those whom he hath decreed to leave in perdition, is so shut up the entrie of life, that either they are left continually corrupted in their blindnes, or els if grace be offered, by them it is oppugned and obstinatly refused; or if it seme to be receaved, that abideth but for a tyme only, and so they returne to their blindnes, and croked nature, and infidelitie agane, in which finally they justly perishe."[40]

The obvious dependence of Knox upon the aforesaid men, however, is simply a reflection of his dependence upon Scripture. Indeed, throughout the volume Knox shows himself to be an able exegete as well as an able controversialist. He exegetes almost every passage in both Old and New Testaments which could be said to have any bearing upon his subject.

The issue of reprobation is a fundamental element of the Reformed doctrine of predestination, and Knox turns to that issue to deal with his opponent's claim that God could not reprobate someone made in his own image since this would be contrary to the inherent love and justice of his divine nature. Knox responds by emphasizing the seriousness of the Fall. In this context he develops the parallel between Adam and Christ which is so

---

[39] ibid., p. 32.

[40] ibid., p. 42.

fundamental to federal theology, including a clear statement of the imputation of Adam's sin to his posterity.[41]

The question of the love of God is raised in the course of this argument. After all, if one holds to the doctrine of reprobation one must be prepared to ask if God truly loves all men, or if he has a love only for the elect. Knox is in no doubt,

> "You make the love of God common to all men; and that do we constantly deny, and say, that before all beginning God hath loved his Elect in Christ Jesus his Sonne, and that from the same eternitie he hath reprobate others, whom for most just causes, in the tyme appointed to his judgement, he shall adjuge to tormentes and fier inextinguible."[42]

Like Calvin, Knox stresses that election was not dependent upon anything in man:

> ". . . God's Election dependeth not upon man, upon his will, purpose, pleasure, or dignitie; but as it is free, proceeding from grace, so is it stable in God's immutable counsel, and is reveled to God's Elect at such tyme as he knoweth most expedient . . ."[43]

Nevertheless, Knox will not allow his opponent to suggest that election and reprobation are of the same order. Indeed he challenges anyone to prove that he, or any other of the Reformers, has taken such a position:

> "Shew, if ye can, in any of our writings, that we affirm, that wheresoever there is Election there is also Reprobation of the same sorte. Shew that clause, I say, of the same sorte, and I will confesse that ye have read more then I have done of that matter, which, nevertheless, I hardly can believe."[44]

Rather, he suggests that the proper way to view the matter is to see the sin and disobedience of mankind which rightly brings God's judgement. The picture Knox paints suggests the whole

---

[41] ibid., pp. 59-61.

[42] ibid., p. 61.

[43] ibid., p. 70.

[44] ibid., p. 124.

mass of mankind heading for an eternity in Hell and God reaching down to save some by free grace. Those who are lost cannot blame God's reprobation because they know themselves to be sinners deserving God's wrath, while those who are saved know that they do not deserve it and hence can only praise God. He is quite certain that the reprobate by their own sin and refusal of grace, have brought judgement upon themselves.[45]

Thus Knox insists that no violence is offered to the will of man in election or reprobation.[46] And to those who reply that violence is done in so far as man cannot avoid the destiny mapped out by God, Knox replies in the words of Paul from Romans 9:20, which verse he takes to be the response of Paul in an identical discussion.

When his opponent begins to challenge the exegesis of the Reformed position, Knox responds in kind. In respect of the crucial passage from Romans 9[47] the Anabaptist argued that the 'Jacob' and 'Esau' who were 'loved' and 'hated' before birth were not individuals but nations.[48] Knox will have none of it, and insists that Romans 9 is speaking of the eternal destiny of individuals.[49]

Knox is quite clear also that the doctrine of election has its corollary in the doctrine of the perseverance of the saints. When his opponent suggests that an elect believer could ultimately lose salvation, Knox responds,

> "The chief Proposition which ye maintein to the end of this your book is, That the Elect may fall from their Election. To the which I answer, That if ye understand that those whom God the Father hath Elected in his eternall counsel to life everlasting in Christ Jesus, may so fall from their Election that finally they perish; if this (I say) be your understanding, then I feare not to affirme that proposition to be

---

[45] ibid, p.125 cf. The different words used in the *Westminster Confession of Faith* for God's action in election and repentance.

[46] op. cit., p. 144.

[47] ibid., p. 146

[48] ibid., p. 146.

[49] ibid., pp. 147-157.

utterlie fals, erroneous, and damnable, as it doeth expressedly repugne
to God's plaine Scriptures; for Christ Jesus doth affirme that so many
as his Father hath given to him shall come unto him. And to such as
do come, he promiseth life everlasting; which he hath in himself for
the salvation of his flock, whereof none shal perish, for furth of his
hands can none be pulled away."[50]

His opponent, however, was arguing that a believer's election
was 'in Christ' and hence if that believer by breaking the covenant
and forsaking the promise effectively refuses Christ, he then loses
his election. Knox' grasp of the relationship between the doctrines
of grace and his grasp of Calvin's system of theology, leads him
to dismiss this as being "a thing impossible".[51] The seriousness
of Knox in respect of the critical importance of the doctrine of
perseverance to a proper doctrine of election is signified by the
fact that he devotes about forty pages to dealing with his
Anabaptist opponent on this point.[52]

John Knox, then, specifically affirmed his allegiance to
Augustine, Calvin and Beza in respect of the doctrine of
predestination. He confirmed this by his treatise on the subject
which contains nothing with which Calvin and the Westminster
Divines could not wholeheartedly agree.

This evidence of Knox's own view of election must surely
stand in opposition to the interpretation of that view offered by
J. S. McEwen who writes, "Certainly, when he folds his
speculative wings, it is to a simple Christocentric faith that he
returns . . . Knox's Christocentric faith . . . is this: that the
immediate object of God's election is Christ, not men. It is by
Christ's calling of us, and in our union with him, that we partake
in this election of God. It is not ours directly, but only mediately,
through Christ."[53] This must also surely cast doubt on McEwan's

---

[50] ibid, p. 254.

[51] ibid, p. 279.

[52] ibid, pp. 267 ff.

[53] op cit., pp. 78, 79.

interpretation of the *Scots Confession* which we quoted earlier.

1560-1645

Now it is proper to consider certain aspects of the period 1560-1645, the years between the *Scots Confession* and the *Westminster Confession of Faith*. First, the reaction against Arminianism will be discussed, and then second, the doctrine of election in the other Reformed Confessions of the period will be surveyed.

1. Arminianism[54]

Jacobus Arminius (1560-1609)[55] was educated in Switzerland and then served for a time as minister of a Church in Amsterdam, during which period he began to question some of the tenets of Calvinism. After various disputes on these matters he left his charge and became Professor of Theology at the University of Leyden. In his work *The Declaration of Sentiments*[56] he outlined his doctrine of election in terms of four Divine decrees (the order being logical and not historical). C. Bangs notes that from Arminius' criticism of his opponents emerge ". . . some parameters within which the four decrees must be defined. Predestination must be understood Christologically; it must not make God the author of sin; it must not make man the author of salvation; it must be scriptural not speculative; and it must not depart from the historic teaching of the Church . . ."[57]

The four decrees are, first, the election of Jesus Christ: Election is 'in Christ' and hence Christ is "more than just a means for

---

[54] A.W. Harrison *The Beginnings of Arminianism* (University of London Press, London, 1926).

[55] C. Bangs *Arminius* (Abingdon Press, New York, 1974).

[56] J. Nichols *(ed) The Works of Arminius* (Longmans, London, 1825) vol. 1.

[57] op cit., p. 350.

carrying out a prior non-Christological decree."[58] Second, the election of the Church: By this Arminius means that God decided to accept those who would repent and believe (cf. his exposition of Romans 9). Third, the appointment of means: The avenue whereby men come to the father—the preaching of the Gospel, the hearing of it in faith and the response to it. Fourthly, the election of individuals: The argument here is that by his Divine foreknowledge God knew those who would believe and persevere and those who wouldn't. This being the case, he predestined the former to eternal salvation and the latter to eternal damnation.

After his death, the followers of Arminius formulated his teaching in a five point document entitled *The Remonstrance* and this was published in 1610.[59] Those who held to its teaching were called the 'Remonstrants'. This was a document of battle, and the five points were points of departure from Calvinism:

1. God's eternal decree was to elect those who would believe in Christ and reject those who would not believe (i.e., God's salvific choice is concomitant with foreknowledge).

2. Christ died for all men and not just the elect, but only believers benefited from it.

3. The necessity of the work of the Holy Spirit in renewing man.

4. Grace is not irresistible although it is the cause of man's redemption.

5. It is possible for believers to fall from grace.

This Arminian system of doctrine was condemned at the Synod of Dort in 1618/19.[60] Five counter theses to the Arminian

---

[58] ibid., p. 351.

[59] P. Schaff *The Creeds of Christendom* (Hodder & Stoughton, New York, 1881/82) vol. 3, pp. 545-549

[60] D. Jellema "Synod of Dort" *NIDCC*.

ones already quoted were put forward and accepted at the Synod. They were:

1. Total Depravity—the totality of human nature was affected by the fall and as a direct result of this man cannot discover truth about God or attain to God's standards, rather he must be redeemed by grace.

2. Unconditional Election—man is chosen for salvation due to the free and sovereign will of God and not because of any works done by the man, or indeed of God's foreknowledge of such.

3. Limited Atonement—some are predestined to heaven and others are predestined to hell. Christ died for the former and his death is effective but only to them. In other words, all men deserve to go to hell, but God picked out some individuals and decided to save them. In order to do this however it was necessary to satisfy the Law which required that punishment be enacted, and so Christ came to take the penalty which was due to the group of people whom God had decided to save.

4. Irresistible Grace—those individuals whom God chose before the foundation of the world to be saved *will* be saved because God's choice cannot in any way be frustrated.

5. Perseverance (final) of the saints - it is not possible for the elect to fall from grace since God will not allow this to happen. The thought here is more one of 'preservation' than 'perseverance'.

It was over 60 years after the publication of the *Scots Confession* when Arminianism began to spread to Scotland,[61] the first man to advocate the position being John Cameron who

---

[61] G.D. Henderson *Religious Life in Seventeenth Century Scotland* (CUP, Cambridge, 1937) pp. 77-99.

became Professor of Theology at Glasgow University in 1622.[62] He had studied and taught on the continent before taking up his chair. He attacked the Calvinist position along the lines which Arminius had followed in Holland. Cameron's disciple Amyrauld established his teaching as an independent school of thought (this school was mentioned at the Westminster Assembly under the name 'Amyraldism').[63]

The 'Aberdeen Doctors'[64] also rejected a number of the tenets of 'high' Calvinism and were among the first to be tried and deposed after the Covenanting Assembly of 1638.[65] There were, of course, extreme forms of Arminianism and indeed some men (e.g.) John Crighton[66] took a stance which even many committed Arminians would have found difficult to accept. The Aberdeen Doctors themselves took up, as one might expect, a moderate line, this task being made more awkward by the fact that both the Scottish and English Anglo-Catholics with whom they were in sympathy were extreme Arminians.[67] One of the Aberdeen Doctors went so far as to publicly dispute with Samuel Rutherford on the Arminian issue.[68]

A study of the history of theology shows that doctrines are usually worked out in times of crisis and not peacefully in the study. The doctrines of the great Creeds and Confessions of the Church were only formulated when incorrect statements were made and these had to be corrected. The doctrines of the Trinity

---

[62] D. Macmillan *The Aberdeen Doctors* (Hodder & Stoughton, London, 1909) p. 107.

[63] Mitchell & Struthers op cit., p. 167.

[64] D. Macmillan, op. cit.

[65] ibid., p. 109.

[66] ibid., p. 110.

[67] ibid., p. 111.

[68] ibid., p. 111-113.

and the Person of Christ are good examples.[69] This was, to some extent, the case with the rise of Arminianism and the subsequent efforts of Calvinist theologians to refute it. When the Westminster Assembly met, therefore, it was inevitable that the doctrine of election would be stated much more clearly and explicitly than had been the case in the 1560 document, especially since a number of the Westminster Divines had been involved personally in the struggle against Arminianism. The doctrine of election then, as we find it stated at Westminster, must owe its existence at least partly, to the determination of the Divines to wipe out once for all this heresy. In other words, the doctrine of election as agreed at Westminster was not contrary to what was agreed at Edinburgh in 1560. It is simply that the doctrine had to be spelled out and clarified in response to the challenge of Arminianism.

2. The Reformed Confessions

Another way to explode the notion of a "pure pristine Calvinism" in 1560 which was perverted by federal theology before 1645 is to demonstrate that all the Reformed Confessions of the period took essentially the same position and that the development in the doctrine of election was a gradual and natural progression rather than a deviation.

In 1561 the *Belgic Confession*[70] was printed in Rouen and article xvi "of eternal election" tells us that God is "merciful" in so far as he ". . . delivers and preserves from perdition all whom he . . . hath elected in Christ Jesus . . .", and that he is "just" when it comes to his ". . . leaving others in the fall and perdition whereby they have involved themselves." Already we have the concepts of election and reprobation spelled out.

---

[69] L. Berkhof, op. cit., pp. 94-122.

[70] *A. Cochrane, op. cit., pp. 185-219.*

The next important document is the *Lambeth Articles*[71] of 1595. This was a Calvinistic appendix to the *Thirty Nine Articles*[72] written by Whitaker, Regius Professor of Divinity at Cambridge University, in opposition to the nine propositions of Barrett.[73] There is no doubt as to the doctrine of election in these few articles since almost nothing else is touched upon.

Here are a selection of its theses:

"1. God from eternity hath predestinated certain men unto life; certain men hath he reprobated . . .

3. There is predetermined a certain number of the predestinate, which can neither be augmented nor diminished . . .

4. Those who are not predestined to salvation shall be necessarily damned for their sins . . .

9. It is not in the will or power of every one to be saved."

Next, consider the *Irish Articles* of 1615.[74] Here we have the clearest statement of the later 'Westminster' doctrine of election. The articles begin with the doctrine of Scripture, then proceed to the doctrine of the Trinity before coming to the doctrine of election. The similarity with the Westminster Confession does not end there, however, since some of the language in the Westminster Confession is practically identical to that of the *Irish Articles* (for example, compare the *Westminster Confession of Faith* chapter 3 section i and the *Irish Articles* section ii). This is the first instance of the 'eternal decrees' coming in such a position. This is further confirmed when we reach the section on election:

". . . God hath predestinated some unto life, and reprobated some

---

[71] *P. Schaff The Creeds of Christendom* (Hodder & Stoughton, New York, 1881,82) vol. 3, pp. 523-525.

[72] *ibid., vol. 1, pp. 658-662.*

[73] Strype *Whitgift* vol. 3, p.3 20.

[74] P. Schaff op cit., vol.3, pp. 526-544.

unto death: of both which there is a certain number, known only to God, which can neither be increased not diminished."

Finally, the last document in this brief 'tour' is the *Aberdeen Confession* of 1616[75] (this title arises from the fact that the General Assembly of the Church of Scotland met in Aberdeen that year). Once again the section on election is quite clear, "Before the foundation of the world, God, according to the good pleasure of his will, did predestinate and elect in Christ, some men and angels unto eternal felicity, and others he did appoint for eternal condemnation . . ."

It is quite clear, then, that there was no sudden change in the doctrine of election between 1560 and 1645. Rather, we can see that each of the Reformed documents of the period takes the same position.

J. B. Torrance disputes this, however, and offers an alternative view. He says that when we consider a number of reformed confessions which were written between 1553 and 1658 we see two things,

> (a) the growing emphasis on election and the doctrine of the decrees of God—on double predestination, and

> (b) the decided move to a view where election precedes grace, so that the interpretation of the Person and Work of Christ is subordinated to the doctrine of the decrees, and seen as God's way of executing the decrees for the elect. The result is that grace is limited to the redemption of the elect.

> Thus the doctrine of the decrees of God in the tradition of Theodore Beza and William Perkins becomes the major premise of the whole scheme of creation and redemption. This is clearly a move away from the *Scots Confession*, where election is placed after the Article on the Mediator, in the context of Christology. It is also a move away from Calvin who expounds election at the end of Book Three of the Institute as a corollary to grace, after he has expounded all he has to say about

---

[75] *Booke of the Universall Kirk of Scotland* (Bannatyne Club, Edinburgh, 1845) pp. 1132-1139.

the work of Father, Son and Holy Spirit, and after his exposition of Incarnation and Atonement."[76]

Torrance is arguing that Calvin placed the doctrine of predestination at the end of Book Three in the *Institutes* so that it would be understood Christologically and that he was followed in this by the writers of the *Scots Confession*. He is further arguing that Beza, Perkins and the Puritans departed from Calvin and placed predestination at the beginning of their schema and then deduced all the other doctrines from that primary doctrine. This error, we are told, inevitably led to a doctrine of limited atonement and a false understanding of both election and grace.

One of Professor Torrance's students, M. C. Bell, takes a similar line and writes,

> "Calvin did not begin his theology with a statement of the order of God's decrees and then proceed in logical exposition. Calvin purposefully withholds discussion of predestination in his Institutes until Book 3, and after he has fully discussed the knowledge of God the Creator and Christ the Redeemer. After a discussion of the Christian experience, he turns to predestination to help explain why some fail to believe savingly. Predestination is, therefore, an 'implicate of grace'. Furthermore, though Calvin can be said to teach a double decree, it is, as it were, 'out of balance'; the stress is on election, not on reprobation."[77]

Paradoxically, however, the most decisive argument against Professor Torrance's position comes from his erstwhile teacher, Karl Barth. In his historical analysis of the doctrine of predestination Barth shows that Calvin,

> ". . . did partly share and partly inaugurate four different conceptions of the place and function of the doctrine of election."[78]

If this is so, then surely Calvin did not himself regard the

---

[76] "Strengths and Weaknesses of the Westminster Theology" in A.I.C. Heron (ed) The Westminster Confession in the Church Today (St Andrew Press, 1982), p. 4 6.

[77] Calvin & Scottish Theology (Handsel Press, 1985), p. 26

[78] Church Dogmatics (T & T Clark), Vol. 2 Part 2, p. 86.

'place' of predestination in his system to be as significant as J. B. Torrance would have us believe.

Barth shows that in the first draft of the *Institutes* (1536) Calvin followed the pattern of Luther's Smaller Catechism where election appeared in the second chapter, and that in the first draft of his Catechism (1537) and later drafts of the *Institutes* he abandoned that pattern and placed election after Christology.

To this extent he agrees with Torrance. Barth, however, goes on to demonstrate that in the final form of the Catechism (1542) Calvin returned to that original pattern. That would surely suggest that the shift between 1536 and 1537 was not as significant as it is sometimes portrayed. Then we must note that in the 1559 form of the *Institutes* he again has election after Christology at the end of Book Three.[79]

In other words, Calvin changed his mind at least three times concerning the place given to the doctrine of predestination in the schema of doctrine. For Torrance and others, then, to try and negate or undermine the strength and clarity of Calvin's doctrine of predestination by suggesting that the place given to it in the schema in some way alters its force and significance is clearly misguided.

There are, of course, two points in Professor Torrance's argument. The argument about the actual place given to the doctrine by Calvin in his schema is not, it would seem, a sound one. The other point concerns the way in which the doctrine of predestination was used to determine all the other doctrines which followed in the schema.

The suggestion is being made by Torrance and Bell that the doctrine of predestination as taught by the Calvinists, because of its content and the place given to it in the schema, led directly to a doctrine of limited atonement, whereas in Calvin this was not the case.

---

[79] ibid, pp. 76-93.

Once again it is Karl Barth's masterly history of the doctrine which challenges this view. Barth says that neither Calvin nor the later Reformed dogmaticians established the doctrine of predestination . . .

"... as a basic tenet from which all other doctrines may be deduced."[80]

Indeed he writes that in the *Westminster Confession of Faith*,

"... it was not a matter of deducing all dogmatics from the doctrine of predestination. If we read their expositions connectedly we are more likely to get the impression that from the standpoint of its systematic range and importance they gave to the doctrine too little consideration rather than too much."[81]

On the argument that the later Calvinists were forced to create a doctrine of limited atonement because of the place they gave to the doctrine of predestination in the schema, Barth insists that Calvin himself ought to have followed the same line because the "Grim doctrine" of limited atonement, "... does follow logically from Calvin's concept of predestination."[82]

Thus Barth fundamentally disagrees with Professor Torrance's argument. He denies any significance to the place which Calvin gives to the doctrine of predestination in his schema; he disagrees with Torrance in respect of the use made of the doctrine by the later Calvinists; and he insists that Calvin's doctrine of predestination does lead logically to the doctrine of limited atonement. Torrance and Barth, then, are at one in attempting to build a theology on the foundation of Christology but Barth does not try to mould Calvin to suit that theology, rather he is prepared to say that he disagrees with Calvin.

Conclusion

On the basis of the above evidence one can argue that the

---

[80] ibid, p. 86.

[81] ibid, p. 78.

[82] Church Dogmatics, Vol. 4 Part 1, p. 5 7.

theology of the *Westminster Confession of Faith* is a natural development from the theology of the *Scots Confession* and that any apparent changes are simply making explicit what is implicit. More particularly, we would argue that the doctrine of election as found in the *Westminster Confession of Faith* is already present in the *Scots Confession*, this being evidenced both by the few references in the text itself and by the published views on the subject of its main author, John Knox.

One can further argue that the attempts to place a wedge between these Confessions have been driven by a predetermined theological agenda rather than by a genuine comparison and study of the text of the documents and the theological positions held by their respective authors.

Scotland and the Westminster Assembly

W. D. J. McKay

I. The Background to Scottish Participation

The accession of Charles I to the throne in 1625 marked the beginning of a time of great turmoil for his northern kingdom of Scotland[1]. In the political and economic spheres he caused consternation by issuing an Act of Revocation by which he annulled all grants of former church land which had been made by his father, James VI, and by himself while Prince of Wales. It represented, as Rosalind Mitchison states,

> a plan for the reconstruction of Scottish landed society, which was in part to put the clock back behind the revolutions of 1560 and 1567, when the aristocracy had annexed much of the wealth of the Church.[2]

---

[1] Charles was not actually crowned King of Scotland until his visit of 1633.

[2] Rosalind Mitchison, *Lordship to Patronage: Scotland, 1603-1745*, (London, 1983), p29. The Revocation is considered in depth by Walter Makey in *The Church of the Covenant* 1637-1651, (Edinburgh, 1979), cpt 1. In the course of his book Makey argues that the "Scottish Revolution" of these years brought about the end of feudalism in Scotland as well as establishing the power of laymen in the Kirk. In contrast, David Stevenson considers the Revolution to be fundamentally conservative. See D. Stevenson, *The Scottish Revolution 1637-44. The Triumph of the Covenanters*, (Newton Abbot, 1973) and *Revolution and Counter-Revolution in Scotland*, 1644-1651, (London, 1977)

In keeping with modern trends in historiography which have led to a

Many stood to lose under the new arrangements and such grievances were exacerbated by resentment over levels of taxation, which affected all classes of society, and over the use which the King made of bishops exercising civil authority as members of the Privy Council in Scotland.

The ecclesiastical policy pursued by the King also gave cause for alarm. As a Stewart, Charles had no liking for Presbyterian church government or forms of worship. His father, in spite of the teaching of George Buchanan and the rebukes of Andrew Melville, had been firmly wedded to Episcopacy and to the belief that the King was Head of the Church as he was of the State. Such a view was enshrined in the "Black Acts" of 1584, and in spite of Presbyterian success in 1592, James succeeded in having Episcopacy restored by the General Assembly in 1610. At its most succinct, James' view was "no bishop, no king". In the Five Articles of Perth (1618), which required among other things kneeling at Communion and confirmation by bishops, the King began to exercise authority over the worship of the Kirk.[3]

Such was the inheritance of Charles I. Whilst his father had boasted that he "knew the stomach" of his Scottish subjects, and so had stopped short of provoking open revolt, Charles clearly did not and so embarked on a course of ecclesiastical innovations which eventually led to military confrontation with the Scots. Space does not permit a detailed account of the conflict, but the

---

revisionist movement in the treatment of Scottish history, a writer such as Makey considers the period entirely in political and sociological terms. He has little sympathy for the theology of the Covenanters, viewing it solely in terms of political maneuverings, and no room for spiritual issues. Older writers sympathetic to the Covenanters tended to consider the spiritual issues very seriously, but gave little attention to the social context in which they arose. A balanced history of the period which takes all factors into account has still to be written. For all its defects, Makey's work contains a wealth of material from original sources which sheds considerable light on life in the Church of Scotland of that time.

[3] A useful summary is provided by J. D. Douglas, *Light in the North*, (Grand Rapids, 1964), cpt 1.

broad outline of events is necessary to explain the outlook of the men who in 1643 required a religious as well as a political alliance with the Parliament of England which was then engaged in a civil war with the King.[4]

From the outset there was alarm at the resurgence of Roman Catholicism in Charles' court and the Arminian sympathies of the younger bishops. Against this background Charles attempted to finish the job his father had begun. Encouraged by his Archbishop of Canterbury, William Laud, Charles tried in January 1636 to impose a Book of Canons on the Scottish Church, solely on his own authority, without the sanction of either Parliament or General Assembly. This was followed in 1637 by a Liturgy, in anticipation of which George Gillespie wrote his first great polemical treatise *A Dispute Against the English Popish Ceremonies* in which he argued that these were matters of "very great consequence"[5]. Violence erupted when the Liturgy was used for the first time on 23 July 1637 in St Giles', Edinburgh, and decisive action to redress both political and ecclesiastical grievances resulted in the drawing up of the National Covenant of 1638. In the words of J. H. S. Burleigh,

> It is certain . . . that the Covenanters were not all of one mind, but the Covenant was as truly national as any such document can ever be.[6]

In November of 1638 a General Assembly met in Glasgow, its Moderator Alexander Henderson and its Clerk Archibald Johnston of Warriston being two men who would exercise great influence in the Covenanting movement of the next few years. The Assembly

---

[4] The detailed account is supplied by Gordon Donaldson, *Scotland: James V - James VII* (Edinburgh, 1965) and David Stevenson *The Scottish Revolution*. A staunchly Presbyterian account is that of W. M. Hetherington, *History of the Church of Scotland*, 5th edition, (Edinburgh, 1844).

[5] George Gillespie, *A Dispute Against the English Popish Ceremonies*, (Edinburgh, 1637). In *The Presbyterian's Armoury* edition (Edinburgh, 1844), p(x).

[6] J. H. S. Burleigh, *A Church History of Scotland*, (Oxford, 1960), p218.

continued to sit in defiance of the royal Commissioner, the Marquis of Hamilton, and proceeded to depose the bishops, restore Presbyterian polity and condemn the Book of Canons, the Liturgy and the Five Articles of Perth. The independent spiritual jurisdiction of the Church had been successfully reasserted.[7]

All through this period, however, politics and religion were thoroughly intertwined. Charles responded to events in Scotland with armed force which was met by a well-prepared army mustered by the majority in Scotland sympathetic to the Covenant. The First Bishops' War in 1639 ended without actual warfare when Charles retreated before the Scots and signed the Pacification of Berwick. In the Second Bishops' War the following year the Covenanters marched into England and defeated Charles at Newburn on 28 August. The negotiations following this defeat were to be of great significance in preparing the way for Scots' involvement in the Westminster Assembly.

To begin with, Charles had been compelled to summon what became known as the Long Parliament in 1640 in order to obtain the money needed to pay an indemnity to the victorious Scots. His twelve years of rule without a Parliament had come to an end, and the forces of popular resistance to the King's policies in both civil and ecclesiastical spheres were unleashed. The confrontation between King and Parliament was to lead to the outbreak of the Civil War in August, 1642.[8]

---

[7] A full account of the Glasgow Assembly is provided by J. King Hewison, *The Covenanters*, (Glasgow, 1908), vol 1, cpt 10. The official record of events is contained in the *Acts of the General Assembly*, which are to be found in various printed editions. The edition used in this study is *A True Copy of the whole printed Acts of the Generall Assemblies of the Church of Scotland, Beginning at the Assembly holden at Glasgow the 27. day of November 1638; and ending at the Assembly holden at Edinburgh on the 6. day of August 1649*, (1682).

[8] A concise outline of events in England during the period 1640-42 is provided by W. M. Hetherington, *History of the Westminster Assembly of Divines*, 3rd edition, (Edinburgh, 1856), pp 81-101.

The negotiations between Charles and the Covenanters which began at Ripon were transferred to London, thus beginning an important and fruitful contact between Scottish Covenanters and English Puritans eager for reformation in their own Church. Many protests against Laud's promotion of the High Church party in the Church of England were presented to Parliament, culminating in the Root and Branch Petition of 1640 which contained 15,000 signatures. Into this volatile situation came the Scots who had already fought and won their struggle for ecclesiastical independence and reformation.

One of the Scots Commissioners drawing up the treaty with Charles was Alexander Henderson, of whom it has been said, "his commanding powers and unfailing sagacity made him the helmsman of the Church".[9] Along with him came such significant leaders as Robert Baillie, whose letters provide such a vivid portrait of the period, George Gillespie and Robert Blair. The personal contacts and public preaching[10] of the Covenanters won them many friends in London, the city where English Presbyterianism was particularly strong. In Baillie's words,

> The town of London, and a world of men, minds to present a petition, which I have seen, for the abolition of bishops, deans and all their appurtenances . . . Huge things are here in working. The mighty hand of God be about this great work.[11]

It was also during this period that Henderson published in London his concise treatise entitled *The Government and Order of the*

---

[9] Alexander Smellie, *Men of the Covenant*, 1924 edition, (Edinburgh, 1975), p 10.

[10] A sample of Henderson's preaching from a few years earlier is his address on Psalm 110:3 preached at the signing of the National Covenant in St. Andrews, reprinted in James Kerr, *The Covenants and the Covenanters*, (Edinburgh, 1895), pp 54-76.

[11] Robert Baillie, *Letters and Journals*, edited by David Laing, (Edinburgh, 1841-2), 1.218ff. See also J. K. Hewison, op. cit., vol 1, pp 354-369.

Church of Scotland[12] which set out clearly the Scottish understanding of Presbyterianism, first with regard to officers and then to assemblies.

As the temperature of the political and ecclesiastical struggles in England rose, a significant proportion of Puritans recognised their close affinity with the Scots and the value of closer links between the two. This was expressed graphically in a letter brought by Henderson to the General Assembly in Edinburgh on 9 August 1641, in which "some Ministers in England" state,

> these Churches of England and Scotland may seem both to be imbarqued in the same botomme, to sink and swim together, and are so near conjoyned by many strong tyes, not only as fellow-members under the same Head Christ, and fellow-subjects under the same King; but also by such neighbour-hood and vicinity of place, that if any evil shall much infest the one, the other cannot bee altogether free: Or if for the present it should, yet in processe of time it would sensibly suffer also.[13]

They go on to express their fear of Independency replacing Episcopacy and seek the advice of the General Assembly. The Assembly in its reply set out in detail its view of Presbyterian church government and expressed itself "not a little grieved" that any Reformed minister should be otherwise minded. The Assembly's prayer and desire is for closer unity in regard to confession of faith, directory for public worship, catechism and form of church government, arguing that "where the hedge of Discipline and Government is different, the Doctrine and Worship shall not long continue without change."[14]

The opportunity to realise this desire came in the middle of 1643. The Civil War had of late been going badly for the

---

[12] *Alexander Henderson, The Government and Order of the Church of Scotland,* (London, 1641). Although his name does not appear on the pamphlet, it is reliably ascribed to Henderson.

[13] *Acts of the General Assembly*, 9 August 1641.

[14] Ibid.

Parliamentary armies and several reverses brought it home to their leaders that the help of a Scottish army would be necessary to revive their cause. Approaches were therefore made to the Scottish Parliament and to the General Assembly regarding an alliance. The chief men among the Scots, including Alexander Henderson, had at first been reluctant to take sides, seeing their role in the Civil War as possible intermediaries. A meeting between the King and the Earl of Loudon and Alexander Henderson, representing the Scots, had taken place at Oxford in the spring of that year. Charles had been assured that the only way to prevent Scottish intervention on the Parliamentary side was to agree to reform of the Church of England, but it was clear that Charles would not make the necessary concessions.

In response to a Scottish invitation, commissioners arrived from England on 7 August to meet with both the Scottish Parliament and the General Assembly which were meeting in Edinburgh.[15] After some tough negotiations the Solemn League and Covenant was approved by Parliament and Assembly on 17 August and sent to England for consideration. After debate and emendation the Covenant was approved by the English Parliament and was signed by the members of the House of Commons and of the Westminster Assembly on 25 September[16] and by the House of Lords on 15 October.

Among other things, the signatories of the Covenant swore "to preserve the rights and privileges of the Parliaments, and the

---

[15] Propositions from the English Commissioners, a Declaration from the Lords and Commons, a letter from some English ministers and one from the Westminster Assembly of Divines are included in the *Acts of the General Assembly*, 10-17 August, 1643.

[16] The sermons and addresses delivered at the signing of the Solemn League and Covenant by Philip Nye, Alexander Henderson, Thomas Coleman and Joseph Caryl are printed in James Kerr, op. cit., pp 138-227. The text of the Covenant is usually printed with the documents produced by the Westminster Assembly.

liberties of the kingdoms; and to preserve and defend the King's Majesty's person and authority". In ecclesiastical affairs they undertook to preserve the Reformed faith of the Church of Scotland and to work for "the reformation of religion in the kingdoms of England and Ireland, in doctrine, worship, discipline and government, according to the word of God, and the example of the best reformed Churches." In practice this would mean uniformity "in religion, confession of faith, form of church-government, directory of worship and catechising", remarkably similar to the programme set out in the General Assembly's 1641 letter. To supervise the execution of this plan for unity a number of commissioners were sent to London to meet with representatives from Parliament and the Westminster Assembly, (the "Grand Committee") and in addition they agreed to sit as consultative members of the Assembly.

The aims and motives of the parties to the Solemn League and Covenant have been the subject of endless controversy. To some the Scots were cynical manipulators of the English, to others they were the dupes of the duplicitous English. Neither interpretation fits the facts. The two parties did, however, come with different agendas. Baillie's comment that "the English were for a civill League, we for a religious Covenant"[17] may state the polarity too starkly, but it does highlight a significant problem. The Scots were seeking above all to preserve the spiritual freedoms which they had secured, and a victorious King south of the border would again pose a serious threat. As David Stevenson says, "the only alternatives open to the covenanters were to intervene in England or virtually to surrender by passively awaiting destruction."[18] Their contacts with England since 1640

---

[17] Baillie, op. cit., 2.90.

[18] Stevenson, *Revolution and Counter-Revolution*, p 211. B. B. Warfield's comment that the Scots "had nothing to gain from the alliance which was offered to them, unless they gained security for their Church from future

also indicate their deep-seated desire for ecclesiastical uniformity, obviously on a Presbyterian basis.

Political considerations loomed much larger with the English, for example with regard to the authority of Parliament, but they too were concerned with ecclesiastical issues. At this point, indeed, the Church of England had no offical polity, the bishops having been deposed, and the Westminster Assembly had begun work, according to Parliament's instructions, on reform of the Church's government, liturgy and doctrine as required by the Ordinance of 12 June. The English were, in varying degrees, interested in uniformity with Scotland, but they were not prepared to bind themselves to adopt the Scottish model wholesale. Estimates of the strength of ecclesiastical "parties" in England show wide divergences, partly due to differences of definition. But although a significant proportion were "Presbyterians" in a broad sense, Independency was strong and there were those too who would settle for a modified Episcopacy.[19]

This reluctance to commit themselves fully to the Scottish model is reflected in the Westminster Assembly's report on the Covenant presented to the House of Commons on 31 August, 1643.[20] Two "Explications" are proposed. The phrase in the Covenant "according to the Word of God" is, say the divines, to be understood thus: "So far as we do or shall in our Consciences conceive the same to be according to the Word of God." The term "Prelacy" is also defined very carefully, in such a way that some modified Episcopal polity might be accepted later. The

---

English interference", whilst putting the Scots' "act of high chivalry" in the best possible light, scarcely reflects the seriousness of their situation. See B. B. Warfield, *The Westminster Assembly and its Work*, (New York, 1931) pp 22-23.

[19] R. S. Paul provides a helpful analysis of the parties in *The Assembly of the Lord*, (Edinburgh, 1985), cpt 4.

[20] See *Journals of the House of Commons*, 3.223 (31 August, 1643).

upshot of these deliberations was, as Baillie put it, "to keep a door open to Independency in England",[21] and the stage was set for conflict.

II. The Work of the Scottish Commissioners.

The Commissioners sent by the Church of Scotland included some of her leading theologians, Alexander Henderson, Samuel Rutherford, George Gillespie, and Robert Baillie, and prominent elders such as Archibald Johnston of Warriston and Lord Maitland (later to be Earl of Lauderdale and a persecuter of Covenanters).[22] Not surprisingly it was the ministers who were active in the Assembly debates although Baillie involved himself more in behind-the-scenes lobbying and negotiating. His efforts serve as a reminder that significant work was done outside the debating-chamber, chiefly in the Grand Committee as the direction of the Assembly's work was discussed and compromises to end deadlocksought. Baillie even engaged in writing to Reformed Churches abroad asking them to send to the Assembly letters supporting the Scottish position, although results did not always meet expectations.[23] He was involved in organising opposition in the City of London to some of Parliament's measures relating to church government which, at least in part, backfired, and in the opinion of A. F. Mitchell the Scots at times "had recourse to petty acts of diplomacy"[24] which, when discovered, did not endear them to some of the English.

Whilst the Scots had many friends in London, there were

---

[21] Baillie, op. cit., 2.90.

[22] Biographical details are provided by Hewison, op. cit., vol 1, pp 380-5 and by Hetherington, Westminster Assembly, pp 388-405.

[23] Baillie, op. cit., 2.179,197,252.

[24] Alexander F. Mitchell, *The Westminster Assembly. Its History and Standards*, (London, 1883), p 283.

others who regarded them with considerable suspicion[25]. Aside from the ancient hostility between English and Scots, there was among some of the English a resentment at their need to call on Scottish military help and a fear that the Scots wanted to force their ecclesiastical system on an unwilling Church of England. It was important, therefore, to show the falsity of this supposition.

The Scots were undoubtedly wholeheartedly committed to Presbyterianism. Several of the Commissioners had written treatises in defence of that polity. Along with Henderson's work already mentioned, there were, to name only two, *An Assertion of the Government and Order of the Church of Scotland* by George Gillespie[26] and *A Peacable and Temperate Plea for Paul's Presbytery* by Samuel Rutherford[27]. This was the position to which they were committed by their National Covenant and this, they believed, was enshrined in the Solemn League and Covenant in the words "according to the word of God and the example of the best reformed Churches."

In spite of the anti-Scottish propaganda of both Royalists and Parliamentarians,[28] the Scots were not rigidly inflexible in their demands. This was evident as early as 1641 in a paper prepared by Henderson which was given in to the Lords of the Treaty after negotiations with the King had moved from Ripon to London,[29]

---

[25] In Baillie's words, "the best of the English have a verie ill will to employ our aid." (op. cit., 2.103).

[26] George Gillespie, *An Assertion of the Government and Order of the Church of Scotland*, (Edinburgh, 1641), reprinted in *The Presbyterian's Armoury* edition (Edinburgh, 1846). A full study of Gillespie's views is provided by W. D. J. McKay, *Church Government in the Writings of George Gillespie: An Ecclesiastical Republic*, (Lewiston, 1994).

[27] Samuel Rutherford, *A Peacable and Temperate Plea for Paul's Presbytery in Scotland*, (London, 1642).

[28] Stevenson, *Revolution and Counter-Revolution*, pp 216-218.

[29] *Arguments for the Commissioners of Scotland persuading Conformity of Church Government*, (1641) reprinted in part by Hetherington, Westminster Assembly, pp 372-81.

and in their pamphlet *Reformation of Church-Government in Scotland Cleared from some mistakes and Prejudices* written, probably by Henderson, in reply to the Independents' *Apologetical Narration*:

> we are neither so ignorant nor so arrogant as to ascribe to the Church of Scotland such absolute purity and perfection, as hath not need or cannot admit of further Reformation.[30]

On several occasions Henderson played a mediating role in the Assembly and there were issues on which the Scots did not get their way. They did ensure, however, that in such cases the permissability of their position was safeguarded.

Although it goes beyond the scope of this study, it must be kept in mind that the course of the Assembly's work was significantly influenced by the progress of the Civil War. Most significant is a comment of Henderson's, reported by Baillie, that his hopes of the English conforming to Presbyterianism were not great until the Scots army would be in England[31]. The direction of the war effort was entrusted to a Committee of Both Kingdoms set up in February 1644,[32] which met daily and to which the Scots Commissioners were the Earl of Loudon, Lord Maitland, Johnston of Warriston and Robert Barclay, the only one not sitting in the Assembly. Through their correspondence with the Scottish Parliament and with the Committee accompanying the Scottish army the tensions and rivalries of an often stormy alliance can be traced vividly.[33] As Cromwell and the Independents of the New

---

[30] *Reformation of Church-Government in Scotland Cleared from some mistakes and Prejudices*, (London, 1644), p 15.

[31] Baillie, op. cit., 2.104

[32] *Journals of the House of Lords* 5.430 (16 February, 1644). Its work can be followed in the entries in the *Calendar of State Papers, Domestic*, for the relevant years.

[33] See *Correspondence of the Scots Commissioners in London 1644-1646*, edited by Henry W Meikle, (Edinburgh, 1817).

Model Army became so powerful that they could dispense with Scottish help, so the difficulties of the Presbyterians in the Assembly increased.[34]

The Scots Commissioners at the Westminster Assembly moved on an international stage. They kept in close contact with the General Assembly at home, as their letters to each meeting of the Assembly show. Thus in a letter dated 20 May 1644, they report the early stages of drafting the Directory for Public Worship,[35] whilst their letter of 6 January 1645.[36] accompanied the completed Directory which was approved at that meeting of the Assembly. They were very conscious of being representatives of the Scottish nation. There was also opportunity to present their views directly to Parliament as they took their turn preaching the weekly Fast Day Sermons, in which they sought to apply Scripture to the contemporary scene. Most of these were printed and, judging by the length of some of them (two of Rutherford's run to over sixty pages), opportunity was taken to expand the spoken address.[37]

The Solemn League and Covenant served to change the entire direction of the Westminster Assembly's work. The revision of

---

[34] Relations between the Scots and Cromwell were never good. As early as December, 1644, the Commissioners were instructed by the Committee of Estates in Edinburgh, (which guided affairs when Parliament was not sitting), to demand justice for derogatory remarks which Cromwell was alleged to have made about the Scots after the relief of Donnington Castle. In the end this was not done. See Miekle, op. cit., pp 51-52, (17 December 1644).

[35] *Acts of the General Assembly*, 4 June 1644.

[36] *Acts of the General Assembly*, 23 January 1645.

[37] The extant sermons are as follows: Henderson, 27 December 1643 (Commons); Rutherford, 31 January 1644 (Commons); Gillespie, 27 March 1644 (Commons); Henderson, 18 July 1644 (Lords and Commons); Henderson, 28 May 1645 (Lords); Rutherford, 25 June 1645 (Lords); Gillespie, 27 August 1645 (Lords). Two sermons by Henderson and Gillespie were not printed. The Fast Day Sermons are most readily accessible in *The English Revolution I. Fast Day Sermons to Parliament*, general editor Robin Jeffs, 34 volumes, (London, 1970-71).

the Thirty-nine Articles, which had been Parliament's first assignment, was halted and a new programme was undertaken in pursuance of the four parts of uniformity, namely Directory of Worship, Form of Church Government, Confession of Faith and Catechism. The contribution of the Scottish Commissioners to each of these areas will now be examined.

(a) The Directory for the Public Worship of God.

In contrast to the area of polity, with regard to public worship there were no fundamental differences of principle between Puritan and Covenanter, although on a few issues debate was keen. Into this first of the Westminster documents to be completed the Scots were able to have a very significant input.

On 16 December 1643, a committee consisting of five members of the Assembly, Marshall, Palmer, Goodwin, Young and Herle, was appointed to meet with the Scots to draw up a Directory for Public Worship which, rather than providing a set liturgy, would provide general guidelines for the conduct of worship services.[38]

In the allocation of the sections of the Directory the Scots were given public prayer and the administration of the sacraments. The profound spirituality of the Scots is evident in the rich and full prayers which they produced, although these were not intended to be read word for word in a service. The suggestions for prayer before the sermon provide a full course in theology, embracing the entire sweep of the plan of redemption, the mediatorial work of Christ, the spread of the gospel and the fall of Antichrist, the needs of Church and State in the convenanted nations, the constant need of grace for minister and congregation.

---

[38] It is perhaps surprising that George Gillespie's *Notes of Proceedings of the Assembly of Divines*, which cover most of the period during which the Directory was drafted, make not a single mention of the document or the debate it occasioned.

Although they "judge this to be a convenient order", they give freedom for petitons to be interchanged with the prayer after the sermon. It is also significant that the basic structure of the Sabbath service follows the pattern set out in the Scots' Book of Common Order ("Knox's Liturgy"). A service according to the Westminster Directory would be immediately familiar to a Scottish Covenanter.

Other parts of the Directory did not proceed so smoothly. It appears that Goodwin, who had no specific assignment, proved difficult to work with and when the sections on preaching (by Marshall) and on catechizing (by Palmer, a renowned catechist) were presented to the committee the Scots were not satisfied. Both sections were given to the Scots for revision and as a result all were satisfied.

On a number of issues the Scots were able to secure the acceptance of their viewpoint in the Assembly,[39] for example in the condemnation of private baptism, a practice which was widespread in England. Yet they were not always successful, the office of "Reader" was not accepted, even though the custom in Scotland had been for a reader to take the first part of a service with the minister sometimes not entering the church until it was time to preach.

The manner of observing the Lord's Supper proved to be a contentious issue. As B. B. Warfield put it,

> It was over the mode of celebrating the Lord's Supper, however, that the most strenuous debates were held. The manner of celebrating the rite prevalent among the Independents, seemed to the Scots to be bald even to irreverence; while many of the details of the Scottish service were utterly distasteful to the extremer Puritans.[40]

---

[39] Only the latter stages of the debate about the Directory are included in the printed *Minutes of the Assembly*, which begin with Session 324, 18 November 1644. See A. F. Mitchell and J. Struthers (eds), *Minutes of the Sessions of the Westminster Assembly of Divines while engaged in preparing their Directory for Church Government, Confession of Faith and Catechisms (November 1644 to March 1649)*, (Edinburgh, 1874).

[40] Warfield, op. cit., p 50.

To take a significant example, the custom of the Scots was for communicants to sit at tables for the sacrament and to serve each other with the elements, a pattern to which they held very strongly. The final form of the Directory provided a compromise which allows but does not mandate the Scottish pattern, speaking of the communicants sitting "about [the table] or at it" and referring simply to the elements being "distributed amongst the communicants". It was the House of Commons which struck out a reference to "as in the Church of Scotland."

Differences of opinion were also evident with regard to the qualifications for communicants and the nature of the profession to be made by parents presenting their children for baptism. In regard to communicants, a form of words was sent up to Parliament containing a phrase suggested by Henderson in order to promote agreement with the Independents.[41] Although the Commons removed the whole paragraph and substituted a short phrase of its own, the Scots' willingness to be flexible is noteworthy. With regard to baptism, however, at the very last stage of debate in Parliament the Scots succeeded in having removed from the Directory three vague questions which the Assembly had recommended to be put to parents, thus safeguarding the Scottish custom of requiring a fuller profession of faith.[42]

The magnitude of some of the concessions made by the Scots is highlighted by Warfield[43] when he points out that after 1637 the General Assembly was deeply concerned about "novations"

---

[41] The phrase was "who give just grounds in the judgement of charity to conceive that there is faith and regeneration wrought in them "although Scottish Reformed theologians generally held that seeking evidence of regeneration was beyond the brief or ability of any eldership. See John Macpherson, *The Doctrine of the Church in Scottish Teology*, (Edinburgh, 1903), Lecture 2. For the wording of the Assembly's paragraph see A. F. Mitchell, op. cit., pp 216-217.

[42] See *Journals of the House of Lords*, 7.264, and Mitchell, op. cit., pp 218-219.

creeping into the worship of the Kirk through the influence of English Puritans and of Scots exiles returning from Ulster. In Warfield's words,

> By these "novations" the use of "read prayers", and even of the Lord's Prayer, in public worship, was discountenanced, as was also the use of the Gloria Patri, and of the Apostles' Creed in the administration of the Sacraments, and the habit of the minister to bow in silent prayer upon entering the pulpit.[44]

With regard to the last-mentioned item, the Puritans held that all private prayer should cease on entering a gathering for public worship. To combat the "novations" the Assembly decided in 1643 to produce a revised Directory of Worship,[45] Henderson, David Dickson and David Calderwood being assigned the task. In view of the work which the Westminster Assembly was undertaking, however, this mandate was not put into effect and eventually the Directory which was adopted countenanced some of the very "novations" which the Scots had sought to eliminate. As will be seen, however, the Scots safeguarded their practices when they adopted the Westminster Directory.

(b) The Form of Presbyterial Church-Government.

To trace the course of the debates on church government in the Westminster Assembly in even a general way would go far beyond the space available. R. S. Paul has provided a very thorough study of the "Grand Debate" between Presbyterians and Independents,[46] and Wayne Spear has shown in detail the influence of the Scots on the Form of Presbyterial Church-Government.[47] Only a few

---

[43] Warfield, op. cit., pp 46-47.

[44] Warfield, op. cit., p 47.

[45] *Minutes of the General Assembly,* 15 August, 1643

[46] R. S. Paul, op. cit.

[47] Wayne R. Spear, *Covenanted Uniformity in Religion: the Influence of the Scottish Commissioners upon the Ecclesiology of the Westminster Assembly*, unpublished PhD thesis, University of Pittsburgh, 1976.

comments on the Covenanters' input can be provided here.

In all the debates regarding church government the Scots played a very full part. The names of Henderson, Rutherford and Gillespie occur constantly in the minutes and throughout their time at the Assembly they were among the most frequent speakers.[48] The Positions which they defended seldom provide any surprises in the light of the works which they had already written in defence of the Scottish model of Presbyterianism. While the Assembly was sitting they produced several more volumes surveying the whole subject,[49] and no-one could fail to be aware of their views as Gillespie presented Copies of *Aaron's Rod Blossoming* to the Prolocutor and the members of the Assembly.[50]

It was the debate regarding Independency that, as everyone had expected, proved to be the most fraught. Although small in number, the Independents were very vocal and were encouraged in their Opposition by the growing power of Cromwell and the New Model Army which included all kinds of sectaries. The majority in the Assembly were opposed to the Independent viewpoint and after allowing its supporters three weeks to argue their case (2 to 22 February 1644), all their arguments were voted down.[51] The polarisation which the confrontation of debate caused may have thwarted possibilities for rapprochement, as seen for example in Rutherford's comment on reading *Keys of the Kingdom of Heaven* by the Independent John Cotton—"I thought it an easy

---

[48] See the statistics provided by Spear, op. cit., Appendix C, p 362.

[49] Samuel Rutherford, *The Due Right of Presbyteries, or a Peaceable Plea for the government of the Church of Scotland*, (London, 1644) and *The Divine Right of Church Government and Excommunication*, (London, 1646); George Gillespie, *Aaron's Rod Blossoming or the Divine Ordinance of the Church Government Vindicated*, (London, 1646).

[50] *Minutes of the General Assembly*, p 261, 30 July, 1646.

[51] See R. S. Paul, op.. cit., pp 249ff; W. M. Hetherington, *History of the Westminster Assembly*, pp 180ff.

labour for an universal pacification, he comes so near unto us."[52]
It is significant that Henderson was the one to propose the setting
up of a committee to try to find an accommodation with the
Independents.[53] Considerable common ground was identified but
final agreement proved to be impossible. The Independents could
not concede to synods and presbyteries the kind of authority which
Presbyterians believed was essential and biblical.

The Scots were concerned to establish the "divine right" of
the Presbyterian system in all its fulness[54] and in this endeavour
they encountered great difficulties. Many in the Assembly who
voted with the Scots were willing to accept Presbyterianism on
prudential grounds, as permitted by Scripture and as most likely
to result in a single national church,[55] but they balked at accepting
"divine right". As Wayne Spear demonstrates, of fourteen
controversial issues in the Form of Church Government which
were important to the Scots, conclusions were reached that were
generally satisfactory to the Scots in thirteen, yet in only two,
namely the office of deacon and a congregation's right to reject a
minister for just cause, was "ius divinum" accepted. All the other
aspects of Presbyterianism were classed as "recommendations"
or as "permissable".[56] Thus on the one hand the Scots exercised

---

[52] *Minutes*, p 60, 17 February 1645 [1644 Old Style].

[53] Hetherington, *History of the Westminster Assembly*, pp 204-5. Hetherington
speculates that the committee was manipulated from the outset by Cromwell
as a delaying tactic.

[54] A sample of the Scots' arguments for "divine right" with regard to higher
church courts is provided by Gillespie in a *Memorandum* which he wrote
during the debates and included in his Notes between 9 and 10 May 1644
(pp 6l-2)

[55] This is brought out by Iain H. Murray in "The Scots at the Westminster
Assembly: with Special Reference to the Dispute on Church Government
and its Aftermath" in *The Banner of Truth*, Issue 371-2 (August - September
1994), pp 19-23. The effect of the Scots' commitment to a national Church
on their views of church membership is clearly shown.

[56] Spear, op. cit., pp 342-343.

considerable influence in shaping the Form, yet on the other they failed to obtain all that they sought. They argued vigorously, for example, for the scriptural nature of the office of ruling elder, the Form speaks only of "other church governors" who may join in government "when called thereunto", providing only Romans 12:7-8 and I Corinthians 12:28 as proof texts. English congregations would not be obliged to have ruling elders.

The other debate in the Assembly which must be noted is that with Erastianism.[57] Although few in the Assembly supported this position, the outlook of Parliament was decidedly Erastian. The civil rulers proved very reluctant to allow the Church independent jurisdiction with regard to discipline and the Propositions setting out the doctrinal foundations for church government and ordination never received the sanction of the English Parliament. The present Form of Presbyterian Church-Government is the practical Directory which the Assembly went on to draft with considerable input from Henderson.

One of the few Erastian divines in the Assembly was Thomas Coleman whose remarks in a sermon preached to the House of Commons on 30 July 1645[58] sparked a vigorous exchange of pamphlets with Gillespie, especially with regard to the Kingship of Christ.[59] Mention should also be made of Gillespie's reply to the Erastian Hebraist John Selden which has passed into Assembly folklore[60]. After a speech of vast learning by Selden which silenced the Assembly, Gillespie was said to have stood up and, without any notes, swept aside every argument presented by Selden,

---

[57] See Hetherington, *History of the Westminster Assembly*, cpt 4.

[58] Thomas Coleman, *Hopes Deferred and Dashed*, (London, 1645).

[59] Gillespie's contributions were *A Brotherly Examination,* (London, 1645), *Nihil Respondes*, (London, 1645) and *Male Audis*, (London, 1646). The debate with Coleman is discussed at length by McKay, op. cit., cpt 2.

[60] Recounted by Hetherington, *History of the Westminster Assembly*, pp 201-202.

leaving him without reply[61]. It is clear that Gillespie's speech was delivered on the following day, after an evening for consideration, whilst the speech given immediately after Selden's contribution was by Charles Herle.[62]

(c) The Confession of Faith

Although the Westminster Confession of Faith is thought of as the quintessential expression of Scottish Calvinism, the Scottish Commissioners did not play an outstanding role in its composition. Neither the Scots not the English could offer a suitable confession for adoption or revision and so a new confession was drafted, drawing heavily on the work of James Ussher in the *Irish Articles* (1615)[63] B. B. Warfield has traced in great detail the influence of this source on the Confession's chapter on Scripture.[64]

The Assembly was slow in getting down to the drafting of the Confession, not least because of the wrangling over church government. When the Scottish Commissioners returned from laying the Directory for Worship and the Propositions touching Church-government and Ordination before the General Assembly, they brought with them a letter urging the Westminster divines on in completing the work of uniformity.[65] Material from the committees drafting the Confession, which had been working

---

[61] Gillespie's own account of his speech is to be found in his *Notes*, pp 25-26.

[62] According to the manuscript minutes, Selden and Herle spoke on 20 February 1644, whilst Gillespie spoke on 21 February 1644. See A F Mitchell, op. cit., p 288.

[63] *The Irish Articles of Religion* are to be found in *The Creeds of Christendom*, edited by Philip Schaff, 1831 edition, (Grand Rapids, 1983), pp 526-44. See the opinion of Mitchell, op. cit., pp 375ff

[64] Warfield, op. cit., pp 169-175. Warfield goes on to compare the Confession's chapter with Ball's Catechism and Ussher's *Sum and Substance of the Christian Religion*.

[65] *Minutes*, p 77, 9 April 1645; *Acts of the General Assembly*, 13 February 1645, for the text of the letter.

since the previous August, was soon before the Assembly, but Gillespie's hope that "we may be as quickly at home as possible"[66] was not to be realised.

Although the divines were at one in their commitment to the Reformed faith, there was considerable scope for variation in the statement of doctrines and within the Calvinism they espoused there were differences of opinion on some matters. In the Assembly there were even some who held an Amyraldian view of the atonement. Precise wording was vitally important and so the three revisions through which the committees' material passed took a great deal of time. The material for discussion was provided by three committees and in these the Scots no doubt played a full part. No record of their discussions was kept and so precise estimates of the influence are impossible. The reports of debate in the Minutes are seldom any more helpful, the most information that is provided usually being "Ordered . . ." or "Resolved upon the Q[uestion]", with an occasional notice of dissent.[67]

Although specific Scottish influence on the Confession cannot usually be traced, there is one point where it does seem that Gillespie had a direct input in the final wording. In Confession 1.5, regarding the reasons why we believe that Scripture is the Word of God, (the "heavenliness of the matter", etc) there are very definite verbal echoes of a passage written by Gillespie and included in the posthumously-published *Treatise of Miscellany Questions*, chapter 21, entitled "Of an assurance of an interest in Christ by the marks or fruits of sanctification, and namely by love to the brethren." The relevant parts of the chapter are worth quoting for the sake of comparison with the Confession:

> The Scripture is known to be indeed the work of God by the beams of divine authority which it hath in itself, . . . such as the heavenliness

---

[66] *Minutes*, p 77.

[67] e.g. *Minutes*, p 297, 21 October 1646, recording dissenters from the Confession's statement of the power of civil magistrates in religious matters.

of the matter, the majesty of the style, the irresistible power over the conscience, the general scope to abase man, and to exalt God; nothing driven at but God's glory and man's salvation, . . . the marvellous consent of all parts and passages . . .[68]

Although, as Warfield says, much of this was common currency at the time and could be paralleled in the work of other divines, his conclusion seems correct that "the phraseology seems too closely similar for there not to have been some literary connection."[69]

The concern of the Scots for strict accuracy of expression is demonstrated by Gillespie's request, at the final reading of the Confession before it was sent to Parliament, that in the chapter on the civil magistrate (cpt 33), three references to "Christ" should be changed to "God" in case it appeared that the Assembly believed that the magistrate held his office from Christ as Mediator.[70] The Assembly accepted Gillespie's amendment, with Burgess dissenting, and included this Memorandum: "This vote was not intended to determine the controversy about the subordination of the Civil Magistrate to Christ as Mediator."[71]

(d) The Catechism.

It comes as a surprise to many to realise that the Scottish Commissioners had very little to do with the drafting of the Catechisms. The details are not entirely clear, but it appears that the Scots had a catechism almost ready by the end of 1644, whether

---

[68] George Gillespie, *A Treatise of Miscellany Questions*, (Edinburgh, 1649) cpt 21. *In The Presbyterian's Armoury* edition, pp 105-6.

[69] Warfield, op. cit., p 176.

[70] This view of Christ's reign over nations as Mediatorial King, though held by later Covenanters, was vigorously rejected by Rutherford, Gillespie and many others. It was the view espoused by Erastians and featured in the Gillespie-Coleman debate. See McKay, op. cit., cpt 2.

[71] *Minutes*, p 308, 4 December 1646.

their own work or a revision of Palmer's catechism.[72] It seems that the Scots endorsed Palmer's method of asking questions which required a "yes" or "no" answer, but the Assembly rejected this method in favour of that used in their catechisms, which gave fuller answers to the questions. Another committee appointed to draft a catechism made little progress and the work eventually had to begin over again, this time with two catechisms in view. Only after the completion of the Confession was this serious work on the catechisms undertaken, from April 1647 onwards.[73]

In July 1646, Henderson was sent to Newcastle to try to convince the King, who had surrendered to the Scottish army, to sign the Covenant, without success. He left Newcastle exhausted and died in Edinburgh on 16 August 1646. Towards the end of 1646 Baillie requested permission to return to Scotland to report to the Commission of the General Assembly on the work of the Westminster Assembly in preparation for the meeting of the General Assembly in August 1647. Gillespie also returned to Edinburgh in time for that meeting at which the Confession of Faith was approved[74]. These dates serve to disprove another of the pious legends relating to Gillespie, namely the story that the answer to the Shorter Catechism question "What is God?" is a transcript of his prayer for guidance in the drafting committee. He was in Edinburgh in May 1647, and three months later he reported to the General Assembly that the Westminster divines had not yet completed the Larger Catechism and had not had time to do anything regarding the Shorter Catechism. As Mitchell says, the answer to the question "What is God?" had at that time

---

[72] In 1644 a catechism was published - *The New Catechism according to the forme of the Kirk of Scotland*. See A. F. Mitchell, Catechisms of the Second Reformation, (1886).

[73] The clearest account of the history of work on the catechisms is by Warfield, op. cit., pp.62-9.

[74] *Acts of the General Assembly*, 27 August 1647.

not even been adjusted for the Larger Catechism.[75] Work on the Shorter Catechism did not begin in earnest until 5 August 1647[76]. Only Rutherford and Baillie stayed for the completion of the Larger Catechism and left before the Shorter Catechism was finished, considering the work of uniformity to be completed.

III. Ratification of the Documents and Beyond.

(a) Ratification of the documents.

The way in which the various documents of the Westminster Assembly were ratified by the Scots, particularly by the General Assembly, provides further insight into their thinking on a number of issues.[77]

(I) The Directory for the Public Worship of God was ratified by the General Assembly on 3 February 1645, "without a contrary voice." The precise wording of the Act is significant: ratification is "according to the plain tenor and meaning thereof, and the intent of the Preface." This reflects a vigorous debate in the Westminster Assembly as to the status such a directory should have. With bitter memories of Laud's attempts to force on the Scots the use of a liturgy in 1637, they were determined that the Directory should not now become a new liturgy. Thus in the drafting of the Preface, in which Henderson played an important part, the Church of England's liturgy was roundly condemned as "an offence, not only to many of the godly at home, but also to the Reformed churches abroad", in spite of the protests of Puritans such as Burgess and Calamy.

---

[75] Mitchell, op. cit., p 429.

[76] *Minutes*, p 408, 5 August 1647.

[77] The *Acts of the General Assembly* ratifying the documents are generally printed in editions of the *Confession of Faith*, etc.

In describing the Directory itself it was necessary to find a compromise which would satisfy those who wanted to use it as a liturgy and those who did not want to be bound by any written forms. To satisfy the latter, including the Scots, a change was made in the wording of the Preface, replacing "those things that concern the service and worship of God" with "those things that concern the substance of the service . . ." .[78] The Scots in underlining their commitment to the Preface were seeking uniformity not in details but in the matters of substantial importance relating to worship. Their view was well expressed at an earlier stage by George Gillespie who opposed the strict imposition of the Directory with the argument that "the more straitly it is imposed, it will the more breed scruples and create controversies which wise men should do well to prevent."[79] In writing to the General Assembly which was debating the Directory, the Scots Commissioners stress the goal of unity which should not be forfeited by disagreement about details,[80] and the letter from the Westminster Assembly which Gillespie and Baillie brought with them denies any desire to enforce the Directory rigidly.[81]

In its ratifying Act the General Assembly also sought to protect distinctively Scottish customs which might have appeared to be threatened by the Directory. Thus specific mention is made of the Directory's instructions regarding communicants sitting about or at the Table, which, says the Assembly, is not to be interpreted

---

[78] See the final paragraph of the Preface. See also Mitchell, op. cit., p 227n.

[79] Baillie, op. cit., 2.506.

[80] "If there be any particular differences among some Brethren; which are not determined, but passed over in silence in the Directory . . . we hope that in your wisedome ye will so consider of them, that they may be layde aside in due time, and that in the mean while, till the Directory be concluded and put in practice, there be no trouble about them, for that were as Snow in Summer, and as Rain in Harvest". Printed in *Acts of the General Assembly*, 23 January 1645.

[81] *Acts of the General Assembly*, 23 January 1645.

as if, in the judgement of this kirk, it were indifferent and free for any of the communicants not to come to, and receive at the table; or as if we did approve the distributing of the elements by the minister to each communicant, and not by the communicants among themselves.

Whilst unity in fundamentals is gladly accepted, the details of traditional Scottish practice will be preserved. Only a specific prohibition in the Directory would overrule custom. As the Assembly puts it:

It is also provided, That this shall be no prejudice to the order and practice of this Kirk, in such particulars as are appointed by the books of discipline, and Acts of General Assemblies, and are not otherwise ordered and appointed in the Directory.

Scots Presbyterians would not see many changes in their services with the implementation of the Directory.

(ii) The documents relating to church government were not dealt with in such a straightforward way. The Propositions, dealing with the doctrinal foundations for government and ordination, were brought, along with the Directory for Public Worship, by Baillie and Gillespie to the General Assembly in February 1645. Although the Propositions set out the fundamental form of Presbyterianism as the Scots knew it, some including David Calderwood raised strong objections. Calderwood held that congregational elderships were not a separate church court but were in fact nothing more that sub-committees of presbyteries,[82] a view for which he could perhaps garner some support from a certain imprecision in earlier Scottish documents.

In the end the Propositions were approved, pending approval of the English Parliament, but they were regarded as a stage on the way to uniformity, with further discussion on some issues, such as "the distinct rights and interests of presbyteries and people in the calling of ministers", being required.[83] As Baillie expresses it, the Propositions were "shuffled by through the pertinacious

---

[82] Mitchell, op. cit., p 262-3.

[83] *Acts of the General Assembly*, 10 February 1645.

opposition of Mr David Calderwood and two or three with him."[84] As it turned out, the English Parliament approved only a radically revised version of this document.

The Westminster Assembly's second document, the practical Directory, was presented to the General Assembly in 1647. It was printed and sent to Presbyteries for comment, although the following year reports were deferred and it would appear that no further official action was taken by the General Assembly, the deteriorating political situation no doubt being a significant factor. By 1651 the General Assembly was so divided that it did not meet for some forty years. Nevertheless what is now known as the Form of Presbyterial Church-Government was reprinted in 1690 and eventually came to be included in the standard collection of Westminster Assembly documents, preceded by the Act of the General Assembly which approves only the earlier Propositions.

The Form does not establish Presbyterianism on a ius divinum basis such as the Scots had argued for in the Westminster Assembly and among its defects is a lack of any consideration of excommunication, which was considered in the Propositions. Wayne Spear is surely correct in attributing the Form's replacing the Second Book of Discipline in Scotland to the Scots' commitment to the vision of the Solemn League and Covenant.[85]

(iii) The Confession of Faith was described by the General Assembly in its ratifying Act as "the chiefest part of that uniformity in religion which, by the Solemn League and Covenant, we are bound to endeavour"[86] After thorough examination the Assembly found the Confession to be "most agreeable to the word of God,

---

[84] Baillie, op. cit., 3.59.

[85] "In view of the inherent imperfections of the Form of Church Government, and its comparative inferiority to other Scottish documents, it appears that its long-standing acceptance in Scotland must be attributed to the influence of the covenanting tradition in the nation." Spear, op. cit., p 346.

[86] *Acts of the General Assembly*, 27 August 1647.

and in nothing contrary to the received doctrine, worship, discipline, and government of this Kirk". In general there was hearty approbation of the Confession both from the point of view of its truth and also in view of the uniformity which it would promote in the three kingdoms. Only two qualifications were stated in the Act.

First, the Assembly states that the absence of any reference in the Confession of ecclesiastical officers and assemblies was not to be taken as undermining biblical teaching on these subjects. The Scots' input to the Westminster Assembly underlined how very important these issues were, and the Act anticipates the full expression of "the truth of Christ in these particulars" in the Directory of Government, which, as we have seen, had not yet been ratified in its entirety.

Second, the Assembly explains its understanding of the second article of Chapter 31 of the Confession which deals with the power of the magistrates to convene ecclesiastical assemblies. To avoid, as they saw it, any hint of Erastianism, the Scots indicate that the powers set out in this article are to be exercised only with reference to "kirks not settled, or constituted in point of government". In such cases a magistrate's call was sufficient authority for a court to meet, or ministers could meet by virtue of their own authority, without being delegated by their churches, but neither course was to be regarded as normal. The power of magistrates was clearly limited in ecclesiastical affairs and could not be used to prevent church courts meeting. Had not the 1638 General Assembly continued to meet in defiance of the royal Commissioner?

It should not be concluded, however, that the Scots thought of Church and State as two utterly separate institutions. They insisted that although Church and State had separate God-given jurisdictions, the "godly magistrate" was keeper of both Tables of the Law and had weighty responsibilities for suppressing heresy and promoting the truth. This view was argued at great length by, to take only one example, Samuel Rutherford in his 1649 treatise on liberty of conscience.[87] The vision of the Covenant, as understood by the Scots, was of Church and State working in close harmony, so that, for example, civil and ecclesiastical discipline would go hand in hand. As Rutherford put it:

the magistrate [is] obliged to follow, ratifie, and with his civil sanction to confirme the sound constitutions of the Church: But conditionally, not absolutely and blindely, but in so far as they agree with the Word of God.[88]

The magistrate was thus put in the position of evaluating church decisions in the light of Scripture, and, according to Rutherford, when he conducts the civil trial of one subject to ecclesiastical discipline he may arrive at a different verdict.

Whilst civil and ecclesiastical jurisdictions are separate, the magistrate is to heed the censures of the Church, and church courts, as Gillespie argues in *Aaron's Rod Blossoining*, must give satisfactory explanation to civil rulers regarding decisions which those magistrates consider unjust.[89] Although the magistrate cannot judge how sincerely his commands are obeyed, Rutherford contends that he must use his civil power to ensure that true doctrine is preached and may call errant ministers to account[90]. Although, as the Confession states, civil rulers could not prevent the meeting of ecclesiastical assemblies, the Scots expected that such meetings would normally be with the sanction and representation of the King.[91]

The very close cooperation envisaged by the Scots may raise

---

[87] Samuel Rutherford, *A Free Disputation Against pretended Liberty of Conscience*, (London, 1649).

[88] Samuel Rutherford, *The Divine Right of Church-Government and Excommunication*, (London, 1646), cpt xxvi, Q 22, p 579.

[89] George Gillespie, *Aaron's Rod Blossoming*, (London, 1646), Part 2, Cpt 8, pp ll7-118, in *The Presbyterian's Armoury* edition.

[90] Rutherford, *Divine Right*, cpt xxiv, Q 20.

[91] Henderson, *Government and Order*, Part 2, Sec 6, pp 56-7.

many questions about the separation of civil and ecclesiastical jurisdictions in practice, but the General Assembly believed that the necessary separation had been secured and to set out its position ordered the printing of Gillespie's *One Hundred and Eleven Propositions*[92] at the same time as it ratified the Confession.

(iv) Issues of church government and of Church-State relationships play only a small part in the Larger Catechism and are entirely absent from the Shorter Catechism. Thus the General Assembly was able to give a hearty and unqualified approval to the two documents which bore least evidence of Scottish influence.[93]

(b) The failure of the Covenant.

The course of Scottish history after the surrender of Charles I to the Scottish army at Newark on 8 May 1646 can be traced in any of the standard histories.[94] It makes sorry reading as splits and disagreements tore Church and State apart. It includes the Engagement with Charles I established by political leaders in 1648, but rejected by the General Assembly, which led to defeat by Cromwell and the execution of the King; the crowning of Charles II by the Scots in 1650 and the subsequent defeat of the Scots army by Cromwell at Dunbar; the divisions in the Church as spiritual requirements for service in the army were relaxed, pitting Resolutioner against Protester, Baillie against Rutherford, Maitland against Warriston; further defeats, the period of Cromwellian rule and in 1660 the Restoration of a covenant-breaking King Charles II.

The hopes of uniformity entertained by the Scots when the

---

[92] *George Gillespie, One Hundred and Eleven Propositions concerning the Ministry and Government of the Church*, (Edinburgh, 1647). See Acts of the General Assembly, 31 August 1647.

[93] *Acts of the General Assembly*, 20 July and 28 July 1648.

[94] See G. Donaldson, op. cit., pp 335-357.

Solemn League and Covenant was signed were not to be realised. Historical events put that realisation far out of reach. Despite the scope and grandeur of its vision, two significant weaknesses are evident in that Covenant.

First, it is clear that the Covenant tried to combine a religious and a political commitment: it was both a covenant and a treaty. Consonant with biblical covenants, there is a spiritual commitment to God, an undertaking to "live in faith and love". This implies a living spiritual experience which cannot be coerced. On the other hand, there is a commitment to engage in various political actions "to preserve the rights and privileges of the Parliaments, and the liberties of the kingdoms". Thus the Scottish Parliament sought to enforce the swearing of the Covenant, on pain of civil punishment, as a test of loyalty and fitness to hold office. This fundamental tension between a free heart-response to God's grace and a binding political treaty led a later Covenanter, Alexander Shields, to conclude that two covenants, one religious and one political, would have been preferable.[95]

In the second place, as has already been indicated, the Scots and the English entered the Covenant with different aims and consequently interpreted it in different ways. In the Scottish view, the Covenant committed the signatories to establish a single Reformed, Covenanted, Presbyterian Church, apart from which no public expression of Christianity would be legal. As time went on, however, it became clear that a degree of toleration of religious views would be permitted in England which was totally unacceptable to the Scots. The resulting recriminations were bitter, with Rutherford stigmatising the English Independents as worse

---

[95] See J. D. Douglas, *Light in the North*, (Exeter, 1964), p 33. Note also the comments of J. G. Vos in *The Scottish Covenanters*, (Pittsburgh, 1980), pp 42-44. For a sample of the General Assembly's enforcement of the Covenant, see *Acts of the General Assembly*, 7 August 1648.

than pagans, having sworn the Covenant "in a Jesuiticall reserved sense"[96] The unfaithfulness of one party, the Covenanters believed, could not lessen the obligation of the Covenant.

Although for the majority the Solemn League and Covenant was relegated to the museum of historical curiosities, its vision lived on in the hearts of the Scottish Covenanters who have never given up hope that it might one day be realised by the power and grace of God.

---

[96] Rutherford, *Free Disputation*, xxi, p 262.

The Battle for the Westminster Confession of Faith in Australia

Stewart D. Gill

Introduction

On June 2, 1992, the Presbytery of Sydney met at the Presbyterian Theological Centre in Burwood in order to discuss a sermon delivered by the Rev. Dr. Peter Cameron, the Master of St. Andrews College at the University of Sydney, at the Dorcas Diamond Jubilee Service on Monday, March 2, in the Ashfield Presbyterian Church. The discussion of the sermon had begun almost immediately and concerns advanced at the April meeting of Presbytery. At the June meeting the Presbytery decided to continue down the line of discipline and they set a date for a brotherly conference. Cameron warned his brother presbyters:

> ... I must admit I don't relish the prospect myself, but I am sure that it will damage the Church far more than it will damage me. After all, I have recently come from Scotland and I will eventually return to Scotland, and my theological position raises few eyebrows there. ...
> It is probably as unremarkable in Scotland as Samuel Angus' views were in Europe and America sixty years ago when the Presbyterian Church of Australia was taking such offence at them. And that is what I mean: this case threatens to become as unpleasant and as farcical as the Angus case, and all it will achieve will be to bring

home to people outside just how little theological progress the Presbyterian Church of Australia has made since those days.[1]

The Presbytery held the brotherly conference on 23 June when Cameron faced fifty ministers and elders. The Rev. Chris Balzer, lecturer in theology at the Presbyterian Theological Centre, soon got to the crux of the problem with three prepared questions. Balzer asked first whether Cameron stood by two extracts of his sermon; second, whether the extracts were consistent with various phrases in the Westminster Confession of Faith; third, whether homosexual practice by Christians was contrary to God's will. Cameron, obviously self-assured, answered Balzer without pausing to think. He subsequently wrote:

> I replied that he could have saved himself (and everyone else) the trouble of reading out half a sermon by simply asking whether I still stood by the whole sermon, which I did; that **the Westminster Confession of Faith wasn't my bedside reading so that I couldn't possibly answer the question without studying the relevant phrases in detail**; that in any case even if we did disagree on these matters it would probably be on the meaning we ascribed to expressions in the Westminster Confession of Faith like 'inspired,' 'rule of faith' and so on; and finally that I did not think homosexual behaviors necessarily inconsistent with Christianity.[2]

The replies were telling and led to a protracted trial through Presbytery and the General Assembly as Cameron, accused of 'heresy,' decided to fight the accusation. The central issues were Cameron's understanding of two documents, the Bible and the Westminster Confession of Faith. The Cameron case has merely been the most recent incident in a long running battle over the Westminster Confession of Faith in Australia. Three famous 'heresy' trials, starting with Charles Strong in the 1880s and continuing with Samuel Angus in the 1930s and finally Peter Cameron, exemplify the battle over the Confession within the

---

[1] P. Cameron, *Heretic*, Sydney, 1994, p. 70.

[2] *Ibid.*, p. 71. Empahsis mine.

Presbyterian Church in Australia. The history of Christianity can on the whole be written as the story of its 'heretics' and orthodoxy's response.[3] The Christian Gospel is a simple message, relatively easily grasped, although only believed and accepted by those who receive the gift of faith. To some, like Strong, Angus and Cameron, this simplicity was and is offensive. After discussing the historical origins of the Presbyterian Church of Australia, this paper will consider the development of the Westminster Confession of Faith through the three aforementioned cases.[4]

Background

The Presbyterian Church of Australia is a compilation of various constituent parts representing the diversity of British Presbyterianism.[5] Scottish emigrants to Australia each brought a fresh experience of the Scottish church and society, an image frozen in time at the point of departure. The Scottish Presbyterian emigrant

---

[3] See H.O.J. Brown, *Heresies*, New York, 1984. Brown writes: "The history of Christian theology is in large part a history of heresies because Jesus and the claims he made, as well as the claims his disciples made about him, seemed to be incredible." (p.xxiii).

[4] This chapter does not pretend to be a comprehensive coverage of the history of the Westminster Confession of Faith in Australia but instead looks at specific challenges to the Confession in Australia and how the Church responded. Various theses have been written which are more comprehensive in scope in the period up to 1901 and the formation of the Presbyterian Church of Australia. See C.D. Balzer, "Australian Presbyterians and the Westminster Confession of Faith, 1823-1901." M.Th. Australian College of Theology, 1989; P. Cooper, "Some Nineteenth Century Challenges to the Westminster Confession of Faith in the Presbyterian Church of Victoria." M.Th. Melbourne College of Divinity, 1989; R.S. Ward, "Divisions and Unions in Australian Presbyterianism.1823-1901. With Special Reference to the Church's Attitude to its Creed." Th.D., Australian College of Theology 194; P. Barnes, "Living in a Half-Way House: The Rise of Liberal Evangelicalism in the Presbyterian Church of New South Wales, 1865-1915." Th.D., Australian College of Theology, 1995.

[5] See R.S. Ward, *The Bush Still Burns*, Melbourne, 1989.

of 1800 was different from that of 1850 or 1950, as each brought a fresh image of the church they had left behind and perhaps attempted to recreate, find, or even flee from such a church on the Australian landscape. From the very beginning there were a variety of responses to the Westminster Confession of Faith as the founding ministers represented different theological traditions.

Settlers from Scotland, and to a lesser extent from Ulster, established the Presbyterian Church in Australia. During the 18th and 19th centuries the Scottish Church suffered schism and re-union, although the various sections continued to hold to the same basic polity and standards. These were the Presbyterian form of government, the Scriptures as the supreme standard of faith and doctrine, and the Westminster Confession of Faith of 1647 as the subordinate standard. The various Scottish schisms affected the development of Presbyterianism in Australia.

Each main division in the Scottish churches found representation in Australian Presbyterianism. The Church of Scotland arrived with John Dunmore Lang in 1823, the Free Church effected divisions in Australia in 1823, and the United Presbyterians arrived in 1847. Each section of the Church adhered to the Westminster Confession of Faith as its subordinate standard. However, as the 19th century progressed, and the various Presbyterian churches united, (1859 in Victoria, 1863 in Queensland, 1865 in South Australia and New South Wales) and in common with an encroaching liberal theology, strict adherence to creeds and confessions began to be questioned. The challenge to the Westminster Confession of Faith by Charles Strong, minister of the influential Scots Church, Melbourne, is of importance here. Strong's attack upon the Westminster Confession of Faith led to the 1882 Declaratory Act in the Presbyterian Church of Victoria that sought to explicate the teaching of the Confession and clarify what subscription to the Standards involved. The 1882 Victorian Declaratory Act provided the basis for the Declaratory Statement drawn up by the state churches uniting together in 1901 to form the Presbyterian Church of Australia.

During the 1920s and again in the 1950s, as the ecumenical movement developed world-wide, a section of the church put forward proposals to unite with the Methodist and Congregational churches. Organised opposition to these plans soon mounted as more conservative elements realised that union would mean a watering down of the traditional Presbyterian beliefs in the Bible as "the Word of God written" denoted in its credal statement, the Westminster Confession of Faith. On the other hand, church union found support among those of a more liberal theological persuasion who wanted to escape from what they saw as the fetters of credal subscription.

While the 1924 Plan of Union failed there were those within the Presbyterian Church who continued to attack the Confession during the 20th century, not least among these was Samuel Angus. This led to the formation of the Uniting Church in 1977 and a smaller continuing Presbyterian Church that adhered to the Confession as subscribed to by the fathers of the 1901 union. However, there has continued to be a group within the Presbyterian Church of Australia that has put a liberal interpretation on the Confession. In recent days, Peter Cameron has represented the more extreme views of this group.

Charles Strong

The Victorian Background

The Rev. James Clow, a retired East India Company chaplain, was the pioneer of Presbyterianism in Victoria. Settling in Melbourne in December 1837 for health reasons he conducted services for the many "Scotch" settled in the town. The Rev. James Forbes followed in January 1838 and took up the work under the authority of John Dunmore Lang's Presbytery of New South

Wales.[6] The Presbytery, founded in 1832

> in accordance with a formal enactment of the Church of Scotland
> which was adopted in 1833 for the purpose of declaring the relations
> which she sustained to Presbyterian Churches formed in the colonies.[7]

The Church of Scotland had passed a Declaratory Act in 1833 that made it necessary for such "colonial" presbyteries and synods so associated to adhere to the standards of the Church of Scotland. Consequently, the Presbytery of New South Wales and later the Synod of Australia, founded in 1840, and the Presbytery of Melbourne constituted in 1842 adhered to the Westminster Confession of Faith. In 1842 the Church of Scotland linked all the Presbyterians in Victoria and consequently they had the Westminster Confession of Faith as their subordinate standard.

With the Scottish "Disruption" of 1843 the Presbyterian scene changed dramatically, as Forbes broke away and formed the Free Church of Australia Felix. His first task was to send an urgent request for additional ministers from the Free Church in Scotland. The Scottish church had its own problems and was unable to respond immediately. However, the Rev. Thomas Hastie joined Forbes from Tasmania and in 1847 the Rev. John Ziegler Huie arrived from Scotland sent by the Ladies' Association of Ayrshire. The latter settled in Geelong but soon the Rev. John Tait, the leader of the Free Church party in the Synod of Australia, replaced him. Tait became one of the leaders in the negotiations that led to Presbyterian re-union in 1859 and the formation of the Presbyterian Church of Victoria.

The Free Church Synod of Australia Felix (Victoria) was constituted on 9 June 1847 by the Revs. James Forbes, Thomas

---

[6] See R.S. Ward, "James Forbes (1813-1851): 'Abundant in Labours' in R.S. Ward ed., *Presbyterian Leaders in Nineteenth Century Australia*. Melbourne, 1993, pp. 37-53.

[7] R. Hamilton, *A Jubilee History of the Presbyterian Church of Victoria*, Melbourne 1888, p. 17.

Hastie, John Zeigler Huie and Mr. Henry Bell (elder). A year later, on 9 May 1848 the church adopted the Fundamental Act that set out the distinctive principles of the new denomination:

> . . . done in accordance with a formal enactment of the Church of Scotland which was adopted in 1833, for the purpose of declaring the relations which she sustained to Presbyterian Churches formed in the colonies.[8]

On the surface it appeared that the new church had accepted the Confessional stand of the Church of Scotland. Section III of the Act modified the Confession with regard to the place of the civil magistrate:

> And this Synod do condemn, and by God's help resolve ever to testify against all interference of civil magistrate with the spiritual affairs of Christ's house, and against all ecclesiastical bodies countenancing or submitting to such interference, either directly or indirectly: and against all tenets, principles, practices, and acts by which such interference on the part of the civil magistrate, or such submission on the part of ecclesiastical bodies may be countenanced.[9]

In 1850, the third major strand in Victorian Presbyterianism arrived with the formation of the United Presbyterian Church of Victoria. The new denomination adhered to a "summary of doctrine" rather than the Westminster Confession of Faith. The summary was not considered binding. The intention of the Summary was outlined as

> The following summary of doctrine is submitted as a general statement of the great principles of truth and practice 'most surely believed amongst us'. It is thought to be sufficiently defined to exclude fatal error, and sufficiently general to permit that variation of sentiment on minor points which seems to be incident to our present imperfect state.[10]

Any appeal on doctrinal matters was to be to the written Word of God alone.

---

[8] R. Sutherland, *A History of The Presbyterian Church of Victoria*, London, 1877, p. 84.

[9] *Ibid.*

[10] Quoted in F.M. Bradshaw, *Scottish Seceders in Victoria*, Melbourne, 1947, p. 162.

Many of the problems that were to face the Presbyterian Church of Victoria in the late Victorian period could be traced to developments which took place in the 1850s. In 1851 the colony had separated from New South Wales and almost immediately gold was discovered. These factors transformed the state beyond recognition. In the period from 1850 to 1855 the population quadrupled and the churches had the problem of coping with increased numbers. A visitor to Melbourne in 1853 noted the impact that the discovery of gold had on the social and religious life of the town:

> Since 1850, the discovery of gold in Victoria having attracted to its shores multitudes of people, I found the population of its capital, including its immediate suburbs, estimated at not less than 80,000, of whom, however, 8,000 were living in tents, in and about the city. . . . Some frightful cases of wickedness have undoubtedly occurred in Melbourne, a result which might fairly have been expected from the sudden influx of a tainted population from a neighbouring colony, on the discovery of gold; but it is now prevented by a prompt and effective administration of law. Besides the arrival of vast numbers of highly respectable immigrants has, no doubt, exerted a collective and highly beneficial influence upon the city. The religious state of the community, however, is far from being satisfactory. It is true, places of worship are numerous and generally well attended and the Sabbath is outwardly observed, and benevolent institutions liberally supported; yet the prevalence of intemperance and gambling is deeply affecting, and, if not checked, will ruin many a family, if not the city itself.[11]

This situation, where the various Presbyterian bodies were in competition and manpower was over stretched, was one of the main issues leading to union negotiations during the 1850s. Adam Cairns, who was the leading Free Churchman of the period in Victoria expressed concern that the Christian gospel was losing out because of a spirit of competition.[12] Cairns was concerned

---

[11] The visitor was Dr. Robert Young, a British Methodist, who reported on his visit in *The Southern World, Journal of a Deputation to Australia and Polynesia* which was published in 1855. It is reprinted in I.H. Murray, *Australian Christian Life,* Edinburgh, 1988, pp. 200, 203.

[12] On Cairns, see S.D. Gill, "Adam Cairns," B. Dickey, ed., *The Australian*

with the spiritual state of Melburnians, and in a sermon preached in 1856 he repeated the views expressed above. "The first and most observable sign of this moral degeneracy," he wrote, "is a forsaking of the assemblies of the saints, and of the ordinances of God's public worship."[13] The trend was for men and women in their move overseas to depart from religion and to leave the church of their fathers. He was particularly dismayed by the number of his compatriots who faced with the greater freedoms of the new society and, while still professing to be Christians, profaned the Sabbath and "were thus despising the privileges of the Gospel". Accompanying non-attendance at worship he also noted a fall in the numbers attending prayer meetings and among his congregation a fall in regular family worship. He concluded: "Their (the Scots) piety has been withered, as by a blast from the desert . . .".[14]

As a consequence of the condition of society Cairns argued that it was a matter of urgency that the churches in the colony cooperate. He wrote on the need for unity in spreading the Gospel.

> To our mind, the moral condition of colonial society is such as to call for the undivided solicitude of every Church and minister to stem the torrent of ungodliness that pollutes the whole land and to get a hearing from the multitudes who are perishing for the lack of knowledge, for the tidings of mercy sufficient for the chief of sinners.[15]

While he recognised that there were differences between churches he argued that it was wrong to major on these distinctions in the colonial situation. He thought that the various denominations should seek "to know nothing in the colony but Christ Jesus and Him crucified.". This was not to suggest that

---

Dictionary of Evangelical Biography. Sydney 1994, pp. 63-4; S.D. Gill, "A Presbyterian Baptist: Adam Cairns and Baptism" *Reformed Theological Review,* Vol. 48, No. 2, pp. 63-70; J.G. Divorty, "Adam Cairns, D.D.," in *A Memorial of the Disruption Worthies, 1843,* Vol. 1, ed. J. Wylie, Edinburgh, 1881; R.S. Ward, "Adam Cairns (1802-81): Evangelical Leader" in R.S. Ward ed., *Presbyterian leaders. . . .*

[13] A. Cairns, *New Year's Sermon with remarks suggested by the decease of the late governor Sir Charles Hotham K.C.B.* (Melbourne, 1856), p. 12.

Cairns was an early ecumenist. He was one of the prime movers that brought about the formation of the Presbyterian Church of Victoria in 1859, but his vision for union did not extend beyond the bounds of Presbyterianism. Cairns saw the unity between the evangelical churches as being necessary for the evangelization of Victoria.

As a consequence of union negotiations some agreement had to be established between the various Presbyterian branches as to their commitment to the Westminster Confession of Faith. Eventually, in October, 1857, at the suggestion of the Free Church of Scotland, the United Presbyterian Synod of Victoria resolved,

> The Synod . . .to remove all existing doubts and to prevent any future misconceptions on this subject, hereby enacts and declares that the Standards of the United Presbyterian Church in Scotland are the Standards of this Church. . . .[16]

Negotiations took place from 1851 to 1859 and culminated on 7 April 1859 with a union between twenty ministers of the Synod of Victoria (Church of Scotland), twenty-seven from the Free Church Synod of Victoria, and four each from the United Presbyterian Synods of Victoria and Australia to form the Presbyterian Church of Victoria. In their Basis of Union the signatories accepted the old formularies of the Church of Scotland namely:

> I. That the Westminster Confession of Faith, the Larger and Shorter Catechisms, the Form of Presbyterian Church Government, the Directory for Public Worship, and the Second Book of Discipline be the Standards and Formularies of this Church[17].

But, Article II gave liberty of conscience and the right of private judgement in the area of adherence to the teaching of the Confession on the Civil Magistrate:

---

[14] *Ibid.*, p. 12.

[15] A. Cairns, Baptism . . ., p. 2.

[16] R. Hamilton, *A Jubilee History* . . ., p. 158.

[17] R. Hamilton, *A Jubilee History* . . ., p. 172.

II. That inasmuch as there is a difference of opinion in regard to the doctrines contained in these Standards relative to the power and duty of the Civil Magistrate in matters of religion, the office-bearers of this Church, in subscribing to these Standards and Formularies, art not to be held as countenancing any persecuting or intolerant principles, or as professing any views inconsistent with the liberty of conscience or the right of private judgement[18].

Although it did not provide an unqualified approval of the Confession, this article did limit the area of dissent. The Formula which ministers had to sign made this clear.[19]

The first years of the Presbyterian Church of Victoria were dominated by Adam Cairns and what could be called conservative Free Church of Scotland orthodoxy. This period of orthodoxy was to last until 1881 as Cairns was the initiator of and dominated theological education within the new church. Cairns upheld the verbal inspiration of the Bible and believed strongly in confessional Calvinism. In a speech reported in 1863 he stated:

... and I candidly own that I did look forward with considerable interest to a time when I should be able to give myself unreservedly to this one pursuit, and do my utmost to leaven the young preachers of our colonial church with a sound Calvinism—that is with a dear and comprehensive understanding of that system of Divine truth which is revealed in the Word of God, and embodied in our well-known confession of faith.[20]

He was strongly opposed to new German ideas, especially the views of Hegel and Schleiermacher. In 1866 he was appointed as the Principal of the Theological Hall. One historian of the Theological Hall speaks of it being dominated in this period by

... the conservative evangelical Calvinism of the Hall, which stood squarely on the standards of the Westminster Confession and the

---

[18] *Ibid.*,p. 172.

[19] "I do hereby declare that I do sincerely approve and accept the Standards and Formularies enumerated in the foregoing Articles as the confession of my faith, with the declarations and provisions contained in the second Article ...". Quoted from *Ibid.,* p. 172.

[20] *The Presbyterian Magazine*, September, 1863, p. 296.

Second Book of Discipline: the ultimate "standard" of course being the Bible interpreted according to the theory of plenary inspiration. The doctrinal and disciplinary demands of the Victorian Church on its members were more stringent than those of any other colony.[21]

Cairns' orthodoxy was supported by the other professors, J. O. Dykes, Peter Brown, A. R. Boyd McCay, T. Mckenzie Fraser and A. J. Campbell. The principal text-book for theology was A. A. Hodges' *Outlines of Theology*.

While in this period Cairns managed to retain the Theological Hall as a bastion of orthodoxy there were those appearing in Victoria who would seek to scale the ramparts. There was the Rev. William Henderson of Williamstown who had trained in Germany. Hamilton reported that "His current thought seemed to run considerably in the German channel."[22] However, Henderson's book, *Christianity and Modern Thought* did not find many readers in Victoria. Henderson proposed at the Victorian Assembly in 1870 that elders in the church be asked to subscribe to the Shorter Catechism with a general adherence to the doctrines, discipline and worship of the church.[23] By a majority of one it was decided to pass the proposal down to the lower courts for comment. This perhaps signalled that changes were afoot in the Presbyterian Church of Victoria. R. S. Ward comments correctly that "Henderson had exploited the poor drafting in the 1859 Basis of Union which required one to own and accept *all* the subordinate standards."[24] Another critic of orthodoxy was the Rev. Dr. Adam

---

[21] D. Chambers, *Theological Teaching and Thought in the Theological Hall of the Presbyterian Church of Victoria, 1865-1906.* Melbourne, 1967, pp. 6,7.

[22] R. Hamilton, *A Jubilee History . . .*, p. 82. See also pamphlet by D. Blair, *Carlylism and Christianity. Notes on a lecture by the Rev. W. Henderson,* Melbourne, 1865.

[23] Minutes of the PCV Assembly, November 1870. Also reported in *The Christian Review,* December 1870, p. 15.

[24] R.S. Ward, "Divisions and Unions in Australian Presbyterianism, 1823-1901 . . .", p. 167.

Turnbull from Tasmania who addressed the General Assembly of the Presbyterian Church of Victoria in 1865 and stated that "he preferred the old Scottish Confession, to the Westminster Confession of Faith."[25]

While Robert Swanton concluded that the Theological Hall retained its conservative Free Church theological tradition until well into the twentieth century, this was not the case in the Church as a whole and indeed highly debatable even with regard to the Victorian Hall. The Presbyterian Church of Victoria's orthodox foundations were soon threatened by the Strong case.

The Strong Challenge to Orthodoxy[26]

Charles Strong was born at Dailly in Ayrshire, on 26 September 1844, the son of a clergyman. He attended the University of Glasgow from 1859 to 1867 where his chief mentor became John Caird.[27] Under Caird, Strong was first introduced to a more liberal form of religion. Caird had become Professor of Theology at Glasgow in 1862 and introduced Hegelian analysis to the Scottish classroom, departing from traditional Scottish

---

[25] R. Sutherland, *A History of The Presbyterian Church of Victoria,* p. 302.

[26] See C.D. Balzer, "Australian Presbyterians and the Westminster Confession of Faith, 1823-1901." M.Th., Australian College of Theology, 1989, pp. 81-116; P. Cooper, "Some Nineteenth Century Challenges to the Westminster Confession of Faith in the Presbyterian Church of Victoria." M.Th., Melbourne College of Divinity, 1989, R.S. Ward, "Divisions and Unions in Australian Presbyterianism, 1823-1901, With Special Reference to the Church's Attitude to its Creed.." Th.D., Australian College of Theology 1994, pp. 165-186; C.R. Badger, The Reverend Charles Strong and the Australian Church, Melbourne, 1971; C. R. Badger, "Charles Strong" Australian Dictionary of Biography, VI, pp. 208- 209; A.M. Harman, "Charles Strong: Dictionary of Scottish Church History and Theology. Edinburgh, 1993, p. 802. Badger's account is written from a sympathetic point of view while the other works are more critical of Strong.

[27] A good introduction to Caird is to be found in A.P.F. Sell, *Defending and Declaring the Faith. Some Scottish Examples 1860-1920*. Exeter, 1987.

realism. Badger writes of Caird:

> He was a notable teacher as many of his students and especially the more able, such as Charles Strong, testified. His method was precisely the opposite of that of his predecessor in the Chair of Divinity, in that he sought to teach theology from its philosophic and not from its dogmatic side. An excellent example of his method of setting out both sides of each question is to be seen in his Gifford Lectures, *Fundamental Ideas of Christianity* (1899). He taught his students to have no fear of the exercise of their minds, but to go to the bottom of each question. His conception of theology saw it not as a cast-iron system of dogma, demanding unqualified assent, but as an expanding body of thought and enquiry.[28]

Caird represented the views of many in the mid-nineteenth century, a period in which Calvinistic orthodoxy in most churches in the Western world was being steadily eroded by the onslaught of a so-called more "scientific" and "rational" approach to Christianity. For the Church the latter half of the nineteenth century was an age of revolution and great change. The events and movement that were occuring in Britain, Europe and North America were paralleled in Australia. The Christian Church changed from being generally Biblically orthodox (in mid-century) to being by and large "critically" orthodox (by around 1914).

Progress was the major certainty of Victorian culture and the extent of progress was invariably measured in material terms. People believed from the 1850s onwards, with the discovery of gold in Victoria, that everything was improving, and they sustained this belief by counting the increase in population and the rising acreage of agricultural production. Progress became a principle of social development. The present would inevitably lead on to a boundless and abundant future. The idea of progress and its place in Victorian culture, however, is more complex than this generalization might suggest. Far from being an exclusively materialistic and secular ideology, the belief in progress

---

[28] C.R. Badger, *The Reverend Charles Strong . . .*, p. 26.

encompassed a series of religious ideas that deeply coloured the way Victorians described the world.

After 1860 it seemed that the Bible and the orthodox Christian faith was being attacked by the forces of modernity, which sought to remove traditional beliefs concerning the origin of all things and the supernaturalness of the gospel of Jesus Christ. The Bible was being attacked on two levels during the latter half of the nineteenth century. On the one hand, it was challenged by scientists especially in the area of the origin of life; and on the other, by theologians who were adopting a higher critical view of the Bible.

Between the years 1800 and 1850 there was a great upsurge of interest in the geological investigation of the earth. This development led to the Bible being challenged along geological lines. The idea that the earth was much older than Genesis appeared to allow became popular. The second scientific challenge to the Bible came from biology. On November 24, 1859, Charles Darwin's book, *On the Origin of Species By Means of Natural Selection* was published. This book marked the beginning of a new era in human thought and philosophy. The vast age of the earth as claimed by the new geology seemed to allow for the time required for life to have evolved. This was the biological challenge to the Bible.

The principal challenges to the Christian faith were in the area of attempting to question the authority of the Bible. The Genesis account of the creation and the fall was questioned and discarded. If creation and the fall were questioned then so was the whole biblical-theological structure of the Christian faith with Christians believing as they did in the creation and the fall leading to redemption in Jesus Christ. The claim that there was purpose in the natural world was also questioned and discarded. Finally, the existence of the God of the Scriptures was reduced to at best an absent God who was merely the first cause of the universe—

a kind of benevolent clockmaker. At the worst God was eliminated altogether as the earth was portrayed as the natural world and not the work of supernatural creation.

In Australia the linking together of the geological and biological challenges to Christianity strengthened the hand of the "free thinkers" who were attacking the Bible and Christianity in the 1870s and 80s. The "free thinkers" used the scientific advances to attack the faith from outside the Churches. Meanwhile some ministers trained overseas and some native-born Australians who were interested in science used scientific advances to modify the faith from within.

At first the conservatives were uncertain how to react to the rising tide of doubt inspired by science. As the challenge grew after 1875 the reaction by the Churches to the scientific revolution took on a different complexion. In 1876 Dr. Z. Barry a Sydney Anglican preached a series of sermons against "free thought". Meanwhile, Dr. R. B. Vaughan, the Roman Catholic Archbishop of Sydney, lectured against "the shallowness of infidelity and the reasonableness of Christianity".

Nevertheless, by the time of Darwin's death in 1882 it appears that the intelligentsia had been won over to Darwinian ideas. We can get some indication of the completeness of the victory from articles that appeared in *The Victoria Review* and *The Sydney University Review* which set forth the so called truthfulness of Darwin's ideas. Once this occurred, it was not long before many of the clergy came to accept the "truth" of geology and biology as the spectacles through which they would interpret the Bible.

During the nineteenth century many of the brightest British theological students studied in Germany and became advocates of the higher critical school of thought. In 1860 a book entitled *Essays and Reviews* published in Britain, led to a great controversy. Alec Vidler wrote of the impact of the work:

> The time has come, when it is no longer possible to ignore the results of criticism. And that was the theme of the whole volume—in so far as

it had a single theme. It was an attempt to acclimatize in the Church of England the critical and historical study of the Bible, which had been actively engaging the minds of German thinkers for fifty years and more.[29]

In Scotland there were similar issues being debated and these ideas were eventually exported to the British colonies.

During the 1870s in Australia, questions began to be asked about the interpretation of the Bible. N. H. Wollaston, a Melbourne Anglican, started the ball rolling by suggesting that the Bible is full of contradictions. He claimed that while the Bible contained the Word of God it was not of itself the Word of God. The major debate of the period revolved around Charles Strong of Scots Church, Melbourne. Strong was chosen in May 1875 to replace the doctrinally orthodox Rev. Irving Hetherington as the minister of Scots Church. Hetherington had been the minister almost from the time that Forbes had departed to form the Free Church in 1846. The spirit of the age ensured that Strong had many philosophical soul mates, although not many were to be found among his Presbyterian brethren. Unlike Hetherington, Strong was a vibrant and attractive preacher and soon gathered a large and enthusiastic congregation open to more liberal views.[30] Under Caird's influence, Strong had rejected orthodox Calvinism even before his ordination in 1868 and with his coming to Melbourne,

> ... brought with him the assumption that if Christianity did not adjust its grounds of authority and orientation towards modern man it would inevitably become obsolete.[31]

In the 1876 Assembly William Henderson, now of Ballarat, once again raised the issue of the Standards of the Church and a

---

[29] A. Vidler, *The Church in an Age of Revolution: 1789 to the Present Day.* London, 1962, p. 125.

[30] See J. Roe, "Challenge and Response: Religious Life in Melbourne, 1876-86," *Journal of Religious History,* Vol. 5, no. 2 (1968); S. Macintyre, *A Colonial Liberalism: The Lost World of Three Victorian Visionaries,* Oxford, 1991. See especially chapter 2 in Macintyre on George Higinbotham.

[31] J.Roe, "Challenge and Response . . ." p. 162.

committee, with Strong as a member, was appointed to look into it. There was no outcome from the labours of the committee. However, Strong's views were already well known, namely, that the Confession was not the final word in doctrinal matters. Nevertheless, it was not until 1877 that those who disagreed with him began to consider taking action. Strong's opponents were moved by an anonymous pamphlet which appeared, entitled *Presbyterian Apostasy*. The author considered that the Presbyterian Church of Victoria was turning a blind eye to ministers who held unorthodox views. He charged that there were those in pulpits who amongst other things: denounced the creeds and confessions; scoffed at orthodoxy; were deceitful in their use of words; denied the supernatural and attempted to explain away Biblical miracles; avoided teaching redemption through the death of Christ and sin; downplayed the work of Christ; they denied the inspiration of the Old Testament; and denied a belief in the punishment of the wicked, the general resurrection and last judgement.[32]

In 1878 J. Oswald Dykes, who had been a foundation Professor in the Theological Hall with Cairns, delivered a lecture in which he said that it was not advisable to revise the Standards "until the new ideas, brought out in connection with modern religious thought, have become crystalized."[33] The 1878 Assembly again considered the question of subscription and subsequently Henderson stirred the pot by writing an article in *The Review*, provoking a reaction. One anonymous author, using the nom de plume of "Orthodox," wrote:

> But my difficulty is this—the Confession is either Scriptural, or it is not;—if it be not, those who ask for change should come boldly forward and show us where it is not Scriptural, and on that ground demand a change, but, if it be Scriptural, then surely our duty is to try, by exposition and reasoning, to remove doubts and objections,

---

[32] C.R. Badger, *The Reverend Charles Strong . . . p. 38-39.*

[33] *The Presbyterian Review and Monthly Record*, April, 1878, p. 69.

and so educate people up to the level of our standards, and not lower our standards to the level of the meagre faith of some of the people.[34]

The following month, Henderson replied that the need was not to revise the Confession but to ease the form of subscription in order to provide "a general assent to the teaching of the church".

By 1880 Strong expressed similar views to Henderson, seeing that the only way around a literal interpretation of the Confession was to loosen subscription. In the same year a group of more theologically conservative Presbyterian ministers began to meet together in order to discuss Strong's views. They were D. S. McEachran, Murdoch Macdonald, J. L. Rentoul and F. R. M. Wilson. The meetings were stimulated by an article published by Strong in 1880 on the atonement.[35] He began the article speaking of the historical relativeness governing the interpretation of the atonement:

> The doctrine of the Atonement is that which treats of reconciliation between a holy God and sinful man, and also between man and man through selfishness estranged from each other. Like every other doctrine of our creeds, the doctrine of reconciliation has a history, apart from which it cannot be rightly understood, either in its form or in its religious consciousness of the Christian Church, while its form has been determined by the particular experience, the mode of thought, and the speculations peculiar to individual Christians, or to the age in which they have lived. Like a stream flowing over different soil, it has taken its colouring from the moral and intellectual soil over which, from age to age of the church's history, it has passed. Hence we find this doctrine assuming Pauline or a Johannine, a Platonic or a scholastic, a deeply spiritual or a coldly legal and logical form.[36]

---

[34] *Ibid.*, October 1879, p. 184.

[35] *Victorian Review*. November, 1880. The *Review* had appeared for the first time in 1879 with an article by Marcus Clarke, "Civilization without Delusion." Clarke is best known for his "gothic horror" novel, *His Natural Life,* published in 1874 and dealing with convictism in Van Diemends Land. Clarke called for a new religion in his article stating: "the tender time of trustfulness in the supernatural is well nigh over, and . . . the faith of our fathers is passing away from us." With such an illustrious pedigree the *Victoria Review* was a suitable vehicle for Strong's article.

[36] Reprinted from the *Victorian Review* in the George Tait Clippings, Book 1, PCV Archives, Melbourne.

Strong's theological views are evident from the article, not so much by what is written but rather by what is left out. For instance, his choice of modern theologians includes Maurice Jowett, William Robertson (Unitarian), and John McLeod Campbell. None were renowned for their orthodoxy.

In December 1880 proceedings were commenced in the Presbytery of Melbourne in order to investigate Strong's doctrine, but because of various delays, the matter was not dealt with until March 1881. In the intervening months Strong became a *cause celebre* in the secular press.[37] This is not surprising as Scots Church was one of the centres of intellectual life in Melbourne, and Strong was a leading figure in society.[38] Strong had the support of most of his congregation and one of his elders wrote to him on 31 December 1880 applauding him for entering the Presbyterian Church of Victoria with his advanced views with the aim of bringing change[39]. This casts Strong in the role of an *agent provocateur.* He also gained much support because he was regarded highly in Melbourne society as a "do-gooder." A Presbyterian wrote:

> It is patent to all who have eyes and ears and who use them, that numbers of the more intelligent and thoughtful of our people have parted or are parting with one after another of the dogmas which they drank with their mother's milk. To many the doctrines of the Confession of Faith and other standards of the Church they no longer yield a blind and unreasoning belief. . . . There is no doubt that the Presbyterian Church is advancing with the rest of the world . . . and it is idle for fossil theologians and heresy-hunters to attempt to arrest progress.[40]

---

[37] E.g., *The Argus*, December 29, 1880, p. 7; December 30, 1880, p. 7; December 31, 1880, p. 6; January 1, 1881, p. 5.

[38] At the time Strong is reputed to have been paid three times more than any other Presbyterian minister which was a sign of the high regard in which he was held by his congregation and the wealth of influence of his congregation.

[39] C.R. Badger, *The Reverend Charles Strong* . . . p. 167.

[40] *The Argus*, January 5, 1881, p. 6.

On 30 January 1881 Adam Cairns died and it appears so did the orthodoxy of the Presbyterian Church of Victoria. The Presbytery meeting in March established a committee to investigate Strong's article. At a subsequent meeting the committee reported that

> ... while the article does not contradict in categorical propositions and express terms the doctrine of the Atonement contained in the Confession, it is nevertheless unsatisfactory, as fitted by the method of treatment followed and by the negative character of its teaching, to depreciate that doctrine, and in particular to obscure the essential relation in which the death of Christ as an expiatory sacrifice and propitiation stands to reconciliation.[41]

The committee went on to suggest that there was room for doubt and that Strong should be given further opportunity to explain himself, and in particular his doctrine of Scripture. Strong refused to discuss this issue further with the Presbytery and the case dragged on until 1883. However, in the interim the Victorian Church commenced work on a Declaratory Act in order to clarify subscription.

The catalyst for this was once again to come from Scots Church. The secular press reported a speech by Mr. J. C. Stewart, an elder, at a congregational meeting held in August 1881. *The Argus* reported:

> He (Mr. Stewart) could appreciate the position of the accusers if they themselves adhered to those standards but he would ask what minister amongst them believed in all the doctrines they contained? (Hear, hear.) Indeed he would venture to say that there was not a man in the church who could truthfully declare that he asserted, maintained, and defended the whole of the Confession of Faith. If then other ministers had a right to say that certain of these doctrines could not now be believed, why had not Mr. Strong the same liberty? (Hear, hear.) Why should Mr. Strong be called a dishonest man because he did no more than his brethren did? They could not be expected to implicitly believe what their forefathers in 1643 said was truth. In the Confession of Faith he found stated "That the world and all the things therein, whether divisible or indivisible, were created in the space of six days

---

[41] George Tait Clippings, Book 1, PCV Archives, Melbourne.

of 24 hours." (Laughter.) Did any man believe that at this time? No, this point was conceded. Further, the same book taught them that in order to satisfy the justice of God, and work out the scheme therein propounded, millions and millions of God's people had been sent to eternal perdition simply because they never knew of Christ. Again it stated that there were "elect" and "non-elect," and that the elect, whether they liked it or not, would be saved, and that the non-elect, do what they could, could not be saved. Still further the Confession went on to say that there was such a thing as the eternal damnation of infant babies who had never lisped a name. Now the man who pretended that he asserted, maintained, and defended all the doctrines in the book was a dishonest man. (Applause.)[42]

The conservative, Rev. Murdoch Macdonald did not help to clarify what was meant by adherence to the Confession when he delivered two lectures, in which he stated that he signed the Standards in a "general way".[43] His remarks were not lost on Strong's supporters who were able to use them in order to press for some modification of the Standards. They did not have long to wait as almost immediately after Stewart's comments were reported, a number of Presbyteries sought to take action in order to clarify the issue. The Presbytery of Melbourne censured Stewart and then virtually removed him from Presbytery. Strong defended Stewart in no uncertain manner:

> The plain question was, what does subscription to the Standards mean?—that *is* the question of (sic) Mr. Stewart has raised—he says it could mean either *verbatim et literatim,* the meaning a lawyer would be inclined to give it, or it means that each member signs only what he believes to be the essence of the Standards.

> I feel that this is a very solemn crisis in the Church and those that are at the helm of affairs just now are driving on rocks ahead if the motion is all the answer which the Church is going to give to the seething doubts and perplexities of men in the present day, then our Church's existence will be of very short duration indeed.[44]

---

[42] *The Argus,* August 9, 1881.

[43] C.R. Badger, *The Reverend Charles Strong . . .* p. 53.

[44] C.R. Badger, *The Reverend Charles Strong . . .* p. 53-54.

The 1881 Assembly upheld the actions of the Presbytery of Melbourne against Stewart. The commissioners also considered a number of options with regard to the Standards. They looked at modifying, preparing a compendium, revising them and preparing some kind of declaratory statement. The resolution adopted was to appoint a committee to draw up a Declaratory Act "setting forth the sense in which the Church understands the statements in the Confession of Faith" concerning a number of controversial issues. These were then listed and included the following: the Divine decrees, the salvation of children dying in infancy; the dealing of God with the heathen; and the creation of the world in six days. Obviously, the issues raised by Strong and Stewart had helped to set and clarify the agenda. "Heresy" had led to action in order to define orthodoxy.

The Church considered the issue so urgent that the Committee had a draft statement prepared for the Commission of Assembly meeting in May 1882. The Commission was then able to send an agreed text down under the Barrier Act for approval at the 1882 Assembly. The 1882 Assembly approved of the Declaratory Act and it became the first of its kind in Australia. The first clause of the Act dealt with predestination and stated that the Presbyterian Church of "Victoria adheres to chapter III Section 1 of the Westminster Confession." There follows a discussion that God is not the author of sin nor is violence offered to the will of man. It further stated that this doctrine is held in harmony with the free offer of the gospel to all men.[45] Clause 2 dealt with the problematical question of the salvation of infants who have died. That clause affirmed that salvation is by Christ alone, and the fact that "the outward and ordinary means of salvation for those capable of being called by the Word are to the ordinances of the

---

[45] *The Subordinate Standards and Formularies of the Presbyterian Church of Victoria*, Melbourne, 1893, p. 327.

Gospel".[46] Being pastorally sensitive, the clause also makes it clear that those who accept the Standards are not required to hold that "any who die in infancy are lost or that God may not extend His grace to any who are without the pale of ordinary means. . . ."[47]

The third clause on liberty of opinion is the one which proved to be most controversial. It allowed liberty only "on such points in the Standards not essential to the system of doctrine therein taught" and gave creation in six days each of twenty-four hours as an example of such "non-essential" things. The clause also went on to state that the Church guards "against the abuse of this liberty to the injury of its unity and peace". This suggested that the Church could limit the claim on liberty by an office-bearer if it proved harmful to the Church as a whole.

Clause four dealt with subscription to the Formula. It restated the phrase "To own and believe the whole doctrine contained in the Standards" and interpreted it as

> . . . the system of doctrine in its unity, formulated in the Confession of Faith, catechetically exhibited in the Larger and Shorter Catechisms, implied in the statements of the Directory for Public Worship, the Form of Presbyterian Church Government, and the Second Book of Discipline, and historically known as the Calvinistic, or Reformed System of Doctrine.
>
> . . . to give a chief place to the central and most vital doctrines thereof, with those objective supernatural facts on which they rest, especially the Incarnation, the Perfect Obedience and Expiatory Death, and the Resurrection and Ascension of the Lord. . . .[48]

This picked up on the very issues raised by Strong in his article on the atonement and the action taken by the Presbytery of Melbourne in 1881, which urged Strong to make these facts prominent in his preaching in the future.

The Declaratory Act had been drafted in a brief time, arising

---

[46] *Ibid.*, p. 327.

[47] *Ibid.*, p. 327.

[48] *Ibid.*, p. 328.

as it did, primarily, as a response to Strong and his supporters. Although it was the first of its kind in Australia, it was not formulated in a vacuum. The United Presbyterian Church of Scotland had introduced a Declaratory Act in 1879 and the Victorian was to a large extent based upon this.[49] However, there was an important difference between the two Acts relating to liberty of opinion. While the Scottish Act uses the phrase "not entering into the substance of the faith", the Victorian spoke of things "not essential to the system of doctrine therein taught", which in Section 4 is defined as that "historically known as the Calvinist, or Reformed System of Doctrine" Consequently, the Victorian statement was designed to keep tighter control over what and what could not be believed. One historian of the Victorian Church, D. Macrae Stewart speaks of the effect of the Act, saying "the doctrinal statements of the Church's creed were brought more closely into line with its living and working faith."[50] Stewart summarised the practical effects of the Declaratory Statement:

> No office-bearer of the Presbyterian Church of Victoria is required to give literal adhesion to all the separate doctrinal statements of the Confession of Faith. The Church is content that its signatories should bind themselves generally to the system of doctrine set forth in the Confession, and simply reserves the right of enquiring into the use which individual men make of their liberty as occasions may arise. By the Declaratory Act of 1882 there is large room left for the exercise of individual conviction on matters not essential to the integrity of the Christian faith.[51]

---

[49] For a brief history of the United Presbyterian Church see S.D. Gill, "United Presbyterian Church' in *Dictionary of Scottish Church History and Theology*, pp. 839-840. The Scottish Statement arose out of a doctrinal controversy on the extent of the atonement. Robert Swanton in *Our Heritage and Destiny*. Melbourne, 1975 notes that the Scottish Statement "was calculated to modify and reduce the Calvinism of the Confession." (p. 3). On the other hand, the Victorian Statement was designed "to safeguard the Confessional doctrine of the very nature of the atonement." (p. 3).

[50] D. Macrae Stewart, *The Presbyterian Church of Victoria: Growth in Fifty Years: 1859-1909*. Melbourne, n.d., p. 76.

[51] *Ibid.*, p. 76.

This was a fair summing up of the Declaratory Statement which led to a tightening up but also some loosening with regard to doctrinal matters. Robert Swanton noted that the Victorian Statement was to have a lasting effect on the shaping of Australian Presbyterianism. He writes:

> In turn, this Victorian Declaratory Statement was to have an important bearing on the Declaratory Statement of the Basis of Union of the Presbyterian Church of Australia, 1901, in which the Victorian Church, through not only its numerical strength but its tested theological tradition was to have a predominant influence.[52]

If any commissioner of the 1882 Assembly thought that the Declaratory Statement would mean the end of Charles Strong they were wrong. The Strong affair raised its head again in July 1883 when the Presbytery of Melbourne had drawn to its attention reports in the secular press that Strong was promoting a position on the Sabbath contrary to the Confession. Strong appealed to the liberty of opinion clause in the Declaratory Statement; nevertheless, the presbytery censured him.

Strong's standing in the Presbyterian Church of Victoria was made more precarious by a lecture given in Scots Church on 1 August 1883 by Mr. Justice Higinbotham.[53] Higinbotham was a well-known Melbourne controversialist who held advanced views on the subject of religion, ascribing to a form of Unitarian theology. Strong had chaired the meeting of the Scots Church Literary Society on the topic of "Science and Religion." Higinbotham attacked the churches inability to accept science and to nourish the needs of an educated laity. He went on to attack credal religion as outmoded and as that which took away from the sublime teachings of Christ. Since the clergy continued to be stubborn in their narrowness, Higinbotham called on the laity to

---

[52] R. Swanton, *Our Heritage and Destiny*, p. 3.

[53] See S. Macintye, *A Colonial Liberalism.* . . . pp. 124-127; J. Roe, "Challenge and response . . ." p. 164.

rise up and withdraw from the churches. Macintyre notes that

> Higinbotham's address appeals to principles to which most liberals
> subscribed: the rejection of claims of the clergy to offer authoritative
> spiritual guidance; the impossibility of subscribing to beliefs that
> cannot satisfy the intellect; the continuing need for inspiration for
> the 'welfare of humanity'. Such attitudes were hardly novel.[54]

The speech was clearly opposed to the Presbyterian Standards and Strong's Presbytery was appalled that he allowed such an address to be given in Scots Church. Consequently, at the next meeting of Presbytery the Rev. D. S. McElachran gave notice that at the next meeting he would charge Strong with heresy. He charged Strong with

> promulgating and publishing heretical and unsound doctrine by his
> action in connection with the recent lecture of Mr. Higinbotham and
> otherwise; Also, with being guilty of teaching and conduct tending
> to destroy the order, unity, and peace of the Church; Also, with failure
> to assert, maintain, and defend the doctrine of the Church when it
> was in his power to do so; And further, with failure to comply with
> the instructions of the Presbytery to give prominence in his teaching
> to the Incarnation, the Atoning Life and Death, and the Resurrection
> and Ascension of Our Lord.[55]

Strong immediately gave notice of his intention to resign from Scots Church and as a minister of the Presbyterian Church of Victoria. Acting according to the procedure laid out in the Victorian Code, the Presbytery then deferred any action until the congregation had been heard. Consequently, the next meeting of Presbytery saw McEachran proceeding with his charges of heresy and the whole matter was referred to the Assembly.

The 1883 Assembly invited Strong to be present in order to answer the charges that had been laid against him. Strong chose not to appear and left Victoria during his "trial". He was found guilty *in absentia* and the Assembly dissolved his tie with Scots Church. Ward has rightly argued that Strong should have had his

---

[54] S. Macintyre, *A Colonial Liberalism.* . . . p. 124.

[55] *Minutes of the Presbytery of Melbourne*, August 7, 1883.

day in court in order to defend himself. Ward goes on to show that the Church did not act in the case according to its due process in a heresy trial[56]. In spite of this procedural reservation, Strong was guilty and his true colours revealed in the foundation of the Australian Church in 1887[57]. "The Strong Case," concludes Ward, "was a watershed not because it showed a Calvinistic phalanx against any deviation from orthodoxy, but because it showed that there was no Calvinistic phalanx."[58] There was surprising unity in Victoria between evangelicals and a developing and growing group of liberal evangelicals against the theologically radical Strong.

---

[56] R.S. Ward, "Divisions and Unions in Australian Presbyterianism., . . ." p. 178-180.

[57] The *Presbyterian Monthly and Messenger of the Churches* reported on April 1, 1887: "The foundation-stone of the "Australian Church" was laid on Saturday, the 19th ult., and the occasion has elicited considerable comment in the daily and weekly Press of Melbourne. The ceremonies which took place have not commended themselves to the approval of the general religious public. *The Southern Cross* describes them as 'semi-heathen pomp,'" or, at least, "Masonic rather than Christian," and says "the actual stone was baptised with wine, and the whole was crowned with a champagne lunch:" while the *Daily Telegraph* speaks of them as "mystic formulae," not quite proper to the foundation of a "Christian Church; and the *Spectator* remarks "that under the circumstances connected with the formation of Mr. Strong's new sect, it appears to us a singular thing that the Masons should become, in this public manner, parties in an ecclesiastical strife." . . . "the Masonic Church would not be as high-sounding a title as the Australian Church, but it certainly would be more appropriate." The *raison d'etre* of the New Church is thus given by the Rev. C. Strong himself: "We have felt it to be our duty to leave the older ecclesiastical organisations, because their machinery seemed hurtful to the spirit life; because their binding formula of subscription to the teachings of another age, and their theological tests, seemed to us to obscure the light of to-day.". . . For anything its founder has yet formulated and given to the world, it may be pronounced *creedless*. The *Southern Cross* remarks that "the Divine and Redeeming Christ finds no place in the theology of the Australian Church." The *Age* says "its creed is a negation." And again, "the Australian Church seems to have no theological hypothesis peculiar to it, and its *raison d'etre* centres in the Rev. Charles Strong." (pp. 101-102).

[58] R.S. Ward, "Divisions and Unions in Australian Presbyterianism," p. 181.

The Declaratory Statement did not however turn back the clock, for the impact of theological modernism in Australia continued to grow. It turned the Bible from being a unique book ("The Word of God in the words of men") into being the religious history of ancient Israel and first-century Christianity. It led to a rapid decline in any type of doctrinal or confessional Christianity, and it stimulated Church union efforts as the way to strengthen the Church rather than evangelism. It promoted as the primary message of the Christian Church social action, rather than gospel preaching and social action. It brought the demise of personal and evangelical faith and stimulated the growth of "Churchianity." Finally, it introduced a materialistic world view into the Australian Church rather than a supernaturalistic world view.

Samuel Angus

From Strong to Angus

In the period from Charles Strong until the turn of the century, Presbyterian Churches in each of the Australian states had one consuming passion, namely, federal union. A so-called Federal Assembly consisting of representatives of the Presbyterian Churches of New South Wales, Victoria, Queensland, South Australia and Tasmania convened at the instigation of the Victorian Church in Sydney in July, 1886. While this body could deal with common interests, it had no legal authority. However, at subsequent meetings, it prepared what was designated the Scheme of Union, which became the basis on which the six state churches (including Western Australia) united on 24 July 1901. The process of union was not an easy one to achieve.

It was to take fifteen years from the first Federal Assembly until union was consummated in 1901. There was a parallel political movement as the states met together for the first time in 1886 and finally came together in the Commonwealth of Australia in 1901. Political federation was certainly an important stimulus in bringing about Presbyterian union. It was believed that a united Australia needed, even demanded, one Presbyterian church. An alternative to federal union had earlier been discussed of a union between New South Wales and Queensland; and another between Victoria, South Australia and Tasmania; but the preference of one great union eventually over-rode all other plans. In the closing years of the nineteenth century, the spirit of union was in the air, and the vision of church extension into the outback and to foreign fields demanded that practical responses replace pious expressions of Presbyterian brotherhood.

The tradition of the Presbyterian Church of Victoria, composed predominantly of the Free Church-Secession background, predetermined its leadership in the union movement. Both components were more dynamic and more "Australian" in their outlook than the Kirk branches in Australia. The Free Church-Secession tradition exemplified itself in a growing awareness of "Australianism" and from early on had attempted to achieve independence from the parent bodies in Scotland, devoted to the principle of voluntarism, aggressively expansionist in both home and foreign mission work. By contrast the Kirk tradition, the predominant factor in New South Wales, was still closely tied psychologically and physically to Scotland.

From a Victorian point of view the hero of the hour was the Rev. Dr. Meiklejohn of South Melbourne who from 1892 led the Victorian negotiating team for union. Despite Victoria leading the charge there was considerable opposition to union from within the Victorian Church. The opposition was led by Dr. Alexander Marshall and Professor J. Laurence Rentoul, one of the prosecutors of Charles Strong. Both were opposed to the method used to bring about union and also to the Plan of Union. Rentoul favoured a simplified statement of belief, impressed by the English and South African Churches acceptance of a shorter and simpler restatement of the Church's Creed. In 1898 Rentoul had unsuccessfully tried to obtain such a restatement of the Church's Creed.[59] He finally settled for a simplification of the Declaratory Statement.[60]

A compromise was finally worked out which proved acceptable to the negotiating churches and the Federal Assembly. Robert Swanton has demonstrated that the final 1901 Declaratory Statement was based upon the 1879 Act of the United Presbyterian Church of Scotland and owed much to the Victorian statement of 1882[61]. The Basis of Union stated that:

I. The supreme standard of the united church shall be the Word of God contained in the Scriptures of the Old and New Testaments.

II. The subordinate standard of the united church shall be the Westminster Confession of Faith read in the light of the following declaration.

The Declaratory Statement then dealt with five issues. First, the doctrine of redemption, which obviously arose out of the 1882 Victorian Act where one of the commitments a minister made was "to give a chief place in their teaching . . . to the message of redemption and reconciliation implied and manifested in them."[62] The second clause dealt with the doctrine of God's eternal decree while the third and fourth had as their main emphases sin and salvation.

Clause five was the one which caused the most difficulty and has continued to be hotly debated in the Presbyterian Church of Australia. Clause five stated:

---

[59] *Minutes of the Union Committee of the Presbyterian Church of Victoria*, July 21, 1898.

[60] See R. Swanton, "The Westminster Confession of Faith and the Declaratory Statement," *Reformed Theological Review.* XLIV (January-April 1985) p. 17.

[61] *Ibid.*, p. 18.

[62] M. Bradshaw, *Basic Documents on Presbyterian Polity.* Lawson, NSW, 1984, p. 93.

> That liberty of opinion is allowed on matters in the subordinate
> standard not essential to the doctrine therein taught, the church
> guarding against the abuse of this liberty to the injury of its unity and
> peace.[63]

Robert Swanton again sees similarities between the 1901 liberty
of opinion clause with that of 1882. There is, however, one small
difference in the 1901 phrasing where the framers resorted to the
Scottish Act of 1879. The words "matters in the Subordinate
Standard not essential to the doctrine therein taught" is substituted
for the wording of the Scottish act of 1879: "such points in the
standards not entering into the substance of the faith." Swanton
comments:

> . . . considering the logical nature of the Confession would appear to
> be an abbreviated equivalent to the more explicit "system of doctrine"
> used in the Victorian Act. "Otherwise," comments F. Maxwell
> Bradshaw, "the section is virtually meaningless, for unless doctrine
> is read as suggested the 'doctrine' must surely mean the whole
> teaching of the Confession, and it would be hard to find 'matters in
> the subordinate standard' not essential to the **whole** teaching it
> contains."[64]

Chris Balzer has disagreed with this interpretation and
suggested that the framers of the 1901 Statement were seeking to
weaken the Calvinistic "system of doctrine in its unity" and
replace it with the "evangelical supernaturalism of the
Confession."[65] In the light of the times and the men involved in
drawing up the statement, like Rentoul, one has some sympathy
for Balzer's interpretation. However, the liberty of opinion clause
undoubtedly limited the extent to which there could be freedom.
As Swanton understands it, this liberty was limited in three ways:

> 1. By the declaration on Redemption. . . . There is no liberty as to this
> basic doctrine.

> 2. The declaration that "liberty of opinion is allowed on matters in
> the Subordinate Standard not essential to the doctrine therein taught"

---

[63] *Ibid.*, p. 95.

[64] R. Swanton, "The Westminster Confession of Faith," pp. 18-19.

... follows the Victorian Statement. This elsewhere designates the doctrine of the Confession as that "historically known as the Calvinistic or Reformed System of Doctrine . . .". There is thus no freedom to diverge from this.

3. Again this "liberty of opinion" is limited in our Basis of Union by the ordination and induction formula for ministers, in which the promise is given: "I . . . to the utmost of my power shall, in my station, assert, maintain and defend the doctrine . . . of this Church." (The doctrine of the Church being the Westminster Confession and the 5 explanations in the Declaratory Statement.) This means the liberty conferred is only one of private personal opinion and does not cover an official function such as the preaching office.

It is therefore clear that this Church through its ministry is closely bound to its Confession.[66]

The new Presbyterian Church of Australia contained obvious but minor divergences of opinion regarding such things as modes of worship and political inclinations, but such differences were unimportant compared to the particular traditions common to most Australian Presbyterians. The uniting churches shared in common a single Scottish and Scotch-Irish tradition and on paper, at least, an adherence to the basic doctrines of the Westminster Confession of Faith. While the Declaratory Statement of 1901 was put in place as a safeguard against "heretics" such as Charles Strong it did go some way to replace a strict adherence to the traditional Calvinistic reformed faith with an adherence to the "fundamentals of the faith." In fact from the 1860s onwards there had been a steady decline from conservative reformed evangelicalism towards liberal evangelicalism.[67] The Kirk element, predominant in New South Wales, contained some "high" churchmen for whom ritualism and ecclesiastical legalism held a strong appeal, but the major influence came through the strong Free Church-Secessionist

---

[65] C.D. Balzer, "Australian Presbyterians and the Westminster Confession of Faith . . .", p. 136.

[66] R. Swanton, *Our Heritage and Destiny*, p. 138.

[67] P. Barnes, "Living in a Half-Way House . . .".

traditions of evangelicalism, voluntarism, and Australianism, present in the Presbyterian Church of Victoria. Theologically the latter element had begun to be influenced by the Hegelian rationalism of German theology and the Wellhausen interpretation of the Old Testament. The former element was greatly influenced by Tractarianism and its Scottish counterpart, the Church Service Society, which introduced changes to the traditional Presbyterian worship service.

Strength through unity was certainly the theme of union in 1901, and Australian Presbyterians had shown the way not just to divided Presbyterians in other countries but to other Protestant denominations in Australia (e.g., the Methodists completed their union in the following year). Certainly the moves for union between the various Presbyterian denominations and later moves towards union with other denominations caused a lessening of adherence to doctrinal distinctives and consequently the Westminster Confession of Faith. The new Church rapidly assumed the interests of the two most dynamic and dominant elements, the Presbyterian Church of Victoria and the Presbyterian Church of Australia in the State of New South Wales. As the twentieth century progressed this led to less of an interest in theology and towards an emphasis upon social matters.

By the turn of the century many of the larger Australian towns, particularly Sydney and Melbourne, were beset by social problems related to industrialization, urbanization, affluence and a rampant materialism. The increased prevalence of labour unrest, Sabbath breaking, alcoholism, prostitution, gambling, substandard housing, child abuse, "sweat shop" employment, abortion, pornography, racial prejudice, political corruption and a host of related evils distressed concerned Victorians and the Presbyterian churches in each of the states were at the forefront of many of the movements to bring about change in society. Poverty of mind and body in the midst of plenty, social injustice in a so-called Christian nation, sin rampant among church-going people—these were the diseases, and "practical Christianity" was the proposed remedy.

Certain basic beliefs were held by Social Gospelers that cut across confessional Christianity—the belief that perfection was attainable in this world, that social conditions must be improved if man were to achieve that perfection, that collective action must replace individual efforts to effect changes, that legislation could produce morality, or at least produce a social milieu conducive to morality. The sum of these ideas were generally included in "liberal theology," or the "new theology," which assumed the findings of higher critics regarding the Old Testament and tended towards humanism, anti-dogmatism and anti-confessional religion. In late nineteenth, early twentieth century, Australia, where individual responsibility in business, politics, social behaviour and personal salvation had so long been the unquestioned rule of life, the Social Gospel was new, exciting, promising, or dangerous, depending upon one's convictions.

Another major influence upon the Presbyterian Church of Australia in the first part of the twentieth century was that of war. One of the myths in Australian history is that the nation came of age during the First World War. If there was a spirit of triumphalism in the nation about war then there was little cause for rejoicing in the Presbyterian Church. From the Great War onwards it appears that all the mainline churches declined in Australia.

Many churches had concluded that the only way to survive in this more secular society was to render Christianity more appealing by making it more secular in both form and content. This change was most apparent in sermon style. Traditional expository preaching was in decline. Sermons were becoming less doctrinal and more narrative in character. The Moody style of preaching was having an immense impact in Australia. His sermons were anecdotal. They featured bits of biography and graphic stories from everyday life. Whenever Moody did refer to

Scripture or retold biblical event, he did so in a fashion that made the characters and stories more contemporary.

A Victorian Presbyterian elder, James Balfour was a prime mover and chief financier of the missions of Dr. J. Wilbur Chapman and Charles Alexander, the most celebrated American revivalists since Moody and Sankey. Twice Balfour tried to induce Moody and Sankey to visit Australia. Chapman and Alexander were more open. The first visit in 1909 received much publicity, and Balfour believed because of the success that it should be repeated as soon as possible. The second Chapman-Alexander mission of 1912-13 ran into financial problems, and Balfour had to save the mission.

Indeed, there was little evidence of a rejuvenation of Christianity in Australian society during the first decade of the twentieth century, and it was in this atmosphere of being unable to stem the tide of secularisation that the long pre-war church union discussions took place between the Congregational, Methodist, Presbyterian and for a while Anglican churches. The challenge that many within the churches thought was confronting them was whether Australia would remain a Christian nation. Not only were the churches struggling against the inroads of secularisation and competition in an evermore consumer-oriented society, but they were faced with the tremendous task of attempting to Christianize the growing number of immigrants who did not share the same religious heritage as the Protestant mainstream. The evangelical churches in Australia had been long cooperating with each other in temperance crusades and other moral reform activity and more recently in urban revivalism as a means to combat the powerful forces of social vice, religious apathy, and secularisation.

The idea of church union—essentially an expression of liberal Christianity—was firmly tied to the optimistic assumptions that still dominated church life. Denominationalism and church doctrines according to liberal religious thought were considered the product of history and civilization, not of God or the Bible. They were not necessarily the embodiments of essential and enduring Christian truths; on the contrary, they were barriers to the building of the Kingdom of God. The great hope was that a united Protestant church would be free of the doctrines that obstructed faith. The act of union would strip away everything that was not vital. Furthermore, it would be efficient in its mission work and more effective in Christianizing the social order by bringing about moral and social reforms, such as temperance and Sunday observance. A national church would ensure that Australia was a Christian society. On one level the church union movement was consistent with the tenets of liberal theology and it can be considered as an advance of both Methodism and Presbyterianism. Indeed it was entirely consistent with both the decline of distinct denominational identities based on rigid orthodox doctrines and the emergence of modern evangelicalism that had characterised recent developments in both churches. Church union had its roots deep in the theological and historical developments that were underway in the 1880s and 1890s.

After a generation of accommodation with secular forces the churches had lost confidence in their message and mission, the very thing that was necessary if they were to withstand the increasing pressure of secularisation. This troubled situation, in which a weakened church, uncertain about its doctrine and mission, had to confront a number of challenges that undermined its role and authority in Australian society, was not the result of an abrupt break from the past. Rather, it was the culmination of a long process of religious beliefs and institutions being adapted to social, cultural, and intellectual change.

While church union negotiations were staggering forward, the realization was also gradually dawning that a quest for Christian renewal through accommodation with secular society was itself hastening the tide of secularisation. As the trend of secularisation forced churches to reconsider the accommodations being made with modern society, there was serious questioning whether the church's broadened mission and more liberal discipline were having the desired effect. The modernization of Christianity was not leading to a revival of faith in terms of either inspiring people to stronger and more certain belief or encouraging them to a more consecrated life and greater commitment to the church. As a result, the optimistic assumptions behind the spirit of accommodation, liberal theology, and the social gospel had to be questioned. The outbreak of the First World War and the horrific consequences of that struggle sharply focused this critique.

Walter Phillips in his book, *Defending "A Christian Country,"* concludes that after some initial resistance the majority of Australian churchmen came to terms with modern science and higher criticism".[68] He goes on to admit that there were still pockets of fundamentalism in places like Sydney but that in general theological liberalism predominated among Protestants. In Britain and the U.S.A., the drift towards theological liberalism of the nineteenth century had turned into a full-blown avalanche during the early years of the twentieth and created a strong reaction of resistance from evangelicals. What happened in Australia?

Walter Phillips has argued that it was commendable that "notwithstanding some tensions (Australia) avoided the serious ruptures or schisms that occurred in the United States through the Fundamentalist-Modernist controversy." One of the most notable characteristics of the Australian scene has been the lack of any major ecclesiastical controversies which have been trans-denominational in effect. Controversies of a Modernist-fundamentalist character have been restricted to individual denominations and have been scattered throughout the twentieth

---

[68] W. W. Phillips, *Defending A Christian Country. Churchmen and society in New South Wales in the 1880s and after*. St. Lucia, 1981.

century. Russel Ward in *The Australian Legend* suggests that the national Australian outlook is different from the American, although both have been influenced by frontiers.[69] Australians are more collectivist in attitude while Americans are individualists. Consequently, it is less likely that controversies would develop on the schismatic scale that they have in the U.S.A.

Moreover, the Australian Churches in the early years of the twentieth century were busy in matters apart from doctrine. They were establishing themselves across the nation, developing federal structures, making approaches to union within and across denominations, and expanding their missionary outreach beyond the continent. They were also busy coping with issues relevant to their roles in and their relationships with the society of which they were a part (such as education, social reform and the consequences of the nation's involvement in the Great War).

Opposition to modernism in Australia is most clearly seen in the development of para-church organizations as the energy of evangelicals was re-directed from their denominations into anti-modernist resistance movements outside of their churches. For the sake of unity, such movements tended to be pietistic and un- or even anti-doctrinal in approach, and almost always when there was a particular theology, Arminian. Here we can think of the development of missionary agencies, evangelistic campaign organisations, convention movements, Bible Colleges and groups like the Australian Fellowship of Evangelical Students, the Bible Union and the Australian Institute of Archaeology.

Faith missions as they developed in Australia have reflected the phenomenon elsewhere in the world. It is the pietistic qualities (operating on a religious, rather than on an intellectual level) which have been largely responsible for the high degree of motivation, spirit of sacrifice, and intensity that have been obvious features

---

[69] R. Ward, *The Australian legend.* Melbourne, 1958.

of the faith missions movement. They have also been responsible for steering the movement into an isolationist situation and away from overt dispute with movements of other views. They have also tended to inhibit the development of a strong intellectual tradition which might have conducted a constructive debate at a more sophisticated level.

The Keswick Movement has had an enormous impact on evangelism in Australia from its commencement in 1891. It has differed from similar developments in Britain and the U.S.A. Whereas the millenarian emphasis was predominant in American thinking, in the Australian scene it was tempered by British pietism. It has been pietistic holiness that has dominated, and again, this has led to a non-confrontational approach to theological issues.

The Bible College movement has been closely associated with faith missions, evangelistic campaigns, and the convention movement. From its origin, it had associations with the fundamentalist movement both overseas and in Australia. They were practically oriented, Bible-centred agencies, offering spiritual training in the pietistic tradition to equip intending missionaries, evangelists and lay-workers. In the context of what was regarded as a steady threat from the pressures of liberalism and defective views of Scripture, the colleges were usually assumed to be bastions of orthodoxy, and as such they were seen as sound alternatives to the denominations and their theological colleges. However, the fact that the colleges needed to draw their support from members of the main denominations meant that there was no large-scale separatistic movement stemming from the colleges. The aim of the colleges to aid denominations in their overall ministry helped to prevent such a movement from developing.

Through a wide range of activity, these parachurch organisations have played a major role in the fundamentalist movement in Australia. Evangelical unity is expressly taught in many areas of the movement as a biblical *desideratum*. This is especially the case in the Keswick convention movement, with its motto, "All one in Christ Jesus." However, unity of this kind is often promulgated at the expense of real doctrinal differences, which are, by tacit agreement, often conveniently set aside without adequate resolution.

Samuel Angus and the Confession

Samuel Angus arrived on the scene as the various transformations described above were taking place. He would become the major representative of the liberal theological view within the Presbyterian Church of Australia during the first half of the twentieth century. Angus was an Ulster-Scot, born in County Antrim on 27 August 1881. His father, a moderately "well-tae-dae" farmer, was conservative and orthodox in terms of his theology and, according to Angus's latest biographer, represented "a passionless Punisher, akin to the vengeful Calvinist God he (Angus) later rejected."[70] By contrast Angus's mother is described in Emilsen's psychological analysis of his childhood in this way:

> Memories of his mother were characteristically associated with images of intimacy and acceptance: sitting on her knee hearing the "stories of Jesus". . . . In his maternal lineage, Angus perceived a more generous and educated spirit, and a more intuitive approach to religion. If John Angus, at least in part, was the model of a vengeful deity, his mother became the model of a gentle, loving deity, waiting beyond death with a tender and unaccusing embrace. Sarah Harper Angus was the dominating influence of Angus's childhood and remained so even in his middle age.[71]

He studied at Queen's College, Galway and then went on to enroll concurrently at Princeton Seminary and University in order to undertake theological and classical studies. This was a seminal experience in his life. Princeton Seminary in 1903 was still the institution dominated by B. B. Warfield and the works of the

---

[70] S. Emilsen, *A Whiff of Heresy: Samuel Angus and the Presbyterian Church in New South Wales.* Sydney, 1991, p. 47.

[71] *Ibid.*, p. 48.

Hodges, holding to confessional orthodoxy. However, it was his study at the university that was to be a life transforming experience. In mid-1906 he left Princeton with a doctorate from the University but no theology degree. He spent the next few years teaching in various institutions in America. From 1908 until 1910 he taught principally at Hartford Seminary, spending his summers in Germany imbibing deeply from German thought. He became convinced that Germany was the centre of all theological thought. In 1910 he crossed the Atlantic in order to settle in Edinburgh and the years from 1910 to 1914 were spent in further research and writing. He also decided that he had better commit himself to a church if he wanted to teach in a theological institution. Consequently he sought licensing in the United Free Church of Scotland. Angus found the theological climate of Edinburgh in 1910 conducive to his own developing theological views. Emilsen notes:

> . . . that the Presbyterianism Angus encountered in Edinburgh after 1910 was significantly different from that espoused at the Princeton Seminary. Sermons emphasised the practical and the spiritual at the expense of the doctrinal. The Westminster Confession of Faith was viewed widely as a historical document rather than a fixed standard of orthodoxy. Theological discussion occurred in an environment in which the only unforgivable sin was bitter antagonism. Attention was being given to the possibility of a new or revised creed and the necessity of loosening subscription requirements for licentiates and ordinands.[72]

In June 1911 he was licensed, experiencing no pangs of conscience in subscribing to the Confession. Edinburgh became a home base for his frequent trips to the continent, and especially Germany. He studied dogmatics with Adolf Harnack and New Testament with Adolf Deissmann, both were to have an enormous impact in the formation of his theology and his later teaching in Australia[73]. In 1914 reluctantly he allowed his name to go forward

---

[72] *Ibid.*, p. 66.

[73] See A. Dougan, *A Backward Glance at the Angus Affair:* Sydney, 1971, p. 25. "Samuel Angus 1881-1943" *Australian Dictionary of Biography* VII p. 73.

for the position of Professor of New Testament Exegesis and Historical Theology at the Presbyterian Theological Hall, St Andrew's College, Sydney, Australia.

The new, young professor arrived in Sydney on 26 February 1915 and was ordained and inducted into his office on 2 March. In the course of the service he subscribed to the Westminster Confession of Faith with the explanations contained in the Declaratory Statement "as an exhibition of the sense in which he understood the Holy Scriptures, and as a confession of his own faith". The years progressed quietly for Angus as he settled into the routine of teaching and preaching the occasional sermon. Meanwhile, after the 1914-18 War the fundamentalist-modernist controversy began to gain some momentum. While Angus kept his distance from the controversy there continued to be a growing concern amongst some in the Church, especially the younger ministers, that credal revision had to take place. At the 1922 State Assembly the Reverend C. N. Button, minister of the Glebe Presbyterian Church raised the issue of credal revision. Although he was unsuccessful, the idea was never far from the minds of many in the church over the next few years.

At the request of several students who were members of the Student Christian Movement at the University of Sydney, in 1923 Angus published a small leaflet on his approach to religion. While in this document he more or less called for a non-credal religion, it was to be another ten years before Angus was charged with "heresy."[74] Why did it take so long to charge Angus with heresy

---

[74] Reprinted in Emilsen, *A Whiff of Heresy* . . . pp. 138-141. Angus stated: "No statement of the Christian faith can properly insist on demanding more than Jesus asked men to believe. The framers of all the historic creeds have been so absorbed in dogmatic conceptions and actuated by controversial interests that they have overlooked this obvious condition. Their yoke has been burdensome. Jesus never exacted the elaborate theological propositions and highly debatable affirmations which form the ingredients of the standard creeds. His demands were few and clear as the sun at noonday. Men could not argue them: they had to accept or reject. All revolved around *personal*

as he so clearly expounded teachings that were at divergence with the Confession? It appears that there was no clear leadership or direction for those who held to orthodoxy within the Presbyterian Church in New South Wales. Presbyterian evangelicals tended to seek refuge in the non-confrontational pietism of inter-denominational societies.

This situation changed as some Methodist students began to raise questions as to Angus's orthodoxy and a Presbyterian student, J. T. H. Kerr, took extensive notes of Angus's lectures in order to provide his minister, Robert J. T. McGowan of Ashfield with a copy. It was McGowan that was to lead the charge against Angus for the next ten years. The campaign was well publicised as the media reported on the progress of the various heresy trials in the Presbytery of Sydney, the General Assembly of New South Wales and the General Assembly of Australia. While Angus's old liberal theology was seen by some like McGowan to be out of step with the new attackers of orthodoxy, the neo-orthodox thinkers, yet the main issue again appeared to be the Confession. "Angus," writes Emilsen, "in common with numerous overseas scholars, had persistently expressed his rejection of existing credal statements."[75] He gave public expression to his views in *Truth and Tradition,* published in 1934, which was particularly polemical, designed to shock his opponents.[76] In that

---

loyalty to Jesus and *the acceptance of the Father's will* for each life. One wonders what Jesus would say of the incomprehensibility of the Athanasian or Nicene creeds, or of that weird compromise which the theologians of three Christian Churches of Australia have accepted as the basis of union!" (p. 138). Unlike his fellow professors in Sydney, during the 1920s Angus was an anti-unionist, this was to change in the 1930s under the influence of Adolf Deissmann. (See S.D. Gill, "Preserving Presbyterians: Links Between Canadian and Victorian Anti-Union Forces in the 1920s" and M.D. Prentis, "Church Union Debates in Australia 1901-1925: Canadian Links and Resonances" in M. Hutchinson ed. et al, *Ties That Bind*, Sydney, 1996.)

[75] Emilsen, *A Whiff of Heresy . . .*, pp. 200-201.

[76] S. Angus, *Truth and Tradition. A Plea for Practical and Vital Religion and for a Reinterpretation of Ancient Theologies.* Sydney, 1934.

regard it did nothing to placate the worst fears of the more conservative elements in the church. In 1939 he published *Essential Christianity* which was a less polemical and, consequently, less controversial work.[77] Nevertheless he was still explicit in his opposition to creedal religion. Creeds, he argued, needed to be constantly revised:

> The individual must apply constantly both moral and intellectual tests to his creed; but the ultimate test of any creed or expression of faith is, whether it holds in the storms of life, enabling the holder fearlessly to confront life with the resources of the Eternal God at his disposal. . . .
>
> But a corporate or institutional creed cannot to-day escape criticism. It must be tested as truly by the members of the society holding it as a personal creed by the individual holding it.[78]

According to Angus, the new creed had to be formulated not out of theological battles but in the battlefront of life, through personal experience.

While Angus's opponents demonstrated that he diverged from the Standards of the Church on a number of points, yet through his scholarly reputation, debating skills and friends he was able to delay the progress of heresy charges at each stage. He constantly argued that he remained true to his ordination vows and the Spirit of the Confession. By the time of his death in 1943 the issue had still not been settled, but the controversy left a legacy of deep divisions within the Presbyterian Church in Australia, Opposition to Angus's views were particularly strong in Victoria, where there were still memories of the Strong case. Strong, himself, was jubilant, stating that the fact Angus was never convicted of heresy showed at last that the Church had caught up with his 1883 position.

From Strong to Cameron

Long before Strong's death, the mainstream theological

---

[77] S. Angus, *Essential Christianity.* Sydney, 1939.

[78] *Ibid.*, p. 195.

thinking within the Presbyterian Church had moved from liberalism to neo-orthodoxy. The post-WWII years were marked by an increased and deep interest in the new wave of theological thought pouring out of Switzerland, Germany and the United States. The earlier influence of Karl Barth and his "neo-orthodoxy" which had attracted many Australian Presbyterian theologians there was now augmented by the likes of Emil Brunner, Dietrich Bonhoffer and Paul Tillich. The writings of these men were now appearing in English translations and challenging the postwar generation to re-assess its own religious thinking. The influence of these "post-Barthian" scholars on Australian Presbyterian thought is difficult to estimate—the impact of their writing was felt primarily in the Theological Halls and among the younger generation of professors and students before being transmitted in more popular forms from the pulpit to the congregations. Nevertheless *The Presbyterian Messenger* and *Australian Presbyterian Life* continued to assume the role of theological educator-at-large by publishing series of popular theological articles particularly promoting a more liberal and ecumenical perspective.

A related trend was the ecumenical movement which swept most denominations in every continent in the postwar period. In Australia there was a resurgence of interest in church union between Methodists, Presbyterians and Congregationalists. Born of war-time experiences of the Christian churches in both Allied and Axis countries, the search for Christian fellowship and understanding on both international and interdenominational levels obviously drew on a long tradition of co-operation already established.

Such interest in "new" theology and the ecumenical movement was not, however, without its opponents among Australian Presbyterians, many of whom believed that association and co-operation with "liberal" denominations would undermine traditional standards and doctrinal purity of their church. In Victoria this led to the organisation of such groups as the Calvinist Society in 1939 with the Reverend Arthur Allen of the Free Presbyterian Church, the Reverend Professor John Gillies, and F. Maxwell Bradshaw, an elder in the Presbyterian Church of Victoria, as the founders. The same men, along with Robert Swanton, were involved in the inauguration of the *Reformed Theological Review,* and all would become virulent opponents of Church union. The conflict between ecumenical and confessional interests in the Australian Church was not new—it had appeared occasionally during the 1930s, even after the defeat of the unionists in the 1920s, and could be traced in part to the reaction against theological liberalism of the anti-union movement in the pre- and post-First World War period. The new spirit of ecumenism which appeared at the close of the Second World War once again forced into the open these long-standing differences.

The rise of modern biblical criticism caused both conservatives and liberals to look beyond their own denominations in order to join kindred minds in other churches whether in defense of verbal inspiration or in exploration of new views. The Keswick Bookshop and the SCM Bookroom in Melbourne, and the use of either Scripture Union or Bible Reading Fellowship Notes became the means used by each group for disseminating their respective theological positions. The "Lenten Bible Studies" published by the Joint Board for Christian Education prior to union in 1977 also encouraged the necessary experience of ecumenism and doctrinal similarity which would assist the vote for union. Conservatives formed and developed transdenominational links through Keswick Conventions at Upwey (prior to its move to Belgrave Heights) in Victoria and Katoomba in New South Wales, and the Bible College movement (with Bible Institutes in Adelaide, Melbourne, Brisbane and Sydney Missionary and Bible College).[79] Those with

---

[79] Sydney Missionary and Bible College had helped to lead the charge against Angus.

ecumenical sympathy had the Australian Student Christian Movement Conferences. Each one of these movements provided a focal point around which people polarised into two theological positions: the conservatives and liberals. These movements provided informal encouragement to either resist or accept union.

The encouragement toward union was often undertaken by ministers who had a great deal in common theologically with their ministerial peers in the other denominations. The Melbourne College of Divinity, and in particular the United Faculty of Theology (Presbyterians and Methodists which accepted Jesuits into its midst in 1972), played its part in fostering an openness to union. Many of these ministers who graduated from an ecumenically oriented education in Melbourne, Sydney, Brisbane or Perth, for social and theological reasons, saw union as a positive expression of their Christian faith and their understanding of what was essential truth. The Basis of Union which was first drafted in 1963, and subsequently revised, was not just a theological document, but one which altered the practices of the Presbyterian Church. It effectively severed it from its historical roots, despite explicit wording which recognised the Presbyterian Church's historical roots in the Westminster Confession. The Presbyterian Church Association took up the gauntlet and fought during the 1960s and 1970s for the preservation of the Presbyterian Church and its standards. The Association sponsored the publication of material attacking union on the basis of polity and doctrine.

With the creation of the Uniting Church in 1977 a dramatic shift took place within the Presbyterian Church in Australia as the Church moved back to a firmer adherence to its Confession. It is notable that Robert Swanton, Principal of the Victorian Theological Hall, saw the Confession as being central to the direction and ethos of the continuing church. Swanton, according to his biographer, "a man who did not write books", took up his pen to expound on the Confession and the Declaratory Statement.[80] In 1983 an Australian sociologist who is a member of the Uniting Church observed

> ... continuing Presbyterians in Australia tend to be more conservative theologically than those Presbyterians who joined the Uniting Church. Nevertheless, the continuing Presbyterian Church, especially in NSW, contains a sizeable minority of clergy whose theological position is at least as liberal as that of the majority of former Presbyterian clergy in the Uniting Church. What has happened within the Presbyterian Church the balance of power between the theologically conservative and liberal wings.[81]

It was that mixed NSW Church as described above that Peter Cameron was to join in 1991.

Peter Cameron

Opposition to the Confession in the period since 1977 has tended to center around interpretation, in particular the meaning of the Declaratory Statement and the Liberty of Opinion Clause. Long before Cameron appeared in Australia there were groups, particularly in NSW and Victoria, who opposed a strict adherence to the teachings of the Confession[82]. Opposition has tended to center on the question of the ordination of women and the Confession has always been seen as a secondary factor. Even in the Cameron case, the defendant and the media tried to convince the public that the issue at stake was the status of women in the Presbyterian Church of Australia rather than the Word of God or the Westminster Confession of Faith.

Unlike the Strong and Angus "heresy" trials, Cameron's was properly pursued by his Presbytery, with the drawing up of a libel.

---

[80] See B. Bayston, "Robert Swanton" in *Australian Dictionary of Evangelical Biography,* p. 362. R. Swanton, "The Westminster Confession and the Declaratory Statement". . . .

[81] A.W. Black, "Church Union in Canada and Australia: A Comparative Analysis," *Church Heritage*, vol. 3, no. 1 (1983), p. 120.

[82] The Presbyterian Association in NSW and The Burning Bush Society of Victoria.

The case centred around the sermon mentioned in the introduction of this chapter and Cameron's denial of the infallibility of Scripture, and the Westminster Confession of Faith's teaching upon Scripture. The trial and the events leading up to it were surrounded by a media circus which had not been seen in the Strong or Angus cases. In addition to the print media were added radio and television. In an age less tolerant of anyone who appears intolerant, the Presbyterian Church of Australia was portrayed as some kind of medieval inquisition sniffing out a witch in its midst. Meanwhile, Cameron appeared to revel in the publicity portraying himself as the champion of rational thought in what he saw as a continuation of the modernist-fundamentalist debate.

Dr. Peter Cameron was born in 1945 and attended Fettes College, a boarding school for the well-to-do in Edinburgh. From there he flirted with a career in music before receiving a law degree at the University of Edinburgh, a decision which would prepare him for his later battles in Australia. After a number of years practising as a solicitor he returned in 1973 to Edinburgh University to study theology at New College. He studied as a private student rather than as a candidate for ordination and went on to graduate studies at Cambridge. On completing his Cambridge doctorate he returned to a legal career. Finally in April 1984 he was ordained and inducted to St. Phillip's Church in Edinburgh. Ominously he later reflected on that event:

> I suppose there were about a dozen ministers who came forward with their gowns flapping and their hands outstretched, their faces solemn and dignified as I knelt at the front of the church. And the combined weight of their hands oppressing down on my head as the officiating minister intoned the ritual words produced in me an extraordinary sensation: it was both awesome and repulsive. I felt simultaneously in-ed and trapped, rooted in a life-giving tradition and anchored in a dead past. The ceremony seemed at once to legitimise my intentions and to deprive me of the power to carry them out. I was as it were initiated and emasculated at the same time.[83]

---

[83] P. Cameron, *Heretic*, pp. 17-18.

In 1987 Cameron moved on from St. Phillip's to become the Meldrum Lecturer at New College. At the end of three years he became disillusioned with University theology. He had failed, he later said, to find God in the university or the church. Subsequently, he accepted in 1991 the appointment as Principal of St. Andrew's College in the University of Sydney.

Cameron kept a fairly low profile in the Church, emerging from the College to preach the occasional non-controversial sermon from his Scottish days. He was aware of the existing tension between the Presbyterian Church and St. Andrew's College and the suspicion with which the Principal was held. Samuel Angus had not been forgotten and Cameron wrote:

> . . . in the context of the relations between college and Church, the name of Angus has always been symbolic: on one side, of an institution which embodies academic independence, and intellectual freedom, and honesty; and on the other side, of an institution which is a thorn in the flesh of orthodoxy, and which corrupts the minds of the young and innocent. . . . The Puritan in the Presbyterian Church of Australia is constantly haunted by St. Andrew's College. And Puritanism, hand in hand with Fundamentalism, has been on the increase in the Presbyterian Church of Australia for some years. It has always been there of course. . . . But in the days of Samuel Angus, for example, they were in a minority vociferous, indeed clamorous, but still a minority.[84]

The heresy trial took place on 18 March 1993 before the Presbytery of Sydney. The meeting was held at the Presbyterian Theological Centre in Burwood, the training College for Presbyterian candidates in the Presbyterian Church in NSW. It was difficult to gain entry as various journalists and television news crews jockeyed for prime position The media were locked out as the Presbytery determined to meet in private.

Cameron was duly accused of teaching what was first inconsistent with Chapter 1 of the Westminster Confession of Faith and second inconsistent with the teaching of the Bible on homosexuality. The first charge was upheld by the Presbytery

---

[84] *Ibid.*, p. 34-37.

while the second was dismissed. The Rev. Bruce Christian, who acted as prosecutor led the charge by centering upon Cameron's contradiction of the Confession. "In the last twenty years," insisted Christian, "we have positively reaffirmed our confessional doctrinal position in direct opposition to the view of the Bible and Westminster Confession of Faith which is presently being espoused by Dr Cameron."[85] Cameron appealed to the NSW General Assembly. The following Sunday he appeared on the television affairs show "60 Minutes." The next few months were busy for Cameron as the media continued to hound the "heretic" and his accusers. Meanwhile the St. Andrew's Principal dug his heels in and entered upon a quest to "liberate the non-Fundamentalist from the stranglehold of the Fundamentalist interpretation of the Bible."[86]

There were two appeals heard, the first from the decision of the Presbytery in February 1993 on the relevancy of the libel, and the second from its decision at the trial in March 1993. Both appeals were lost and Cameron turned to the supreme court, the General Assembly of the Presbyterian Church of Australia, which was due to meet in September 1994. However, he resigned as a minister of the Presbyterian Church of Australia prior to the Assembly meeting. In his statements following his resignation he demonstrated a new honesty about his position as a minister. He wrote:

> I entered the ministry as in some sense an impostor, a double agent, hoping to change things from within. That is no longer possible for me. . . .
>
> Because I don't at all mean that I have given up on God or withdrawn from the quest. . . . I suspected from the beginning that God was not to be found in the Church. . . .

---

[85] Minutes of the Presbytery of Sydney 18 March 1993 in *Peter Cameron Papers,* PCNSW, 1993.

[86] P. Cameron, *Heretic,* p. 139.

> Previously it was a question of abandoning a secular career in order
> to explore within the Church the possibility of God: if he existed
> good and well; if he did not exist, then no secular career was worth
> pursuing anyway. Now I am to abandon an ecclesiastical career in
> order to continue the search—because if God is not to be found in
> the Church, then no ecclesiastical career is worth pursuing either.[87]

The Westminster Confession of Faith has recently enjoyed a
revival in Presbyterian circles. For much of the twentieth century
it had disappeared from sight in the Presbyterian Church of
Australia. A former teaching associate tells the story that when
he was a student in the post-1945 Victorian Theological Hall the
Westminster Confession of Faith was almost unknown amongst
the students and was unavailable from the Presbyterian
Bookroom.[88] 1992 saw the publication of two commentaries on
the Confession by Australian Presbyterians which have gained
acceptance and are used widely throughout Presbyterian Churches
in Australia.[89] A regular column authored by Tom Wilkinson
expounding the Confession has also appeared in the national
journal, *APL Today*, since January 1994.

In a style reminiscent of previous generations, a pamphlet war
has also broken out on the subject of the Confession. For example,
the attack on the Confession and the Declaratory Statement has
continued through the publications of the Burning Bush Society.[90]

---

[87] *Ibid.*, p. 210-211.

[88] The Rev. Dr. T.L. Wilkinson taught in the Reformed Theological College in
Geelong and after his retirement in the Presbyterian Theological Hall in
Melbourne from 1984 until 1993.

[89] T.L. Wilkinson, *The Westminster Confession Now*. Melbourne, 1992. R.S.
Ward, *The Westminster Confession for the Church today*. Melbourne, 1992.
Wilkinson is a minister of the PCA and Ward of the Presbyterian Church of
Eastern Australia.

[90] A.T. Stevens, *An Appraisal of the so-called 'Five Points of Calvinism.'*
Bendigo, 1994. H.A. Stamp, *The Word of God in the Bible*. Bendigo, 1994.
Both are retired ministers. Alex Stevens was for a number of years a lecturer
in New Testament at the Melbourne Bible Institute (now the Bible College
of Victoria) and defends the Arminian point of view. Arthur Stamp, like

These works have been received well by those who already accept a more liberal interpretation of the Confession and the Bible but pose no serious threat to the advance of orthodoxy within the Presbyterian Church of Australia. The Professor of Theology at the Presbyterian Theological College in Melbourne, Douglas Milne, has responded to such attacks and has adequately dealt with the old liberal and Arminian arguments.[91]

Conclusion

The battlefield over the Westminister Confession of Faith in Australia is littered with many dead. Tensions over the Westminster Confession of Faith were evident from the beginnings of Presbyterianism in Australia as each branch exported its own stand to the Subordinate Standards. This is perhaps best exemplified in the three case studies considered in this chapter. Charles Strong, Samuel Angus and Peter Cameron were each produced by churches overseas that were questioning the legitimacy of a firm adherence to the Westminster Confession of Faith. They merely tried to recreate the beliefs of their home church in their adopted home. They were imports who brought with them an imported theology. Meanwhile, many Presbyterian evangelicals retreated into a pietistic world view often unconcerned about doctrinal orthodoxy.

The Strong Case was central as it led to the creation of a Declaratory Statement within the Presbyterian Church of Victoria, leading to the 1901 Statement and has since proved to be at the centre of any debate on the Westminster Confession of Faith.

Cameron, is a graduate of Cambridge University and immediately after union taught Hebrew in the Victorian Theological Hall. He tends to favor the old liberal interpretation of the Scriptures; i.e., like Angus. In 1994, the Burning Bush Society produced an edition of the Westminster Confession of Faith with the Declaratory Statements.

[91] D.J.W. Milne, *The Bible IS The Word of God. The Five Points of Calvinism ARE essential to the Presbyterian Church today.* Melbourne, 1994.

The number of words expended upon the 1901 Basis of Union with its Declaratory Statement "qualifying" adherence to the Westminster Confession of Faith demonstrates its central importance in the battle. Some have argued that it weakened adherence to the Confession and others that it strengthened adherence. Whatever the case, as the Presbyterian Church of Australia looks forward to the year 2000 there has been a real return to Confessional orthodoxy and the church that had once lost its way has found it again.

Calvin, Westminster and Assurance

Mark E. Dever

Introduction

To face a holy God when one is in opposition to Him is a terrifying prospect. And yet, according to the words of the Bible, this is the fate of each one who is outside of Christ. Apart from the salvation brought by the work of the triune God, we have no hope. So it is that the assurance one has of this salvation is to be of the greatest concern. The fact that it has not been in recent decades in much of the English-speaking protestant world can be attributed to a diminishing concern about the reality of this prospect of facing Almighty God in judgment. On the one hand, many protestant churches have assured their hearers that either God's character is not one which is so bothered by sin, or if it is, then He has predisposed Himself to forgive all those He has made in his image. This is the challenge of modern liberalism to the Christian faith. On the other hand, many other protestant churches have assured their hearers that the memory of a momentary decision or an apparently sincere religious experience of confession is all that is required to avert the judgment of God. If this is the case, then it is no wonder that the assurance of one's salvation has been of so little concern to modern protestants. What was once accepted by grace can now better be said to be taken for granted. This dilemma is the challenge of a contemporary casual sub-evangelical message. It must be confessed that both liberal universalism and sub-evangelical voluntarism leave the believer with the impression that their position before God is settled, but is it?

In his second letter, the apostle Peter exhorted some early Christians to "make their calling and election sure," (1:10). The exhortation itself would seem non-sensical to some. "God has settled this—surely He has elected all in Christ." To others who would be more likely to be reading the second paragraph of an article buried deep in a book celebrating the 350th anniversary of the Westminster standards, Peter's exhortation would not be so surprising. Instead, what might be surprising is how Peter, in the context, seems to suggest that this be done—by finding increasing evidences of the Spirit's work in our lives. This seems to be what Peter clearly says (in concert with many other Biblical authors). He does not exhort his readers to remember a decision made, to recall a prayer prayed; rather, he calls them to an examination of the course of their lives.

It is at this point that John Calvin, William Perkins, and the whole host of the Westminster Divines have been brought into the discussion. With a remarkable regularity (which alone suggests something), Calvin has been brought in as the representative of the "freeness" (stated positively) or "sheerness" (stated more critically) of salvation in the protestant understanding of the gospel. The later English puritans, so this theory goes, while supposing themselves to be his followers, actually were the subverters of his teaching. They subverted it by the simple re-introduction of works into the equation. The theological distinction between works being a ground of salvation and an evidence of salvation is taken as having been too slight for the laity to comprehend, so that in Christian experience, the looking to one's life for evidence of salvation is seen to be practically indistinguishable from auto-soterism—that is, from saving oneself by one's own life. If this charge is true, it is a damning indictment of the gospel presented by the Westminster standards. As much as may be admirable in a vessel, a small hole in the right place can sink the whole ship. Such a crucial error in such a central doctrine would do just that to any concept of salvation by the grace of God.

One of the central difficulties in establishing whether this has been the actual situation is the problematic nature of synthetic studies. By synthetic studies is meant studies which span a number of theologians, particularly if those theologians studied are themselves of different nations and times. Even though no theology is all context,[1] all theology is contextual. The very characteristics which attract us to some of the sweeping studies of Perry Miller, R. T. Kendall or Alister McGrath should also caution us. Surveys naturally have difficulty taking the varying contexts of contemporary discussions into account. Themes are easier to trace through various authors than they are to find in them. That is to say, it is easier to find something many places in Calvin, for example, than it is to hear it from him. The latter hearing requires a longer and more careful understanding of Calvin in the breadth of his writings and in the context (intellectually and socially) of his work, whereas the former finding can easily be done by a scholar with a thesis and a good notation system. It is the difference between exegesis and eisegesis. Certainly our knowing is neither purely inductive nor purely deductive; but what should be moving, developing spirals (e.g., Ecclesia Reformata, semper reformanda secundum verbum dei) can easily become stationary circles (e.g., Rome's semper eadem) if the texts studied are not given time and space to speak for themselves about their own concerns. This is as true in our work for the classroom as it is in our work for the pulpit. Even as

---

[1] In the sense of being "only context."

liberal 19th-century students of the life of Jesus could look down the long well of history to find Jesus, and see only their own reflection, so many a modern researcher (friendly or hostile to Calvin or the puritans) can be trapped by their own methods into learning nothing by their studies, but merely appearing to prove what they already knew even before they began.

And so it is that this author comes to present a brief, synthetic survey of his own! The only defense for this to be offered (other than the request of the editors) is that this survey is based on a much larger study undertaken by the author of a single individual in his context. Having listened to this late sixteenth-, early seventeenth-century theologian (without initially intending to explore his teaching of assurance), this author is convinced that some modern controversies about the Puritans have been caused by anachronistic readings, insensitive to the original theological or pastoral contexts of the theologians in question. It is the hope of this author that this short study will be of some help to Christians today who wish to listen to these teachers of the past on this crucial topic of assurance.

The Setting

By the latter days of Elizabeth's reign, the focus of puritan divinity seemed to have shifted from the controversies of the 1570's to more pastoral, less contentious concerns. "The bitter arguments over the precise form of a Christian church laid down in the New Testament, which twenty years previously had absorbed so much of the energy of Cartwright and Whitgift, had given way to a more pacific school of writers who put far more emphasis on practical Puritan piety."[2] Not that controversies ceased. Peter Milward's works have highlighted in a most helpful way the continuing religious controversies of the Elizabethan and

---

[2] Claire Cross, *Church and People*, p. 161.

Jacobean ages.[3] But there was along side the controversial literature a growing literature of personal devotion and piety, concerned with preparation for salvation and assurance of it. This is the literature which history has, with reason, taken to be typical of that company usually referred to as "the English Puritans."

It was exactly this popularly pious character of much of these preachers' writings which has led scholars for the last century to affirm the necessary existence of some kind of theological discontinuity—witting or unwitting—between these English divines, and their continental predecessors. Most influential in asserting this has probably been Perry Miller. He referred to the "drastic alterations" which these men made on the theology that they had inherited.[4] Miller was certainly neither the first nor the last to discern this theological rift between the reformed English divines of the seventeenth century and their continental co-religionists. George P. Fisher, writing two generations earlier, identified what was to become the standard location suggested for this theological divide. He asserted that it was the special use of the covenantal scheme in particular that had "softened the rigor of Calvinistic teaching by setting up jural relations in the room of bare sovereignty."[5]

Having been repeated almost countless times since then, this suggestion has received its fullest recent exposition from R. T. Kendall. In his provocative book *Calvin and English Calvinism to 1649*, Kendall asserted that there were fundamental differences between the faith expressed in the Westminster Confession, and that of John Calvin.[6] Indeed, Kendall concludes that "Westminster

[3] Peter Milward, *Religious Controversies of the Elizabethan Age: A Survey of Printed Sources* (London: The Scolar Press, 1978); Peter Milward, *Religious Controversies*

[4] Perry Miller, *The New England Mind: The Seventeenth Century*, p. 92.

[5] George P. Fisher, *History of Christian Doctrine* (Edinburgh: T. & T. Clark, 1896), p. 348.

[6] R. T. Kendall, *Calvin and English Calvinism to 1649* (Oxford: Oxford University Press, 1979).

theology hardly deserves to be called Calvinistic—especially if that term is to imply the thought of Calvin himself."[7] Kendall suggests that this discontinuity was introduced on the continent by Calvin's successor, Theodore Beza, and in England, by William Perkins. This "turn to the subject" in late sixteenth century reformed theology was brought about, he suggests, by the introduction of the doctrine of Christ's limited atonement. Once this doctrine was accepted, introspective questions of whether one possessed a truly saving faith could no longer be answered simply by a Luther-like (or, as Kendall would suggest, a Calvin-like) appeal to the cross. Christ's death on the cross may not have been "for" the one questioning. In this theological context distinguishing between saving and temporary faith became important. And it was in the pietistic and covenantal language of early Stuart puritanism that these issues were to be worked out to their logical (and un-Calvinistic) conclusions in the doctrines of preparation for grace and in the questions of personal assurance of salvation.

And yet, for all of the helpful clarification which may come by noting these differences, shifts of emphasis, and even innovations, severe difficulties arise if this divide is presented too radically. Most English divines of the period both admired Calvin, and understood themselves to be the inheritors of his tradition. Richard Hooker, in the preface to his *Of The Laws of Ecclesiastical Polity*, called Calvin "incomparably the wisest man that ever the French church did enjoy, since the hour it enjoyed him."[8] The decrying of Calvin and other reformers by William Barrett in a University Sermon preached at Great St. Mary's, Cambridge, on 29 April 1595 and the stinging rebuke he met with from the university authorities clearly show that the

---

[7] Kendall, *Calvin and English Calvinism*, p. 212

[8] Richard Hooker, *Of The Laws of Ecclesiastical Polity*, ed. Ronald Bayne (London: J.M.Dent & Co., 1907, vol. 1.), p. 77.

identification with Calvin was so strong that to attack him publicly was to go beyond the theological pale.[9]

Not only did these theologians reckon themselves to be part of the same theological tradition as Calvin, and others of the reformed camp, but their presentation of theological issues anthropological and soteriological did not, in fact, differ in substance from Calvin's so much as some have suggested. George Marsden has presented a concise, perceptive examination of Perry Miller's Calvin/Puritan distinction, concentrating upon the misrepresentation of the former.[10] John von Rohr has more recently and more fully criticized this same distinction, concentrating more upon the misrepresentation of the latter.[11] Roger Nicole has presented a searching critique of the soteriological divide posited between Calvin and the English Puritans, concentrating especially upon R. T. Kendall's portrayal of Calvin's teaching on the atonement.[12] All of these studies are helpful in that they enable one to lay aside the suggested distinctions which have dominated the search for the Puritan theological identity for the last century, but which increasingly seem at least facile, if not entirely misleading. To find the nature of English Puritan divinity in a distinction from Calvin which did not in fact exist, is to misunderstand puritanism itself.

---

[9] H.C. Porter, *Reformation and Reaction in Tudor Cambridge* (Cambridge: Cambridge University Press, 1958), pp. 344-363.

[10] George Marsden, "Perry Miller's Rehabilitation of the Puritans: A Critique" *Church History* 39 (1970) 91-105.

[11] John von Rohr, *The Covenant of Grace in Puritan Thought* (Atlanta: Scholar's Press, 1986). Cf. Dewey D. Wallace, *Puritans and Predestination: Grace in English Protestant Theology, 1525-1695*, (Chapel Hill, N.C.: University of North Carolina Press, 1982), p. 197; Harry S. Stout, "Theological Commitment and American Religious History," *Theological Education* Spring 1989, 44-59.

[12] Roger Nicole, "John Calvin's View of the Extent of the Atonement" *Westminster Theological Journal* 47 (1985), 197-225.

What then of the obvious concern about assurance among the English godly divines of late Tudor and early Stuart England? If the suggested theological transformation did not take place, what can explain the pastoral rather than polemical, the pacific rather than controversial nature of puritan divinity? Realizing that what Harry Stout has called "the burden of deity"[13] cannot rightly be borne by the historian in reconstructing the past, and that, as Patrick Collinson has suggested, "Historians are rightly suspicious of mono-causal explanations,"[14] what then can be suggested? It is the purpose of this study to suggest another model which relates English puritanism to its reformed forefathers, which attempts to be more faithful to each theologically and more historically sensitive. This study suggests that they were not so much theological, but historical shifts which brought about the markedly experimental reformed divinity of the English Puritans.

The Problem of Assurance

Puritan sermonic rhetoric about the doctrine of assurance could be quite equivocal, intending at one moment to assure the doubting believer that their election was based upon nothing in themselves and that their perseverance was assured by the same God who had begun a good work in them, (Philippians 1:6), and at the next exhorting believers to make sure their interest in Christ.[15] Whatever rush of certainty may have attended the initial preaching of the Protestant gospel, by the early seventeenth-century, and probably well before, such preaching, intended as a balm after the Roman "doctrine of doubting," had various effects on its hearers. This is well illustrated by two letters which

---

[13] Harry S. Stout, "Theological Commitment and American Religious History" *Theological Education* Spring 1989, 44-59.

[14] Patrick Collinson, "Shepherds, Sheepdogs, and Hirelings" in *Studies in Church History* 1990, p. 219.

Lady Joan Barrington received from younger relations (daughter and nephew, respectively) in 1629 and 1630.

Lady Elizabeth Masham had obviously often heard such exhortations to assurance, and found them a spur to spiritual progress. In a letter written to her mother, Lady Joan Barrington, in early 1629, she "confesed" that "I daly se more and more that there is noe hapynes in any thing but in getting asuranc of God['s] love in Christ, and 'tis the only thing, I thank God, which I take comfort in, and I know that you will say the like your self."[16] Others, however, did not find the doctrine so spiritually comforting. A year later Thomas Bourchier, Lady Joan's nephew, wrote to her a pathetic, mainly melancholic letter, lamenting the state of his own soul.

> Madame of late I have had such infinite sadnes springinge from feares of my union with Christe, that truli I have scarce bin able to subsiste. My feares are not about his faithfulnes, with whome I knowe there is no shadowe of chainge, but they arise from secret doubtes of the truthe of grace (without which all prophession does but aggravate condemnation). I knowe the spirit of man onely knowes what's in man, experience tho of God's dealing in strates gives no small lighte to another wounded. Give me leave therefore humbli to supplicate your ladyship to sende some balme to him whoe indeed does not a little langwish in the inwarde man. Tho thus I complaine, (I blesse God) when I am at the poynte of deathe I still hope, and indeed some tymes have such refreshings, that the sweet thereof invites to truste tho God kill . . . tho I am confident that that precious blood which some yeares since I have applied does perfectli justifie me and in some measure by its efficaci I am clensed, yet the thoughtes of wastinge my marrow in vaniti does manye tymes produce stronge assaultes.[17]

---

[15] E.g. John Calvin, *The Sermons of M. John Calvin upon the Fifth Booke of Moses Called Deuteronomie*, trans. Arthur Golding, (London, 1583), p. 519.b.

[16] *Barrington Family Letters, 1628-1632*, ed. Arthur Searle, (London, 1983), p. 56.

[17] *Barrington Family Letters, 1628-1632*, ed. Arthur Searle, (London, 1983), p. 176.

If sincere confusion could be created in the hearts of earnest listeners who saw their souls at stake in the early seventeenth century, much more easily can confusion creep into the modern reader's discussion of assurance or certainty.

Any discussion of assurance which is unclear in the object of assurance can hardly be expected to be clear in any other matter. It is vital to know whether one is discussing the objective assurance of faith that Christ is all he professes to be,[18] and that he will freely save whoever believes in him, or the subjective assurance of faith in which one is assured of one's own salvation.[19] The former use of assurance was prominent throughout the century following the reformation, particularly in anti-Roman polemics.[20] The latter emphasis, though always present and distinct in the Reformed tradition, becomes more clearly distinguished, and more prominent in the English church due perhaps to the increased attention given pastoral issues over polemical ones in printed books as the Protestant succession seemed more certain, and the Elizabethan settlement more settled. Such a distinction is essential in clearly considering the Reformed background of the Westminster statements on the assurance of salvation.

Robert Middlekauf has written that "The most familiar figure among Puritans is the tormented soul, constantly examining his every thought and action, now convinced that hell awaits him, now lunging after the straw of hope that he is saved, and then once more falling into despair. He wants to believe, he tries, he

---

[18] Even this is to be distinguished from mere "notional" knowledge, or "historical" faith, which, while essential to any saving faith, is not really in view here.

[19] For a brief, accurate, systematic distinction of these two, see Louis Berkhof, *Systematic Theology*, (Grand Rapids, Michigan, 1939), pp. 507-509.

[20] Dewey D. Wallace, Jr., *Puritans and Predestination: Grace in English Protestant Theology, 1525-1695*, (Chapel Hill, North Carolina, 1982), pp. 63-65; cf. Peter Lake, Moderate Puritans and the Elizabethan Church, (Cambridge, 1982), pp. 98-106, 166-167.

fails, he succeeds, he fails—always on the cycle of alternating moods."[21] John Calvin had complained that this was exactly the "assurance mingled with doubt" that some "half-papists" were teaching in his own day. They taught that

> Whenever we look upon Christ, they confess that we find full occasion for good hope in him. But because we are always unworthy of all those benefits which are offered to us in Christ, they would have us waver and hesitate at the sight of our unworthiness. In brief, they so set conscience between hope and fear that it alternates from one to the other intermittently and by turns. . . . Thus, when Satan once sees that those open devices with which he formerly had been wont to destroy the certainty of faith are now of no avail, he tries to sap it by covert devices.[22]

Was this teaching of "half-papists," which Calvin lamented, the teaching of his Reformed heirs, and particularly of the Westminster standards?

The Roman Catholic Position

The tradition against which this Reformed understanding of assurance was preached—one of the most truly catholic traditions overturned by the Reformers—was the tradition concerning assurance of salvation codified by the Roman Catholic Church at Trent.[23] In their Sixth Session in 1547 they produced the "Decree

---

[21] Robert Middlekauff, "Piety and Intellect in Puritanism," *The William and Mary Quarterly*, 3rd series, XXII, no. 3 (July, 1965), 459. For a careful accounting of the most celebrated case of a search for assurance see George H. Williams, "Called by Thy Name, Leave us Not: The Case of Mrs. Joan Drake," *Harvard Library Bulletin* (1968), 111-128, 278-300. Cf. the case of John Overall at Epping, recounted in Porter, *Reformation and Reaction*, pp. 285-286.

[22] Calvin, *Institutes*, III.ii.24. Cf. Makfred K. Bahmann, "Calvin's Controversy with Certain 'Half-Papists,'" *The Hartford Quarterly*, V/2 (Winter, 1965), 27-41.

[23] On disagreements at Trent over the doctrine of assurance, see Reinhold Seeberg, *The History of Doctrines*, trans. Charles Hay (??German, 1898; rpt Grand Rapids, Michigan, 1977), II.435-438.

on Justification."[24] Following Aquinas, rather than Duns Scotus, the Council defined justification in a non-punctiliar fashion. The Tridentine explanation of the life of a Christian was that the Christian's initial justification in baptism could be lost through mortal sin.[25] Final justification, that justification which most Christians would have in view in their earthly life, necessarily followed sanctification, because, essentially, God could not justify sinners as sinners.[26] Normally, the righteousness of Christ had to be imparted to them and, to grow throughout their lives by God's grace administered through the seven sacraments of the church. In chapter IX, the Decree stated what logically followed from such an understanding of justification, i.e., that "no one can know with a certitude of faith which cannot be subject to error, that he has obtained God's grace." Chapter XII was directed explicitly against those who thought that they could definitely know that they were among the elect, apart from special revelation.[27] To propagate a teaching of assurance of final justification, then, was taken as teaching sinners to think themselves perfect, a damning error.[28]

John Calvin

John Calvin wrote of salvation as if it included assurance one moment,[29] and yet also conceded that "we cannot imagine any

---

[24] "Decree of Justification," reprinted in *The Christian Faith in the Doctrinal Documents of the Catholic Church*, rev. ed., ed. J. Neuner and J. Dupuis, (New York, 1982), pp. 554-570.

[25] Decree on Justification, Chapter XV.

[26] Decree on Justification, Chapters VII and XIV.

[27] So too Decree on Justification, Canon 16.

[28] Decree on Justification, Chapter XIII contained the "doctrine of doubt" that is, that a Christian ought to doubt his salvation, which became infamous among Protestants.

[29] E.g., his comments on Galatians 4:6 in his *Commentaries on the Epistles of Paul to the Galatians and Ephesians*, trans. William Pringle, (Edinburgh,

certainty that is not tinged with doubt. . . ."[30] This was not to suggest, he insisted, the Roman position, "that faith does not rest in a certain and clear knowledge, but only in an obscure and confused knowledge of the divine will toward us,"[31] because "even if we are distracted by various thoughts, we are not on that account completely divorced from faith. . . . We see him [God] afar off, but so clearly as to know that we are not at all deceived."[32] Instead of experiencing lack of assurance from putting one's faith in an unsure source of salvation, Calvin said believers should "deeply fix all our hope [on God's promise], paying no regard to our works, to seek any help from them" in regards to the basis of salvation. That was not to say, however, that the believer should not regard works when considering the question of whether one has this salvation established on the basis of Christ's righteousness alone.[33] Assurance, in this sense—having a certain basis of salvation—is inherent in true faith.

Calvin taught that while it was theologically necessary to distinguish between justification and sanctification, they were never separable in the true believer's experience.[34] This inseparability of justification from sanctification in Calvin may go some way to explaining a certain amount of confusion regarding Calvin's position on assurance. Calvin has often been taken as affirming that saving faith necessarily included assurance,

---

1854), 121 (yet it should be noted that Calvin makes this comment in the context of anti-Roman polemics); Calvin, *Institutes*, III.ii.7.

[30] Calvin, *Institutes*, III.ii.16 and 17. Cf. III.ii.18, 37; xiii.3; xxiv.6.

[31] Calvin, *Institutes*, III.ii.18.

[32] Calvin, *Institutes*, III.ii.18-19; cf. III.ii.14.

[33] Calvin, *Institutes*, III.XIII.4; cf. xiv.18; Lynn Baird Tipson, Jr., "The Development of a Puritan Understanding of Conversion," (Ph.D. dissertation, Yale University, 1972), 102-104, concluding that "Calvin very cautiously accepted the confirmatory evidence of good works while insisting that true faith was its own assurance."

[34] Calvin, *Institutes*, III.xxiv.1.

with the implication being that the two were almost identical.[35]

---

[35] This posited identification in Calvin, and their obvious separation in later Reformed thought, has, along with the related issue of covenant, been the moving force behind the idea that Calvin's heirs in England in the century following his death radically altered his theology. E.g., George Fisher, *History of Christian Doctrine*, (Edinburgh, 1896), 274, 299. Perry Miller, in what amounts to an extreme form of this understanding of assurance in Calvin, represented Calvin as even denying that people should attempt to look into the matter of their own salvation at all. Yet he did so by quoting a passage from Calvin in which he was reprimanding the desire to search the hidden will of God. (See Perry Miller, "The Marrow of Puritan Divinity," *Publications of the Colonial Society of Massachusetts*, XXXII [1937], 252.) He then went on to suggest that the anxiety arising from this uncertainty was deliberately exploited by the following generations of Reformed theologians. To do so, Miller suggested, they constructed covenant theology, with mutual obligations, which both God and the believer were bound to respect. Ingenious as this reading was, it was clearly a mis-reading not merely of covenant theology (as has been shown in Chapter 5) but also of Calvin on assurance. In his 1956 collection of some of his previously published articles (*Errand into the Wilderness*, [Cambridge, Massachusetts, 1956]) he included "Marrow" unchanged, and mentioned in his introduction to it his indebtedness to Fisher and A. C. McGiffert for noting the modification in Calvinism brought about by the advent of the covenant idea (48). Many writers followed Miller, et al., in positing this substantial modification in Reformed theology. Miller has been specifically criticized for exaggerating the difference between Calvin and the later puritans by his misunderstanding of Calvin by Ian Breward, (Breward, *The Work of William Perkins*, [Appleford, Abingdon, Berkshire, 1970], 92-93. The most influential work recently to equate saving faith and assurance in Calvin has been R. T. Kendall, *Calvin and English Calvinism to 1649*, (Oxford, 1979), 13-28, 196. Kendall presented some idiosyncratic views (e.g., Calvin believed the "atonement" essentially occurred in Christ's intercession after his ascension, rather than on the cross [16], therefore the idea of a limited atonement as classically stated was not held by Calvin.) Such suggestions stirred a large critical response, most of which have been in the theological journals (unfortunately for historians, who, therefore, have tended to rely on Kendall uncritically, e.g. Lake, 322 [n. 217], 329, [for which G. F. Nuttall criticized Lake in his review of Lake's book, in *Heythrop Journal*, XXVI/1 (Jan. 1985), 95] On the other hand, the contemporary master of the history of theology, Jaroslav Pelikan, has recently referred to Perry Miller as "the leading scholar of Puritan thought", [Pelikan, *Reformation of Church and Dogma (1300-1700)*, (Chicago, 1984), 372]). One of the best summaries of criticisms of Kendall's

Yet many statements of Calvin (some quoted in this section) show the fallacy of a simple identification of fides and fiducia in Calvin.[36] Thus while Calvin could be read as including assurance in initial, saving faith only by controverting other clear statements of his, he may more satisfactorily be read as affirming assurance as part of the Christian's normal, life-long experience of saving faith.[37] In such a way, and only in such a way, does assurance

---

thesis, based on a much more careful look at Calvin, was by Roger Nicole, "John Calvin's View of the Extent of the Atonement," *Westminster Theological Journal*, XLVII (1985), 197-225; cf. Paul Helm, *Calvin and the Calvinists*, (Edinburgh, 1982). Kendall also suggested that Calvin could allow Christ alone as the ground of assurance because of the universal reference of Christ's death, and that subsequent Reformed theologians had to find other grounds as they limited the effect of Christ's death (e.g., 32), yet even if Kendall's treatment of Calvin here were taken as accurate, and the inferences about assurance to follow (which is questionable), such a limited intercession then in Calvin would have left him with essentially similar pastoral problems to the ones had by those that followed him. Kendall's main fault in this study, however, is the presentation of Calvin's views exclusively in dialogue with those of his Reformed followers, without taking sufficient cognizance of their original context (both textually and historically). Most importantly, there is no significant mention of the Roman Catholic doctrine against which Calvin's presentation of the gospel is made. Therefore, statements about "assurance" are set in the context of a contrast with later statements by Reformed divines in a very flat way, when their respective contexts no doubt helped to shape the ambiguities and assertions of all of their expressions on assurance. It is as if Calvin's dialogue has been kept from a conversation where the partner has been replaced, and the topics changed. The most persuasive and thorough treatment of Calvin on faith and assurance is found in Joel R. Beeke, "Personal Assurance of Faith: English Puritanism and the Dutch 'Nadere Reformatie'" From Westminster to Alexander Comrie (1640-1760)," (Ph. D. dissertation, Westminster Theological Seminary, 1988), 44-78.

[36] In Calvin, *Institutes*, III.XIII.5.

[37] In personal conversation, Tony Lane has suggested to the author that this distinction between initial and life-long is an anachronistic distinction, foreign to Calvin. (Cf. A.N.S. Lane, "Calvin's Doctrine of Assurance," *Vox Evangelica* 11 [1979], 47-48). Yet while this verbal distinction itself may be anachronistic, precisely this idea seems to summarize well Calvin's own teaching.

become an experience of all Christians, though not at all times, gratuitous, and yet clearly related to sanctification.

In 1539, Calvin prayed to God, remembering the situation before the Reformation, a situation in which "That confident hope of salvation, which is both enjoined by thy Word and founded upon it, had almost vanished. Indeed it was received as a kind of oracle; it was foolish arrogance, and, as they said, presumption, for any one to trust in thy goodness and the righteousness of thy Son, and entertain a sure and unfaltering hope of salvation."[38] In Calvin's teaching and preaching, the sudden acquisition of certain salvation—what Max Weber has referred to as the "powerful feeling of light-hearted assurance, in which the tremendous pressure of their sense of sin is released, apparently breaks over them with elemental force"[39]—would have likely been the experience of his previously Roman Catholic hearers as they came into the Protestant evangelical gospel, being taught for the first time that their justification was not dependent in any sense upon their sanctification, and that therefore assurance was more available than most of them had previously imagined. The simple perseverance in abstaining from Roman practices and attending Protestant worship became an act of and an evidence of true faith. With such polemic dominating "Calvin's whole development" of faith, according to Wendel, it is only natural that he should stress the primacy of the work of Christ.[40]

Even among those inwardly embracing the promises of God,[41]

---

[38] John Calvin, "Reply to Sadolet" [1539], trans. J. K. S. Reid, *Calvin: Theological Treatises*, (London, 1954), 247. "The Institutio was addressed to men suffering under the pastoral cruelty of the mediaeval church," (T. H. L. Parker, *John Calvin: A Biography*, [London, 1975], 36).

[39] Max Weber, The Protestant Ethic and the Spirit of Capitalism, trans. Talcott Parsons, (London, 1930), 101.

[40] Francois Wendel, *Calvin: Origins and Development of His Religious Thought*, trans. Philip Mariet, (London, 1963), 262.

[41] Calvin, *Institutes*, III.ii.16; cf. xxiv.4.

Calvin clearly spoke of "degrees of assurance" saying that they were "certainly well known in the faith."[42] Calvin encouraged his hearers, in order to get this "assurance of the kingdom of heaven," to look to the "pledge" which God had given believers "in the death and passion of our Lorde Jesus Christ."[43] "Christ . . . is the mirror wherein we must . . . contemplate our own election."[44] Yet Calvin also taught that though any assurance of salvation based on one's own righteousness was impossible,[45] "we do not forbid him from undergirding and strengthening this faith by signs of the divine benevolence toward him."[46] Believers should consider their "experience"[47] as a "confirmation of our fayth."[48] Though never saving, a righteous life was essential to "ratify"[49] the covenant God made with believers. Finally, realizing the problems of hypocrisy,[50] Calvin also stressed the need for the witness of the Holy Spirit as

---

[42] John Calvin, *Sermons on 2 Samuel*, trans. Douglas Kelly, (Edinburgh, 1992), 199-201; cf. John Calvin, "Catechism of the Church of Geneva," [1545], trans. Reid, 104.

[43] John Calvin, *The Sermons of M. John Calvin upon the Fifth Booke of Moses Called Deuteronomie*, trans. Arthur Golding, (London, 1583), 28.b.40; cf. 913.a.10; Calvin, *Institutes*, III.xxiv.5.

[44] Calvin, *Institutes*, III.xxiv.5; cf. III.xvii.10; III.xvi.1; Calvin, Deuteronomie, 532.a.10.

[45] Cf. Calvin, *Institutes*, III.xvii.5; cf. xiii.3; xiv.20.

[46] Calvin, *Institutes*, III.xiv.18; cf. 19-20; Galatians, 121. William K. B. Stoever has maintained that this is the basis for the practical syllogism in Calvin, (Stoever, '*A Faire and Easie Way to Heaven': Covenant Theology and Antinomianism in Early Massachusetts*, [Middletown, Connecticut, 1978], 223, n. 16).

[47] Calvin, *2 Samuel*, 201.

[48] Calvin, *Deuteronomie, 240.b.10;* Calvin, *Institutes*, III.viii.1; Cf. Calvin, *A Commentary on the Harmony of the Gospels*, trans. T. H. L. Parker, (Edinburgh, 1972), II.194.

[49] Calvin, *Deuteronomie*, 316.b.50; cf. 326.b.50; 554.b.50; 915.b.30-60; *Institutes*, III.vi.1; III.xvi.1; John Calvin, Commentaries on the Catholic Epistles, trans. John Owen, [Edinburgh, 1855], 376-378.

[50] Calvin, *Institutes*, III.xvii.5.

the "seale of our adoption."[51] Therefore

> every one of us must have an eie to himself, so as the gospel be not preached in vain nor we beare the bare name of Christians, without shewing the effect of it in our deedes. For until our adoption be sealed by the holy Ghost, let us not thinke that it availeth us any whit to have herd the word of God. . . . But when we have once a warrant in our hearts, that his promises belong unto us, & are behighted unto us, by reason that we receive them with true obedience, & sticke to our Lord Jesus Christ, suffering him to governe us: that is a sure seale of God's chosing of us, so as we not onely have the outwarde apparance of it before men, but also the truth of it before our God.[52]

So, Calvin taught that subjective assurance was distinct from saving faith, and came not through simply reflecting on one's own process of believing, but through looking to Christ as the sole basis of salvation, living a Christian life, and the direct witness of the Holy Spirit in the believer's heart.[53]

The English Reformers[54]

William Tyndale is often recognized as being at the head of the stream which culminated in the English Puritan divinity so well exemplified by the Westminster Assembly's statements. Tyndale, in his *Parable of the Wicked Mammon* (1527), early on maintained that after God's Spirit convicted the elect of sin, "Then, lest they should

---

[51] Calvin, *Deuteronomie*, 913.b.60; cf. 316.b.50-317.a.10, 915.a.60; Galatians, 121; Institutes, III.ii.24.

[52] Calvin, *Deuteronomie*, 440.a.30.

[53] Breward has mistakenly portrayed Calvin as only presenting looking to Christ (though through church, word and sacraments) as the avenue of assurance, (Breward, 45). Therefore, the later prominence of assurance among the puritans Breward portrays as coming from Perkins.

[54] For brief sketch of assurance in first century of English Protestantism, see Breward, *The Work of William Perkins*, pp. 93-99; and Lynn Baird Tipson, Jr., "The Development of a Puritan Understanding of Conversion," (Ph.D. dissertation, Yale University, 1972), pp. 76-78; also, specifically on Theodore Beza (pp. 118-121), John Bradford (pp. 139-142), Richard Greenham (pp. 180-183), Dudley Fenner, (pp. 187-188).

flee from God by desperation, he comforteth them again with his sweet promises in Christ; and certifieth their hearts that, for Christ's sake, they are received to mercy, and their sins forgiven, and they elect and made sons of God, and heirs with Christ of eternal life: and thus through faith are they set at peace with God."[55] Later in the same treatise, Tyndale referred to "the earnest of the Spirit" that testifies and bears witness "unto his heart that God hath chosen him, and that his grace shall suffice him. . . ."[56] And finally, as did Calvin, Tyndale also affirmed that the "fruit of the will of God" in the life of the believer "testifieth that God hath blessed us in Christ."[57]

In most of the writings of the English reformers, the doctrine of assurance had been important, primarily in anti-Roman apologetics.[58] In the Marian martyr John Bradford, faith and assurance seem to be at points identified,[59] and at other points

---

[55] William Tyndale, *Parable of the Wicked Mammon*, reprinted in *Doctrinal Treatises*, ed. Henry Walter, (Cambridge, 1848), p. 89. Kendall ignores this side of Tyndale, presenting him as basing assurance merely on obedience to the law (Kendall, *Calvin and English Calvinism*, pp. 42-43). It is due to this under-representation in his picture of Tyndale, that he then contrasts Tyndale and Bradford, (p. 44). In the differences Kendall presents between Tyndale, Bradford and Richard Greenham, he might have noticed that his quotations are taken largely from different sources for each, (respectively, polemical theology, personal writings, and sermons) which would go some way to explaining the different presentations of assurance and faith.

[56] Tyndale, *Wicked Mammon*, p. 101; cf. p. 113; Tyndale, *Exposition of the First Epistle of St. John* (1531) reprinted in *Expositions and Notes*, ed. Henry Walter, (Cambridge, 1849), pp. 186, 207.

[57] Tyndale, *Wicked Mammon*, p. 113; cf. Tyndale, *Exposition of First Epistle of St. John*, p. 207.

[58] E.g., "The Examinations of John Philpot," (1555) in *The Examinations and Writings of John Philpot*, ed. Robert Eden, (Cambridge, 1842), p. 140; cf. the examination of Mr. Careless in John Foxe, *Acts and Monuments*. It was still so in 1607 when the anti-Presbyterian, anti-Sabbatarian Thomas Rogers, chaplain to Archbishop Bancroft and Rector of Horninger, Suffolk, asserted that the "Papists" were in error when they held "that all and every man is to remain doubtful whether he shall be saved or no . . . ," (Thomas Rogers, *The Faith, Doctrine and religion, professed, & protected in the Realm of England*, [1607; rpt. Cambridge, 1854], p. 113).

distinguished.[60] To one female friend, Bradford wrote in 1554,

> I exhort you, my good sister, diligently to labour, as by continual reading and meditation of God's holy word, so by earnest prayer and other godly exercises to maintain and increase the same, that, by the feeling of God's gracious Spirit working in you such good fruits as witnesses of your faith, you may grow in strength thereof and certainty of God's good favour and good-will towards you. . . . Labour therefore for this certainty of faith through Christ: whensoever you doubt, you heap sin upon sin.[61]

It is particularly illuminating to note that in his public utterances Bradford seemed to unite both senses of assurance polemically, in order to clear the field of a Roman understanding of the gospel; however, in his private writings Bradford distinguished pastorally between assurance of Christ's sufficiency alone, and assurance of one's own apprehension of that.[62]

In 1561, Thomas Becon, former Chaplain to Cranmer, published a dialogue entitled "The Sick Man's Salve", in which at one point one participant, the sick man in question, asked from his bed, "What if I be not of the number of those whom God hath predestinate to be saved?"[63] His neighbour, Philemon, still in the first flush of Protestant certainty, responded by assuring him of his election on the basis of his evident repentance, earnest faith in the blood of Christ, baptism, coming with a fervent desire to the Lord's table,

---

[59] E.g., "Sermon on Repentance" in *The Writings of John Bradford*, ed. Aubrey Townsend, (1553; rpt.; Cambridge, 1848), pp. 76-77; "Against the Fear of Death," in *Writings*, p. 344.

[60] E.g., "Meditations" prefixed to Tyndale's New Testament, in *Writings*, p. 252; Letter to Robert Harrington and His Wife, in *The Writings of John Bradford*, ed. Aubrey Townsend, (Cambridge, 1853), pp. 116-117.

[61] Letter to Mary Honywood, *Writings* (1853), p. 132; cf. another pastoral letter to Mary Honywood on the topic of assurance, pp. 151-156.

[62] William Cunningham suggested a similar distinction, between polemics and personal experience, as an explanation of the inconsistencies found in the Reformers on assurance, (Cunningham, *Reformers*, p. 113).

[63] Thomas Becon, "The Sick Man's Salve" in *Prayers and Other Pieces of Thomas Becon*, ed. John Ayre, (Cambridge, 1844), p. 172.

his desire to pray and, supremely, his attendance of preaching, for "there is not a more certain sign that any man is predestinate to be saved, than when he hath a mind to hear the word of God. . . ."[64] Philemon then dismissed as "the doctrine of the papists, both wicked and damnable" the teaching that "no man in this world is certain of his salvation." In the same way, then as in Calvin, assurance was equated with saving faith, if the assurance in view was that Christ's righteousness alone was the only adequate basis for salvation.[65] The distinction in Becon is less clear, and would be clarified again as the church's pastoral experience of doubt in the midst of an assured gospel grew.

In what was perhaps the most celebrated Anglican/Roman controversy, John Jewel, Bishop of Salisbury, and Thomas Harding, of Louvain, exchanged almost a score of books and treatises between them during the first decade of the Elizabethan settlement.[66] In the final exchange between Harding and Jewel, Harding attacked the Protestants' "presumptuous doctrine of your certainty of grace and salvation."[67] Jewel responded by quoting Paul in Romans 8 and then Tertullian, Clement of Alexandria, Cyprian, Prosper of Aquitaine and even Antonius Marinarius, a Tridentine theologian, all affirming the real desirability and

---

[64] Becon, p. 174.

[65] Thomas Becon, "The Sick Man's Salve" in *Prayers and Other Pieces of Thomas Becon*, ed. John Ayre, (Cambridge, 1844), pp. 176-178. Cf. Becon, "The Actes of Christe and Antichrist," in *Prayers and Other Pieces of Thomas Becon*, p. 531.

[66] The intricacies of almost identical titles in various editions in this controversy (and others related) is ably made perspicuous in Peter Milward, *Religious Controversies of the Elizabethan Age: A Survey of Printed Sources*, (London, 1978), pp. 1-24.

[67] In John Jewel, *A Defense of the Apologie of the Church of England, Conteining an Answer to a certaine Booke lately set forth by M. Harding*, in *The Works of John Jewel* vol. III., ed. John Ayre (1570; rpt. Cambridge, 1848), p. 241.

possibility of the individual Christian's assurance of faith.[68] Jewel concluded with the riposte, "Certainly, M. Harding, it were a very presumptuous part to say that these fathers, Greeks, Latins, new, old, your own, and ours, were all presumptuous. . . . Thus, M. Harding, to be assured of our salvation, St. Augustine saith, it is no arrogant stoutness: it is our faith. It is no pride: it is devotion. It is no presumption: it is God's promise."[69]

The practiced polemicist William Fulke, Master of Pembroke College, Cambridge, evidently spent much of his time defending the faith against English Roman Catholic writers who were confused by the Protestant equivocation on assurance. Nicholas Sanders, an English Roman Catholic priest on the continent had published a defense of the papacy in English in 1567, in which he had asked the Protestants "Why then are you so presumptuous as even by faith to assure yourselves of your salvation?"[70] Fulke responded that "it is no presumption to assure ourselves that the promises of God are true. . . . As for the deep secrets of God's predestination, we take not upon us to know them, otherwise than they be revealed by His word."

Gregory Martin, an English Roman Catholic at Rheims had evidently also noticed such equivocal usage of "assurance" in the Protestant theologians, and following the Decree of Justification at Trent,[71] attacked them more clearly than Sanders had done, for

---

[68] Jewel, *A Defense of the Apologie*, in *Works of John Jewel* vol. III., p. 245.

[69] Jewel, *A Defense of the Apologie*, in *Works of John Jewel* vol. III., p. 245, 247.

[70] William Fulke, *A Discoverie of the Daungerous Rocke of the Popish Church*, in 1580 rpt; Stapelton's *Fortress Overthrown . . .*, ed. Richard Gibbings, [Cambridge, 1848], p. 229.

[71] See Decree on Justification, chapter IX, and canons XIII-XV. This lack of clarity seems endemic to almost all early Protestant statements perhaps, as has been suggested, by the desire to draw the contrast with the prevalent Roman doctrine. For example, note the language of the Augsburg Confession (Part I, Article IV) which, in 1530, spoke of those who are justified as being justified freely "for Christ's sake, through faith, when they believe that they are received into favor, and their sins forgiven for Christ's sake, who by his

saying that "If he be not by faith as sure of this [his election] as of Christ's incarnation, he shall never be saved." In his 1583 response to the then-deceased Martin, Fulke clearly asserted that all Christians should be certain that the Creed is true "being inwardly taught by the Spirit of truth, that he is the child of God, and consequently elect, and predestinate unto eternal salvation."[72] Yet while every Christian should know such certainty, Fulke specifically denied that such assurance of the truth of one's own interest in Christ was necessary to salvation. In fact, he said, perhaps overstating his case "that a man shall never be saved, except he have such certainty of this faith, as the truth of God's promises doth deserve, none of us doth teach, none of us doth think. Fore we know our own infirmity . . . nevertheless we acknowledge . . . that these things standing upon the immoveable pillars of God's promises . . . ought to be most certain unto us."[73]

William Perkins

The person most often cited as the turning point for theology between Calvin and Westminster is William Perkins. Perkins taught that assurance was the supreme case of conscience.[74] Though believers differed in the degree of

---

death hath satisfied for our sins. This faith doth God impute for righteousness before him." The point clearly was what they were believing, i.e., that they were "justified freely for Christ's sake through faith" and that "their sins [could only be] forgiven for Christ's sake, who by his death hath satisfied for our sins" and on no other basis. Unlike the Lutheran symbols, the Reformed confessions (e.g., Scottish Confession of Faith of 1560, Belgic Confession of 1563, Helvetic Confession of 1566) tended to avoid such ambiguity.

[72] William Fulke, *A Defense of the sincere and true Translations of the holie Scriptures into the English tong*, (1583 rpt; Cambridge, 1843), p. 415.

[73] Fulke, *A Defense*, pp. 415-416.

[74] William Perkins, *The Whole Treatise of the Cases of Conscience*, (Cambridge, 1606), 73-87.

assurance they enjoyed, he suggested that one could be sure by examining oneself to see if one's faith did "purifie thy heart, and cleanse thy life, and cause thee to abound in good workes."[75] Not that Perkins suggested that good works could save a person; they merely witnessed to the reality of saving faith.[76] Because, Perkins taught, election, vocation, faith, adoption, justification, sanctification and glorification, though partially sequential, "are never separated in the salvation of any man, but like inseparable companions, goe hand in hand,"[77] evidence of any one of them could serve as well for all the others. Furthermore, Perkins set forth the internal witness of the Spirit[78] (which comes usually "by the preaching, reading, and meditation of the word of God; as also by praier, and the right use of the Sacraments" and by the "effects and fruits of the Spirit"[79]) and the witness of the believer's sanctified spirit, or conscience (evidenced by grief for sin, resolution to repent, "savouring" the things of the Spirit, and appropriate works) as the two testimonies of adoption. Even if the fruit were small, Perkins encouraged his hearers to believe. It was like

> The man that is in close prison, if he sees but one little beame of the Sunne, by a small crevisse; by that very beame he hath use of the Sunne, though he seeth not the whole body of the Sunne. In like manner, though our faith, the hand of our soule, be mingled with weakness and corruption; though we feele never so little measure of God's grace in us; yea though our knowledge be never so small; yet it is an argument, that the Spirit of God beginnes to worke in our harts, and that we have by Gods mercie, begunne to lay hold on Christ.[80]

---

[75] William Perkins, *A Clowd of Faithful Witnesses, Leading to the heavenly Canaan: Or, A Commentarie upon the 11. Chapter to the Hebrewes, preached in Cambridge*, (n.l., 1609), 26.

[76] William Perkins, *A Commentarie, or, Exposition Upon the five first Chapters of the Epistle to the Galatians*, (Cambridge, 1617), 186, 502.

[77] Perkins, *Cases*, 74. So too, Calvin, *Institutes*, III.xvi.1.

[78] Cf. William Perkins, "The Foundation of Christian Religion Gathered into Six Principles", reprinted in Breward, 155-156, 158.

[79] Perkins, *Cases*, 76.

[80] Perkins, *Cases*, 347 (cf. 78).

Perry Miller and many following him since have used just this teaching in Perkins to suggest the striking contrast between Perkins and Calvin: "that the minutest, most microscopic element of faith in the soul is sufficient to be accounted the work of God's spirit. Man can start the labor of regeneration as soon as he begins to feel the merest desire to be saved. Instead of [Calvin's position of] conceiving of grace as some cataclysmic, soul-transforming experience, he [Perkins] whittles it down almost, but not quite, to the vanishing point."[81] Yet, compare Perkins' illustration cited here with the illustration Calvin used to make the same point:

> When first even the least drop of faith is instilled in our minds, we begin to comtemplate God's face, peaceful and calm and gracious toward us. . . . It is like a man who, shut up in a prison into which the sun's rays shine obliquely and half obscured through a rather narrow window, is indeed deprived of the full sight of the sun. Yet his eyes dwell on its steadfast brightness, and he receives its benefits. Thus, bound with the fetters of an earthly body, however much we are shadowed on every side with great darkness, we are nevertheless illumined as much as need be for firm assurance when, to show forth his mercy, the light of God sheds even a little of its radiance.[82]

Whatever architectonic differences there may have been between Perkins' presentation of theology and Calvin's, in the substance of their teaching on assurance, there was little difference. So Perkins exhorted his doubting hearers to "beginne with faith, and in the first place, simply beleeve Gods promises; and afterward we come, by the goodnes of God, to feele and have experience of his mercie."[83]

Jacobus Arminius

One of Perkins' theological opponents on matters of predestination and election was the Dutch theologian, and former

---

[81] Miller, "Marrow," 255.

[82] Calvin, *Institutes* III.ii.19.

[83] Perkins, *Cases*, 347.

student of Beza, Jacobus Arminius. In his "Declaration" given before the States of Holland at the Hague on 30 October, 1608, Arminius, like his other Reformed contemporaries affirmed the possibility of certainty and assurance for the individual believer, "that he is a Son of God, and stands in the grace of Jesus Christ."[84] He proceeded to develop the doctrine similarly to Perkins, suggesting that it was the work of the Holy Spirit and the believer's conscience.[85] In his third lecture given in the chair of divinity at the University of Leyden five years earlier, Arminius, disputing the Roman claim to the title of the true church, suggested to his hearers that certainty or assurance of truth could only come about by the primary work of the Holy Spirit, and, in this case, with the use of His Word as the instrument.[86] Similarly, in his Declaration, Ariminius went on to separate carefully the certainty of one's own salvation, from the certainty of God and that salvation is only possible in Christ, suggesting that the former can never be as certain as the latter. Both, however, he presented as fundamentally the work of the Spirit, and instrumentally, of the Word. One further consideration, however, vitiates any substantial similarity between Arminius' view of assurance, and the Reformed position, regardless of any methodological similarities. Arminius' lack of certainty about perseverance meant that any assurance of

---

[84] Jacobus Arminius, "A Declaration of the Sentiments of Arminius," in *The Works of James Arminius*, Vol. I, trans. by James Nichols, (London, 1825), p. 603.

[85] Cf., Jacobus Arminius, "Oration I: The Object of Theology," in *The Works of James Arminius*, Vol. I, trans. by James Nichols, (London, 1825), pp. 276-277; Jacobus Arminius, "Oration III: The Author and the End of Theology," in *The Works of James Arminius*, Vol. I, trans. by James Nichols, (London, 1825), p. 294; Jacobus Arminius, "Oration IV: The Priesthood of Christ," in *The Works of James Arminius*, Vol. I, trans. by James Nichols, (London, 1825), p. 362. Though there may be other misjudgments in the chapter, in his section on Arminius, R. T. Kendall has rightly noted the formal similarity between Arminius and his Reformed contemporaries, (Kendall, *Calvin and English Calvinism*, pp. 143-150).

faith the believer may have gained, however similarly to the way Perkins laid out, could not be taken as certainty of final salvation, but only as certainty that one was in the way of salvation.[87] Thus, for all its formal similarity, Arminius' position essentially was much closer to that of Rome, than of the Reformers.

Other Reformed Confessional Statements

A number of confessional statements on assurance were made during the years between Calvin's ministry in Geneva and the meeting of the Westminster Assembly. The Lambeth Articles of 1595 were composed by William Whitaker in the days before his death. The sixth of these articles, if read carefully, affirms basically that a justified man is capable of knowing as much (not that he necessarily will).[88] More clearly, James Ussher in the Irish Articles

---

[86] Jacobus Arminius, "Oration III: The Certainty of Sacred Theology," in *The Works of James Arminius*, Vol. I, trans. by James Nichols, (London, 1825), p. 336; cf. pp. 318-319.

[87] Jacobus Arminius, "A Declaration of the Sentiments of Arminius," in *The Works of James Arminius*, Vol. I, trans. by James Nichols, (London, 1825), pp. 600-603. Arminius, similarly to the Roman Catholics, asserted that, given the propensity of humans to hypocrisy, a doctrine of assurance combined with a doctrine of perseverance would naturally lead to "security", and, that implied, antinomianism. This was, in fact, criticism latent in the basic Roman objection to justification by faith alone. See Jacobus Arminius, "Certain Articles to be Diligently Examined and Weighed," in *The Works of James Arminius*, Vol. III, trans. by William Nichols, (London, 1875), p. 726. Cf. Francis White's objection to Thomas Morton's espousal of assurance of salvation at the York House Conference, recorded in "The Conference at York House," in *Works of the Right Reverend Father in God John Cosin*, vol. II, (Oxford, 1845), p. 58. Sibbes objected to this division, made by Arminius and some Lutherans, "what kind of assurance is it to be in the state of grace to-day, and not to be to-morrow?" (CSCO.III.468).

[88] "The Lambeth Articles", in Philip Schaff, ed., *The Creeds of Christendom with a History and Critical Notes*, vol. III (6th ed., New York, 1931), p. 524. Cf. Cunningham, *Reformers*, pp. 132-133. H. C. Porter has noted the role John Whitgift had in toning down Whitaker's language of certainty, (see Porter, *Reformation and Reaction in Tudor Cambridge*, [Cambridge, 1958], 335-336, 365-371).

of 1615 stated that "a true believer may be certain, by the assurance of faith, of the forgiveness of his sins, and of his everlasting salvation by Christ."[89] A few sentences later, Ussher allowed that this "true and lively faith" may be "discerned, as a tree by the fruit" by good works. The Canons of the Synod of Dort, composed in the heat of the controversy surrounding the deceased Arminius' teachings, specifically allowed for the regenerate to "sometimes lose the sense of God's favor, for a time" by sin.[90] Article IX, recognizing the different degrees of faith even in the regenerate, taught that true believers "may and do obtain assurance according to the measure of their faith" (cf. Article XI). Such assurance was to come from God's promises revealed in his Word, from the testimony of the Holy Spirit, and "lastly, from a serious and holy desire to preserve a good conscience, and to perform good works."

William Ames

William Ames, a disciple of Perkins, first published his celebrated *Medulla theologica* in Amsterdam in 1623 (first translated into English in 1638 as *The Marrow of Sacred Divinity*). In it, Ames admitted that faith "appear[ed] weaker in this or that person than the assent of knowledge" because of the inclination from which faith came.[91] Though he taught that "Justifying faith of its own nature produces and is marked by a special, sure persuasion of the grace and mercy of God in Christ,"[92] Ames

---

[89] "The Irish Articles of Religion", in Philip Schaff, ed., *The Creeds of Christendom with a History and Critical Notes*, vol. III (6th ed., New York, 1931), p. 534.

[90] Fifth Head, Article V, "Canons of the Synod of Dort", in Philip Schaff, ed., *The Creeds of Christendom with a History and Critical Notes*, vol. III (6th ed., New York, 1931), p. 593.

[91] William Ames, *The Marrow of Theology*, 3rd ed., trans. John Dykstra Eusden (1629; rpt. Durham, North Carolina, 1968), p. 81.

[92] Ames, *Marrow*, p. 163.

clearly distinguished between faith in God, and the "certain and absolute confidence of future good."[93] Following Perkins in talking of degrees of faith, Ames wrote that

> It may and often does happen, either through weakness of judgment or various temptations and troubles of mind, that a person who truly believes and is by faith justified before God may for a time think that he neither believes nor is reconciled to God. Second, there are many degrees in this persuasion. Believers obviously do not have the same assurance of grace and favor of God, nor do the same ones have it at all times. But this cannot be said of justifying faith itself, without considerable loss in the consolation and peace which Christ has left to believers.[94]

Ames then allowed for sure knowledge of truth ("mere assent"), saving faith based on the assurance of Christ's Word, and assurance that one had personally and graciously appropriated that second kind of knowledge—saving faith. The second kind of knowledge—saving faith—differed from the first kind—assent—by the necessary involvement of the will.[95] The final kind of assurance came from Christ[96] by the witness of the Spirit,[97] and was confirmed by "inward signs" (such as love of the brethren, zeal for holiness) which was evidenced in true repentance, good

---

[93] Ames, *Marrow*, p. 82; cf. p. 245; also, p. 83, where Ames stated that "experience teaches that particular certainty of the understanding may be lacking in some at times, even though they have true faith hidden in their hearts." And again, "assurance of salvation is not, properly speaking, justifying faith but a fruit of such faith," (Ames, *Marrow*, p. 167). For a typically careful discussion of despair see Ames, *Marrow*, p. 249.

[94] Ames, *Marrow*, p. 163.

[95] For Ames' change from Calvin and Perkins, by championing the centrality of the will, see John Dykstra Eusden's "Introduction" to Ames' *The Marrow of Theology*, pp. 47-51 (yet, see Calvin, *Institutes*, III.ii.8); cf. Von Rohr, *Covenant of Grace*, p. 65.

[96] Ames, *Marrow*, p. 148. Kendall under-emphasizes this aspect of Ames' theology, (Kendall, *Calvin and English Calvinism*, pp. 151-164).

[97] Ames, *Marrow*, p. 167.

works and a good conscience.[98] Contrary to his Roman and Arminian opponents, Ames did not see hope and fear as antithetical virtues in the Christian experience because "the orientation is not the same: Hope looks to the grace of God and fear looks to the just merit of our sins."[99] The final kind of assurance—that of one's own salvation—was to be sought, whatever degree of faith the believer might presently have.[100]

Richard Sibbes

Richard Sibbes (Master of St. Catharine's College, Cambridge, and Preacher of Gray's Inn, London) presented assurance as a secondary act of faith, not given to all Christians, but available depending upon the will of God and the actions of the believer.[101] Since it was possible for true Christians to doubt their salvation, and for hypocrites to delude themselves, assurance of salvation was necessarily to be sought. Theologically, the assurance sought by Sibbes was typical of Protestants. It was not, as Roman polemicists necessarily saw it, a prediction, so much as a diagnosis. The matter which was uncertain in Sibbes' discussions of assurance was not salvation itself, as Trent had said must necessarily be the case, but rather merely the perception of it. While Sibbes and his friends did clearly teach (as had their Reformed predecessors, including Calvin) that "good works" were confirming of salvation, they did not teach that such works were either present or obvious at all times to the elect, or that they were present only in the elect. Sibbes affirmed what might well be called the Reformed tripartite basis of assurance—the

---

[98] Ames, *Marrow*, pp. 248, 223-224.

[99] Ames, *Marrow*, pp. 249.

[100] William Ames, *An Analytical Exposition of both the Epistles of the Apostle Peter*, (London, 1641), pp. 162-163.

[101] See Stoever, 129-137.

consideration of the objective work of Christ, the inner testimony of the Spirit, and the answering works of the regenerated life.[102]

Remembering the different concerns (polemical and pastoral) being addressed in Bradford and others above, it should be noted that Sibbes' public works were primarily pastoral, and were polemical only in a secondary sense, as were all sermons of the time. Given this, it is not surprising that there should be ambiguity in many of Sibbes' exhortations to assurance. With pastoral issues in the fore, it was not always clear whether his hearers were being exhorted to conversion, or to assurance that they had been converted.[103] Yet such ambiguity is to be expected in sermons to a covenanted community which would be composed largely of two sorts of people: those who had been either committed by others, but not self-consciously converted by God (who must be exhorted to trust God themselves); and those who have experienced self-conscious conversion, but yet doubt. To both groups within the covenant, Sibbes urged the same action. Since faith is the gracious gift of God based on the work of Christ, and since faith comes by hearing the Word of God with the working of the Spirit, and since faith was strengthened by the sacrament of the table and by exercises—since faith was and came by and was strengthened by all this, Sibbes taught as the Westminster Confession would teach, and as Reformed Protestants before him taught, that assurance had essentially three bases. Sibbes, citing I John 5:7-8, exhorted his hearers to look to these three bases for assurance: the "sweet motions of the Spirit", sanctification, and, the one place where Sibbes said "there was always comfort"—"the blood of Christ."[104]

---

[102]Cf. Heinrich Heppe, *Reformed Dogmatics Set Out and Illustrated from the Sources*, trans. G. T. Thomson, (London, 1950), 585-589.

[103]Sibbes, *Works* I.415-417; VI.353-4; VII.187; VI.8; II.264.

[104]Sibbes, *Works* III.464; cf. WS.VII.376-377; John Downame, *The Christian Warfare*, (London, 1608), 231, 277-278; similar passage in Theodore Beza, *A Brief and Pithy Sum of the Christian Faith*, trans. Robert Fyll, (London, 1585), 71-72.

Consistent with his pastoral setting, Sibbes particularly focused on the continuing reality of doubt in the believer's life. Though this element is present in all of those mentioned above, it is more prominent in pastoral writings than in polemical writings, and similarly, but not identically, is more clearly defined over time. The life of the believer is, Sibbes stressed, always evidence of his spiritual state, but not always discernable. At times of particular need, the Spirit witnessed internally to the troubled believer. Yet, throughout his preaching, Sibbes was always clear that the objective work of Christ was the sole basis, not merely of salvation in abstraction, but of one's own participation in it.

John Preston

John Preston, too, clearly taught "degrees in faith" along with the duty to attain full assurance.[105] In a sermon on faith, he exhorted his hearers to "labour to get full assurance; the more assurance you have, the more love . . . you shall doe the more work when once you are assured that your labour shall not be in vaine in the Lord. . . ."[106] Thomas Goodwin later remembered

---

[105] John Preston, *The Breast-Plate of Faith and Love*, (London, 1630), I.110. Preston's words on the necessity of assurance in his second sermon on effectual faith (particularly I.164) could easily be taken to imply that assurance was a part of conversion, but this would be to mistake his words. His point is simply that the Holy Spirit must work saving faith in the heart of a believer.

[106] John Preston, *The Breast-Plate of Faith and Love*, (London, 1630), I.110; cf. I.242; cf. III.146-147. Perry Miller has mis-represented Preston's idea of evidences of assurance as essentially prices to be paid for salvation, ("The Marrow of Puritan Divinity," p. 271). Again, this is fundamentally related to his misunderstanding the covenant as an essentially bi-lateral agreement, while "the horrified ghost of Calvin shuddered to behold his theology twisted into this spiritual commercialism," (Miller, *The New England Mind: The Seventeenth Century*, p. 389). This is typical of the way Miller treated the Puritan doctrine of assurance throughout *The New England Mind: The Seventeenth Century*, pp. 49-53, 55, 370-371, 385-390 (p. 387 has something of a qualification of this, but is still so incomplete as to be mis-leading,

Preston as someone who spent his thoughts and breath "in unfolding and applying, the most proper and peculiar Characters of Grace, which is Gods Image; whereby Beleevers came to be assured, that God is their God, and they in covenant with him."[107] As faith initially came, Preston taught that assurance came by the Holy Spirit through hearing the Word (though one could hear the Word without experiencing the heart-work of the Holy Spirit).[108] To those within the covenant, Preston also said that "you may much more easily and fully come to this assurance, because yee have the fruits of the Spirit in you, which are the seales of his love," and, when particularly mindful of one's sins

---

particularly in context); cf. Kendall, *Calvin and English Calvinism*, p. 208; M. Charles Bell, *Calvin and Scottish Theology: The Doctrine of Assurance*, (Edinburgh, 1985), pp. 7-11. Yet note the essential unilateral basis and certainty of the covenant which Preston presented in *Breast-Plate*, I.38-39. A helpful correction to Miller's distortion has been presented by John von Rohr, "Covenant and Assurance in Early English Puritanism," *Church History* 34 (1965) 195-203. An even more thorough correction of Miller was George Marsden, "Perry Miller's Rehabilitation of the Puritans: A Critique", *Church History* 39 (1970), pp. 91-105. One of Marsden's closing statements has, unfortunately, been born out: "As for the thesis that the covenant of grace represented a revision of Calvinism, Miller has created a myth that has been so elegantly presented and widely repeated that it will be difficult to destroy," (p. 105). See, too, Tipson's conclusion that "Miller misrepresented Calvin's position, over-emphasized the difference between Calvin and the Puritans, and placed far too much emphasis on the use of the covenant in conversion," (Tipson, "Conversion," pp. 232-233). George Selement has particularly criticized Miller's selective use of sources, ("Perry Miller: A Note on His Sources in *The New England Mind: The Seventeenth Century*," William and Mary Quarterly, 3rd series, vol. XXXI, no. 3 [July, 1974], 453-464). See too, Richard A. Muller, "Covenant and Conscience in English Reformed Theology: Three Variations on a 17th Century Theme" *Westminster Theological Journal* 42 (1980) pp. 308-334; Michael McGiffert, "Grace and Works: The Rise and Division of Covenant Divinity in Elizabethan Puritanism." *Harvard Theological Review* 75 (1982), pp. 463-505. John von Rohr revised and expanded his criticisms in *The Covenant of Grace in Puritan Thought*, (Atlanta, 1986), pp. 17-22, 30-33.

[107]Thomas Goodwin, "To the Reader," in John Preston, *Life Eternall; or a . . . Treatise . . . of the Divine . . . Attributes*, (London, 1631).

to regard the sincerity of one's heart.[109] The uses of such assurance he said were primarily two. First, that comfort could be taken from any amount of true faith: "It is true, when a man is within the doore, there are greater degrees, he may goe farther into the house, or a little way in, but all is well when he is in once. . . : and therefore cast not away your hope, but labour to know, that though you be but as smoaking flax, yet there is fire there, as well as if it were all on a flame."[110] And the second use that Preston drew out was the desirability of growth in faith, filled out with many advantages to that.[111]

William Gouge

William Gouge, member of the Westminster Assembly and frequent moderator during William Twisse's absences from the chair, in his sermons on Hebrews preached at St. Anne's

---

[108]Preston, *Breast-Plate*, I.164-165.

[109]Preston, *Breast-Plate*, III.145-147.

[110]John Preston, *The Breast-Plate of Faith and Love,* (London, 1630), I.110, 112. Cf. ". . . we [ministers] are to doe as the Shepheards doe there with their Flocks, some Sheepe are weake, and are not able to goe the pace of the rest; some are broken, some are lost, and some are gone astray, and some are great with young: our businesse is to seeke those that are lost, to drive on according to the pace of the weakest, to bind up the broken, to carrie them in our armes: thus Christ did, and if we faile in this, Christ, who is the great Shepheard of the flock, he sees it; if we goe astray, he fetches us in; if we be broken, and have lost our wooll, and be not in right order, he binds us up, he feeds us, and tenders us; thus Christ dealeas with you. And therefore be not discouraged, though thou be not so strong as the strongest, yet if thou be a Sheepe, if thou be in the fold, if thou hast the least degree of faith, it is able to make thee partaker of this righteousnesse, although thou have not the highest degree, though thou have not that excellencie that others have," (I.113).

[111]Preston, *Breast-Plate*, I.113-114. Cf. Fifth Head, Articles XII, XIII, "Canons of the Synod of Dort", in Philip Schaff, ed., *The Creeds of Christendom with a History and Critical Notes*, vol. III (6th ed., New York, 1931), p. 595.

Blackfriar's, London, referred to the assurance of salvation as the death of Christ, and to the seal of salvation as the Holy Spirit and the believer's own faith and hope.[112] God's children are marked by confidence in professing Christ and his gospel, in approaching God and calling him Father, and by perseverance. Lack of any of these things, Gouge suggested, was cause to doubt one's salvation. This was not to suggest that all true Christians always experienced assurance. "I will not deny but that believers, by reason of the mixture of the flesh with the spirit in them, have many times occasions of fear, grief and perplexity; yet not such as depriveth them of the rejoicing here intended." "From the flesh cometh doubting, wavering, and all manner of weakness, Mat. xxvi.41. But as the spirit getteth strength, and prevaileth over the flesh, so will this doubting and wavering be more and more dispelled, and assurance more and more increased."[113] Such sorrow of the godly, Gouge taught, led to repentance. Assurance of salvation was an encouragement to the individual, but should never be used as an excuse for carnal security.[114]

Gouge said that the believer in order to gain assurance was to "acquaint ourselves with all the evidence's of God's favour that we can, and meditate on his promises, and duly weight his properties, as his free grace, rich mercy, almighty power, infallible truth, everywhere present, with the like. Let us go out of ourselves, and behold him inviting all to come to him, and accepting all that come."[115] Again,

> If we think assurance of hope worth the having, let us do to the utmost
> what God enableth us to do for attaining thereunto. Let us acquaint

---

[112] William Gouge, *Commentary on Hebrews*, (London, 1655), i.161; cf. iii.62. In iii.66 Gouge specifically denied the "papist" error that hope necessarily implied uncertainty.

[113] Gouge, *Hebrews*, vi.80.

[114] Gouge, *Hebrews*, vi.75.

[115] Gouge, *Hebrews*, iii.61.

ourselves with the grounds of hope, God's promises and properties, and frequently and seriously meditate thereon. Let us conscionably attend God's ordinances, and earnestly pray that God would add his blessing to our endeavour. We are of ourselves backward, dull, and slow to believe and hope; we are much prone to doubting. In these respects we ought to use the more diligence, and to quicken up our spirits unto this full assurance, and not cease till we have attained some evidence thereof.[116]

Assurance then, for Gouge, was a duty, and a privilege.[117]

The Westminster Standards

Though the topic of this article is, in part, the Westminster Standards, their statements on assurance need occupy little space. Only the relation of this teaching to the earlier Reformed tradition has stirred controversy. The substance of their teaching is clear and concise. In many ways, the Assembly's teaching acts as a fine summary to the Reformed doctrine of assurance in the previous century.[118] Instructed by long experience of anti-Roman polemics and pastoral ministry, the Assembly produced a balanced statement protecting against hypocrisy on the one hand, and an uncritical identification of saving faith with assurance on the other. Questions 80 and 81 of the Larger Catechism affirmed the possibility and even normalcy of assurance, while also admitting the reality of doubt (though never utter despair) among true believers. In the Confession, Chapter XX dealt with assurance. It contained four articles. In the first, the possibility of assurance was set forth, though clearly distinguished from the vain deceits

---

[116]Gouge, *Hebrews*, vi.80.

[117]Gouge, *Hebrews*, x.131.

[118]This statement is in contrast to William Cunningham's reading of saving faith in Calvin, as including assurance, which therefore leads him to see Perkins, and finally the Westminster Assembly as espousing in specifics, if not generally, a different understanding of faith and assurance, (Cunningham, *Reformers*, pp. 123-125).

of hypocrites. In the second, the foundation of this assurance was said to be the "divine truth of the promises of salvation" and the inward evidence "the testimony of the Spirit of adoption witnessing with our spirits that we are the children of God." In the third, this assurance was distinguished from the "essence of faith", and yet, since it was attainable, "it is the duty of everyone to give all diligence to make his calling and election sure; that thereby his heart may be enlarged in peace and joy in the Holy Ghost, in love and thankfulness to God, and in strength and cheerfulness in the duties of obedience, the proper fruits of assurance: so far is it from inclining men to looseness." And, in the final article, the shaking, diminishing and intermitting of assurance in the experience of believers was clearly allowed.

Conclusion

In this century, an interesting confluence of historical and theological studies have suggested that the puritans undermined reformed theology. Both drawing on earlier observations, but apparently independently of each other, in the middle of this century Perry Miller and Karl Barth suggested that this undermining had, in fact, occurred. Though the two men and their concerns could hardly have been more different—Miller, a confidently atheistic American historian, Barth, a devout Swiss Reformed theologian—both came to strikingly similar conclusions about the effects of covenant theology on Reformed thought, albeit for different reasons. Miller's optimistic rationalism clearly left him puzzled by the Reformed roots of his own New England. Looking back at Calvin, and disliking what he took to be the irrationalism he saw, Miller observed a growing reliance on and confidence in reason in Calvin's later heirs, particularly among the covenant theologians. Barth, on the other hand, as an unabashed champion of Calvin, saw in the more explicit covenant formulations which followed a creeping anthropocentrism which obscured grace. Though Miller in particular has influenced later theological interpretations of seventeenth-century puritanism, and many following him, it was the even more powerful combination of these concerns by church historians such as Basil Hall and J. B. Torrance which gave them particular weight with other historians who were ready to cede all knowledge of things theological to experts trained in that field.

The most influential recent study to reinvigorate debate on this issue is Kendall's *Calvin and English Calvinism to 1649*. Though Kendall's work has been mentioned repeatedly in the footnotes of this study, it should be noted here that Kendall's work, though widely quoted as theologically authoritative by recent historians of the period, is flawed by factual, interpretive and methodological errors. If one of the advantages of large studies like Miller's and Kendall's is that they can be enormously helpful in digesting, summarizing and organizing information, one of the disadvantages conversely is the potential for consequent ignorance of particulars and slighting of specifics. For example, factually, Kendall was incorrect in dating Richard Sibbes' birth and admission to St. John's, in accepting his deprivations, and in suggesting that Sibbes' sermons "do not delve into ecclesiology at all."[119] His interpretation of Calvin and the subsequent Reformed tradition on assurance has been questioned above. Finally, by simple constraints of space and time, such a sweeping synthetic study as Kendall undertook is easily flawed in its methodology. To extract figures from different eras and situations in order to compare their views is a task as difficult to do well as it is needful. That it can be done and done well, this author has no doubt. Yet Kendall's scant attention to the historical setting would seem to have rendered Kendall's study less helpful than it appears. It becomes, in fact, misleading, as Calvin's statements uttered in

---

[119]Kendall, 103.

the context of polemic against the form of Christianity all around him and ever-beckoning to the inhabitants of Geneva, are put "in conversation" as it were, with statements made by English preachers fifty and one hundred years later in a national Protestant church. The hermeneutics involved in getting the two situations to "speak" to one another do not present insuperable barriers; yet they have not been overcome in Kendall's work. Though this present study is in no way as sweeping a work as Kendall's it does at least raise a serious question against historians' ready acceptance of his work, and of the ever-popular "Calvin against the Calvinists" theme, at least in so far as it has been built upon the assumption of the fundamental incompatibility of covenant and Reformed theology as seen in the teaching of the Westminster divines on assurance.

For followers of Jesus Christ around the world who have never heard of the Westminster Assembly and its products, nor even of John Calvin, the assurance of salvation is a matter of the utmost importance. In this matter, the Westminster divines well summarized the teaching of Scripture, as did John Calvin before them.

Revision of the Westminster Confession (Declaratory Act of 1892)

J. L. MACLEOD

1. Introduction

When the Free Church of Scotland was founded as a result of the Disruption of 1843, Dr. Buchanan told that historic first Free Church General Assembly in Edinburgh that although they had separated from the Church of Scotland,

> We do not separate from the Confession of Faith, which we do truthfully and assuredly regard as the sound and scriptural exposition of the word of God.[1]

Fifty years later, another Free Church of Scotland minister could say that "The truth in the Confession of Faith we receive as the truth of God's Word" and he could in the same speech remark that the Westminster Confession of Faith was "one of the bulwarks of our beloved Free Church."[2] If the Free Church of Scotland stood for anything, it seemed, it stood for undiluted adherence to

---

[1] *Proceedings and Debates of the General Assembly of the Free Church of Scotland* (hereafter *PDGAFC*), 1843, 26, 27.

[2] *The Free Church Declaratory Act. A Criticism and Protest. Being the Speeches Delivered at a Public Meeting Held in Glasgow On Thursday, 18th February, 1892* (Glasgow, 1892), 3. The Disruption Father Robert Candlish said, in a lecture at New College, Edinburgh, in March, 1864, "By

the Westminster Standards. And yet the remarkable fact is that in 1892 the Free Church overwhelmingly passed a Declaratory Act which in several important ways qualified the operation of the Westminster Confession of Faith, and which provoked the biggest secession in a Scottish church since the Disruption. How this came about is the subject of this chapter.

2. The Free Church of Scotland, 1843-1893

What seemed so extraordinary, viewed from the standpoint of 1843, was that the Free Church of Scotland had decided to qualify the Westminster Confession of Faith at all. At the time of the Disruption of 1843, the Free Church which it had produced was recognized throughout the world as a bastion of Reformed, "Orthodox" Calvinism.[3] The Free Church of men like Thomas Chalmers, Robert Candlish and William Cunningham had rejoiced in the title of a "champion of orthodoxy"[4] and basically stood foursquare by the Westminster Confession of Faith. The Free Church of 1843 seemed to hold the Westminster Confession aloft as a banner—symbolic of, if not as important as, "Christ's Crown and Covenants".

---

all means, let them (the Westminster Standards) stand untouched, as monuments of the vast erudition and mental power of other days, and as safeguards of truth and bulwarks against error for ages yet to come." (R. S. Candlish, *The Fatherhood of God. Being the First Course of the Cunningham Lectures Delivered Before the New College, Edinburgh, in March 1864* (Edinburgh, 2nd edition, 1865), 285).

[3] There were, for example, French and Dutch delegates present at the first General Assembly of the Free Church in 1843. The English Baptist preacher C. H. Spurgeon spoke in 1882 of "the high reputation that the Free Church has hitherto held among the evangelical churches of Christendom." ("Mr. Spurgeon on Professor Bruce", *The Signal*, September 1882, 11).

[4] eg "The Coming Struggle in the Free Church Assembly and its Issues", *The Signal*, May 1883, 66, which bemoaned the damage which the case of William Robertson Smith had done to "the good name of the Free Church, as a champion of orthodoxy."

Revision of the Westminster Confession
(Declaratory Act of 1892)

There were, however, even in 1843, signs on the horizon that all was not rosy for the traditional interpretation of Calvinism within the Free Church. The world in which the Free Church of Scotland had cast its lot was a world of almost unprecedented change. As Professor Marcus Dods of New College, Edinburgh, observed in 1889, "Every department of human thought and activity has felt the touch of the new influences".[5] The Free Church prided itself on being what Richard Riesen has called "as well-educated a church as any in history, laity as well as clergy",[6] and Free Church laymen held prominent places in a wide range of disciplines. This meant that the Church could not wrap itself in the cloak of the Westminster Confession and shelter itself from the changes in society and in academic thought. Even the most conservative of Free Churchmen could hardly turn his back and ignore the changing world; and many issues, while notionally unrelated to ecclesiastical affairs, came to have a considerable effect on churchmen. In a modern, changing world, the Free Church of Scotland felt that it in turn had to be a modern, changing church. As will be seen, the Free Church was aware that Confessional revision was something which was taking place all over the world, and was in many ways a movement whose "time had come"; a movement which reflected the changes of the modern world.

But more than that, the Free Church of Scotland was a denomination which by the 1890s was irreconcilably divided, and it is even possible to argue that in some ways a schism in the Free Church was inevitable. There were many areas of conflict, but it can perhaps best be summarized as a confrontation between

---

[5] M. Dods, *Recent Progress in Theology. Inaugural Lecture at New College Edinburgh, 1889* (Edinburgh, 1889), 6.

[6] R. A. Riesen, *Criticism and Faith in Late Victorian Scotland. A. B. Davidson, William Robertson Smith and George Adam Smith* (Lanham, MD, 1985), 221.

the new and the old, between a liberal approach to theology and a conservative one. Nowhere was this more clear than in the disputes over the authority and status of Scripture which ruptured the denomination in the nineteenth century. While some in the Church accepted the most advanced conclusions of Biblical Criticism and of Darwinian Science, men like Marcus Dods, A. B. Davidson, Henry Drummond and, most famously of all, William Robertson Smith there were others who were bitterly opposed to what they characterized as the "poison" of criticism and evolutionary science. The conservatives fought as hard as they could but the tide was against them and ultimately it was to be a losing battle. Revision of the Westminster Confession, it is clear, needs to be seen in the context of a time when almost every accepted religious theory was being tested in what Marcus Dods described as the "crucible" of criticism. Men were being confronted with what the biographer of A.B. Davidson called "the riddles to which the spirit of a new age was demanding a solution from every thinking man".[7] Crucially, the Free Church did not make a unified response to these developments, and indeed the different responses produced a lasting bitterness which ultimately contributed to the fragmentation of the Free Church.

Furthermore the Free Church of Scotland was geographically divided. The Church had congregations in both the northern Highlands of Scotland and in the southern Lowland part of the country; between the two regions there was, to coin a phrase, a "great gulf fixed". The two regions had different cultures, different traditions, different histories, different languages and completely different attitudes to religion. On the whole, the Highlanders in the Free Church tended to hold very conservative and traditional attitudes to Scripture, to the Confession, to church government,

---

[7] J. Strahan, *Andrew Bruce Davidson* (London, 1917), 102; Dods, *Recent Progress*, 9-11.

to doctrine and to church practice; generally-speaking, the opposite was the case in the Lowlands. On issues such as Biblical Criticism, the theory of evolution, the exclusive use of psalms in public worship and, crucially, confessional revision, the Highlanders and the Lowlanders within the Free Church usually found themselves on opposite sides of the fence; the day was coming when that fence was going to grow large enough to separate the Free Church into two distinct denominations.[8] But although the Declaratory Act of 1892 is a reflection of a divided denomination, it was also very much the product of the times, and it is to this wider background that we now turn.

3. Confessional Revision in Other Denominations— "The Advancing Tide"

A. C. Cheyne has styled the years between around 1860 and around 1910 as the time of "the Great Confessional Controversy"[9] and even a cursory examination of the available literature testifies to the accuracy of this title. B. B. Warfield wrote in 1889,

> The last few years have been marked, throughout the Presbyterian world, by a widespread agitation regarding the relation of the churches to the Westminster Standards, which has seemed to culminate during the ecclesiastical year which has just closed.[10]

Around 1890, Charles Briggs, Professor of Hebrew and Cognate Languages at Union Theological Seminary, New York,

---

[8] J. L. MacLeod, "The Origins of the Free Presbyterian Church of Scotland" (PhD, University of Edinburgh, 1993); see also J. L MacLeod, "The Influence of the Highland-Lowland Divide on the Free Presbyterian Disruption of 1893", forthcoming in *Records of the Scottish Church History Society* vol XXV (1995).

[9] A.C. Cheyne, "The Place of the Confession through Three Centuries" in A.I.C. Heron (ed), *The Westminster Confession in the Church Today* (Edinburgh, 1982), 125.

[10] B.B. Warfield, "The Presbyterian Churches and the Westminster Confession", *The Presbyterian Review*, vol X, no 40 (October, 1889), 646.

and co-editor with Warfield of the *Presbyterian Review*,[11] described the revision of the Westminster Confession as,

> a product of the evolution of Christian thought in our century. It is the swell on the wave of the advancing tide of Christianity . . . It was but a spark last April . . . and now the whole church is ablaze . . . We are in the beginnings of a theological reformation that can no more be resisted than the flow of a great river.[12]

Revision became the norm, and what was seen as the "harsh" Calvinism expressed in the Westminster Confession was under attack the world over.

In Australia, for example, the case of Charles Strong divided the Presbytery of Melbourne, Victoria; among other things, Strong was accused of failing to "assert, maintain and defend the doctrines of the Confession" and he was ultimately expelled from the church

---

[11] Charles Augustus Briggs was one of the leaders of the revisionist movement in the United States and was involved in a vigourous debate with his more conservative compatriots Archibald Alexander Hodge and Benjamin Breckinridge Warfield (both of whom edited the *Presbyterian Review* with Briggs). The debate produced a multitude of interesting publications, including C.A. Briggs, *Whither? A Theological Question for the Times* (New York, 1889); Briggs (ed), *How Shall We Revise? A Bundle of Papers* (New York, 1890); B.B. Warfield, "The Presbyterian Churches and the Westminster Confession", *The Presbyterian Review*, October 1889; and Warfield, *Ought the Confession to be Revised?* (New York, 1890). Another great Union scholar who became involved was Philip Schaff, the Professor of Church History at Union. He was said to be "overjoyed" when the General Assembly of the Presbyterian Church in the United States seemed set to revise the Westminster Confession in 1889, and was "gravely disappointed that the revision was not adopted in his lifetime." (G.H. Shriver, *Philip Schaff: Christian Scholar and Ecumenical Prophet* (Macon, Georgia, 1987), 87, 88). He wrote several articles on the subject, as well as an influential book: *Creed Revision in the Presbyterian Church* (New York, 1890).

[12] C. Briggs, "The Advance Towards Revision" in Briggs (ed), *How Shall We Revise?*, 1-2. The article was based on an address before the Presbyterian Union of New York in December, 1899. By 1893, Briggs had been tried for heresy and on June 1st he was formally suspended by the General Assembly of the American Presbyterian Church. He was eventually defrocked. See, eg, *British Weekly*, June 15th, 1893, 115 and Shriver, *Philip Schaff*, 88-93.

in 1883.[13] A draft Declaratory Act, qualifying the Westminster Confession, soon followed however, and after consideration by the Presbyterian Church of Victoria in 1882, it was incorporated into the "Basis of Union" which united the Presbyterian churches of Australia in July, 1901.[14] In line with other declaratory statements, this "allowed liberty of conscience in those matters which did not enter into the substance of the faith, and gave the Assembly the right to determine what these matters could be in any given case."[15] Some Free Church of Scotland conservatives, incidentally, much preferred it to their own Declaratory Act; Kenneth Moody-Stuart described it as an Act "which would relieve weak conscience, but would exclude those who held really heretical doctrine."[16] In New Zealand, too, there were passed Declaratory Acts very similar to those in Scotland in order that "difficulties and scruples felt by not a few in signing the Confession of Faith would be removed."[17]

---

[13] R. S. Ward, *The Bush Still Burns. The Presbyterian and Reformed Faith in Australia 1788-1988* (Brunswick, 1989), 250- 269.

[14] *Ibid*, 276-282. The Free Church was well aware of this development, and the Victorian Church's Act appeared in full in an appendix to the Report of the Committee on the Confession of Faith. "Declaratory Act of the Presbyterian Church of Victoria, Approved by the Victorian General Assembly in November 1882", *PDGAFC*, 1890, Report XLII, Appendix III, 24-25. The Report is a valuable gathering of materials concerning Creeds and Creed Subscription from around the world.

[15] G.S.S. Yule, "The Westminster Confession in Australia", in Heron, *Westminster Confession in the Church Today*, 102.

[16] Moody-Stuart, in *The Free Church Declaratory Act and Proposed Alterations to the Questions and Formula. Report of discussions in the Free Presbytery of Lockerbie* (Glasgow, 1893), 9. On another occasion he said, "a Declaratory Act is simply an Act explanatory . . . the Australian Church of Victoria conformed exactly to this ideal." (K. Moody-Stuart, *The New Declaratory Act and Proposed New Formula of the Free Church of Scotland. A Lecture Delivered in Hope Street Free Church, Glasgow, on 28th February, 1893* (Moffat, 1893), 4).

[17] J.Dickson, *History of the Presbyterian Church of New Zealand* (Dunedin, 1899), 296. See also J. R. Elder, *The History of the Presbyterian Church of*

The Presbyterian Church in Canada also found itself having to confront the issue of whether the Westminster Confession was a suitable creed for the late nineteenth century. The case of Daniel James Macdonnell in the mid 1870s which almost split the newly-united Canadian Church, and that of Professor John Campbell in the 1890s, indicated that the traditional view of the Confession was changing. Macdonnell accused some members of the Church of treating the Confession "not as a subordinate standard but as superior to the Scripture itself"; Campbell described sections of the Confession as "exhibiting utter ignorance of biblical criticism and (being) itself unscriptural."[18] Both men were largely vindicated in their trials, and although the Confession was not modified in Canada at this time by an actual Declaratory Act, the attitude towards it had clearly changed to such an extent that a de facto modification had taken place.

In Scotland, the United Presbyterians had set what was at the very least a Scottish precedent of Confessional revision with their Declaratory Act of 1879,[19] although it should be said that the previous year's acquittal of the Revd Fergus Ferguson on charges of holding erroneous doctrines had indicated that the United Presbyterian Church was moving away from a strict adherence to the Calvinism of Westminster.[20] Formal moves began at the

---

New Zealand 1840-1940 (Christchurch, 1940), 169-170; and I. Breward, "The Westminster Standards in New Zealand", in A. I. C. Heron, *The Westminster Confession in the Church Today* (Edinburgh, 1982), 104.

[18] McNeil, *Presbyterian Church in Canada*, 204-210.

[19] Some observers went even further. B. B. Warfield, for example, attributed the "formal beginnings" of the worldwide agitation over Confessional Revision "to the movement which issued in the adoption by the Scottish United Presbyterian Church, in 1879, of a Declaratory Act . . ." (Warfield, "The Presbyterian Churches and the Westminster Confession", 646).

[20] I. Hamilton, *The Erosion of Calvinist Orthodoxy. Seceders and Subscription in Scottish Presbyterianism* (Edinburgh, 1990), 188; "The trials of Fergus Ferguson, and the subsequent toleration of his views all but signalled the final stage in the erosion of Westminster Calvinism within the United Presbyterian Church." (*Ibid*, 145).

Synod of 1877, when a number of overtures were tabled "anent the Revisal of the Subordinate Standards" and the Synod concluded that it should appoint "a Committee to consider the whole subject". [21] The middle course between the "conservative party, favouring no change" and the "progressive or aggressive wing which favoured a shortening and simplification of the Confession of Faith" was to frame a declaratory statement.[22] The final stage was reached in 1879 with the passing of the United Presbyterian Declaratory Act, which sought to "explain" the Confession's position on such points of doctrine as the love of God, the divine decrees, man's total depravity, and the eternal destination of the souls of those who die in infancy or without hearing the Gospel. It also considered the Confession's teaching on Church-State relations and, in a celebrated clause, allowed liberty of opinion on points of the Confession which were "not entering into the substance of the faith."[23] Considerable attention was given to the United Presbyterian Church Declaratory Act around the world,[24] but it was particularly influential at home, in the Free Church of Scotland.

---

[21] Quoted in C. G. McCrie, *The Church of Scotland. Her Divisions and Her Re-unions* (Edinburgh, 1901), 298-299.

[22] *Ibid*, 299.

[23] *Proceedings of the Synod of the United Presbyterian Church*, 1879, 637-638. As one member of the Committee commented at the time, "The great essential truths will, of course, remain, but there is a strong desire for some declaration that will not make predestination the beginning and end of our faith, but Christ as the expression of God's love to the world, putting election in its proper place . . .The wish is felt to leave some of the minor questions for each one to settle in thought by himself." (*Letters of the Rev John Ker D.D. 1866-1890* (Edinburgh, 2nd edition, 1890), 283-284).

[24] "The Act," wrote J.H. Leckie, "has been much derided; but . . . it has been accorded the flattery of being imitated." (J.H. Leckie, *Secession Memories. The United Presbyterian Contribution to the Scottish Church* (Edinburgh, 1926), 233) and it was, for example, cited by Philip Schaff of Union Theological Seminary, New York, in his 1889 article on revision. ("The Revision of the Westminster Confession of Faith", *The Presbyterian Review*,

Clearly, then, Confessional revision was very much on the agenda in the wider Presbyterian world; as Philip Schaff put it in 1889, "Revision is in the air."[25] James Candlish of the Free Church of Scotland had pointed out in 1886 that although every English-speaking Presbyterian church in Britain, Ireland, the Colonies and the United States held the Westminster Confession as their creed, "every single one" had adapted it.[26] As has been seen, the debate during this time included two separate aspects of the Westminster Confession: what could be termed "non-fundamental" doctrines, such as that of Church-State relations: and what were considered to be "fundamental" doctrines like the Confession's pronouncements on the Love of God and Predestination. Revision generally involved the teaching on these two sets of doctrines.

It is also worth noting that not all the critiques of Westminster were gentle academic treatises. While some were prepared to couch both criticism and defence of the Confession in relatively

---

vol X, no 40 (October, 1889), 535). Later in the article, however, he dismissed it as something which produces "two Confessions which flatly contradict each other in three important articles." (*Ibid*, 549). B.B. Warfield also noted it, and was similarly unimpressed; "Its effect is simply to amend the Confession by indirection in certain specified points (and if amendment is to be made, why not do it directly?), while leaving the liberty of the subscriber just as much in bondage to the (now altered) Confession as before; it, therefore, does not in any way supersede the need for a freer formula of subscription." (B.B. Warfield, "The New Creed of the Presbyterian Church of England", *The Presbyterian Review*, vol X, no 37 (January, 1889), 115-116). Charles Briggs said of the United Presbyterian Act, "such an Act only deals with a few of the mooted questions. It virtually sets up two standards of doctrine that are not in harmony. It doubtless has done good service in Scotland, but it would not suit the American Church." (C. Briggs, "The General Assembly of the Presbyterian Church in the United States of America", *The Presbyterian Review*, vol X, no 39 (July, 1889), 469).

25 Schaff, "Revision of the Westminster Confession", 529.

26 J.S. Candlish, *The Relations of the Presbyterian Churches to the Confession of Faith* (Glasgow, 1886), 3.

unconfrontational language, this reserve was not always the case. In the United States, for example, Charles Briggs suggested with characteristic bluntness that it was both unreasonable and unscriptural to think that Divine Revelation had ceased to be brought to bear on the Bible in the Seventeenth Century. Creation, for example, he looked upon as "mere child's play", while he also saw Westminster as being inadequate on the Trinity, on the Being of God and on the Atonement.[27] Philip Schaff described the Confession's teaching on predestination as "in open contradiction to several of the clearest declarations of the Bible",[28] and said of the statements regarding the Pope and the Roman Catholic Church,

> I protest against this judgement as untrue, unjust, uncharitable, and unsuitable in any Confession of Faith. It is a colossal slander on the oldest and largest Church of Christendom. . . . It seems incredible. . . . It outpopes the Pope. . . .[29]

Llewellyn Evans said that the Confession contained,

> statements which are admitted to be non-essential to our system of doctrine; which are not supported by the express declarations of Scripture; which, if not absolutely rejected by the large majority of our ministers, are never preached or urged on others; which are at the best misunderstood by other evangelical believers; and which, as long as they are retained, present our Calvinism to the world as something hard, unsympathetic, unlovely, unattractive, and so far powerless for good. . . .[30]

and Samuel Hamilton, another American Presbyterian, said that the Confession contained "certain statements that horrify men's ordinary sense of justice."[31]

---

[27] Briggs, "Advance Towards Revision", 18.

[28] Schaff, "Revision of the Westminster Confession", 539.

[29] *Ibid*, 547, 548.

[30] L.J. Evans, "Dogmatic Confessionalism Versus Revision", in Briggs (ed), *How Shall We Revise?*, 46.

[31] S.M. Hamilton, "A Non-growing Creed", in Briggs (ed), *How Shall We Revise?*, 133.

In the Church of Scotland, too, there were blunt words for the Westminster Confession. James Stark's *The Westminster Confession of Faith Critically Compared to the Holy Scriptures and Found Wanting*, for example, was a long and at times startlingly brutal critique of the Confession, practically word-by-word. The Confession's sections on Predestination were described thus:

> These clauses, therefore, drawn up on a complete misunderstanding of the Scriptures, are disgraceful perversions of the Scriptures and foul slanders of the God of Love . . . In fact, were these clauses of the Confession true, then the Gospel is offered to man in vain.[32]

Stark described the Westminster position on Predestination and Election as "contrary to the whole tenor of the Gospel scheme of salvation,. . . thoroughly to be detested and abhorred."[33] Reference was also made to "that false doctrine which pervades the whole Westminster Confession", and "jumbled nonsense (which) is then passed off upon our credulity as if it were the word of God and matter for religious faith."[34] Stark concluded that

> all its leading doctrines have no support from Scripture, but are the false inferences of a vain scholastic philosophy, founded on detached passages of Scripture whose true meaning was misunderstood.[35]

This was very far away from being the language of compromise—battle lines were being clearly drawn. It was not really until the 1880's, though, that the more strident voices began to make themselves heard within the Free Church, and it is to this that we shall now turn.

---

[32] J. Stark, *The Westminster Confession of Faith Critically Compared with the Holy Scriptures and Found Wanting; or, A New Exposition of the Doctrines of the Christian Religion in Harmony with the Word of God, and Not at Variance with Modern Science* (London, 1863), 55, 56.

[33] *Ibid*, 64.

4. The Revision Movement in the Free Church of Scotland and the Framing of the Declaratory Act, 1880-1892

Throughout the early 1880s, things had seemed all quiet on the Westminster front. Free Church General Assemblies during this time debated many diverse issues, but left the Westminster Confession alone. The first overture on the subject did not appear until 1887, a full decade after the United Presbyterians had first formally broached the subject. James Candlish, a Professor in the Free Church's Glasgow College, had, however, made his position quite clear the previous year, when he suggested that the Westminster Confession stressed Divine sovereignty to the detriment of Divine love and he had argued for some sort of revision. The United Presbyterian Declaratory Act he described as "a considerable step in the right direction" and he had argued that "the present form of subscription in the Free Church is hardly defensible."[36] During a speech before the Glasgow Presbytery in February, 1887, he had said that,

> It would not be at all unlikely that the Confession, granting that it was the most suitable for the seventeenth century, should be found in this nineteenth century not to be altogether so suitable . . . he did not think that any one could doubt that there were some points on which the statements of the Confession had been proved by the progress of knowledge, in the history and experience of the Church, to be either inaccurate or at least very doubtful.[37]

---

[34] *Ibid*, 274

[35] *Ibid*, 285.

[36] Candlish, *Relations of the Presbyterian Churches to the Confession of Faith*, 18, 24, 25. On Candlish's comment that the United Presbyterian Declaratory Act was a "step in the right direction", one conservative writer commented, "we are as far as possible from believing it to have been (such)." ("Candlish on the Confession", *The Signal*, March 1887, 87).

[37] Candlish, quoted in "Professor Candlish on the Westminster Confession of Faith. Second Article", *The Signal*, April 1887, 99.

Just over a month before the 1887 Assembly another prominent Free Churchman, W. G. Blaikie, had written in the *British Weekly* of the Westminster Confession;

> I am . . . thoroughly persuaded that that creed is not the kind of document to every part of which it is reasonable and scriptural to require an absolute assent from every one who is to be a teacher in the Church. If what appears to be an absolute assent to every part of so comprehensive and minute a document is required, it will inevitably give rise to popular 'understandings', which at once hurt the conscience and interfere with the binding force which a creed ought to have.[38]

The controversial Bible scholar Professor Marcus Dods was never one to remain silent while others spoke out. He had perhaps gone further than the rest when, in the same week as Blaikie's British Weekly article, he had written this:

> It were worthy of any church to consider whether Creeds, used as terms of Office, have not done more harm than good, accentuating peculiarities and perpetuating inconsiderable distinctions;. . . whether a church is justified in holding a creed which cannot be expected ever to become a creed of the Church Catholic, thus dooming herself to everlasting sectarianism; whether a Church is justified in exacting from her ministry any confession of faith beyond the one article of faith in Christ as the Living Supreme, which she is justified in demanding from her members.[39]

Dods had asked rhetorically at the close of the above article where a Calvinistic ministry was going to come from "if the pew is gradually drifting from Calvinism." It was becoming clear, though, that it was many of the most senior and influential figures

---

[38] Blaikie, "Revision of the Westminster Confession", 1. Interestingly, Blaikie was at this time an associate editor of *The Presbyterian Review*, of which the two senior editors were none other than C.A. Briggs and B.B. Warfield.

[39] M. Dods, "The Revision of the Westminster Confession (II)", *British Weekly*, April 22nd, 1887. His views on the need for a creed to embrace the "Church Catholic" are an interesting echo of those of, for example, Philip Schaff, who said, "We need a theology and a confession that is more human than Calvinism, and more divine than Arminianism, and more Christian and Catholic than either." (Schaff, "Revision of the Westminster Confession", 552).

in the Free Church's pulpits and college chairs who were themselves drifting far from the Calvinist consensus of the Westminster Confession.[40] The writing, it seemed, was beginning to appear on the wall. "The Presbyterian creed," commented the *British Weekly* in a review of the year, "is in the crucible, and will certainly not emerge as it went in."[41]

By 1888, more signs were appearing that the process was accelerating. This year saw the publication of a controversial pamphlet on the subject of creed revision by Robert Mackintosh, a Free Church of Scotland junior minister. Its very title *The Obsoleteness of the Westminster Confession of Faith* was a clear indication that the temperature of the debate was rising. Among other things, Mackintosh said that,

> we know that the Confession was meant to teach persecution was, indeed, drawn up with that view . . . it is plain to us as students of history that persecution was an integral part of the Westminster theology-bone of its bone, and flesh of its flesh.[42]

Of the men who drew up the Confession, than whom few were rated more highly by the conservatives in the Free Church, Mackintosh had nothing but contempt. He described them as "intellectually babes, and morally diseased, . . . these blunderers

---

[40] Dods, it should be remembered, was elected to the Chair of New Testament at New College by the Assembly of 1889; an act by which "the movement towards a Declaratory Act was greatly encouraged". (A.T. Innes, *Chapters of Reminiscence* (London, 1913), 223). "Unquestionably," commented Carnegie Simpson, "it was a very significant election. For, in appointing Dr. Dods the Church knew what she was doing. He had never made any secret of his views or stated them with any ambiguity. The election did not mean that the Church had adapted these views, but it did mean she tolerated them and that even in a teacher of her students." (P.C. Simpson, *The Life of Principal Rainy* (London, 2 vols, 1909), vol II, 110).

[41] *British Weekly*, December 30th, 1887, 171. The Confession was thus being placed alongside the Bible which was also being "thrown into the crucible". (Dods, *Recent Progress*, 10).

[42] R. Mackintosh, *The Obsoleteness of the Westminster Confession of Faith* (Glasgow, 1888), 15.

and persecutors", and declared,

> Men all wrong in everything else, where we can test them, are not
> likely to be at all right in the most important point of all, where we
> cannot so easily test them. Men ignorant of apologetics, ignorant of
> toleration, ignorant of scientific interpretation—or, in other words
> ignorant of truth—men who assumed the Bible to contain what it
> does not contain—men who failed when tried by tests of practice—
> are not likely to have been miraculously guided to the truth in their
> hard and inhuman doctrines.[43]

Not surprisingly, the pamphlet provoked an outraged response
from the conservatives. This was partly because they were

> very much afraid that . . . (his views) express the sentiment of not a
> few of the promising young aspirants to the ministry the benefits of
> whose services he (Mackintosh) thinks it would be a sad thing for
> the Free Church to lose.[44]

Sections of the pamphlet were quoted in *The Signal* in order
to show conservatives "what doctrinal views are being entertained
by young men in our Divinity Halls, and thence finding their
way into the pulpits of our Church." "We wish you to see,"
continued the author grimly,

> the full extent of the evil . . . that our congregations be not poisoned
> with the very worst of false doctrine, and the minds of the rising
> generation imbued with opinions contrary to true Christianity and
> directly tending to absolute infidelity.[45]

This was very close to the line taken on biblical criticism; a
feeling almost of panic that not only was the present gloomy, but
that the future seemed to have even worse in store. The sense of
gloom was heightened by The Signal publishing, on the very next
page, an account of a meeting of the Free Presbytery of Dundee
at which the Revd D.M. Ross asserted that "The Westminster
Creed was no longer a faithful reflection of the living faith of the

---

[43] *Ibid.*, 54.

[44] "A Free Church Probationer on the Westminster Confession of Faith," *The
Signal*, August 1888, 229.

[45] *Ibid*, 231.

Church."[46] The conservatives did not like it, but events were soon to prove Ross right.

For by the summer of 1889, the trickle of overtures regarding the Confession of Faith had been transformed into a deluge. The General Assembly of that year received no fewer than 33 of them. About one third of these were in favour of retaining the present relationship between Church and Confession but, significantly, all of the rest betrayed more or less hostility towards Westminster.[47] The movement towards revision had picked up a great deal of momentum between 1888 and 1889, with some of the most senior men in the Church working together with that end in view. A. T. Innes had helped to set up what he called a "caucus" of senior revisionists, made up of men like Walter C. Smith, A. B. Bruce, T. M. Lindsay, James Candlish, Marcus Dods, Ross Taylor and, of course, Innes himself. Significantly, it did not at this time include the most influential man in the Free Church, Robert Rainy, who, in late 1888, had indicated his own reluctance that the Church embark on such a course.[48]

Rainy, ever the aware ecclesiastical politician, knew that action to revise the Westminster Confession would lead to division in the Church. "And," commented one biographer, "the Free Church was divided enough. She sorely needed rest."[49]

Rainy was in Australia as the Free Church of Scotland delegate at the Jubilee of the Presbyterian Church of Victoria when the "caucus" were planning their action; their activities, said Innes, took place "with a queer feeling of uneasiness almost as of mice while the cat was away."[50] The Assembly of 1889 took place in

---

[46] "The Free Presbytery of Dundee and the Confession of Faith," *The Signal*, August 1888, 237.

[47] *Free Church of Scotland Assembly Papers, No 1*, 1888, 329-346.

[48] Simpson, *Rainy*, vol II, 122.

[49] *Ibid*, 122.

[50] Innes, *Chapters*, 223.

Rainy's absence, but it was no less significant for that. Indeed, the debate in the 1889 Free General Assembly on the Confession was one of the clear, almost symbolic, indications of the wide gulf that had come to exist within the pale of the Free Church of Scotland by this time. When William Balfour "trembled" lest the church took steps "which would amount to a virtual surrender of her proud boast to be the church of Knox, Melville, Henderson and Chalmers",[51] the response was applause from the conservatives but laughter from his opponents. He was fearful of a kind of Trojan Horse of revision:

> the advocates of change began by stating that there were one or two little things which required to be rectified, but when they got elsewhere the little things swelled into almost the whole Confession, therefore the members of the House required to be very cautious how they moved in this matter.[52]

On the other hand, to James Smith the Westminster Confession was like an old navigational chart which had long outlived its usefulness. If revision revealed divisions within the Free Church, he believed, it would be because these divisions already existed.[53] Orrock Johnson could argue that all they were doing was changing "trivialities",[54] but at the same time Sheriff Cowan of Paisley believed that,

> Predestination . . .was a repulsive doctrine which kept back many who were attracted by the offer of universal salvation which was to be found in the Bible.[55]

Several speakers—and, indeed several of the Overtures being considered—made reference to bringing the Confession into line with the "Living Faith" or "present Faith" of the

---

[51] PDGAFC, 1889, 133.

[52] *Ibid*, 133.

[53] *Ibid*, 143.

[54] *Ibid*, 145.

[55] *Ibid*, 15.

church[56] and this seemed to be the heart of the matter. To conservatives the "Present Faith" was exactly the same as the faith of 1843—and of the Apostles and of the Reformers—and as Alex Forbes put it, the process should have been to revise the "Living Faith" to fit the Confession, not the reverse. If not, then faith was regulated by "the wayward and ever-shifting imagination of each man's heart."[57] *The Signal*, never a magazine to make use of much circumlocution when blunt terms could be employed, expressed it thus:

> The living faith of the Church! Say rather, the actual unbelief of the Church, or of some in the Church, who ought not to be in it at all, even as members, much less as ministers or elders. . . . God forbid that it should change its Confession to bring it into accordance with their views, or to give them a legitimate standing-place within its pale.[58]

Soon after the debate, James Gibson of Perth said this of the phrase, "living faith";

> It is no secret that for some of the advocates of revision the words mean that they no longer hold (if they ever did hold) certain of the leading doctrines of the Confession.[59]

---

[56] "It is humbly overtured by the Free Presbytery of Dalkeith, to the Venerable General Assembly, to . . . secure fuller harmony between the subordinate standards on the one hand, and the spirit and teaching of Scripture and the living faith of the Church on the other hand." ("Overture Anent Confession of Faith From the Free Presbytery of Dalkeith", *Free Church of Scotland Assembly Papers Number 1*, 1889, 336). David Macrae's plea for revision of the United Presbyterian Church's relationship with the Confession had also - partly - been for this reason. He said, "the professed (creed) is not the actual creed of the Church; . . . our Church is professing one creed while holding, and to a large extent preaching, another." (*Mr Macrae and the Confession of Faith* (London, 1877), 5).

[57] *PDGAFC*, 1889, 142.

[58] "The Free Church General Assembly of 1889: What Ought it to Do?", *The Signal*, June 1889, 165-166.

[59] J. Gibson, *"Buy the Truth:" Thoughts on Creeds and Creed Revision* (Edinburgh, 1889), 33 note 3.

And in an abrasive pamphlet published that year Kenneth Moody-Stuart declared,

> Even now it is difficult to gather from their pleadings how many have changed their faith, and how long they have changed their faith, and how deliberately they have changed their faith . . . (but) they overestimate their numbers when they assert that the whole Church has changed its living faith. . . .[60]

Clearly, then, there were perceived to be two distinct "living faiths" within the Free Church, and towards the end of the debate, Dr Scott of Aberlour made an explicit statement of this fact;

> it had been made clear that they were by no means a united Church. They were, in fact, nearly as far divided as they could be, not only in regard to Biblical criticism, but in regard to such primary doctrines as the plenary inspiration, infallible truth, and divine authority of Scripture.[61]

What it also illustrated, of course, was the age-old divide in the Free Church of Scotland between the Highlands and the Lowlands, with the Highlanders as in other cases around this time—voting overwhelmingly against any change.[62] The conservative side in the Free Church of Scotland were determined, but were heavily outnumbered; at the end of the 1889 debate the anti-revisionists lost by over three votes to one. While the argument over Confessional revision continued, the battle was all but over. The way had been cleared for the Declaratory Act, and bitter schism would soon follow.

The motion which won the day in 1889 made no mention of a Declaratory Act, and indeed did no more than set up a committee whose remit was

> to consider carefully what action it is advisable for the Church to take, so as to meet the difficulties and relieve the scruples . . . it being

---

[60] K. Moody-Stuart, *Why We Do Not Mean to Change Our Confession of Faith* (Edinburgh, 1889), 4.

[61] K. Moody-Stuart, *Why We Do Not Mean to Change Our Confession of Faith* (Edinburgh, 1889), 4.

[62] *Ibid*, viii-xxvi, 154.

always understood, that this Church can contemplate the adoption of no change which shall not be consistent with a cordial and steadfast adherence to the great doctrines of the Confession.[63]

Over the next two years, the Committee deliberated under the convenorship of Robert Rainy, who was now sure that change was inevitable and committed to some form of revision. By the Assembly of 1891 he was able to put forward a draft Declaratory Act which was, in the opinion of the Committee, "the mildest, the least startling, the least offensive way . . . of taking in hand the duty which was committed to them."[64] The Act had six clauses, the first five of which dealt with the love of God, denied "the fore-ordination of men to death irrespective of their own sin", argued that there could be extraordinary means of Grace, qualified the doctrine of total depravity, and disclaimed "intolerant and persecuting principles", a reference to the age-old controversy about the respective roles of Church and State. The sixth clause is worth quoting in full:

> That while diversity of opinion is recognised in this Church on such points in the Confession as do not enter into the substance of the Reformed Faith therein set forth, the Church retains full authority to determine, in any case which may arise, what points fall within this description, and thus to guard against any abuse of this liberty to the detriment of sound doctrine, or to the injury of her unity and peace.[65]

Obviously, definition of what did or did not enter into "the substance of the reformed faith" was going to be extremely controversial.

Rainy argued that the Act did not amount to much,

> The truth was, they were not anxious to do exceedingly much. They were not anxious to do anything that was revolutionary, and they were very well aware that if they had gone a little further, the critics would have said that the committee had now gone over to rationalism,

---

[63] *PDGAFC*, 1889, 137.

[64] *PDGAFC*, 1891, 78.

[65] "Act anent Confession of Faith (No. 8 of Class II.)", *Acts of the General Assembly of the Free Church of Scotland*, 1889- 1893, 478-479.

and had deserted the evangelical faith.[66]

Rainy stressed that what they were proposing would do no more than put the Free Church of Scotland in line with "those sister Churches" which had already taken similar steps. He went on to recommend the Act, in a speech which was received most enthusiastically, and proposed that the Act be sent down to the presbyteries of the Church under the Barrier Act. After a short debate, during which the main anti-Declaratory Act speech was interrupted by a large number of members noisily leaving the Assembly hall, the motion was overwhelmingly passed by a majority of over six to one.[67] Having gone through the presbyteries the Act came back to the Assembly and, after a debate in which the main opposition speech was again interrupted by the noisy departure of many members, it was passed on the 26th of May 1892 by a majority of 346 to 195. The Declaratory Act was now part of the law of the Free Church.[68]

Conclusion

There followed a full year of protest and campaigning, with meetings the length and breadth of Scotland. It was all to no avail, however, and thus on the 25th of May 1893, the Revd Donald Macfarlane, Free Church minister of Raasay in the Scottish Highlands, advanced to the table of the Assembly and read the protest against the Declaratory Act which severed his connection from the Free Church of Scotland.[69] On the 28th of July, in the company of Donald Macdonald, minister of Sheildaig, and Alexander Macfarlane, schoolmaster of Raasay, he formed the "Free Church Presbytery of Scotland", later to become the Free

---

[66] *Ibid*, 78.

[67] *PDGAFC*, 1891, viii-xxvii.

[68] *PDGAFC*, 1892, 145-172.

[69] *PDGAFC*, 1893, 183.

Presbyterian Church of Scotland. Another denomination was born.[70] Macfarlane and Macdonald were followed by some dozen students who had been intending to enter the Free Church ministry, and by thousands of the Free Church's most loyal members and adherents throughout Scotland. There was much bitterness and ill-feeling in the Highlands over the Free Presbyterian Disruption, with precious little brotherly love on view; Macfarlane and Macdonald were evicted from their churches and manses, and one Free Presbyterian's daughter spoke of her father never having forgotten the embittered reaction he and his family received on choosing to follow "the seceders" in Lochcarron in 1893. Much mud, by no means all metaphorical, was slung in their direction.[71]

Although there were soon congregations in such Lowland places as Greenock, Dumbarton, Glasgow and Edinburgh, the vast bulk of the new denomination's congregations were north of the Highland line. While it is difficult to provide certain statistical evidence, it is very probable that the majority of those in the "Lowland" congregations would have been immigrant Highlanders; the Greenock congregation, for example, emerged out of the Free Gaelic congregation.[72] The Free Presbyterians were, almost exclusively, a Highland denomination. It is very difficult to speculate on the numbers involved, and these clearly varied very much from place to place. Estimates on the size of the Secession varied hugely, and the Free Presbyterian's own official history never gave a figure, preferring to refer to "the little band who

---

[70] *Records of the Free Church Presbytery of Scotland* (27th July 1893 - August 31st 1894), 1-4; see also D. Beaton, *Memoir, Diary and Remains of the Rev. Donald Macfarlane, Dingwall* (Inverness, 1929); Beaton, *Memoir, Biographical Sketches, Letters, Lectures and Sermons (English and Gaelic) of the Revd Neil Cameron, Glasgow* (Inverness, 1932); Beaton (ed), *History of the Free Presbyterian Church of Scotland, 1893-1933* (Glasgow, 1933).

[71] Interview with Mrs Jessie MacLeod (nee MacRae), of Lochcarron, 20th December, 1992.

[72] L. MacLeod, "Formation of the Greenock Free Presbyterian Congregation", *The Free Presbyterian Magazine* vol 98, no 9 (September, 1993), 263-266.

faced a hostile world".[73] It was not until 1896 that the Free Church managed to produce their own statistics on the Free Presbyterian Disruption; the total number, according to these official Assembly returns, was 6756 elders, deacons, communicants and adherents over the age of eighteen; this was considerably less than many estimates but is almost impossible to evaluate.[74]

There were also many within the Free Church who, although opposed to the Declaratory Act, remained within that denomination. When the Free Church split again, in the more celebrated division over their union with the United Presbyterian Church in 1900, these conservative opponents of the Declaratory Act remained outside the Union as the continuing Free Church. One of their first acts was to repeal the Declaratory Act, but for various complex reasons, union with the Free Presbyterians has never really been likely; perhaps there had been too much pain involved in the initial separation for reunion to be a viable option. Denominational stratification remains very much a fact of life in Scotland and in parts of the Highlands in particular, tiny communities are served by as many as four different Presbyterian Calvinist denominations.

For us in the twentieth century, the lesson perhaps is that denominations can change position relatively quickly and that "fundamentals" can come and go unless very carefully defined and protected. A church can change its creed and constitution and this is of course right and proper in certain circumstances but what has to be guarded against is compromise on fundamental doctrines. There will not always be many voices raised in defence of a document like the Westminster Confession of Faith, but the continued existence of the Free Presbyterian Church of Scotland is testimony to the fact that in 1893 at least one man was prepared to lift his voice in its defence; there are many who would argue that today that voice needs to be heard once more.

---

[73] Beaton (ed), *History*, 118.

[74] *PDGAFC*, 1896, 91.

Finney's Attacks on the Westminster Confession

MICHAEL S. HORTON

The most famous evangelist of the nineteenth century declared that the Westminster Divines had created "a paper pope" and had "elevated their confession and catechism to the Papal throne and into the place of the Holy Ghost." "It is better," he declared, "to have a living than a dead Pope," dismissing the Standards as casually as the boldest Enlightenment rationalist: "That the instrument framed by that assembly should in the nineteenth century be recognized as the standard of the church, or of any intelligent branch of it, is not only amazing, but I must say that it is highly ridiculous. It is as absurd in theology as it would be in any other branch of science."[1]

Given the unpopularity of Calvinism in particular, and confessionalism in general, all of this might not have raised the slightest hint of impropriety except for the fact that the evangelist was Charles G. Finney, an ordained Presbyterian minister. In his introduction to Finney's Lectures on Revivals of Religion, William McLoughlin wrote the following:

> The first thing that strikes the reader of the Lectures on Revival is the virulence of Finney's hostility toward traditional Calvinism and all it stood for. He denounced its doctrinal dogmas (which, as embodied

---

[1] Charles Finney, *Charles Finney's Systematic Theology* (Minneapolis: Bethany House, 1976), author's preface, xii.

in the Westminster Confession of Faith, he referred to elsewhere as 'this wonderful theological fiction'); he rejected its concept of nature and the structure of the universe . . .; he scorned its pessimistic attitude toward human nature and progress . . .; and he thoroughly deplored its hierarchical and legalistic polity (as embodied in the ecclesiastical system of the Presbyterian Church). Or to put it more succinctly, John Calvin's philosophy was theocentric and organic; Charles Finney's was anthropocentric and individualistic. . . . As one prominent Calvinist editor wrote in 1838 of Finney's revivals, 'Who is not aware that the Church has been almost revolutionized within four or five years by means of such excitements?'

In this brief survey, our purpose will be two-fold: first, to understand the factor that shaped Finney's theology and practice, and second, to appreciate the legacy both for contemporary evangelicalism and especially Reformed faith and practice in the United States.

I. The Man: His Life and Times

We must remember that the period just prior to the Great Awakening was not congenial to an undiluted Calvinism: Jonathan Edwards lost his pulpit in 1750 in large part because he would not moderate his belief in total depravity. Solomon Stoddard, Edwards' grandfather, had softened the Puritan emphasis on conversion in the interests of civil order with his "Half-Way Covenant," and the Enlightenment, having practically extinguished the remnants of orthodox Calvinism in English nonconformity, was threatening the citadels of American learning.

It was in reaction to the spiritual state of New England, ranging in general from nominal to skeptical, that a handful of preachers— Anglican, Presbyterian, Congregationalist, and Dutch Reformed, but Calvinists all, began to recover the evangelical emphasis of the Protestant Reformers, summoning men and women to a confrontation with God through the Law and the Gospel. A cursory glance at the most popular sermon titles illustrates the dependence on classical biblical categories of sin and grace, judgment and justification, Law and Gospel, despair and hope. These gifted evangelists were convinced that the success of their mission rested in the hands of God and their faithfulness to the apostolic proclamation.

In spite of such biblical rigor, matched with evangelistic zeal, the Great Awakening (1739-43) itself was not without its excesses of enthusiastic religion, as Edwards himself was painfully aware. The Princeton divine labored to distinguish between true and false religious emotions. A man of towering presence and celebrated oratory, George Whitefield proved a valuable colleague in awakening sinners to God, and yet, as Harry S. Stout has argued in a controversial work, Whitefield himself may have contributed to some of the seminal features of mass evangelism that would manifest themselves in the revivalism to follow.[2] The Tennent brothers, along with James Davenport, were also accused by some of their brethren as sowing seeds of unwholesome enthusiasm. A host of questions could be raised concerning the Awakening in terms of its ecclesiology and the prominence given to radical individual conversion over and against the more traditional covenantal motifs of Reformed theology. While the "New Light" and "Old Light" factions do not directly parallel the"New School" and "Old School" divisions which follow, they do reflect the controversial innovations introduced by those who sought to wed a pietistic impulse to Reformed orthodoxy, leading to the removal of Gilbert Tennent's "New Light" Presbyterians from the more traditional Philadelphia presbytery in 1741.

However essential it may be to raise those questions within the Reformed family, it is not within the scope of this brief survey to explore them. It is sufficient for our purposes to at least recognize the fundamental Reformed consensus of the Great Awakening on anthropological and soteriological grounds.

---

[2] Harry S. Stout, *The Divine Dramatist: George Whitefield and the Rise of Modern Evangelicalism* (Grand Rapids: Eerdmans, 1991).

Revival was "a surprising work of God," as Edwards expressed it, and depended entirely on divine freedom.

The revivals associated with the Great Awakening created a rift in New England Congregationalism, encouraging many who were offended on grounds of taste and style (as well as by the resurgent Calvinism) to embrace Unitarianism. Edwards provided the intellectual resources for a courageous defense of Calvinism in conversation with, not merely in reaction to, the Enlightenment. Perhaps no other movement has had such a profound hand in shaping the religious character of Revolutionary America and the evangelicalism that is its heir—with the possible exception of the Second Great Awakening.

Following closely on the heels of the first, the Second Great Awakening (1800-10) launched a succession of "revivals" that would last to the present day. However, it was very different both in style and substance from the first. Arthur Schlesinger, Jr., observes, "By the time the revolutionaries came to Philadelphia in 1776, the flames of Calvinism were burning low. . . . Original sin, not yet abandoned, was, like everything else, secularized."[3] Even on the frontier, the experience of the rugged individualist who had pulled himself up by the bootstraps in the wilderness matched that of the self-confident Enlightenment thinker in New England.

In the early part of the nineteenth century, Scots-Irish immigrants brought their tradition of sacramental occasions to the Jacksonian democracy. In Scotland, such festivals would draw Presbyterians from the far reaches, who after preparing for such "Seasons," anxiously anticipated the event which was surrounded with preaching, teaching, and exhortation. Meanwhile, in the academies, some of which had been founded out of the Great Awakening, revival stirred as well. In 1802, Yale's president,

---

[3] Arthur Schlesinger, Jr., *Cycles of American History* (New York: Houghton Mifflin, 1986), p. 5.

Timothy Dwight, led a revival that left one third of the student body converted—a rather significant result considering that all but a few were nominal Christians or skeptics. Still, for Dwight, Calvinism's orthodox convictions and intellectual rigor were considered indispensable to genuine awakening, and the divisions that would come to distinguish "New School" and "Old School" were not yet obvious.

Meanwhile, on the frontier, revival was removed from the watchful eye of New England. By "frontier," we are thinking of western New York, Vermont, New Hampshire, and—to the south, various sections of Virginia, Kentucky, and Tennessee. It was the Presbyterian minister James McGready who, transforming the "Sacramental Season," instigated the Cumberland revival at the turn of the nineteenth century, assisted by Methodists and Baptists. Tents were erected for the "camp meetings," where sinners and saints gathered to experience revival fires." The Cumberland revival was followed a year later by the Cane Ridge meeting, another interdenominational affair with at least ten thousand in attendance. At Cane Ridge, enthusiasm reached a fever pitch, as women's combs flew in the air, and such "exercises" as falling, running, jumping, and "holy jerks" and "holy laughter" amazed those who gathered. The Presbyterian Church's action itself resulted in the formation of the Cumberland Presbyterian Church and a schism led by Barton Stone, who eventually founded the Christian Church (Disciples of Christ), who remarked that he did not have time for creeds and confessions, that he despised Calvinism, and could care less about the doctrine of the Trinity. The Baptists and Methodists, however, were both more enthusiastic and reaped the greatest benefits from these revivals.

Whitney Cross explains the growth of the "camp meeting": "Methodists held camp meetings and permitted physical exercises upon which Congregationalists frowned. Freewill Baptists inclined to tolerate such activities, while Calvinistic Baptists were more strict. . . . Methodists and Baptists, more literal, more emotional, and better understood by common folk, increasingly 'strung Presbyterian fish' and gained adherents more rapidly, just as they had at the expense of the established New England church."[4] Unitarianism was especially popular among many sectarians coming out of the Great Awakening, even of the common sort, including the "Christians" (not to be confused with Disciples or "Campbellites"), weakening the argument that New England Unitarianism was entirely due to an allegedly Calvinistic tendency to ignore Christ and the Holy Spirit in favor of "God" (i.e., the Father).

It became increasingly clear, however, that these meetings could not be dismissed as "mass hysteria" without a backlash from the common folk, and there was no promise that Presbyterians and Congregationalists could dominate the landscape, especially on the frontier, given the remarkable adaptability of the Methodists and Baptists. In part, to consolidate its interests in the face of the growing threat, Presbyterians and Congregationalists in New England decided to throw their common resources behind the missionary effort. The Plan of Union, as it was called, was put into effect in 1801, and those who were bent on recovering losses and maintaining cultural dominance were willing to settle for minimal doctrinal commitments in the interest of success. Cross observes,

> The entire evangelical movement of the first quarter of the century seemed in many respects to stress piety rather than sectarian peculiarities. The Plan of Union itself evinced an early desire to redeem sinners without undue creedal emphasis. The whole string of benevolent societies was nondenominational in form, nondoctrinal in bearing, and at least officially directed toward common Christian goals. It is paradoxical that purportedly nonsectarian revivalism and benevolence should encompass much of the spirit they professed and

---

[4] Whitney R. Cross, *The Burned-Over District: The Social and Intellectual History of Enthusiastic Religion in Western New York, 1800-1850*, pp. 8-9.

yet engender interdenominational strife of a bitterness scarcely to be paralleled.[5]

From the Plan of Union, the old guard recognized a further ecumenical step was required to advance the cause on the frontier, so the Presbyterians and Congregationalists joined the Methodists and Baptists in the formation of the American Home Missionary Society (A. H. M.S.). Nevertheless,

> Fixed in dominant position in the large older settlements, the Presbyterians found themselves losing ground to others in the countryside and the younger towns. This loss may be ascribed to their insistence upon an educated ministry, their emphasis upon settled pastors rather than itinerants, and their conservative, limiting theology. In part consciously, but more largely unconsciously, they set out to overcome these handicaps by zealous effort and by compromise.[6]

In order to participate in the American Home Missionary Society (and attempt to lead it), Presbyterians and Congregationalists had to leave their creed out of the literature and tone things down a bit at their educational institutions, where evangelicals of all stripes were encouraged to attend. Where before Presbyterians and Congregationalists would have held a ministerial hopeful back due to insufficient learning or orthodoxy, William Burchard was declared unfit for his home missionary agency in western New York in 1823 because he did not make "such an appeal to the heart as would have brought the people to take hold of the missionary cause." After all, "Baptists in the region expected that ministers would 'let—the Holy Ghost' prepare their sermons. . . . Even Auburn Seminary dallied with the notion of a short course to stave off the competition of the revivalistic training schools springing up at Troy, Whitesboro, and Rochester."[7] When faced with a choice between marginalization and shared success, the New School Presbyterians were convinced that the

---

[5] *Ibid.*, p. 40.

[6] *Ibid.*, p. 47.

[7] *Ibid.*, pp. 51, 156.

"practical" would have to be allowed precedence, at least for the time being, over the "theological." This fact was generally understood and implied, if not explicitly stated.

Sylvester Finney, a farmer, moved to the frontier from Connecticut with his wife Rebecca and children. The year was 1794, and the Oneida County area of New York had already distinguished itself for its odd spiritual fads. John Humphrey Noyes's perfectionistic Oneida Community had gathered followers who were intent on duplicating the Book of Acts by holding all goods and wives in common. Millerites, Mormons, Campbellites, spirituatists, Swedenborgians, Shakers, Quakers, and a host of sects sharing an enthusiastic, millennial, and Gnostic orientation, found the region's spiritual soil rich for the most fantastic visions, earning the nickname, "Psychic Highway." According to Keith J. Hardman, by 1850 Spiritualism and Mesmerism, antecedents to what one today might recognize as "New Age" ideas, boasted sixty-seven periodicals, thirty-eight thousand mediums and two million followers inside and outside the church.[8]

It was into this "Burned-over District," as it came to be called, that Charles Finney arrived with his family at age two. Handsome and charming, Finney seemed to take up anything to which he set his mind with great skill and energy. Although it is not certain that he actually had been enrolled himself, Finney began teaching elementary school. "There was nothing which anyone else knew," a student later reflected, "that Mr. Finney didn't know, and there was nothing which anyone else could do that Mr. Finney could not do—and do a great deal better."[9]

Finney's parents were not church-goers and in his Memoirs, he could recall nothing religious from his upbringing. However,

---

[8] Keith J. Hardman, *Charles Grandison Finney: Revivalist and Reformer* (Grand Rapids: Baker and Syracuse University Press, 1987), p. 25

[9] *Ibid.*, p. 31.

he did begin attending the services at the Congregational church in Warren, Connecticut, when he lived briefly with his uncle. Peter Starr, whose preaching Finney later recalled with great frustration, became an icon of Old School intellectualism that would inspire the evangelist's caricatures. Evidently, Starr's method of preaching was mundane, dispassionate, and lecture-like; he rarely even made eye-contact with the congregation. And his theology did not fare any better, from the young man's point of view, as Starr was an ardent Calvinist if, indeed, ardor was at all expressed by the minister.

Disinterested in religion, Finney eventually entered the practice of law near his home, but experienced a profound change in direction while walking among the woods in 1821. As he records the event, it was a purely rational decision that suddenly made its impression upon the lawyer's mind, as the resolution to any case in the courtroom. He returned to his office the next day to inform his client that he had a retainer from the Lord to preach the Gospel.

However, it was not an easy thing for a convert to simply decide to become a preacher, as Finney assumed, and the frontier was no exception. His Presbyterian pastor, George W. Gale, with Old School roots, but New School interests, encouraged him to attend seminary and go under the care of presbytery. What followed differs in the accounts of Gale and Finney. According to Finney, presbytery offered him a full scholarship to Princeton Seminary, "but Gale, whose memory played fewer tricks on him, recorded in 1853 that he 'had written to Andover, to Princeton, and to Auburn' for admission for Finney, but received 'no encouragement.'" Finney accounts for the outcome by saying that he declared to the presbytery that, against its protestations, "I would not put myself under such an influence as they had been under; that I was confident they had been wrongly educated, and they were not ministers that met my ideal of what a minister of

Christ should be." "I told them this reluctantly," he added, "but I could not honestly withhold it."[10] One thing of which both his friends and enemies were constantly reminding the self-confident ordinand throughout his life was that his displays of arrogance and conceit could get him into trouble. Even when Gale's generous attempts to secure a place for Finney failed, the pastor convinced presbytery to allow him to personally supervise his instruction, using his own library. Nevertheless, Finney's reminiscences of Gale's generosity included the remark that, ". . . so far as he was concerned as my teacher, my studies were little else than controversy." Hardman's analysis of Finney's recollections are pointed: "It is to be seriously doubted that dignified, competent clergymen of many years' experience would meekly accept the tongue-lashing of a rather arrogant, newly converted law clerk who patently knew nothing of theology and whose application for scholarship aid had just been rejected by three seminaries!"[11]

Finney's remark that Gale taught him "little else than controversy" was probably calculated to leave the impression that anything Finney really learned during those years he had to teach himself. And to some extent, he was correct. Finney refused to follow the systematic thinking that had occupied divines in the past; he was more interested in immediate practical successes. Anti-intellectualism, so much a part of the frontier revivalism that had "burned-over" the region, was very much in evidence in such remarks.

What is rather surprising, even if this tongue-lashing was a figment of Finney's active imagination, is that on December 30, 1823, as Gale was ill and the church was in need of pastoral assistance, the presbytery agreed to license Finney to fill the pastoral ministry there in Adams. This even after one examiner, in passing,

---

[10] *Ibid.*, pp. 50-51.

[11] *Ibid.*

allegedly inquired whether Finney subscribed to the Westminster Standards and the evangelist replied that he had never even read it. "I had not examined it. . . . This had made no part of my study." And yet, as Hardman points out, it would have been inconceivable that a Princeton graduate such as Gale would have ignored the *Confession* in preparing Finney for ministry.[12] Whether this was simply an error of Finney's memory of the events, an attempt to evade his examiners on a subject that would certainly have jeopardized his ordination, or a deliberate attempt to portray his theological convictions as having never changed (as he later insisted), it is rather remarkable to think that one would embark on a ministry in a confessional denomination without ever having even read the document to which he subscribed in good conscience.

At last, on July 1, 1824, Finney preached his ordination sermon and, refusing to mount the exalted pulpit, strolled throughout the congregation and paced the platform. Even before Finney arrived in many towns, revivalism had already produced strange phenomena. The frontier revivalist Peter Cartwright reported that the preachers themselves would become hysterical and Hofstadter describes the scene:

> They laughed senselessly, 'holy laughs,' they called them. And then they jumped around like dogs on all fours and, still barking, 'treed the devil' like dogs chasing a squirrel. When all else failed, they spoke in a gibberish which they believed to be the 'other tongues' used by the apostles in the Bible.[13]

In DeKalb, Presbyterians and Methodists had divided over the phenomenon of "fainting under the power of the Spirit," endorsed by the Methodists. When Finney arrived in 1823, he brought the Presbyterians into agreement with the practice. Indeed, Finney occasionally wondered aloud why he did not become a Methodist

---

[12] *Ibid.*

[13] *Richard Hofstadter, Anti-Intellectualism in American Life* (N. Y. : Vintage, 1963), p. 70.

and praised them as better revivalists than the Presbyterians.[14] According to Cross, "Lawyers, real-estate magnates, millers, manufacturers, and commercial tycoons led the parade of the regenerated."[15]

Finney, however, was not the only evangelist. In fact, not all of the missionaries and evangelists of the frontier were chafing at the strictures of the Calvinistic creed. Asahel Nettleton (1783-1844), for instance, was the leader of revivals in New England and New York before Finney. From the mold of the earlier evangelists of the first Great Awakening, Nettleton emphasized sin and grace, dependence upon the sovereignty of God, and therefore eschewed all forms of emotionalism. His restrained style, however, was now considered passé for the new revivalists, although he had a firm ally in the Boston pastor Lyman Beecher (1775-1863). Born in New Haven, Beecher arrived as a student at Yale and found it in a most ungodly state. . . . Most of the class before me were infidels, and called each other Voltaire, Rousseau, d'Alembert, etc., etc.," (Autobiography, 27). Under Dwight, Beecher became a minister and even studied for a while in the Yale president's home. First, he was committed to opposing the evils of Jacksonian democracy, representing instead the New England establishment and its Congregational dominance. Jeffersonian and Jacksonian trends, he insisted, went hand in hand with religious sectarianism on the frontier. Under the 1801 Plan of Union, he served Presbyterian parishes as well as Congregational and remained a Presbyterian for the rest of his life. Beecher was assisted in his revivalistic opposition to various causes by Nathaniel Taylor, father of the "New Haven Divinity," discussed below. Beecher did not share, therefore, Nettleton's Old Calvinism, but was rather sympathetic to Taylor's optimistic view of human nature. When he became a pastor in

---

[14] Hardman, pp. 67, 108.

[15] Cross, p. 155.

Boston, Beecher bitterly attacked the Unitarians who now dominated. He became president of Lane Seminary, the western outpost for the New School Presbyterians in Cincinnati. Here, his causes included abolition, opposition to Catholic immigration and the defense of America's "manifest destiny." His own trial for heresy in 1835 was a prelude to the schism of the Presbyterian Church, along Old School and New School lines.

Nettleton, however, found in Beecher what he considered a loyal ally in opposing Finney. While Nettleton was opposed for theological reasons, Beecher was opposed on stylistic principles. Because Finney was merely applying Taylor's theology to the frontier, Beecher' s criticisms were of the "New Measures" and the minister's social and intellectual snobbery rather than firm theological grounds. Finney's problem was not that he was introducing Pelagian notions, but that he was upsetting order, both civil and religious. Eventually, that was not enough to keep Beecher in opposition, as the New Lebanon Convention would in 1827. There, a handful of the leading New England ministers met to informally discuss their relationship to Finney. When it appeared that the tide of sentiment was turning in favor of the "New Measures," Beecher declared openly that there was no difference between them and invited the evangelist to Boston. Of course, Nettleton was crushed, but he continued to hold his meetings. Nettleton would visit townspeople in their places of business, at leisure, in their homes by invitation, and in the town square. "But," Hardman notes, "this seemed, for all its success, to be an obsolete approach, and his tenacious insistence on preaching the doctrine of original sin put him increasingly out of touch with Nathaniel Taylor, Lyman Beecher, and Charles Finney."[16]

The New Lebanon Conference was the turning point. No longer was Finney an outcast. The theology and practice that had

---

[16] Hardman, p. 111.

caused the Presbyterian Church, without delay, to oust the Presbytery of Cumberland at the turn of the century, had now become almost officially tolerated. Even the Old School-dominated Presbytery of Philadelphia allowed New School doctrines. When one such pastor invited Finney to that city, he warned his brethren, "To oppose them [the revivals] openly would be unpopular." The conversion of an Old School man to Finney's side led the evangelist to reason, "His love of souls overruled all difficulty on nice questions of theological difference."[17]

While Congregationalists believed that they could hold the fort in New England, there was no question about the success of the Methodists and Baptists on the frontier. While Old School Presbyterians fought the theological and practical dangers, many came to attach themselves to the maxim, "If you can't beat them, join them." As one interpreter put it, "Pragmatism won the day. It was statistics—numbers of converts—that counted. . . ."[18]

In all of this, it is quite naive to consider Charles Finney the father of this shift. The Old School-New School rift had been a long time in the making and Hardman argues that Solomon Stoddard a century and a half earlier had introduced some of these ideas:

> "Stoddard's entire approach assumed that pastors and people could indeed assist in bringing down spiritual fire, and his methodology was the first to delineate the steps necessary to cooperate with God in this."[19]

Even in Puritanism itself, especially in its Congregationalist variety, there is a significant emphasis on separation, conversion, piety and the affections that could sometimes lose sight of the objective focus of redemption. Ever since the Antinomian Controversy in 1636 there had been a cycle of depression and revival, the latter considered a means of repairing whatever ailed

---

[17] *Ibid.*, p. 156.

[18] *Ibid.*, xii.

[19] *Ibid.*, p. 19.

both church and state. What was unique ever since the Second Great Awakening, however, was the explicitly Pelagian theology that undergirded the revivalistic enterprise.

Eventually, there were enough Old School Calvinists to oppose a complete take-over of the Presbyterian Church and throughout the 1830's, New School proponents, such as Beecher, Albert Barnes (the biblical commentator), and professors at Union and Auburn, were tried for heresy in church courts. These tensions led to a schism of the denomination in 1837, when the Old School finally had a clear majority in the General Assembly, and four synods with the membership were cut off from the denomination. In vain the New School attempted to re-enter the General Assembly, but when the decision was final these exiled Presbyterians discovered that they had enough support beyond their region to form their own denomination. No wonder, then, that Finney declared, "No doubt there is a jubilee in hell every year, about the time of the meeting of the General Assembly."[20]

While Finney, therefore, cannot be regarded as the father of a movement, he certainly was the most important catalyst for its success. Cross well summarizes Finney's outlook: "But no individual or school of thought could equal experience as Finney's teacher. His doctrine, in fact, grew out of actions which met the pragmatic test; success could be measured only in numbers of converts and in the apparent intensity of their convictions. Thus it was that Finney's chief contribution in the New York campaigns was not a theology but a set of practices. These devices met effectively the demand for larger revivals, and served to popularize and vitalize the New Haven theology."[21] This fact brings us to the discussion of the theological sources and effects of the revivals.

---

[20] *Charles Finney, Revival Lectures* (Old Tappan, NJ: Fleming H. Revell), p. 269.

[21] Cross, p. 160.

II. The Theology of Charles Finney

A. The New Haven Divinity

Although revivals had been conceived by Puritans such as Solomon Stoddard with somewhat more of a dynamic give-and-take between God and humans, they were still considered, as Edwards put it, "surprising works of God." In short, they were miraculous works of divine favor that in no way depended on the moral or emotional earnestness of sinful creatures. But the Unitarians had already made a break with Calvinism (and indeed orthodox Christianity). In 1757, the Reverend Samuel Webster, a Harvard graduate, wrote *A Winter-Evening's Conversation upon the Doctrine of Original Sin*, in which he rejected the biblical teaching that the sinful condition is inherited by all because of Adam's fall. Before long, this Pelagianizing sentiment extended into full-blown universalism and when linked to the increasingly popular Deism that regarded Jesus as a great moral teacher, but not the God-Man, Unitarian-Universalism became a major force in New England Congregationalism.

Nathaniel W. Taylor (1786-1858), student of and theological successor to Timothy Dwight at Yale, along with Beecher, attacked Unitarians, Episcopalians, and conservative Calvinists (all of whom were opposed to revivalism). Although he authored no magnum opus, Taylor's immense influence lies in the impress of his lectures, as he trained the forces of New England revivalism.

Like Edwards, Taylor was convinced that Calvinism had to interact with the current questions of the day. The Enlightenment made it impossible for Calvinists to simply repeat the old answers without taking into account the new questions that had been raised. Hobbes and Locke had left serious questions about the genuine freedom or even existence of the individual and Calvinism had to be distinguished from materialistic determinism and the moral chaos that could result from Hobbes's Leviathan. Furthermore, the discussions of individual rights, Kantian ethics, and democratic liberties appeared to render Calvinistic theological and anthropological assumptions anachronistic. But unlike Edwards, Taylor was not really convinced that Calvinism had the correct answers in the first place. It was not so much providing a new defense in the light of new questions, but of accommodating Calvinism to the sentiment of the times. Therefore, Taylor dismissed from the Calvinistic corpus the doctrines of original sin, regeneration, and the bondage of the will. Rather, human beings are born neutral, so that their own conversion and regeneration is self-generated by a self-determining will that possesses "power to the contrary." Therefore, humans can overcome sinning if they simply choose to do so.

Another popular figure of the New Haven Divinity was Joseph Bellamy (1719-90), a Congregationalist minister during the Great Awakening and both a student and associate of Edwards who, according to Stephen Berk, "subordinated doctrine to practice" and utility.[22] While retaining an Edwardsean interest in explicating the divine purpose in permitting the Fall and insisting on divine sovereignty over evil, Bellamy also denied original sin and argued that an individual only becomes a sinner by committing the first act. This, of course, affected the doctrine of the atonement. Embracing a governmental theory similar to that of Hugo Grotius (1583-1645), Bellamy and Taylor both emphasized the idea that God punishes sin rather than sinners. It is his justice, rather than his wrath, that is at issue in the work of Christ. Therefore, they argued, Christ did not actually atone for the sins of any individual, but demonstrated divine justice. Further, it exhibited divine love (the moral influence theory). There was no room for the theory of penal substitution, since God was not requiring a legal satisfaction for the guilt of sinners. The atonement should move sinners to turn from their wickedness and simply reorient their

---

[22] Stephen Berk, *Calvinism Versus Democracy* (Berkley: University of California Press, 1968), pp. 59-61.

moral lives, something that was entirely within their power apart from regeneration. That is not to say that God was entirely absent from conversion, but he exercised merely an "influence of persuasion," much the way another person might attempt to convince someone of a particular course of action.

Such sentiments did not rise Phoenix-like from the ashes of a once luminous Calvinism. Richard Baxter had appropriated the Grotian insights two centuries earlier and seventeenth century English Puritanism was filled with accusations and counter-accusations of Antinomianism, enthusiasm, Arminianism, and Socinianism. The affinities between Baxter's arguments in his *Catholick Theologie* and those in Bellamy's *True Religion Delineated* are striking, and Baxter's departures had earned for the English Puritan the ignominious accusation of Socinian and Arminian heresy from no less a person than John Owen.

B. Finney's Lectures on Systematic Theology

In an April 1876 article in *Bibliotheca Sacra*, G. F. Wright criticized Charles Hodge's review of Finney's *Systematic Theology* for representing Finney as "putting the universe in the place of God," but Warfield agreed with Hodge that this is the logical conclusion of his theology.[23] But was this rather severe indictment justified in the light of the evidence?

In the Lectures, Finney demonstrates an unwitting dependence upon the Newtonian metaphysics that conceived of the universe rather mechanically. Frequently, the author will refer to a universal "intelligence," "reason," "law," "government," or "principle," that is supreme and to which even God is subject. As far as the divine attributes are concerned, "All God's moral attributes are only so many attributes of love or of disinterested benevolence,"[24] and

---

[23] *B. B. Warfield, Perfectionism* (Philipsburg, NJ: Presbyterian and Reformed), p. 195.

[24] Finney, *Systematic Theology, op. cit.*, p. 31.

such comments are pronounced without the slightest exegetical appeal, much unlike the *Confession*. In fact, one is impressed throughout the Lectures with the absence of proof texts, the collection reads like a volume of Blackstone's Law.

A traditional method of systematic theology is not attempted and the doctrine of God is strangely deduced from "self-evident principles" rather than from Scripture. The result is a deity whose features are virtually indistinguishable from Islam's "Allah." There is nothing specifically Christian about Finney's doctrine of God, much less is it an explicitly evangelical description.

Finney's anthropology suffers from a similar lack of exegesis and historical-theological reflection. Once again the theory is proved that those who naively and self-confidently presume to be independent of the sources (i.e., "mere men") are often the most easily beguiled by the subtleties of what they do not understand. Finney's anti-intellectualism and self-confidence notwithstanding, he was a mirror reflection of his age. Taylor, in *The Quarterly Christian Spectator*, June 1829, argued that children are not born into the world sinful, but rapidly acquire a self-indulgent disposition by practice and repetition until it becomes a bias. Assuming a Kantian categorical imperative, Finney follows the Taylorites to the conclusion that if God commands something, it must be possible. Edwards, of course, argued that this was acceptable if by "possible" one meant "naturally possible." There is nothing inherent in nature essentially that predisposes one to sin. Sin cannot be attributed to a defective faculty. Rather, human beings are "morally incapable" of doing that which lies within their natural ability. With that distinction denied, the New Haven Divinity embraced Kant's "ought implies can" and Finney took this to mean that if God commands absolute perfection, it must be attainable by human beings according to their present condition. Hodge responded to this aspect of Finney's work in the following manner, "It is merely a dictum of philosophers, not of common people that 'I ought, therefore I can.' Every unsophisticated heart and especially every heart burdened with a sense of sin says rather, 'I ought to be able, but I am not.'"[25]

One need go no further than the table of contents of the Lectures to discern that Finney's entire theology revolved around human morality. Chapters one through five are on moral government, obligation, and the unity of moral action; chapters six and seven are on "Obedience Entire"; chapters eight through fourteen discuss attributes of love, selfishness and virtues and vice in general. Not until the twenty-first chapter does one read anything especially Christian, on the atonement. This is followed by a discussion of regeneration, repentance, and faith. There is one chapter on justification followed by six on sanctification. In fact, Finney did not really write lectures on systematic theology, but lectures on ethics. That is why, in his review, Hodge wrote, "It is altogether a misnomer to call such a book 'Lectures on Systematic Theology.' It would give a far more definite idea of its character, to call it, 'Lectures on Moral Law and Philosophy'.... Let moral philosophy be called moral philosophy and not Systematic Theology."[26]

Nevertheless, the author does make his views quite plain on the essential doctrinal matters in question. For our purposes here, we will restrict the discussion of Finney's anthropology to its soteriological implications, rather than exploring the philosophical assumptions of the New Haven anthropology.

The classical dogma of original sin, embraced by Protestant and Roman Catholics alike, is "anti-scriptural and nonsensical dogma," Finney declared.[27] In explicit language, Finney denied the notion that human beings possess a sinful nature.[28] Therefore,

---

[25] Charles Hodge, "Finney's Lectures on Theology," Biblical Repertory and Princeton Review, April 1847, p. 254.

[26] *Ibid.*, p. 241.

[27] Finney, *Systematic Theology*, p. 179.

[28] *Ibid.*, p. 179

if Adam leads individuals into sin merely by his poor example, this leads logically to the corollary that Christ redeems by offering a perfect example. Guilt and corruption are not inherent, but are the result of choices. The author responds to a number of proof texts commonly adduced in support of original sin. When the Psalmist, for instance, declares, "The wicked are estranged from the womb; they go astray as soon as they are born, speaking lies" (Ps.58:3), Finney replies, "But does this mean that they are really and literally estranged from the day and hour of their birth, and that they really go astray the very day they are born, speaking lies?" In other words, is this verse really telling us the truth? "This every one knows to be contrary to fact," as if "fact" and Finney's interpretation of his experience are synonymous. Therefore, the text must mean, ". . . that the wicked are estranged and go astray from the commencement of their moral agency," in spite of what the text actually says.[29] With Pelagius, Kant, and all who have been unable to accept this rather enigmatic biblical doctrine, Finney simply concludes of original sin, "It is a monstrous and blasphemous dogma, that a holy God is angry with any creature for possessing a nature with which he was sent into being without his knowledge or consent."[30] Later, he wrote, "Original or constitutional sinfulness, physical regeneration, and all their kindred and resulting dogmas, are alike subversive of the gospel, and repulsive to the human intelligence."[31]

The medieval church, of course, entertained a notion of concupiscence, attaching sinfulness to desire—not the desire for a particular thing, but desire in and of itself. Warfield argued that Taylor's and Finney's twist on "concupiscence" "differs from that doctrine at this point only in its completer Pelagianism."[32]

---

[29] *Ibid.*, p. 179.

[30] *Ibid.*, p. 180.

[31] *Ibid.*, p. 236.

[32] *Warfield, Perfectionism*, p. 189.

From the denial of original sin, Finney is free to move to a denial of the doctrine of supernatural regeneration. Like revival, regeneration itself was a gift of God, a "surprising work of God" according to the first Great Awakening. But for Finney, while the Holy Spirit exerted moral influences, "the actual turning . . . is the sinner's own act."[33] The evangelist's most popular sermon, which he preached at Boston's Park Street Church, was titled, "Sinners Bound To Change Their Own Hearts." "There is nothing in religion beyond the ordinary powers of nature," Finney declared, rendering the charge of Pelagianism undeniable. "Religion is the work of man," he said. "It consists entirely in the right exercise of the powers of nature. "It is just that and nothing else. When mankind becomes religious, they are not enabled to put forth exertions which they were unable before to put forth. They only exert powers which they had before, in a different way, and use them for the glory of God." A revival is not a miracle, nor dependent on a miracle, in any sense. It is a purely philosophical result of the right use of constituted means—as much as any other effect produced by the application of means" (emphasis in original).[34]

One notices in the preceding citation the dominance of the mechanical and pragmatic view of the universe. It was, after all, the dawn of the Industrial Age and the human attempt to imitate Newtonian metaphysics by creating an ordered, predictable existence through mechanics and technology. As William James' philosophical pragmatism was well-suited to the American psyche, so Finney's popular version said more about the factors by which he was shaped than about the influences he himself exerted. James (1842-1910) argued, "On pragmatic principles, if the hypothesis of God works satisfactorily in the widest sense of the word, it is true." Thus, James wanted to know "the truth's

---

[33] Cited in above, p. 176.

[34] Finney, *Revival Lectures*, op. cit., pp. 4-5.

cash-value in experiential terms."[35] "Many servants of the Lord," the foreword to a modern edition of Finney's Lectures reads, "should be diligently searching for a gospel that 'works,' and I am happy to state they can find it in this volume." The American pragmatic impulse that produced both Finney and James, and their respective heirs, could not have been more aptly expressed than the former's insistence upon revival depending on the correct techniques rather than on the sovereign freedom and grace of God.

In fact, what is striking at this point is that Finney's theology hardly requires God at all. It is an ethical system based on general self-evident principles that men and women can discover and follow if only they make that choice.

The next domino to fall in terms of the classical construction was the doctrine of the substitionary atonement of Christ. The first thing one must note concerning the atonement, Finney insists, is that Christ could not have died for anyone else's sins other than his own. His obedience to the Law and his perfect righteousness were sufficient for his acceptance before God, but it is legally impossible and unjust to substitute one person on behalf of others. Finney's entire theology is driven by a passion for moral improvement: "If he had obeyed the law as our substitute, then why should our own return to personal obedience be insisted upon as a sine qua non of our salvation?"[36] In other words, if Christ fulfilled the conditions of our obedience and satisfied divine justice for our sins, why would our own obedience be a necessary condition of salvation? Here, Finney is careful to distinguish between ground and condition, as he is in the later discussion of perfection. The believer's perfect obedience is a condition, while God's mercy is the ground, of redemption. How God could be described as being merciful to those who, by their

---

[35] William James, *Pragmatism* (N.Y.: Meridian, 1955), pp. 192-195.

[36] Finney, *Systematic Theology*, p. 206.

obedience, simply merited eternal life is another enigmatic feature of Finney's argument.

In line with the New Haven Divinity, Finney describes the atonement in governmental and moral rather than substitutionary language: "The atonement would present to creatures the highest possible motives to virtue. Example is the highest moral influence that can be exerted. . . . If the benevolence manifested in the atonement does not subdue the selfishness of sinners, their case is hopeless."[37] Notice again the goal of the atonement is not the redemption of sinners from divine wrath, but a moving exhibition designed to exert moral influence to the end of subduing selfishness and the flesh. In other words, the work of Christ itself is a purely ethical. The substitionary view of the atonement is explicitly rejected because it "assumes that the atonement was a literal payment of a debt, which we have seen does not consist with the nature of the atonement. . . . It is true, that the atonement, of itself, does not secure the salvation of any one."[38]

Original sin, divine sovereignty, regeneration, and the substitutionary atonement pushed aside, Finney bravely faced his next challenge: the doctrine of justification sola fide, "by which," according to the evangelical faith, "the church stands or falls." As if he were entirely unaware of the sixteenth century debate between justification through an inherent righteousness and a justification through an imputed righteousness, Finney adopts a view of justification that is as Pelagian as the foundation upon which it was erected.

First, in answer to the question, "Does a Christian cease to be a Christian, whenever he commits a sin?" Finney answers:

> Whenever he sins, he must, for the time being, cease to be holy. This is self-evident. Whenever he sins, he must be condemned; he must incur the penalty of the law of God. . . . If it be said that the precept is

---

[37] *Ibid.*, p. 209.

[38] *Ibid.*, p. 217.

still binding upon him, but that with respect to the Christian, the penalty is forever set aside, or abrogated, I reply, that to abrogate the penalty is to repeal the precept; for a precept without a penalty is no law. It is only counsel or advice. The Christian, therefore, is justified no longer than he obeys, and must be condemned when he disobeys; or Antinomianism is true. . . . In these respects, then, the sinning Christian and the unconverted sinner are upon precisely the same ground.[39]

Finney was convinced that God required absolute perfection, but instead of that leading him to seek his perfect righteousness in Christ, he concluded that ". . . full present obedience is a condition of justification." The position taken by the Council of Trent in the sixteenth century was far more Augustinian. Sanctification, to be sure, preceded final justification, nevertheless, the former was always incomplete in this life and imperfections were covered by Christ's atoning work, mediated through the sacramental and sacerdotal ministry. Finney's gospel, however, is pure law. Regardless of his distinction between works as the condition and works as the ground, Finney embraced a works-righteousness that exceeded the Counter-Reformation position.

"But again," writes Finney, "to the question, can man be justified while sin remains in him? Surely he cannot, either upon legal or gospel principles, unless the law be repealed. . . . But can he be pardoned and accepted, and justified, in the gospel sense, while sin, any degree of sin, remains in him? Certainly not."[40] With the Westminster Confession in his sights, Finney declared concerning the Reformation formula, *simul iustus et peccator*, "This error has slain more souls, I fear, than all the universalism that ever cursed the world." For, "Whenever a Christian sins, he comes under condemnation and must repent and do his first works, or be lost."[41] With regard to the Confession's insistence on the forensic character of justification, Finney makes the following reply:

---

[39] *Ibid.*, p. 46.

[40] *Ibid.*, p. 57.

[41] *Ibid.*, p. 60.

> But for sinners to be forensically pronounced just, is impossible and absurd. . . . As we shall see, there are many conditions, while there is but one ground, of the justification of sinners . . . As has already been said, there can be no justification in a legal or forensic sense, but upon the ground of universal, perfect, and uninterrupted obedience to law. This is of course denied by those who hold that gospel justification, or the justification of penitent sinners, is of the nature of a forensic or judicial justification. They hold to the legal maxim that what a man does by another he does by himself, and therefore the law regards Christ's obedience as ours, on the ground that he obeyed for us.[42]

If Finney had not read the *Confession* prior to his ordination, it is not likely that he gained great familiarity with it afterward, since federal theology insists upon "universal, perfect, and uninterrupted obedience to law" as the proper ground of justification. It is Christ, however, whose fulfillment of this requirement forms the ground of the sinner's justification. Finney, on the contrary, insists that this should refer instead to the believer's obedience:

> The doctrine of an imputed righteousness, or that Christ's obedience to the law was accounted as our obedience, is founded on a most false and nonsensical assumption, for Christ's righteousness could do no more than justify himself. It can never be imputed to us. . . . It was naturally impossible, then, for him to obey in our behalf. Representing the atonement as the ground of the sinner's justification has been a sad occasion of stumbling to many.[43]

Such remarks led Warfield to conclude, "When Finney strenuously argues that God can accept as righteous no one who is not intrinsically righteous, it cannot be denied that he teaches a work-salvation, and has put man's own righteousness in the place occupied in the Reformation doctrine of justification by the righteousness of Christ."[44] Furthermore, the view that faith is the sole condition of justification is "the antinomian view." "We shall see that perseverance in obedience to the end of life is also a

---

[42] *Ibid.,* p. 320-321.

[43] *Ibid.,* p. 321-322.

[44] Warfield, *Perfectionism*, p. 154.

condition of justification," placing justification at the end rather than at the beginning of the Christian life. But that is not all: "Present sanctification, in the sense of present full consecration to God, is another condition . . . of justification. Some theologians have made justification a condition of sanctification, instead of making sanctification a condition of justification. But this we shall see is an erroneous view of the subject." Each act of sin requires "a fresh justification." Referring to "the framers of the Westminster Confession of faith," and their view of an imputed righteousness, Finney wondered, "If this is not antinomianism, I know not what is." The legal transaction is unreasonable to Finney, so he concludes, "I regard these dogmas as fabulous, and better befitting a romance than a system of theology." The doctrine of justification, therefore, is "another gospel." He concludes this section against the Westminster Assembly:

> "The relations of the old school view of justification to their view of depravity is obvious. They hold, as we have seen, that the constitution in every faculty and part is sinful. Of course, a return to personal, present holiness, in the sense of entire conformity to the law, cannot with them be a condition of justification. They must have a justification while yet at least in some degree of sin. This must be brought about by imputed righteousness. The intellect revolts at a justification in sin. So a scheme was devised to divert the eye of the law and of the lawgiver from the sinner to his substitute, who has perfectly obeyed the law."[45]

Finney understood the significance, therefore, of his break and he also exhibited a surprising grasp of the Reformation position. His denial is not the result of confusion, it seems, but was born out of careful reflection, and he was so uncomfortable with the evangelical doctrines of imputation and substitution that he did not trouble himself with the Wesleyan-Arminian compromise. He recognized the implications and, unlike Wesley, found them unavoidable. Therefore, he went the entire distance to Pelagianism.

There are debates as to whether the New Haven Divinity owed

---

[45] Finney, *Systematic Theology*, pp. 326-339.

its origins to Edwards himself or whether it was a reaction to the mentor's strict Calvinism. Allen Guelzo, in favor of the first proposal, argues concerning the New Haven doctrine of the atonement, "Governmental images came easily to the New Divinity, since it was one of the chief philosophic objects of Edwardseanism to prove that God was a moral, not an arbitrary, Governor of creation."[46] After all, Edwards did contribute the preface to Bellamy's *True Religion Delineated* in 1750 and Guelzo argues that his private notebooks, mostly unpublished, confirm a drift toward a governmental view of the atonement. Others argue that Bellamy and Taylor simply rediscovered Hugo Grotius for the "enlightened" moralism of the age.[47] Regardless, the New Divinity and the so-called "Consistent Calvinists" proved the adage, "With friends such as these, who needs enemies?" It was at the hands of these Edwardsean pupils that Calvinism was turned on its head. The New Divinity would have died on its own, but the New Haven theologians, through the zealous fervor of Nathaniel W. Taylor, incorporated it to the revivalistic bloodstream until it reached the western frontiers in the person of Charles G. Finney.

III. The Practice of Finney

A. The "New Measures"

"We must have exciting, powerful preaching, or the devil will have the people, except what the Methodists can save," Finney declared in his 1835 revival lectures.[48] The demand assumed that the preaching Finney heard in his uncle's congregation,

---

[46] Allen Guelzo, "Jonathan Edwards and the New Divinity, 1758-1858," in *Pressing Toward The Mark*, ed. Charles 6. Dennison and Richard Gamble (Philadelphia: The Orthodox Presbyterian Church, 1986). See also his major work on Edwards published by Wesleyan University Press.

[47] Cf. especially Joseph Haroutunian's important work, *Peity Versus Moralism: The Passing of the New England Theology* (New York: Holt, 1932).

[48] Finney's *Lectures on Revival*, second ed. (N. Y., 1835), pp. 184-204.

monotonous, plodding, dispassionate, was the most common. Ever since the Reformation, preaching had been a hallmark of Protestants, both Lutherans and Calvinists insisted that "the preached Word of God is, in a special sense, the Word of God." (Second Helvetic Confession). In the place of idols, God wishes his people to be taught "through the lively preaching of his Word" (Heidelberg Catechism). One cannot read the sermons of the Reformation period, or those of the Puritans, without being moved by the passion and power of the sermon.

However, many sermons in the colonial and antebellum era were dry, formal lectures on various topics and were not, properly speaking, proclamation in their style, content, or urgency of address. While Finney's antipathy to being bogged down by "nice theological questions" and historical as well as exegetical reflection may have led him to exaggerate the conditions, he certainly had many followers for whom the caricature corresponded to a real individual.

The New Measures included the following; First, a direct and confrontational form of address. Informed of the notorious sinners in town before the meeting, Finney would pray publicly for these misguided strangers by name and even point them out in the meeting if they were present. It was high popular drama in an age without television, a combination of whodunit and situation comedy. Second, he would include in these public prayers the names of local clergy who were unsympathetic to the revivals, praying for their souls as if they were unconverted. Third, when Finney came to town, churches suspended their normal services and substituted in their place the "protracted meeting" which would occur nightly for a week or more. A fourth "new measure" is perhaps the most noted. The "anxious bench," a seat up front to which "seekers" and those "under conviction" might move as the meeting progressed. From this practice emerged the "altar call," the practice of calling forward those who were interested in "making a decision for Christ." However, even this innovation was not as controversial as the practice of encouraging women to "testify" in the meetings and even share in public prayer. In antebellum America, both women and men regarded the public speaking of women as degrading and socially unacceptable. This was as true for liberal Unitarians as for conservative Calvinists. However, the sects and revivalists were making room for such practices and it is no surprise that the original leaders of the women's rights movement were converts and associates of such New Measures revivalism. A final "measure" was advance publicity. Sending a team ahead of him, Finney would arrive much as the circus, with a ready-made tent and audience. If revival and religion in general were not supernatural, but "philosophical results of the right use of constituted means," such measures seemed best suited to the times. As Finney put it, "The evangelist must produce excitements sufficient to induce sinners to repentance."[49] Sydney Ahlstrom observed the connection between theology and practice at this point: "Finney's emphasis on the human production of conversions was not the only point on which he strayed from strict Westminster standards. And far from concealing the fact, he proclaimed it. From the first he demanded that some kind of relevant social action follow the sinner's conversion, and in time this led to an even more disturbing emphasis on 'entire sanctification.'"[50] In a letter on revival, Finney stated the following:

> Now the great business of the church is to reform the world—to put away every kind of sin. The church of Christ was originally organized to be a body of reformers . . . to reform individuals, communities, and governments. . . . Look at the Moral Reform movement. A few devoted, self-denying females, engaged in a mighty conflict with the great sin of licentiousness. This struggle has been maintained for

---

[49] *Ibid.*

[50] Sydney Ahlstrom, *A Religious History of the American* People (New Haven: Yale University Press, 1972), p. 460.

years; and yet how few comparatively of the churches as such have treated this effort in any other way than with contempt. A few devoted Christian women in various churches form societies to aid in this work: but where are the churches themselves as a body? Where are these sworn reformers—these men and women who profess to be waging everlasting war against every form of sin?

"Moral suasion" being Finney's watch-phrase for evangelism and social reform (one and the same), the revivalist contended that

> Law, rewards, and punishments—these things and such as these are the very heart and soul of moral suasion. . . . My brethren, if ecclesiastical bodies, colleges, and seminaries will only go forward— who will not bid them God speed? But if they will not go forward— if we hear nothing from them but complaint, denunciation, and rebuke in respect to almost every branch of reform, what can be done?[51]

Therefore, as Cross relates, for Finney, "Pulpit manners matched the burden of the address. The imitator of Finney and Nash 'must throw himself back and forward just as far as they did; and must if strong enough, smite as hard upon his chair, besides imitating their wonderful drawl and familiarity with God.' Hand clapping, wild gesticulation, and the shift of voice from shout to whisper added visual and auditory sensation to a theatrical performance." These revivalists could reuse their sermons, but the average pastor had to develop a long-term preaching ministry. Those who could not imitate the revivalist were often suspect. "Finney's relatively sane popularizing tendency grew among his emulators into a mania."[52]

This attachment to popular forms, which, more than theology, drew the ire of so many among the established New England clergy, was pointed out by the Presbyterian and later German Reformed theologian, John Williamson Nevin (1803-86), who insisted in *The Anxious Bench* that he did not oppose revivalism because of its earnestness. "Its professional machinery, its stage

---

[51] Donald W. Dayton, *Discovering An Evangelical Heritage* (San Francisco: Harper and Row, 1976), p. 20. Finney's "Letters on Revival-No. 23."

[52] Cross, p. 175.

dramatic way, its business-like way of doing up religion in whole and short order, and then being done with it—all made me feel that it was at best a most unreliable mode of carrying forward the work and kingdom of God."[53] Nevin complains, "All is made to tell upon the one single object of effect. The pulpit is transformed, more or less, into a stage. Divine things are so popularized as to be at last shorn of their dignity as well as their mystery. Anecdotes and stories are plentifully retailed, often in low, familiar, flippant style. . . . The preacher feels himself, and is bent on making himself felt also by the congregation; but God is not felt in the same proportion" (emphasis in original).[54] For Nevin, the issue of style was no less indicative of one's theological convictions than the matter of creed. There was not only a Reformation theology, but a Reformation style of evangelism and churchly life as well. Nevin added the following introduction to his rather lengthy critique of the revivalistic enterprise:

The system of New Measures has no affinity whatever with the life of the Reformation, as embodied in the Augsburgh Confession and the Heidelbergh Catechism. It could not have found any favor in the eyes of Zwingli or Calvin. Luther would have denounced it in the most unmerciful terms. His soul was too large, too deep, too free, to hold communion with a style of religion so mechanical and shallow. Those who are actively laboring to bring the Church of Luther, in this country, into subjection to the system, cannot be said to be true to his memory or name. . . . The system in question is in its principle and soul neither Calvinism nor Lutheranism, but Wesleyan Methodism. Those who are urging it upon the old German Churches, are in fact doing as much as they can to turn them over into the arms of

---

[53] John Williamson Nevin, Catholic and Reformed: *Selected Theological Writings of John W. Nevin*, ed. by Charles Yrigoyen, Jr. and George H. Bricker (Pittsburgh: The Pickwick Press, 1978), p. 5.

[54] *Ibid.*, p. 93.

Methodism. This may be done without any change to denominational name. Already the life of Methodism, in this country, is actively at work among other sects, which owe no fellowship with it in form. . . . And whatever there may be that is good in Methodism, this life of the Reformation I affirm to be immeasurably more excellent and sound. . . . If we must have Methodism, let us have it under its own proper title, and in its own proper shape. Why keep up the walls of denominational partition in such a case, with no distinctive spiritual being to uphold or protect? A sect without a soul has no right to live. Zeal for a separate denominational name that utters no separate religious idea, is the very essence of sectarian bigotry and schism.[55]

Although Nevin and Schaff, with roots in Princeton's Old Calvinism, did not always see eye to eye with Hodge and Warfield, the Mercersberg Theology sought to recover not only the theology, but the liturgical style and form of the Reformation. When matched with the penetrating theological critiques of their close colleagues and mentors, Hodge and Warfield, the combined resources appear striking.

But Finney's revivals encouraged further measures as well, including an emphasis on healing and the "prayer of faith," requiring absolute trust on the part of the entire congregation, uniting in a common feeling of expectation. Finney complained that more orthodox prayers were a "mockery of God," since they lacked a sense of expectation and depended too much on divine sovereignty.[56] "Rumors, dreams, and visions went hand in glove with religious excitement," Cross relates. "The revival engineers had to exercise increasing ingenuity to find even more sensational means to replace those worn out by overuse. In all of these ways the protracted meeting, though only a form within which the

---

[55] *Ibid.*, pp. 12-13.

[56] Cross, p. 179.

measures operated, helped the measures themselves grow even more intense, until the increasing zeal, boiled up inside of orthodoxy, overflowed into heresy "[57]

In addition to the "New Measures," and partly because of them, Finney's revivals also produced a spirit of divisiveness. Ironically, this had been the standard criticism of orthodox churchmen and their commitment to creeds and confessions. And yet, nowhere was sectarian zeal more acutely realized than on the western frontier. Enthusiasm proved to be an even more unstable guarantor of unity than theological conviction, as the former is inherently more subjective and individualistic than the latter. The result of fanaticism and "no creed but Christ" was that the sects most confident of the latter-day overthrow of church, tradition, creed and the alleged disunity created was that, as one wag reported, the churches were "split up into all kinds of Isms . . . [that] hardly any two believe alike."[58] Enthusiasm, not theology, emerged as the agent of discord. While Finney may have objected to a "paper pope" in the Westminster Standards, the nineteenth century created scores of living ones.

Nevertheless, New School presbyteries (and even some traditionally dominated by Old School men) increasingly accommodated themselves to the New Measures. In spite of its opposition to the measures, the Oneida Presbytery, for instance, invited him anyway. And why? "'God was with him,' and their hands were tied."[59] Success seemed to seal divine approval.

IV. The Legacy of Finney

A. Theological

Edwin H. Rian, in *The Presbyterian Conflict*, observes that theological modernism was "the child of New School theology,"

---

[57] *Ibid.,* p. 182-184.

[58] *Ibid.,* p. 315.

[59] *Ibid.,* p. 162.

and George Marsden points out that the "New School" was composed of Lyman Beecher and other New England Congregationlists who, under the Plan of Union, had embraced Presbyterianism and the Awakening. Eventually, however, the New England tradition clashed with the more orthodox Scots-Presbyterians and brought about the schism of 1837.[60] Samuel Hopkins emphasized moral government, but the Princetonians judged it to be within confessional bounds. It was Taylor who made the break, although it was his students who would actually reap the whirlwind. Throughout the 1820's, the Old Schoolers launched heresy trials for Beecher, Barnes, and others, but unsuccessfully as the New Schoolers were able to secure a looser view of confessional subscription. Remarkably, Marsden argues that the popularity of Taylor's New Haven Divinity waned in the New School Presbyterian Church by the time it reunited with the Old School in 1869.

As W. Robert Godfrey has explained, with the retirement of "Old School" theologian W. G. T. Shedd in 1890 Union Seminary's confessional Presbyterianism came to an end. In the following year, Charles Augustus Briggs became professor of biblical theology. In his inaugural address, Briggs championed German criticism and insisted that if Presbyterians and evangelicals generally would adapt themselves to the scientific advances and the modern world-view, they would hasten the dawn of the millennium. These evangelical Presbyterians wanted nothing more than to see the success of Christianity, but to appeal to the modern world, certain accommodations had to be made.[61] Just as Taylor's New Haven Divinity felt the burden of making Calvinism

---

[60] *George Marsden, "The New School Heritage and Presbyterian Fundamentalism" in Pressing Toward the Mark, op. cit.,* 169-179

[61] W. Robert Godfrey, "Haven't We Seen The 'Megashift Before?'", in Modern Reformation(January-February, 1993), pp. 14-18. Quoted in Marsden, 174-175.

relevant to an Enlightenment culture, and Finney sought to accommodate evangelical faith to the practical experience of the Jacksonian democracy, so the evangelicals at Union simply wanted to advance the Christian cause and fortify Christian America's moral and political destiny.

Hegel's spirit of enlightened modernity and Romanticism, mediated through Harnack, permeated the period, with the secular dogma of historical progress virtually indistinguishable from Christian eschatology. Perhaps even more powerful than the New Haven theology was German idealism in general and the thought of G. F. W. Hegel in particular. Marsden mentions one Laurens P. Hickok (1790-1888), a New School professor at Auburn. Hickok was widely recognized outside of theological circles as a pioneer of American idealism. While Hickok warned against a transcendental pantheism, he did advance Hegel's philosophy. The New School's concern, however, seemed to have had more to do with "the practical results in Sunday balls and theatres," as their journal cautioned.[62] One cannot help but notice the parallels between the Joachamist vision of history as progress toward pure spirit, through seismic advances in human betterment, to which Hegel explicitly acknowledged an obvious debt, and the postmillennial moralism of the New School activists.

When wedded to the Romantic pietism of Friedrich Schleiermacher (1768-1834), evangelicals, in the name of evangelicalism, reduced Christianity to feeling. When wedded to the thought of Albrecht Ritschl (1822-89), evangelicals, in the name of evangelicalism, reduced Christianity to morality and the Kingdom of God to social advances. What these accommodations share in common is not only a desire to make Christianity relevant, but a Pelagianizing tendency. If Warfield was correct in asserting that Pelagianism is the religion of universal heathenism and of

---

[62] Hodge, *op. cit.*

the natural man, these developments, from Taylor to Finney to the liberal evangelicals of the late nineteenth century, constitute a common drift toward the accommodation of Christianity to natural theology. Even when Arminian revivalists championed healing, for instance, it was not conceived as a supernatural intervention, but as a scientific, natural effect of universal laws. Taylor and Finney had denied original sin, supernatural regeneration, a substitutionary atonement, justification by an imputed righteousness, and had substituted modernity's confidence in human potential, moral and social redemption, a moral influence and governmental concept of the atonement, and the collapse of justification into the notion of naturalistic perfectionism. But their theological descendants, aided by German pietists, would see the modern project to its ultimate destination in what is now regarded as theological liberalism.

What must not be overlooked, however, is the fact that both fundamentalism and liberalism are heirs of this evangelical trend. The upheavals of the 1920s and '30s between fundamentalists and modernists must not obscure the fact that both were indebted to the legacy of Taylor and Finney. Much as Beecher was offended by Finney's style but eventually embraced the evangelist because of their common theological convictions, modern liberals and fundamentalists differed on substantial matters while they both nevertheless carried the Pelagian virus. This is why J. Gresham Machen found himself odd man out, not only in his own Presbyterian Church, but in the sea of fundamentalism, with its revivalistic, millennial, and moralistic orientation.

Even though it shares affinities with Enlightenment modernism (such as optimism concerning human nature, faith in progress, and an emphasis on morality), Marsden insists that fundamentalism is the true heir to the New Divinity. Just as New Haven was reacting against Unitarianism, fundamentalists were reacting against modernism, and everyone was reacting against

Calvinism for different reasons.[63] However, I would argue that both fundamentalism and modernism owed a debt to this "megashift." Taylor's sophisticated humanism fits with liberal sentiments, while Finney's Pelagianism paved the road for enthusiastic revivalism. Finney was too self-confident and anti-intellectual to acknowledge his debt to Taylor, just as fundamentalism fails to see its inheritance from Enlightenment dogmas. If this fact is true, it comprises one of the strangest ironies in American religious history. Fundamentalism and Modernism are cousins with a common theological ancestor and a remarkably similar soteriological creed, aside from issues of biblical inerrancy and the historical veracity of Christian truth claims concerning Christ's person and work.

This point was not lost on B. B. Warfield, who, in 1920, responded to a proposal that would have Presbyterians accept a common "evangelical creed" as a basis for evangelistic cooperation in the most unmerciful terms. It is utterly reductionistic, something that a sacerdotalist or rationalist could sign in good conscience, he says:

> There is nothing about justification by faith in this creed. And that means that all the gains obtained in that great religious movement which we call the Reformation are cast out of the window. . . . There is nothing about the atonement in the blood of Christ in the creed. And that means that the whole gain of the long mediaeval search after truth is thrown summarily aside. Anselm goes out of the same window with the Refomation. There is nothing about sin and grace in this creed. So far as this creed tells us, there might be no such thing as sin in the world; and of course then no such thing as grace. . . . Augustine shares the same fate of Anslem and the Reformers. It is just as true that the gains of the still earlier debates which occupied the first age of the Church's life, through which we attained to the understanding of the fundamental truths of the Trinity and the Deity of Christ are discarded by this creed also. There is no Trinity in this creed; no Deity of Christ or of the Holy Spirit. Are we ready to enter a union based on the elimination of these principles? Are we ready to

---

[63] *Ibid.*

say in effect that we will not insist, in our evangelistic activities, on any mention of such things as salvation by faith only, dependence for salvation on the blood of Christ alone, the necessity for salvation of the regeneration of the Holy Spirit. Is this the kind of creed which twentieth-century Presbyterianism will find sufficient as a basis for co-operation in evangelistic activities? Then it can get along in its evangelistic activities without the gospel. For it is precisely the gospel that this creed neglects altogether. 'Fellowship' is a good word, and a great duty. But our fellowship, according to Paul, must be in 'the furtherance of the gospel.'[64]

As surely as Romanticism produced Schleiermacher, it simultaneously created an idealistic and pietistic impulse in revivalism that led to a popular emotionalism paralleling the urbane intuitionalism of the transcendentalists. Both tendencies tested truth by its pragmatic usefulness or its experiential and emotional cash-value (to paraphrase William James), and thereby shifted theology and apologetics from the objective to the subjective, from the external to the internal, from the public to the private, from the grand to the trivial, from the rationally defensible to the experientially satisfying.

Lest Finney and his antebellum associates be regarded as an aberration in the history of evangelicalism, it is good to remember that the entire revivalistic tradition, from Finney to Billy Graham, whatever subtle differences may exist, was united in its general theological and practical distinctives. Son of Lyman Beecher, Henry Ward Beecher (1813-87) was the most prominent preacher and, in Milton J. Coalter, Jr.'s description, preached a mixture of civil religion and Christianized Social Darwinism. He largely ignored the substance of his Calvinist upbringing to popularize a romantic view of God superintending a natural evolution toward ever greater heights of human unity, order, and freedom. He believed that the United States led the world as the pinnacle of human development. His liberal theology matched a social

---

[64] *B. B. Warfield, The Shorter Writings, Volume I* (Philipsburg, PA: Presbyterian and Reformed), p. 387.

conservatism allowing for mild reforms based on the duty of the more fortunate to lift up the less advanced under God.[65]

The postmillennialism, Romanticism, idealism, and Pelagianism of the New Haven tradition fit perfectly with Social Darwinism's Hegelian eschatology. Departures from orthodoxy could be justified by the dogma of progress, since everyone embraced it. Those who opposed innovations in faith or practice were constantly having to defend themselves against the horrific charge of refusing to cooperate with the inevitable progress of history. As Martin Marty relates, "Once the Puritan faith had centered on the supernatural; but Lyman Abbott saw [Henry Ward] Beecher making religion seem a natural experience, 'something to be enjoyed' for everyday use," and here he was saying nothing that Finney had not declared earlier.[66] Christianity was practical and "testimonies" were now an important part of making that case.

Wheaton College's first president, Jonathan Blanchard (b. 1811) was deeply committed to the perfectionistic principles of Charles Finney. In fact, in an address for Oberlin College in 1839, titled, "A Perfect State of Society," Blanchard declared that when the laws of God become the laws of the land, the kingdom of God will come to the earth. It is "not so much . . . the doctrines of Christ, as the form they will give society, when they have done their perfect work on mankind," he insisted, for "every true minister of Christ is a universal reformer, whose business it is, so far as possible, to reform all the evils which press on human concerns." Donald Dayton cites Blanchard's remark that what "John Baptist and the Saviour meant when they preached 'the kingdom of God' was 'a perfect state of society.'"[67] A fierce abolitionist and temperance man, Blanchard was committed to

---

[65] Donald K. McKim, ed., *Encyclopedia of the Reformed Faith* (Louisville, KY: Westminster/John Knox, 1982).

[66] Martin Marty, *Pilgrims In Their Own Land* (N.Y.: Penguin, 1984), p. 312.

[67] Donald W. Dayton, *op. cit.*, pp. 7-14.

the idea of the kingdom and the Gospel in very this-worldly terms and the theology of perfectionism created an enormous amount of zeal in social, moral, and political activism.

D. L. Moody (1837-1899), heir to Finney's anti-intellectual and anti-theological sentiments as well as an Arminian in conviction, would add, "Whenever you find a man who follows Christ, that man you will find a successful one."[68] Under Moody's revivalistic ministry, the world of big business became the target group, and Carnegie, Wanamaker, Dodge, and a host of other Wall Street names helped finance the campaigns. P. T. Barnum even produced the tents. According to Richard Hofstadter, revivalism "evolved a kind of crude pietistic pragmatism with a single essential tenet: their business was to save souls as quickly and as widely as possible. For this purpose, the elaborate theological equipment of an educated ministry was not only an unnecessary frill but in all probability a serious handicap; the only justification needed by the itinerant preacher for his limited stock of knowledge and ideas was that he got results, measurable in conversions. To this justification very little answer was possible."[69] Moody declared, "It makes no difference how you get a man to God, provided you get him there."[70] Sam Jones (1847-1906), mocking "the little Presbyterian preacher," cried, "Oh, that preachers would preach less doctrine and more of Jesus Christ!" and yet, he obviously was doing theology without knowing it. In his own crude manner he displayed his debt to Taylorism, mediated through Finney. Of the substitutionary atonement, he stated, "It's a lie! It's a lie! God never was mad, nor did he ever shoot the javelin from his great hand at the heart and

---

[68] Richard Hofstadter, *op. cit.*, pp. 59 ff.

[69] *Ibid.*

[70] Ibid, 115.

[71] Cited by Tom Nettles, "A Better Way: Church Growth Through Reformation and Revival," in *Power Religion: The Selling Out of the Evangelical Church?* (Chicago: Moody Press, 1993), p. 182

body of his Son."[71]

Later, an ex-baseball-player-turned-evangelist, Billy Sunday, held dramatic revivals that included breaking baseball bats on the stage. By now, the pragmatic and consumeristic sentiments had deteriorated even further. "What I'm paid for my work makes it only about $2 a soul, and I get less proportionately for the number I convert than any living evangelist."[72] A true heir of Finney, Sunday, for whom prohibitionism was his greatest obsession, declared, "I believe there is no doctrine more dangerous than to convey the impression that a revival is something peculiar in itself and cannot be judged by the same rules of causes and effects as other things."[73]

In his classic study of perfectionism, Warfield explained the relationship of Finney to the evolution of the various "holiness"movements that were gaining ground in Britain and America. In revivalism, the Word is substituted for the evangelist and there is an *ex opere operato* effect in his very person. "By a mere gaze, without a word spoken, Finney says he reduced a whole room-full of factory girls to hysteria. As the Lutheran says God in the word works a saving impression, Finney says God in the preacher works a saving impression. The evangelist has become a Sacrament."[74] Warfield also argued the connection, theologically, between Oberlin Perfectionism in America and the Keswick Convention in England ("Victorious Life Movement"):

> Perhaps as the old Egyptian monarchs, in taking over the structures of their predecessors, endeavored to obliterate the signatures of those from whom they had inherited them, these later movements would be glad to have us forget the sources out of which they have sprung. But the names of the earlier Egyptian kings may still be read even in their defaced cartouches, so the name of Oberlin may still be read stamped on movements which do not acknowledge its parentage, but

---

[72] Hofstadter, p. 115

[73] Cited by Sidney E. Mead, *The Lively Experiment* (N.Y.: Harper and Row, 1963), pp. 114-115

[74] Warfield, *Perfectionism*, p. 135

[75] ibid., p. 124

which have not been able to escape altogether from its impress.[75]

Much of the Keswick Holiness movement's success in America was found not as much in Pentecostal or Wesleyan circles, but in New School Presbyterianism. Warfield describes the Presbyterian Mr. Boardman: "We have one process for acceptance with God," he says; "that is faith; and another for progress in holiness, that is works. After having found acceptance in Jesus by faith, we think to go on to perfection by strugglings and resolves, by fasting and prayers, not knowing the better way of taking Christ for our sanctification, just as we have already taken him for our justification." Thus, says Warfield, this "is not one indivisible salvation, but is separated into two distinct parts, received by two distinct acts of faith." "When we read it in its intended sense, it is as pure a statement of the Wesleyan doctrine of the successive attainment of righteousness and holiness by separate acts of faith as Wesley himself could have penned."[76] Today, its leading popular representatives are still often Presbyterians (Bill Bright, Lloyd Ogilvie, the late Lewis Sperry Chafer). The implications are beyond the scope of this article, but well worth exploring, especially as it anticipates the so-called "lordship controversy" of recent years.

Marsden even notes the New School roots of American Dispensationalism. Samuel Cox, for instance even seems to have arrived at the scheme of seven dispensations prior to C. I. Scofield's famous efforts, but both were Presbyterians. "Even more direct continuity can be demonstrated by the participation of former New School men in the International Prophecy Conferences which marked the first stages of the organized

---

[76] ibid., pp. 226-228

[77] Marsden, *"The New School Heritage and Presbyterian Fundamentalism,"* pp. 177-178. I am not taking issue with Marsden here, but simply widening the influence beyond fundamentalism. If Finney did not directly influence the drift of Presbyterianism toward modernism, he certainly was himself

movement that later became known as fundamentalism."[77] Could it not be the case that the Pelagianism that combined with postmillennialism created the Social Gospel, while the merging of Finney and premillennialism led to Dispensational Fundamentalism.

The Old School-New School division within fundamentalist ranks is clearly seen in the rift between J. Gresham Machen and "Old Princeton" Calvinists on the one hand, and Carl McIntire, Lewis Sperry Chafer, and prophetic revivalists on the other. One side was committed to historic Calvinism, the spiritual nature of the church, and Christian liberty; the latter insisted on loose subscription to fundamentals, moral and political crusades, and strict codes of personal conduct. By now, the activist impulse of the New School Presbyterians itself divided between those who supported more liberal causes and those who were more politically and socially conservative. Where originally "New School" meant civil rights for minorities and women as well as prohibition of alcohol and moral legislation, the Social Gospel split into two ideological tendencies, but retained their common debt to Finney and revivalism. Once more, therefore, we see how much more alike Modernism and Fundamentalism are than either to Old School Calvinism. Neither version of New School thinking could suffer the burden of theological orthodoxy, since it stood in the way of the idea of a Christian America brought about by the enthusiasm and might of interdenominational cooperation and moral campaigns.

---

carried along by the same winds that eventually accomplished just that. The perfectionistic impulse, carried over into radical political and social movements, surely assisted in preparing the way for an acceptance of German idealism. That many of the pioneers of "Modernism" in the Presbyterian church were simply representing themselves as champions of "evangelical" Christianity over rigorous confessionalism is demonstrated in *The Presbyterian Controversy* by Bradley J. Longfield (Oxford University Press, 1991).

But more important than these theological symptoms is the heart of the soteriological "megashift" that has occurred more recently within evangelicalism. Some would argue that so-called "progressive" or "liberal" evangelicals today are simply the Old Liberals of yesteryear. While the theological affinities are certainly there, historically, we have seen that it is possible to be a fundamentalist (revivalistic, millennial, with a literalistic hermeneutic) and every bit as naturalistic or Pelagian in soteriology as any friend of Ritschl.

Finney's legacy is explicitly acknowledged and celebrated in contemporary evangelicalism. Dayton observes, "As late as the 1940s and the 1950s V. Raymond Edman, Wheaton's fourth president, called the Evangelical world back to Finney as 'the most widely known and most successful American evangelist.' Edman's book, *Finney Lives On*, carried an endorsement from Billy Graham." Harvard University Press considered Finney's *Revival Lectures* to be of such significance in shaping American culture that in 1960 they reissued the work in a critical edition.[78] Bethany House Publishers, Revell, Scripture Press, and a host of other evangelical publishers have helped revive an interest in Finney over recent decades and the leaders of the "Jesus Movement" of the 1960s and '70s reappropriated Finney's theology and style for a new generation. Keith Green, Jimmy Swaggart, and Youth With A Mission are among the individuals and groups that have actively promoted the revivalist's theology, while mainstream evangelicalism has continued to regard Finney in heroic terms even when not entirely aware of his theological convictions. In a recent interview, Jerry Falwell claimed Finney as "one of my greatest heroes,"[79] and yet he is also hailed by Christians from the "left."

---

[78] Donald W. Dayton, op. cit. p. 15

[79] Jerry Falwell, interview in *The Horse's Mouth* (September, 1994) published by CHRISTIANS UNITED *for* REFORMATION (CURE), in Anaheim, California

In February 1990, *Christianity Today* ran a cover story on "The Evangelical Megashift," and a growing flank of evangelical scholars are making adjustments in evangelical theology that appear to be extensions of these earlier departures. The practical effects of Finney's legacy are ubiquitous throughout the evangelical empire of voluntary associations that bear his imprint. Evangelistic practices, "seeker-sensitive" approaches, church growth strategies that emphasize technique, political activism on the part of the church, nationalism, moralism, and a host of other interests are directly descended from the anthropocentric theology at the heart of Finney's rejection of the Westminster Standards.

Lord of Lords and King of Commoners: The Westminster Confession and the Relationship of Church and State

WILLIAM S. BARKER

One of the special beauties of the Presbyterian and Reformed confessional statements is that they point to the Bible as the only infallible rule of faith and practice. Acknowledging that synods and councils of the church may err, the Westminster Confession of Faith is itself subject to amendment as the church gains further light on its interpretation of certain parts of Scriptural teaching. The area of church and state relations is the outstanding example of this principle as American Presbyterianism has found it necessary—primarily because of new historical circumstances— to amend the Westminster Confession in three places that referred to the civil magistrate. As modern culture moves increasingly in a totally secular direction, the church may have to continue examining whether our confessional standards sufficiently summarize the Bible's teaching on this complex area of church-state relations, while at the same time maintaining the Scriptural principles expounded by the Confession of Faith.

At the time when the Westminster Assembly was meeting, 1643-1648 a civil war was being fought between King and Parliament, with religious issues very much at stake, and as a result of this war a republic would (temporarily) replace the monarchy. The members of the Westminster Assembly, nevertheless, were all agreed on the establishment of a national church in England (and/or Scotland). The two issues under debate in the area of church and state were those of toleration (largely between the Presbyterians and the Independents in the Assembly) and of the church's prerogatives in doctrine and especially discipline (largely between the Presbyterians and the Erastians in the Assembly and in Parliament).

In the midst of these unusual historical circumstances the Westminster Assembly succeeded in maintaining two exceedingly important principles: (1) the integrity of the individual's conscience as subject only to Christ and the word of God and (2) the autonomy of the church in matters of doctrine and discipline. In both of these principles the Westminister Confession was declaring the lordship of Jesus Christ over his church, whether considered corporately or as individual believers. The relationship to the state nevertheless presented, and continues to present, some complex issues which we shall describe in the context of the Westminster Assembly itself, then in the context of American Presbyterianism, and finally on into the 21st century.

1) The Westminster Assembly's Conflict with Erastianism

By the 16th century the European church had been living with a Constantinian cooperation of church and state for well over a millennium. Although Bible-believing groups like the Waldensians, the Lollards, and the Hussites had experienced persecution from a professedly Christian state, it was still assumed by all but scattered groups of Anabaptists that the church should be established and supported by the state. The Reformation in Germany and in Switzerland was accomplished with the aid of the civil magistrate.

The English Reformation in particular was an act of state, the break with the Pope coming by King Henry VIII's being declared the supreme head of the church in England. In Scotland the Protestant faith was championed by a churchman, John Knox, and in spite of the opposition of Mary Queen of Scots; nevertheless, there too it was established by the state.

When almost a century later, in 1643, the Solemn League and Covenant provided opportunity for the church in England to be reformed along the lines of the church in Scotland, the differing experiences of these two lands with church-state relations produced some not very surprising tensions even for those agreed on the goal of ecclesiastical reform in doctrine and worship. The Church of England from the beginning of the Reformation and throughout the reigns of Elizabeth I (1558-1603) and James I (1603-25) had displayed its Erastian character—that is, that the final say in matters of the church's doctrine and especially discipline should lie with the civil authority. Now that Parliament was winning out over the realm, even the Puritans in the House of Commons or the House of Lords were not inclined to surrender the final verdict to ministers, elders, and theologians on matters crucial for life in a society more thoroughly influenced by religion than American society in the 20th century.

In the Westminster Assembly the question of excommunication arose early in 1644. The learned John Selden, a member of Parliament as well as of the Assembly, argued that Matthew 18:15-18 was referring to civil courts in the Jewish context rather than to what in the Christian context would be church courts. According to William Hetherington, ". . . the ostentatious display of minute rabbinical lore which he brought forward, seems to have somewhat staggered the Assembly"; however, the young Scottish minister and theologian George Gillespie provided an effective answer:

> But Gillespie saw through the fallacious character of Selden's argument; and in a speech of singular ability and power completely refuted his learned antagonist, proving that the passage could not be interpreted or explained away to mean a mere reference to a civil

court. By seven distinct arguments he proved that the whole subject was of a spiritual nature, not within the cognizance of civil courts; and he proved also, that the Church of the Jews had and exercised the power of spiritual censures. The effect of Gillespie's speech was so great as to astonish and confound Selden himself, who made no attempt to reply; and the result was that the Assembly soon afterwards decided that the negative arguments of Selden and the Independents were not conclusive, and the proposition was affirmed.[1]

The most serious conflict with Erastianism came, however, in the spring of 1646, when Parliament sought to establish in every county civil commissioners to whom appeals from the church courts could be brought. The assembly presented a petition that such an arrangement would violate their consciences, and the House of Commons resolved, by a vote of 88-76,[2] that this petition constituted a breach of the privilege of Parliament and sent a delegation, in effect, to dress down the Assembly. After receiving the delegation's speeches in silence, the Assembly proceeded to a day of prayer and fasting and then heard an address from the Scottish ruling elder and lawyer, Archibald Johnston, Lord Warriston. Included in his speech were these claims:

> ... that Christ lives and reigns alone over and in his Church, and will have all done therein according to his word and will, and that he has given no supreme headship over his Church to *any pope, king, or parliament whatsoever.* Christ's throne is highest, and his privilege supreme as only head and king of his Church, albeit kings and magistrates may be members in it. There is no authority to be balanced with his, nor post to be set up against his post, nor the altar of Damascus against his altar, nor strange fire against his fire, nor Corahs to be allowed against his Aarons, nor Uzziahs against his Azariahs. Is it so small a thing to have the sworde that they must have the keys also?[3]

---

[1] William Maxwell Hetherington, *History of the Westminster Assembly of Divines* (Edmonton, Alberta: Still Waters Revival Books, 1993: reprint of 3rd ed. Of 1856), pp. 238-240; cf. pp. 201-202.

[2] Alexander F. Mitchell, *The Westminster Assembly: Its History and Standards,* 2nd ed. (Philadelphia: Presbyterian Board of Publication, 1897), p. 315.

[3] Mitchell, *Westminster Assembly,* pp. 325, 327. The entire speech, somewhat abridged, appears on pp. 323-328.

By the end of 1646 the Assembly had the Confession of Faith ready to present to Parliament. Probably to gain a delay that would render their position more powerful, Parliament required that the Assembly add its Scripture proofs. This was accomplished by April 29, 1647. On March 22, 1648 the House of Commons and the House of Lords conferred on their acceptance of the Confession and found agreement with the Assembly on the doctrinal part, but determined that "particulars in discipline are recommitted," including the 30th chapter "Of Church Censures," the 31st chapter "Of Synods and Councils," and the fourth section of the 20th chapter "Of Christian Liberty, and Liberty of Conscience."[4] This being the final positive act of Parliament on the Confession before Oliver Cromwell's influence predominated, it is apparent that the Erastian issue was not completely resolved for England. Meanwhile, however, the Church of Scotland adopted the Westminster Confession on August 27, 1647.

The Confession's position on church-state relations is summed up by Robley J. Johnston in three points:

> The first fact to note, and one that is deserving of the greatest emphasis, is the insistence of the Confession on a government of the church which is distinct from the civil power. . . .

In the second place, the Confession not only distinguishes between civil and ecclesiastical government but it also outlines the duties of each. To the church belongs the administration of the Word and sacraments and the power of the Keys of the Kingdom of heaven, while it is the magistrate's office to have the "power of the sword, for the defence and encouragement of them that are good, and for the punishment of evil doers." [Chapter XXIII, section 1] . . .

> Not only does the Confession distinguish between two different kinds of government but, in the third place, it will not allow of the intrusion

---

[4] Heatherington, *History*, pp. 283-285.

of either into the sphere of the other.[5]

When one examines the original version of the Westminster Confession on the civil magistrate (Chapter XXIII, section 3—subsequently revised in American Presbyterianism as will be discussed below), one wonders if the disallowance of mutual intrusion was all that clear:

> ... yet he hath authority, and it is his duty, to take order that unity and peace be preserved in the Church, that the truth of God be kept pure and entire, that all blasphemies and heresies be suppressed, all corruptions and abuses in worship and discipline prevented or reformed, and all the ordinances of God duly settled, administered, and observed. For the better affecting whereof, he hath power to call synods, to be present at them, and to provide that whatsoever is transacted in them be according to the mind of God.[6]

This would be difficult enough with a Puritan ruler like Oliver Cromwell in charge, to say nothing of a worldly king like Charles II. Alexander Mitchell argues, however, that this was a big advance for the time:

> The chapter on the Civil Magistrate, while adhering closely in some parts to the very words of the Irish Articles, emphatically sets out a different doctrine as to the limits of his power. Its doctrine in those days would probably have been admitted by few who did not belong to the Puritan party; but the Revolution Settlement of 1688 rests on it. The question whether the magistrate was under Christ as Mediator was intentionally left open [reference to Minutes of Session 752, Dec. 4, 1646]. The sentiments expressed are in several places nearly akin to those of Article XXXVI. of the Belgian Confession. It is the only chapter in which a close resemblance can be traced between the two, and I consider it not a little remarkable that the Westminster divines should be found turning to Holland just for that which, from its history and conflicts, Holland was best fitted to teach. Some, I know, will have it, that though the limits of civil obedience are rightly

---

[5] Robley J. Johnston, "A Study in the Westminster Doctrine of the Relation of the Civil Magistrate to the Church," *Westminster Theological Journal*, 12:13-29 and 121-135 (Nov. 1949 and May 1950), pp. 128-129.

[6] *The Confession of Faith of the Assembly of Divines at Westminster, From the Original Manuscript Written by Cornelius Burges in 1646*, ed. S. W. Carruthers (London: Publishing Office of the Presbyterian Church of England, 1946), p. 19.

defined in this chapter, too much is allowed to the magistrate in connection with religion. But such should consider that what is here allowed is less than was claimed for him in the old Scotch and other early reformed confessions, and far less than what was conceded in the English and the Irish Articles.[7]

It was not assumed that the civil magistrate would necessarily be friendly to the church. There were too many contrary examples in the recent history of Christendom to substantiate that.[8] But it was assumed that heresies and blasphemies could readily be recognized, and these must be dealt with for the sake of civil order. J. D. Douglas describes the position of the Scottish divine Samuel Rutherford:

> But Rutherford does not hold that the magistrate is to punish false religion as religion, He rather strongly maintains that the civil magistrate never aims at the conscience. The magistrate, he urges, does not send anyone, whether heretic or murderer, to the scaffold with the idea of producing conversion or other spiritual result, but to strengthen the foundations of the civil order. . . .
>
> Such views of the function of the civil Magistrate are a part of the whole ecciesiastico-political theory of the sixteenth and seventeenth centuries, and were intimately connected with their more religious notions of the magistrate. The latter was God's vicegerent in that he stood on a special level above the officers of the Church. This status, however, affected only the external man, and did not apply to a man's soul and conscience. This whole line of argument, echoes of which we have already found in Gillespie, strikes an unreal note, built as it is upon the assumption that the magistrate is himself a God-fearing man, that he, as it were, knows the rules, and has a due awareness of

---

[7] Alexander F. Mitchell, "Introduction," p. lxix, in Mitchell and John f. Struthers, eds., *Minutes of the Sessions of the Westminster Assembly of Divines* (Edmonton, Alberta: Still Waters Revival Books, 1991 reprint of the 1874 edition).

[8] The original version of Chapter XXXI, section 2 of the Confession of Faith read: "As magistrates may lawfully call a synod of ministers, and other fit persons, to consult and advise with, about matters of religion; so, if magistrates be open enemies to the Church, the ministers of Christ, of themselves, by virtue of their office, or they with other fit persons upon delegation from their Churches, may meet together in such assemblies. (*The Confession of Faith*, ed. S.W. Carruthers, p. 23.)

what is involved in being God's vicegerent.[9]

The problem with this understanding of church-state relations is illustrated in the conflict over toleration.

2) The Westminster Assembly's Conflict with the Independents over Toleration

As mentioned earlier, almost all parties in 17th-century England favored having an established national church. This included the Independents in the Westminister Assembly. Realizing that the Solemn League and Covenant between the English Parliament and Scotland was most likely to result in a presbyterian rather than a congregational church polity, the Independents held out for toleration. This toleration *would* not constitute a separation, for the Independents' gathered churches would still be accountable to the state and in communion with the presbyterian churches. The Presbyterians in the Assembly, however, were willing to offer an accommodation whereby some scruples regarding church government could be recognized, but not the liberty to gather churches on a voluntary basis out of other churches, for this would result in a perpetual schism and division in the church.[10]

Robert S. Paul, although at several important points differing with John R. de Witt's analysis of the Westminster Assembly, here builds on de Witt's insight that for the Presbyterians the issue

---

[9] J.D. Douglas. *Light in the North: the Story of the Scottish Covenanters* (Grand Rapids: Eerdmans, 1964), pp. 56-57. A helpful discussion of the political theories behind both sides of the Erastian controversy can be found in Douglas F. Kelly, *The Emergence of Liberty in the Modern World: The Influence of Calvin on Five Governments from the 16th through 18th Centuries* (Phillipsburg, N.J.: Presbyterian and Reformed, 1992), pp. 105-109.

[10] Cf. John Richard de Witt, *Jus Divinum: The Westminster Assembly and the Divine Right of Church Government* (Kampen: J.H. Kok, 1969), pp. 161-162, 118-119, 139-142.

was the authoritative spiritual power which the higher courts and assemblies could exercise within the church:

> This was the essential difference, and despite the quirks of polity, perhaps it was the only essential difference—one side claimed that there was a governing power in the gospel, and the other side thought that such power did not properly belong to the gospel. From that perspective de Witt was entirely right to describe it as the "great continental divide in the history of evangelical church polity," but the division took on these proportions because both sides believed their own position to be *jure divino,* and therefore dared not concede the point to the other.[11]

But the difficulty lay not only with conflicting claims of divine right polity. It was also the threat of persecution or oppression of dissenting views when spiritual authority is joined with the enforcing power of the state in support of an established church.

Much to the embarrassment of the Independents in the Assembly, this point was made clear by the appearance in England of Roger Williams, who had returned from America in 1643 in order to gain approval for his new colony of Rhode Island. His publication of *The Bloudy Tenent of Persecution* in 1644 and the ensuing literary debate with John Cotton of the Massachusetts Bay colony made clear not only Williams' advocacy of complete religious liberty and separation of church and state, but also that the New England Way, though sharing the congregational polity of the Independents in the Assembly, was intolerant of dissent.[12]

---

[11] Robert S. Paul, *The Assembly of the Lord: Politics and Religion in the Westminster Assembly and the 'Grand Debate'* (Edinburgh: T. & T. Clark, 1985), p. 449. In footnote 55 on that page Paul says: "It is possible to believe in the *jus divinum* of the Church itself without using it to justify the details of a particular polity, but that was something neither side was ready to concede. A more pragmatic approach to church order could have accepted the presbyterian system and administered it with 'ministerial' authority rather than the 'magisterial' authority the Independents rightly feared."

[12] Cf. Irwin H. Polishook, Roger Williams, John Cotton and *Religious Freedom: A Controversy in New and Old England* (Englewood Cliffs, N.J." Prentice Hall, 1967), pp. 21-25.

The question in the 17th century was how far even those who advocated congregational polity were willing to go in the direction of toleration. The army of Oliver Cromwell was filled with sectarians of various sorts, yet even when his regime made the influence of the Independents predominant in England, many of the sects (such as the Levellers, the Fifth-Monarchy Men, the Socinians, the Antinomians, and the Quakers) were forcibly suppressed without any opposition being offered by the Independents to this suppression as an intolerant interference with liberty of conscience.[13]

William Hetherington argues that the Independents and the Presbyterians in the Westminster Assembly "misapprehended each other's opinions on the subject of religious toleration":

> What the Presbyterians understood their opponents to mean by that term was what they called a "boundless toleration," implying equal encouragement to all shades and kinds of religious opinions, however wild, extravagant, and pernicious in their principles, and in their evident tendency. And when they somewhat vehemently condemned such laxity and licentiousness, the Independents seem to have thought that they intended or desired the forcible suppression of all opinions that differed from their own.[14]

Hetherington, writing in mid-19th-century Scotland, claimed that the Presbyterian concept of church-state cooperation "could never lead to persecution":

> ... the question is, Ought error also [as truth ought to be encouraged and diffused], and with equal directness, to be suppressed? The best method of obtaining a right answer to this inquiry is, to consult the Word of God, and to investigate the nature of conscience. The Word of God, in almost innumerable instances, commands the direct encouragement of truth, and also the suppression of certain *forms* of error,— as of idolatry and blasphemy; but gives no authority to man

---

[13] Hetherington, *History*, p. 332. For a tracing of the influence of John Owen's view of toleration on John Locke, cf. J.Wayne Baker, "Church, State, and Toleration: John Locke and Calvin's Heirs in England," pp. 525-543 in W. Fred Graham, ed., *Later Calvinism: International Perspectives*, Sixteenth Century Essays and Studies, Vol. XXII (1994).

[14] *Ibid.*, p. 331.

> to judge and punish errors of the mind, so far as these amount not to
> violations of known and equitable laws, and disturb not the peace of
> society. And with regard to the nature of conscience, it is manifest to
> every thinking man, that conscience cannot be compelled.

He stated that it was therefore contrary to both the Word of
God and the nature of conscience "to promote truth by the
compulsive suppression of error":

> But it by no means follows that toleration means, or ought to mean,
> equal favour shown to error as to truth. Truth ought to be expressly
> favoured and encouraged: erring man ought to be treated with all
> tenderness and compassionate toleration; but error itself ought to be
> condemned, and all fair means employed for its extirpation.[15]

The assumption here is that it is easy to identify truth and
error in religious matters. It was simpler to hold such a view where
there was an established church. As Presbyterianism and the
Westminster Confession came to America, the interpretation of
the Scriptures' teaching on church-state relations was worked out
in an increasingly pluralistic context.

3) Modifications of the Confession
in American Presbyterianism

When the Synod of the Presbyterian Church in America
adopted the Westminster Standards on September 19, 1729, the
ministers declared the Confession and Catechisms to be the
confession of their faith, excepting only some clauses in the 20th
and 23rd chapters pertaining to the civil magistrate.[16] Clearly,
from an American perspective, as part of a dozen British colonies
separated from the mother country by the Atlantic Ocean,
Presbyterians here could not expect the support of the civil
magistrate. Indeed in most of the colonies they were a minority
of limited influence. Nevertheless, in the wake of the Great

---

[15] *Ibid.,* pp. 330-331.

[16] Guy S. Klett, ed., *Minutes of the Presbyterian Church in America, 1706-
1788* (Philadelphia: Presbyterian Historical Society, 1976), p. 104.

Awakening, with the reunion of the New Side and Old Side in 1758, the Presbyterian Church launched upon a period of internal harmony and extensive external influence.

In the period leading up to the War of Independence American Presbyterians were almost unanimously in support of opposition to what was viewed as British tyranny. In part this may be explained by traditional Scottish and Scotch-Irish resistance to English domination. In addition to the familiar causes for the American Revolution, Presbyterians also saw the violation of civil liberties as a threat to the security of ecclesiastical and religious liberty. Charles Hodge, in his *Constitutional History of the Presbyterian Church*, traces the tendency of the British government, in South Carolina, Virginia, Maryland, New York, and New Hampshire, to impose Episcopacy on the American colonies as the established church to be supported by all the colonists as a national church:

> The fundamental assumption . . . was that the Episcopal church was the national established church in all the king's dominions, Scotland only, and not the colonies excepted: that other denominations were merely tolerated, and consequently were entitled to nothing more than the act of toleration allowed them; whereas the church of England was entitled to a legal provision, to national support, and the exclusive favour and patronage of the government.[17]

Acknowledging that the particular injuries and indignities of the taxes were not so great as the underlying power that was being claimed and steadily implemented by the British government, Hodge saw the establishment of a national church as part of the same underlying principle as the power to tax:

> The assumption was the same in both cases, viz.: that America was part of the nation of England, that the power of the king and parliament was here what it was there. Hence on the one hand, the inference that the British parliament could here levy what taxes they pleased; and

---

[17] Charles Hodge, *Constitutional History of the Presbyterian Church in the United States of America* (Philadelphia: William S. Martien, 1839, 1840) Vol. II, pp. 381-382.

on the other, that the king's supremacy in ecclesiastical matters, extended to the colonies; that every Englishman who came to America, did but remove from one part of the nation to another; that he stood in the same relation to the national church in this country, as he had done in England.[18]

It is not surprising that the American Revolution was sometimes termed "a Presbyterian rebellion." Presbyterians, as a minority in America, played a major role in gaining the religious liberty that was eventually secured in the First Amendment to the United States Constitution. Hodge concludes concerning the threat of established Episcopacy:

> This controversy had more to do with the revolution than is generally supposed; and a knowledge of the leading facts in the case is necessary to free Presbyterians and other denominations, from the charge of unreasonable and bigoted opposition to a church fully entitled to confidence and affection.[19]

With the gaining of American independence and the formation of the United States, the Presbyterian Church reorganized itself into a General Assembly in 1788. John Witherspoon, Moderator of the First General Assembly in 1789 and the one clergyman to sign the Declaration of Independence, is usually credited with drafting the eight "Preliminary Principles" which served as a preface to the new Form of Government of the church. Among them were the following:

> I. That "God alone is Lord of the conscience; and hath left it free from the doctrine and commandments of men, which are in anything contrary to his word, or beside it in matters of faith and worship": therefore they consider the rights of private judgment, in all matters that respect religion, as universal and unalienable: they do not even wish to see any religious constitution aided by the civil powers, further than may be necessary for protection and security, and, at the same time, be equal and common to all others.

> VIII. . . . Since ecclesiastical discipline must be purely moral or spiritual in its object, and not attended with any civil effects, it can

---

[18] *Ibid.,* Vol. II p. 389.

[19] *Ibid.,* Vol. II, p. 395.

derive no force whatever, but from its own justice, the approbation of an impartial public, and the countenance and blessing of the great Head of the Church universal.[20]

This renunciation of any state establishment of the church was accompanied by revision of the last paragraph of the 20th chapter of the Confession of Faith and the first paragraph (replacing the original second paragraph) of the 31st chapter, along with the third paragraph of the 23rd chapter already excepted to in 1729. This removed the function of the civil magistrate with regard to synods and councils of the church and also with regard to preserving the unity and peace of the church, to keeping pure and entire the truth of God, to suppressing all blasphemies and heresies, and to preventing or reforming all corruptions and abuses in worship and discipline. By the end of the 18th century the American Presbyterian experience had led to the conclusion that the role of the civil magistrate in such matters could be more harmful than beneficial. Presbyterians desired from the civil magistrate only protection and security for their religious freedom on a par with all other denominations.

4) Into the 21st Century

The 19th and 20th centuries saw a number of issues arise that were pertinent to church and state relations that cannot here be described in detail. At the Old School Presbyterian General Assembly of 1861 the "Gardiner Spring Resolutions" were adopted, calling on Presbyterians to support the Union of the States in the just-begun Civil War. Charles Hodge submitted a protest, signed by one-fourth of the voting members of the Assembly: "We deny the right of the Assembly to decide the political question, to what government the allegiance of Presbyterians as citizens is due,

---

[20] Lewis S. Mudge, ed., *Digest of the Acts and Deliverance of the General Assembly of the Presbyterian Church in the U.S.A.* (Philadelphia: General Assembly of the PCUSA, 1938), Vol. I, pp. 73 75.

and its right to make that decision a condition of membership in our church."[21]

The "spirituality of the church," as enunciated by James Henley Thornwell, restrained the Southern Presbyterian Church from addressing social or political issues. By 1973, the year in which the Presbyterian Church in America (PCA) was formed, largely out of the Southern Presbyterian Church (PCUS) the U.S. Supreme Court's ruling in favor of abortion led to the church's feeling an obligation to speak God's truth to an increasingly secular society. The controversy over prayer in the public schools has raised additional questions concerning the relation between church and state, the desire to have neither intrude into the sphere of the other, and the preservation of religious liberty.

As we approach the end of the 20th century, the major question that is emerging is whether the kind of separation of church and state that Presbyterians helped to produce in America leads inevitably to the prevalence of secularism.

Although the current trends are moving powerfully in that direction, the answer is no. But, as in the civil realm, the price for religious liberty is eternal vigilance—plus prayer and energetic obedient activity.

In the Confession of Faith, Chapter XX, section 2, the Westminster Divines made a careful distinction: "God alone is Lord of the conscience, and hath left it free from the doctrines and commandments of man, which are, [1] in any thing contrary to His Word; or [2] beside it, if matters of faith, or worship"[22] Our conscience may not be bound by anything that is contrary to

---

[21] Cf. David B. Calhoun, *Princeton Seminary, Vol. I: Faith and Learning, 1812-1868* (Edinburgh and Carlisle, Pa: Banner of Truth, 1994) pp. 394-396, for a discussion of this matter.

[22] *The Confession of Faith . . . by Cornelius Burges in 1646*, ed. S.W. Carruthers, p. 17.

God's Word. But in matters of faith or worship, our conscience may not be bound even by those commands of men that are merely beside God's Word. Doctrine and worship, those parts of God's law that are summed up by that first and great commandment, "Thou shalt love the Lord thy God with all they heart, soul, mind, and strength," are his special prerogative. There his Word alone must govern his church; the civil government should only guarantee freedom. In those parts of God's law that are summed up by that second great commandment, "Thou shalt love thy neighbor as thyself," the civil government has God-ordained responsibility to administer and enforce law, and we are to obey so long as it is not contrary to God's law.[23]

Approaching church-and-state issues with this distinction in mind will assist us in the myriad complex questions that are bound to arise in the 21st century. The Westminster Confession, from the 17th century to the present, has faithfully upheld two principles vis-a-vis the state: the autonomy of the church and the integrity of the individual's conscience. Thus it has been maintained that Jesus Christ is Lord of Lords and King of commoners.

---

[23] For a further development of exegetical support for this position, based on Matthew 22:15-22, see my chapter "Theonomy, Pluralism, and the Bible," pp. 227-242 in William S. Barker and W. Robert Godfrey, eds., *Theonomy: A Reformed Critique* (Grand Rapids: Zondervan, 1990).

Index

Carlisle, Dr. Charles, 27
Carroll, B. H., 156
Carruthers, Dr. Samuel W., 25, 26, 30
Carson, Dr. John L., 27
Cartwright, 306
Catechism, 235
Catechism for Babes, 151
catechizing, 227
catholicity of the church, 158
Chalmers, Thomas, 344
Chapman, J. Wilbur, 282
Charles I, 213, 214, 216, 219, 243
Charles II, 243
Chesterton, G. K., 35, 37
Cheyne, A. C., 347
Childs, William Robinson, 60
Christ, 198
Christ the Mediator, 106
Christian, Bruce, 298
Christian Liberty, 152
Christ's death, 308
Christ's sufficiency, 322
Christ's work, 154
Church, 113
Church of Scotland, 4, 250, 252, 253
Church-Government, 229
Church-State, 241, 243
civil magistrate, 253, 256, 419
Civil War, 216, 218, 219, 224
Clarendon Code, 149
Clement of Alexandria, 323
Clow, James, 251
Coalter, Milton J., Jr., 405
Coffin, Henry Sloane, 24
Coleman, Thomas, 178, 232
Collinson, Patrick, 310
Commemorations of the
    Westminster Assembly, 1–38
Communion of Saints, 113
Confession, 103, 338
Confession of 1677, 149, 150
Confession of Faith, 8, 13, 163, 240
Confession of Faith and Catechism, 226

confessional revision, 11, 21
confessionalism, 156
Congregationalism, 370
Constitutional History of the
    Presbyterian Church, 424
Cotton, Dr. J. Harry, 24
Cotton, John, 230
Council of Trent, 391
Covenant, 106, 221
Covenanters, 215, 216, 217, 222, 226, 245
Cox, Samuel, 409
Cranmer, 322
creation, 105, 137, 261
creation ordinance, 136
Crighton, John, 205
Cromwell, Oliver, 149, 224, 230, 243
Cross, Whitney, 371, 378, 381, 399
Cunningham, William, 5, 344
Curtis, W. A., 195
Cyprian, 323

D

Dabney, Robert L., 16
Dagg, John L., 155
Darwin, Charles, 261, 262
Davidson, A. B., 346
de Kroon, M., 168
De Witt, John R., 420
deacon, 231
Death, 120
death of Christ, 337
Decalogue, 130, 139, 140, 141
Decrees of God, 105, 153, 189, 202, 208
Defense of the Faith, 51
Deissmann, Adolf, 288
Dendy, Henry B., 59
Dickson, David, 229
dictation theory, 43
Didier, J. C., 174
Dipping, 177

About the Editors and Contributors

Ligon Duncan, PhD, is the Senior Minister of the historic First Presbyterian Church (1837), Jackson, MS, and Adjunct Professor of Theology at the Reformed Theological Seminary (RTS). He was formerly the John R. Richardson Professor of Systematic Theology at RTS. He is a Council Member of the Alliance of Confessing Evangelicals.

W. Duncan Rankin, PhD, is Professor of Systematic Theology at Reformed Theological Seminary in Jackson, MS and Minister of the Lebanon Presbyterian Church in Learned, MS.

Derek W. H. Thomas, PhD, is the John E. Richards Professor of Pastoral and Systematic Theology, and Dean of Chapel at Reformed Theological Seminary. He is also Minister of Teaching at the First Presbyterian Church in Jackson, MS.

Robert C. Cannada, Jr., DMin, is the President of Reformed Theological Seminary which has US campuses in Jackson, MS; Orlando, FL; Charlotte, NC; Washington, DC; and Atlanta, GA.

Stephen R. Berry, PhD (cand.), is the former Archivist of the Reformed Theological Seminary Library, winner of the G. Aiken Taylor Award for American Presbyterian Church History and doctoral candidate at Duke.

Stephen E. Tindall, BA, Biblical and Theological Studies, Gordon College, is a student at Reformed Theological Seminary in Jackson, MS, and currently serves as intern for the Senior Minister at First Presbyterian Church. He is happily married to Sara.

David W. Hall, PhD, was the Senior Fellow of the Center for the Advancement of Paleo-Orthodoxy (CAPO) and former Minister of the Covenant Presbyterian Church in Oak Ridge, TN. He is now Minister of the Midway Presbyterian Church in Powder Springs, GA.

Wayne R. Spear, PhD, is Professor of Systematic Theology and Homiletics at the Reformed Presbyterian Theological Seminary in PA and serves as Clerk of Session of the Reformed Presbyterian Church of North Hills, Pittsburgh.

O. Palmer Robertson, ThD, is President of the African Bible College in Uganda and has taught at Reformed, Westminster, Covenant and Knox Theological Seminaries.

Morton H. Smith, ThD, is Professor of Systematic Theology at the Greenville Presbyterian Theological Seminary. He was the Stated Clerk of the Presbyterian Church in America and a longtime Professor at RTS.

Richard B. Gaffin, ThD, is the Charles Krahe Professor of Biblical and Systematic Theology at Westminster Theological Seminary in Philadelphia, PA.

Timothy George, PhD, is the founding Dean of the Beeson Divinity School, Samford University, Birmingham, USA and is a Senior Editor of both *Christianity Today* and *Books & Culture*.

David F. Wright, DD, is Professor of Patristic and Reformed Christianity and former Dean of the University of Edinburgh, New College, Scotland.

Andrew T. B. McGowan, PhD, is the Principal of the Highland Theological College and a minister in the Church of Scotland.

W. D. J. McKay, PhD, is Professor of Systematic Theology and Christian Ethics at the Reformed Theological College, Belfast, Northern Ireland.

Stewart D. Gill, PhD, is the Dean & Deputy Warden of Trinity College and Senior Fellow, Department of History, University of Melbourne, Australia.

Mark E. Dever, PhD, is Minister of the Capitol Hill Baptist Church in Washington, DC, Senior Fellow of the Center for Church Reform, sits on the Council of the Alliance of Confessing Evangelicals and taught for the Faculty of Divinity at Cambridge University (where he was a J. B. Lightfoot Scholar).

J. L. Macleod, PhD, is a Professor of History at the University of Evansville in Indiana.

Michael S. Horton, PhD, is Professor of Theology at Westminster Theological Seminary in Escondido, CA and President of the Alliance of Confessing Evangelicals.

William S. Barker, PhD, is the former Dean of Westminster Theological Seminary in Philadelphia, PA, formerly Editor of the *Presbyterian Journal* and former President of Covenant Theological Seminary in St. Louis, MO.

Puritan Profiles

*54 Members and Contemporaries
of the Westminster Assembly*

William Barker

"Will Barker's love of biography, historian's eye for detail, his personal devotion to Christ and Scripture make these pages an expertly guided tour of the varied characters and remarkable personalities drawn together by the Westminster Assembly'.

**Sinclair B. Ferguson,
Westminster Theological Seminary,
Dallas Campus, TX**

...insightful, wise and encouraging! Read them, and come away a stronger person.'

**The Late James Boice,
Tenth Presbyterian Church, Philadelphia**

'For those who admire the confessional statements [of the Westminster Assembly] but know little of their origins, this is a wonderful introductory volume. The diversity of the assembly participants with their immense commonalities is amazing. Also of interest are the enormous energy of involved in the debates, the participants' struggles to understand the Bible and freedom to vent disagreement at high decibels while maintaining a spirit of unity.'

John D. Hannah, Bibliotheca Sacra

William Barker is vice-president for academic affairs and Professor of Church History at Westminster Theological Seminary, Philadelphia. He is an ordained minister in the Presbyterian Church in America. His keen interest in contemporary culture and politics ensures that this book is relevant today.

ISBN 1-85792-191-7

An Exposition of the
Westminster Confession of Faith

Robert Shaw

Foreword by Sinclair B. Ferguson

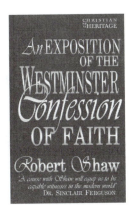

'The fullest and most carefully constructed exposition of the Christian Faith ever written'

**Sinclair B. Ferguson,
Westminster Theological Seminary,
Dallas Campus, TX**

'...one of the best written and helpful expositions ever to appear. ...each category of doctrine is opened up with clarity and applied with warmth and spirituality. It is a handsome volume and is recommended highly.'

Evangelical Times

The Westminster Confession of Faith is the standard of Church beliefs for the Reformed churches worldwide. It is also the most comprehensive statement of biblically based Christian belief available. Hence you have an excellent manual for Christian Doctrine, expertly unpacked by Robert Shaw.

This book is a practical aid to help us understand and apply material in the Confession to our lives - making us live out our confession as individual Christians and as members of a worldwide church.

This book is the recognised companion volume to the Westminster Confession of Faith.

ISBN 0-90673-104-6

Christian Focus Publications

publishes books for all ages

Our mission statement –

STAYING FAITHFUL

In dependence upon God we seek to help make His infallible word, the Bible, relevant. Our aim is to ensure that the Lord Jesus Christ is presented as the only hope to obtain forgiveness of sin, live a useful life and look forward to heaven with Him.

REACHING OUT

Christ's last command requires us to reach out to our world with His gospel. We seek to help fulfill that by publishing books that point people towards Jesus and help them to develop a Christ-like maturity. We aim to equip all levels of readers for life, work, ministry and mission.

Books in our adult range are published in three imprints.

Christian Focus contains popular works including biographies, commentaries, basic doctrine, and Christian living. Our children's books are also published in this imprint.

Mentor focuses on books written at a level suitable for Bible College and seminary students, pastors, and other serious readers. The imprint includes commentaries, doctrinal studies, examination of current issues, and church history.

Christian Heritage contains classic writings from the past.

For a free catalogue of all our titles, please write to
Christian Focus Publications, Ltd
Geanies House, Fearn,
Ross-shire, IV20 1TW, Scotland, United Kingdom
info@christianfocus.com

For details of our titles visit us on our website
www.christianfocus.com